Records
—of—
Egypt Reformed Church
Lehigh County
Pennsylvania

1734–1834

Translated
by
Charles R. Roberts
with Notes

Heritage Books
2010

HERITAGE BOOKS
AN IMPRINT OF HERITAGE BOOKS, INC.

Books, CDs, and more—Worldwide

For our listing of thousands of titles see our website
at
www.HeritageBooks.com

A Facsimile Reprint
Published 2010 by
HERITAGE BOOKS, INC.
Publishing Division
100 Railroad Ave. #104
Westminster, Maryland 21157

Originally published
Harrisburg, Pennsylvania
Harrisburg Publishing Company, State Printer
1905

— Publisher's Notice —

In reprints such as this, it is often not possible to remove blemishes from the original. We feel the contents of this book warrant its reissue despite these blemishes and hope you will agree and read it with pleasure.

International Standard Book Numbers
Paperbound: 978-1-58549-532-0
Clothbound: 978-0-7884-8567-1

PREFACE

These church records have been copied directly from Volume 6, of the Sixth Series of the Pennsylvania Archives which was originally published in 1906. As such, the reader will find some imperfections in the type, i.e broken type as well as typesetting errors.

Such errors should be easily recognized by the reader and it is the reader's prerogative to assume any corrections. It is only in rare instances that corrections were made by the indexer.

As anglicization intruded into the German way of life, the German naming system, etc., we find a great variation in the spelling of both given and surnames. Consideration should also be given to the possibile inability of the original transcriber/ translator to read the old handwritten records in some instances - resulting in additional mis-spellings of names. The reader therefore, should examine all conceivable spellings of any given name in order to provide himself/herself with the greatest possiblity of finding the information which is being sought.

RECORDS OF EGYPT REFORMED CHURCH.

1734.

TRAXEL, DAVID, son of Peter Traxel;[4] b July 27, 1734; bap. Sept. 23, 1734, by Rev. Boehm; sp. Nicolaus Kern[5] and w. Maria Margaretha.

1736.

TRAXEL, JOHANNES, son of the respectable Peter Traxel, church censor of the Reformed congregation here, and wife Juliana Catharina Traxel; b. ———; bap; Oct. 26, 1736, by Rev. Goetschi; sp. Nicolaus Kern, Johannes Egender, Margaretha Egender.

1737.

ROTH, PETER, son of Daniel Roth[6] and wife Anna Margaretha Roth; b. ———; bap. July 27, 1737; sp. the respectable Peter Traxel, deacon of the Reformed congregation here, and wife Juliana Catharina Traxel.

1739.

WUDRING, ANNA BARBARA, dr. Abraham Wudring[7] and Anna Margreth; b. ———; bap. March 22, 1739; sp. Ulrich Burghalter[8] and Anna Barbara.

HOFFMAN, CATRINA LISABETH, dr. Michael Hoffman[9] and Eva Catrina; b. ———; bap. March 22, 1739; sp. Peter Traxel, Catrina Lisabeth Kern, George Kern's wife.

TRAXEL, CHRISTIAN, s. Peter Traxel and w. Juliana Catharina; b. ———; bap. April 16, 1739; sp. Christian Brengel, Peter Traxel, Salome Gut.

TRAXEL, JULIANA MARGARETHA, dr. above-mentioned Peter Traxel and his wife; twins baptized; b. ———; bap. April 16, 1739; sp. Johannes Bertsch, Catharina Elisabetha Kern, Maria Margaretha Neuhart.

BRICKER, JACOB, s. Jacob Bricker and w. Anna Magdalena; b. ———; bap. May 13; sp. Balthasar Gering and Veronica.

ARNDT, CATHARINA, Eva, dr. Clementz Arndt and w. Maria; b. ———; bap. May 13; sp. Henrich Geck, Eva Roth.

KOCHER, ANNA BARBARA, dr. Martin Kocher and Sara; b. ———; bap. June 12; sp. Barbara Burghalter, w. of Ulrich Burghalter, Niclaus Seger.[11]

FLICKINGER, GEORGE, s. Ulrich Flickinger and Lucia; b. ———; bap. June 27; sp. George Kern, Juliana Traxel, w. of Peter Traxel.

SENSINGER, JOH. PETER, s. Ulrich Sensinger and Cathrina; b. ——; bap. Sept. 30; sp. Peter Traxel and Juliana, Anna Mary Traxel, Johannes Traxel's[12] wife, Niclaus Kern.

1740.

The following three children were baptized in the Saucon church by Mr. Inspector Peter Henrich Torchius:

NEUHART, JOH. MICHAEL LORENTZ, s. Friederich Neuhart[13] and w. Margaretha Neuhardt; b. ——; bap. Sept. 23; sp. Lorentz Guth,[14] Michael Neuhardt, Juliana Catharina, Peter Trexal's wife, Engel, daughter of Simon Trumer.

WEBER, JOHANN MICHAEL, s. Johannes Weber and w. Anna Maria; b. ——; bap. Sept. 23; sp. Michel Weber and wife.

SCHNEIDER, MARIA BARBARA, dr. Johann Nicolaus Schneider and w. Eva Schneider; b. ——; bap. Sept. 23, by Inspector T.; sp. Peter Traxel, Paulus Paillet, Maria Margaretha, Nicolaus Kern's wife, Anna Barbara, daughter of Nicolaus Seger.

1741.

Following five children were baptized by Rev. Mr. Boehm:

TRAXEL, GEORG FRIEDERICH, s. Peter Traxel, deacon of the Reformed congregation here, and w. Juliana Catharina Traxel; b. ——; bap. July 28, 1741; sp. Georg Kern, Frederich Neuhart, Salome. Gut, Lorentz Gut's wife, Susanna Ruch, Georg Ruch's[15] wife.

KERN, CATHARINA ELISABETHA, dr. Georg Kern and w. Catharina Elisabetha Kern; b. ——; bap. July 28, 1741; sp. Peter Traxel, church censor here, Roland Schmidt, Maria Barbara Neuhart, Michel Neuhart's wife, Luce Flickinger, Ulrich Flickinger's wife.

FLICKINGER, CATHARINA BARBARA, dr. Ulrich Flickinger[16] and w. Luce Flickinger; b. ——; bap. July 28, 1741; sp. Christian Brengel, single, Juliana Catharina, Peter Traxel's wife, Catharina Elisabetha Kern, Georg Kern's wife.

KNAUS, ————, —— Ludwig Knaus and w. Eva Knaus; b. ——; bap. July 28, 1741; sp. Nicolaus Kern and w. Maria Margaretha Kern.

SCHNEIDER, GEORG JACOB, s. Friederich Schneider and w. Anna Maria Schneider; b. ——; bap. July 28, 1741; sp. Georg Jacob, son of Georg Kern, Anna Barbara, daughter of Nicolaus Seger.

1742.

Notice. Children were baptized by Peter Traxel and Georg Kern. Commencing 1742 were baptized by myself.

JOH. CONRAD WUERTZ, V. D. M.
Helvetio Tigurinus.

FLICKINGER, HANS GEORG, s. Ulrich Flickinger and wife; b. Aug. 1, 1742; bap. Sept. 17, 1742; sp. Christian Brengel, Georg Kern, Juliana Catharina Traxel.

NEUHARDT, MICHEL, s. Michel Neuhardt;[17] b. May 7; bap. Sept. 19, 1742; sp. Peter Traxel, George Jacob Kern, Maria Marg. Neuhard, Cath, Elisabet Neuhard.

ARNER, HEINRICH, s. (Jacob) Ulrich Arner; b. Aug. 10; bap. Sept. 19, 1742; sp. Heinrich Hauser and wife.

PRENGEL, LORENTZ, s. Christian Prengel and Anna Barbara; b. Oct. 17; bap. Nov. 21, 1742; sp. Lorentz Gut, Peter Stoeckel,[18] Anna Maria Traxel, Lucey Flickinger.

1743.

HEUSSLY, ANNA MAGDALENA, dr. Joachim Heussly and Elisabeth Heussly; b. Nov. 23, 1742; bap. March 6. 1743; sp. Johannes Schneid and Anna Magdalena Burckhalter.

SCHNEIDER, JOHANN SAMUEL, s. Joh. Friederich Schneider and Anna Maria Schneider; b. Nov. 20, 1742; bap. March 6, 1743; sp. Johannes Schneider, Samuel Seger, Catherina Eberhardt.

TESCHLER, PETER, s. Adam Teschler[19] and w. Apel Teschler; b. March 18, 1743; bap. April 5, 1743; sp. Peter Traxel, Georg Kern, Friederich Neuhardt, Salome Gut, Susanna Rauch.

WAECKERLY, JOHANNES, s. Abraham Waeckerly and ———; b. April 10, 1743; bap. April 25, 1743; sp. Johannes Schneider and Christina Tanner.

NEUHARDT, PETER, s. Michel Neuhardt and w. Maria Barbara; b. Nov. 15, 1743; bap. Dec. 15, 1743; sp. Peter Traxel, Georg Kern, Friederich Eberhardt, Maria Margaret Neuhardt, Salome Gut, Hann Apel Teschler.

SCHNEIDER, JULIANNA CATHARINA, dr. Joh. Nicolaus Schneider and w. Eva Schneider; b. May 1, 1742; bap. Sept. 25, 1743; sp. Joh. Adam Doeschler, Juliana Catharina Traxel, Barbara Seger.

1744.

SCHNEIDER, PETER, s. Joh. Nicolaus Schneider and wife; b. Aug. 13; bap. Dec. 13, 1744; sp. Joh. Nicolaus Seger,

Johann Peter Trachsel, Peter Trachsel's son, Apolonia Toeschler, Cornela Kern, Nicolaus Kern's daughter.

TRAXEL, MARGARETHA, dr. Peter Traxel and w. Juliana Catharina; b. Oct. 25, 1744; bap. Dec. 21, 1744; sp. Georg Kern, Lorentz Guth, Michel Hoffman, Anna Barbara Neuhart, Apolonia Toeschler, Maria Margaretha Neuhart.

1752.

Math. 19. 14: Suffer little children, and forbid them not, to come unto me, for of such is the Kingdom of heaven.
JOHANNES JACOBUS WISSLER,
Dillenberga Nassauicus pt. p. of Egypt, Jordan and Heidelberg.

Egypt.

HOLTZLEINER, ANNA BARBARA, dr. Michael Holtzleiner and w. Anna Maria; b. Sept. 16; bap. Sept. 24, 1752; sp. Johannes Schneider and Barbara, Leonhard Schlosser's wife.

Heidelberg, Sept. 28, 1752.

REINHARD, ANNA MARGRETHA, dr. Johann Henrich Reinhard and w. Elisabet Maria, of Heidelberg; b. Aug. 7; bap. Sept. 28, 1752; sp. Joh. Henr. Schmid, single, son of Christian Schmid, of Heidelberg, and Anna Margretha Roeder, single, daughter of Henrich Roeder, of Heidelberg.

Egypt, Oct. 3, 1752.

GERSLER, PHILIP JACOB, s. Henrich Gersler and w. Barbara Alimand, of Egypt; b. Aug. 7; bap. Oct. 3, 1752; sp. Georg Jacob Kern, Philip Jacob Schreiber, son of the deceased Jacob Schreiber,[21] Anna, daughter of Johannes Freyvoger, and Margaretha, daughter of Michael Hoffman.

HOFFMAN, JOH. MICHAEL, s. Michael Hoffman and Eva Catharina, of Egypt; b. May 27; bap. Oct. 3, 1752; sp. Adam Deshler and Michael Neuhard, of Egypt; Maria Margaretha, Georg Jacob Kern's wife, and Magdalena, Johannes Draxel's wife.

KREIDLER, DANIEL, s. Johann Georg Kreidler and w. Sybilla; b. Sept. 29, 1752; bap. ———; sp. Samuel Seeger, Anna Eva, daughter of Friedrich Eberhard, Daniel, son of Henrich Sold, and Elisabetha, daughter of Michael Neuhard, all of Egypt.

LEHIGH COUNTY—1734-1834.　　9

Heidelberg.

This child was baptized with Joh. Hen. Reinhard't child.
NEUHARD, JOHANNES, s. Georg Neuhard and w. Anna Catharina; b. May 29; bap. Sept. 28, 1752; sp. Johannes Lamp and w. Susanna.

Egypt.

SCHNEIDER, SARA, dr. Johannes Schneider and w. Anna Margaretha; b. Aug. 16, 1752; bap. ———; sp. Joseph Kennel and W. Sara, of Egypt.

Heidelberg.

FILLER, CATHARINA, dr. Philipp Filler and w. Maria Elisabetha; b. Nov. 13, 1752, between one and two o'clock in the morning; bap. ———; sp. Jacob Benter and w. Catharina.
FUR, SUSANA ELISABETHA, dr. Leonhard Fur and w. Maria Catharina; b. Oct. 51, 1752; bap. ———; sp. Jacob Ferber and w. Susanna.

Egypt.

PALYET, JOH. JACOB, s. Paulus Palyet[22] and w. Maria Magdalena; b. Dec. 23, 1750; bap. ———; sp. Jacob Meckle[23] and Lucae Flickinger.
PALJET, ———, dr. Paulus Paljet and w. Maria Magdalena; b. July 28, 1752; bap. ———; sp. Peter, son of Ulrich Burckhalter, and Maria, daughter of Joseph Kennel, both single and from Egypt.

Jordan.

BRENGEL, PETER, s. Christian Brengel and w. Anna Barbara; b. Nov. 27, 1752; bap. ———; sp. Peter Steckel, Ulrich Flickinger, Anna Barbara, wife of Christian Leibrod, and Anna Barbara, daughter of Tobias Mosser.

1753.

Heidelberg.

OHL, EVA CATHARINA, dr. Michael Ohl[24] and w. Elisabetha Barbara, of Heidelberg; b. Jan. 9, 1753; bap. ———; sp. Andreas, son of Henrich Ohl, Henrich, son of the late Henrich Roeder, Eva Elisabeth, daughter of Bardel Gucker, and Anna Catharina, daughter of Henrich Ohl.

Jordan.

ROTH, EVA CATHARINA, dr. Johannes Roth[25] and w. Dorothea; b. Feb. 25, 1753; bap. ———; sp. Gottfried Knauss[26] and w. Anna Eva.

Heidelberg.

DAUBENSPECK, ANNA MAGDALENA, dr. Jacob Daubenspeck and w. Juliana; b. Feb. 16, 1753; bap. ———; sp. Conrad Bloss and w. Anna Magdalena.

PETER, MARIA MAGDALENA, dr. Jacob Peter and w. Elisabetha; b. Feb. 19, 1753; bap. ———; sp. Rudolph Peter and w. Anna Magdalena, Maria Barbara, daughter of Joseph Kennel.

1755.

RINGER, MICHAEL, s. Chr. Ringer; b. ———; bap. Oct. 5, 1755; sp. Michael Ringer and Catharina ———(?).

SCHNEIDER, MARIA BARBEL, dr. Daniel Schneider; b ———; bap. Oct. 5, 1755: sp. Heinrich Huber (?) and Maria Barbel Burghalter, Catharina Schneider.

1756.

SOLT, ———, ——— Daniel Solt; b. ———; bap. May 2, 1756; sp. Felix Arner and Mari ———(?).

AECKERT, GEORG NICOLAUS, s. Joh. Georg Aeckert and w. Anna Margaretha; b. ———; bap. June 6, 1756; sp. Nicolaus Nehlich, Maria Catharina Altmann, and Jacob Roth and wife.

BRITENNER, ANNA MARIA, dr. Joseph Britenner and w. Anna Maria; b. ———; bap. June 6, 1756; sp. Ulrich Flickinger and w. Lucin.

NEUHART, MARIA MAGDALENA, dr. Michael Neuhart and w. Maria Barbara; b. ———; bap. July 15, 1756; sp. Joh. Adam Docschler, Michael Traxel, Eva. Hoffman, Maria Magdelena ———.

ARNERT, ELISABETHA, dr. Felix Arnert[27] and w. Elisabetha; b. ———; bap. July 15, 1756; sp. Jacob Rex[28] and wife.

HERTZOG, ANNA LISA, dr. Joh. Nicolaus Hertzog and w. Maria Catharina; b. ———; bap. Aug. 15, 1756; sp. Christoph Baer, Christoph Feichterr, Margaretha, Michel Traxel's wife, Margaretha Saeger.

FRANTZ, CHRISTINA BARBARA, dr. Peter Frantz and w. Eva Elisabeth; b. ———; bap Aug. 15, 1756; sp. Samuel Wotring and wife, Johannes Berret, Christina, Jacob Wolff's wife.
RIEBELET, JOHANNES, s. Barthol Riebelet and w. Maria Catharina; b. ———; bap. Nov. 7, 1756; sp. Johannes Turn, Christina Margaretha Leibeguth.

1757.

WOLFF, MARIA MARGARETHA, dr. Jacob Wolff and w. Christina Wolff; b. ———; bap. Aug. 28, 1757; sp. Johannes Berret, Christian Seeger, Margaretha Seger, Barbara Wotring.
ANDREAS, WILHELM, s. Martin Andreas and w. Elisabetha Andreas;[29] b. ———; bap. Aug. 7, 1757; sp. William Wotring, Barbara Flickinger.
MEYER, ———, ——— Martin Meyer and w. Magdalena Meyer; b. ———; bap. June 26, 1757; sp. Elisabeth Mickli.
WOTRING, JOH. PETER, s. Peter Wotring and w. Margaretha; b. ———; bap. ———, 1757; sp. Peter Flickinger, Elisabetha Seger..
KERN, DAVID, s. Leonhart Kern and w. Johannetha Kern; b. ———; bap. Oct. 8, 1757; sp. David Doeschler,[30] Lorentz Neuhart, Margaretha Kern, Catharina Elisabetha Kern.

1758.

ECKERT, MARIA CHRISTINA, dr. Johann Georg Eckert and w. Anna Margaretha; b. May 11; bap. June 25, 1758; sp. Peter Altmann, Peter Wannenmacher, Maria Catharina Altmann, Maria Christina Schutter.
KERN, DANIEL, s. George Jacob Kern and w. Margaretha Kern; b. ———; bap. July 30, 1758; sp. Daniel Traxel,[31] Stephan Schneider, Philip Jacob Schreiber, Eva Catharina Burkhalter, Catharina Elisabetha Kern.
ILLEGITIMATE, ANNA MARIA, dr. of Elisabetha Dieter; b. ———; bap. Aug. 21, 1758; sp. Joerg Kopp, Anna Maria Kopp.
HAHN, MARIA CATHARINA, dr. Johannes Hahn and wife; b. ———; bap. Sept. 3, 1758; sp. Melchior Solt and wife.
MEHRKAMM, CATHARINA, dr. Conrad Mehrkamm and w. Margaretha Meerkamm; b. ———; bap. Sept. 11, 1758; sp. Martin Flick and w. Margaretha Flick.
HOFFMAN, ANNA ELISABETHA, dr. Johannes Hoffman and w. Maria Catharina Hoffman; b. ———; bap. Sept. 11, 1758; sp. Johannes Jundt, Anna Elisabetha Yundt, Anna Hoffman, wife of Michael Hoffman.

1759.

TRAXEL, CATHARINA ELISABETHA, dr. Joh. Michael Traxel and w. Margaretha Traxel; b. ———; bap. April 8, 1759; sp. Johannes Schneider, George Koehler, Catharina Elisabetha Kern, Barbara Neuhardt.

1760.

ARNER JOHANNES, s. Ulrich Arner and w. Margretha Arner; b. ———; bap. Feb. 7, 1760; sp. Johannes Kern, Juliana Catharina Hoffman.

PALLIET, EVA, dr. Paulus Palliet and w. Magdalena; b. ———; bap. March 26, 1760; sp. Johann Nicolaus Schneider, Maria Catharina, w. of Johannes Solt.

FLICKINGER, JOHANN JACOB, s. Peter Flickinger and w. Barbara; b. May 6; bap. June 1; sp. Jacob Flickinger and Eva Schneider.

1761.

On Feb. 8, 1761, were baptized:
ROETHER, ADAM and wife Margaretha Maria Susanna.
TRAXEL ———, wife of Han Nickel Traxel.
SEGER, MARIA SUSANNA, wife of Christian Seger.
SCHRIBER, ———, dr. Jacob Schriber and w. Catharina; b. ———; bap. May 23, 1761; sp. Georg Jacob Kern's wife and Juliana Neuhardt.

KERN, ———, s. Joerg Jacob Kern and w. Maria Gretha; b. ———; bap. July 5, 1761; sp. Georg Kehler.

KOHLER, JOH. PETER, s. Peter Kohler[32] and w. Juliana Margaretha; b. ———; bap. July 28, 1761; sp. Georg Kehler, Catharina Kohler.

1762.

FLICKINGER, JOH. MICHAEL, s. Peter Flickinger and w. Maria Barbara Flickinger; b. Nov. 20; bap. Dec. 5, 1762; sp. Michel Neyhart, son of Michael Neyhart, Catrina Flickinger, daughter of Ulrich Flickinger.

763.

KOHLER, EVA CATHARINA, dr. Peter Kohler and w. Juliana Margaretha; b. ———; bap. March 27, 1763; sp. Peter Roth, Christoph Kern, Margaretha Traxel, wife of Michel Trachsel, Eva Catharina Kohler.

KERN, MARIA ELISABETH, dr. Georg Jacob Kern and w. Margaretha; b. ———; bap. April 12, 1763; sp. Michel Neyhart, Jacob Shreiber, Sofia Traxel, Maria Elisabeth Kehler.[34]

SCHNEIDER, SUSSANA, dr. Hannes Schneider[35] and w. Margaretha; b. ———; bap. April 12, 1763; sp. Peter Burckhalter, Susana Seger.

1765.

BURCKHALTER,[36] MAGDALENA, dr. Peter Burckhalter[37] and w. Eva Catharina; b. April 17; bap. April 28; sp. Philippus Jacobus Schreiber, Peter Doeschler, Magdalena Mickle and Susanna Deschler.

FLICKINGER, CATHARINA ELISABETH, dr. Jacob Flickinger and w. Maria Elisabeth; b. April 7; bap. May 12; sp. Johannes Ries and Catharina Flickinger.

SCHREIBER, JOHANN JACOB, s. Jacob Schreiber and w. Catharina Elisabetha; b. July 1; bap. July 27; sp. Georg Jacob Kern and Juliana Schreiber.

FLICKINGER, JOHANN GEORG, s. Peter Flickinger and w. Barbara; b. Sept. 21; bap. Oct. 20; sp. Jacob Flickinger and w. Maria Elisabeth.

NEUHARD, JOHANN PETER, s. Michael Neuhard and w. Maria Barbara; b. Nov. 16; bap. Dec. 1; sp. Johannes Moritz, Peter Neuhard, Margaretha Buchman, Magdalena Kohler.

SEGER, ANNA MARIA, dr. Christian Segar and w. Susanna; b. ———; bap. Dec. 15; sp. John Seger, Catharina Drachsel, Anna Milia Hahn.

1766.

KOHLER, JOHANN JACOB, s. Peter Kohler and w. Juliana; b. Jan. 10; bap. Jan. 26; sp. Lorentz Gut and Magdalena Kohler.

TRACHSEL, MARIA BARBARA, dr. Nikel Trachsel[38] and w. Catharina; b. March 1; bap. March 9; sp. Peter Kern and Catharina Baliet.

HOFMANN, JOHANN PETER, s. Engelbert Hofman and w. Magdalena; b. Feb. 29; bap. March 16; sp. Peter Neuhard, Rosina Hofmann.

LEIBENGUTH, JOHANN PETER, s. Georg Leibenguth and w. Catharina; b. Feb. 1; bap. March 23; sp. Peter Neuhard, Stoffel Kern, Jeanne Frantz, Margaretha Meyer.

MICKLE, JOHANN JACOB, s. Johann Jacob Mickle[39] and w. Susanna Margaretha; b. April 14; bap. May 18; sp. Peter Doeschler and w. Magdalena, Valentin Fatzinger, Maria Barbara Hofmann.

KERN, MARIA MAGDALENA, dr. Georg Jacob Kern and w. Maria Margaretha; b. ———; bap. June 1; sp. Philipp Jacob Schreiber and Catharina Trachsel.

KELCHNER, JOHANN CHRISTOFFEL, s. Michael Kelchner and w. Elisabetha; b. Aug. 16; bap. Aug. 30; sp. Christophel Schneider and w. Anna Elisabetha.

KOHLER, JOHANNES, s. Jacob Kohler,[40] the younger, and w. Maria Barbara; b. Sept. 6; bap. Sept. 16; sp. Johannes Miller and w. Eva.

MARK, CATHARINA, dr. Joh. Nickel Mark and w. Eva;[41] b. Sept. 25; bap. Oct. 12, sp. Conrad Mark, Adam Maurer, Elisabetha Traxel and Maria Catharina Baliet.

ALLEMAN, CHRISTIAN, s. Jacob Alleman and w. Elisabetha Barbara; b. Dec. 6; bap. Dec. 14; sp. Christian Hunsecker and Catharina Baliet.

1767.

MILLER, PETER, s. Jacob Miller and w. Elisabetha; b. Feb. 17; bap. April 5; sp. Peter Neuhard and Magdalena Kohler.

HOMS, JOHANNES, s. Johannes Homs and w. Barbara; b. Feb. 20; bap. April 5; sp. Johannes Hofmann and w. Maria Catharina.

SCHREIBER, MARIA MAGDALENA, dr. Philipp Jacob Schreiber[42] and w. Catharina Elisabetha; b. Jan. 29; bap. April 5; sp. Peter Doeschler and Maria Elisabetha Koehler.

BECK, PETER, s. Theobald Beck and w. Anna Maria; b. Mar. 17; bap. April 5; sp. Peter Burckhalter and w. Eva Catharina.

DOESCHLER, JOHANN PETER, s. Peter Doeschler[43] and w. Magdalena; b. April 3; bap. April 20; sp. Martin Mickle and Barbara Doeschler.

SCHWAB, JOHANN MARTIN, s. Johann Martin Schwab and w. Anna Barbara; b. Feb. 8; bap. April 20; sp. Valentin Fatzinger and Catharina Doeschler.

VAUDRING, JOHANN NICKEL, s. Abraham Vaudring and w. Maria Margaretha; b. April 6; bap. 9; sp. Nickel Marks, Nickel Vaudring,[44] Magdalena Baliet and Elisabetha Trachsel.

FLICKINGER, MARIA MAGDALENA, dr. Jacob Flickinger and w. Maria Elisabetha; b. April 8; bap. May 10; sp. Michael Ringer and Maria Barbara, w. of Peter Flickinger.

LEIBENGUTH, MARIA MAGDALENA, dr. Christian Leibenguth and w. Magdalena; b. ———; bap. May 31; sp. Georg Leibenguth and Maria Elisabetha Flickinger.

NEUHARD, MARIA MAGDALENA, dr. Michael Neuhard and w. Maria Barbara; b. June 3; bap. June 28; sp. Friedrich Neuhard, Johannes Moritz, Magdalena Neuhard and Barbara Kohler.

KERN, SUSANNA, dr. Georg Jacob Kern and w. Maria Margaretha; b. Sept. 16; bap. Nov. 8; sp. Philipp Jacob Schrieber and w. Catharina Elisabetha.

FUCHS, PETER, s. Johann Nickel Fuchs and w. Margaretha;[45] b. ———; bap. Nov. 25; sp. Peter Roth, Juliana Kohler, Friedrich Neuhard, Barbara Kohler.

HOFMANN, EVA CATHARINA, dr. Johannes Hofmann and w. Maria Catharina; b. Oct. 30; bap. Nov. 22; sp. Jacob Mickle and w. Susanna, Michael Hofmann, Jun., Catharina Kern.

STECKEL, DANIEL, s. Peter Steckel and w. Elisabetha; b. ———; bap. Nov. 24; sp. Daniel Dorni and Appollonia Baehr.

1768.

LEIBENGUTH, SUSANNA, dr. Georg Leibenguth and w. Catharina; b. Nov. 21, 1767; bap. Jan. 3, 1768; sp. Michael Neuhard, Jun., and Maria Magdalena Leibenguth.

NEUHARD, CATHARINA ELISABETHA, dr. Peter Neuhard and w. Magdalena;[46] b. Feb. 25; bap. April 17; sp. Peter Kohler and Maria Elisabetha Kohler.

TRACHSEL, EVA, dr. Nickel Trachsel and w. Catharina; b. ———; bap. June 19; sp. Paul Baliet and wife, Nickel Mark and wife.

FLICKINGER, MARIA BARBARA, dr. Georg Flickinger and w. Eva; b. May 26; bap. July 3; sp. Peter Flickinger and w. Maria Barbara.

1769.

FLICKINGER, JOHANN PETER, s. Peter Flickinger and w. Barbara; b. Dec. 11, 1768; bap. Feb. 19; 1769; sp. Michael Ringer and w. Margreth.

FLICKINGER, CHRISTIAN, s. Jacob Flickinger and w. Maria Elisabetha; b. ———; bap. June 4; sp. Christian Reinert and w. Catharina.

HOFMANN, JOHANNES, s. Johannes Hofmann and w. Maria Catharina; b. May 11; bap. about three weeks after birth; sp. Georg Jacob Kern and w. Margreth.

1770.

WAEBER, MARIA ELISABETH, dr. Daniel Waeber and w. Margaretha; b. ———; bap. Feb. 19; sp. Juliana Kohler, wife of Peter Kohler, Peter Steckle, the younger, Anna Maria Kohler.

BUCHMAN, ——, —— Jacob Buchman and w. Margaretha Buchman; b. ——; bap. Nov. 18; sp. Conrad Marck,[47] Peter Myer, Barbara Neyhart, Maria Barbara Burckhalder.

1771.

ROTH, PETER, s. Philip Roth[18] and w. Catarina Roth; b. ——; bap. Jan. 6; sp. Georg Kehler, Maria Elisabetha Kehler, Peter Kohler, Maria Barbara Kohler.

HOFMANN,[19] MARIA MAGDALENA, dr. Johannes Hofmann and w. Maria Catharina; b. May 18; bap. June 2; sp. Dewald Kendel and w. Maria Magdalena.

NEUHART, MARIA BARBARA, dr. Michael Neuhart and w. Maria Barbara; b. July 2; bap. July 28; sp. Peter Burckhalter and Maria Barbara Neuhard.

TESCHLER, MARIA BARBARA, dr. Adam Teschler, the younger; b. ——; bap. July 28; sp. ——.

KERN, HEINRICH, s. Jacob Kern and w. Maria Margretha; b. July 19; bap. July 21; sp. Adam Teschler, the younger, and w. Maria Catharina.

KELCHNER, PETER, s. Michael Kelchner and w. Elisabeth; b. Aug. 4; bap. Sept. 8; sp. Peter Flickinger and w. Maria Barbara.

KERN, SUSANNA, dr. Peter Kern and w. Catharina; b. Sept. 1; bap. Sept. 22; sp. Peter Stoeckel, the younger, and Catharina Kern.

KERN, JOHANNES, s. Christophel Kern and w. Catharina; b. Aug. 31; bap. Oct. 6; sp. Jacob Schreiber and w. Catharina Elisabetha.

BURCKHALTER, SUSANNA, dr. Peter Burckhalter and w. Eva Catharina; b. Sept. 1; bap. Oct. 6; sp. Peter Kern and w. Catharina.

LEIBINGUT, MICHAEL, s. Christian Leibingut and w. Magdalena; b. Sept. 9; bap. Oct. 20; sp. Michael Neuhart, the younger, and w. Barbara.

MARX, EVA, dr. Nicholaus Marx[50] and w. Eva; b. Nov. 8; bap. Nov. 16; sp. Martin Mueckli and w. Catharina.

GRAF, MAGDALENA, dr. Georg Graf[51] and w. Barbara; b. Oct. ——; bap. Dec. 15; sp. Jacob Neuhard[52] and Maria Kohler.

1772.

MUECKLI, MARIA MAGDALENA, dr. Martin Mueckli and w. Catharina; b. Feb. 5; bap. March 8; sp. Nicholaus Marx and w. Eva.

THORMEYER, ANNA MARIA, dr. Andreas Thormeyer and wife; b. ——; bap. March 8; sp. Christian Jacob and N—— Wolf.

FLICKINGER, JOHANNES, s. Peter Flickinger and w. Maria Barbara; b. Feb. 21; bap. April 5; sp. Michael Kelchner and w. Elisabeth.

KOHLER, SUSANNA, dr. Jacob Kohler and w. Maria Barbara; b. Feb. 5; bap. April 5; sp. Peter Kohler and w. Juliana.

SHREIBER, JOHANNES, s. Jacob Shreiber and w. Elisabeth; b. Jan. 12; bap. April 19; sp. Georg Shrieber[53] and w. Juliana.

HARTMAN, CARL PETER, s. Jacob Hartman and w. Anna Margreth; b. Feb. 22; bap. April 19; sp. Johann Carl Shriebler and w. Anna Margreth.

FLICKINGER, MARIA BARBARA, dr. Jacob Flickinger and w. Maria Elisabeth; b. April 4; bap. May 17; sp. Sebastian Miller and w. Catharina.

HAUESLI, JOHANN HEINRICH, s. Jacob Hauesli and w. Barbara; b. May 29; bap. June 28; sp. Henrich Hauesli and w. Barbara.

WUESS, ANNA MARIA, dr. Georg Wuess and w. Anna Maria; b. —— 21; bap. June 28; sp. Georg Graf and w. Anna Barbara.

PFEIFFER, HENRICH, s. Henrich Pfeiffer and w. Elisabeth Barbara; b. Sept. 20; bap. Oct. 4; sp. Peter Gut [54] and w. Eva Catharina, David Mosgenung and Juliana Meyer

RISCHEL, MARIA CATHARINA, dr. Georg Rischel and w. Anna Maria; b. Sept. 3; bap. Oct. 4; sp. Abraham Martin and Barbara Gerster.

NEUHARDT, MARIA BARBARA, dr. Peter Neuhardt and w. Maria Magdalena; b. Sept. 6; bap. Oct. 18; sp. Joh. Nicolas Fuchs and Maria Barbara Neuhard.

HOFMANN, DANIEL, s. Engelbert Hofmann and w. Magdalena; b. Aug. 28; bap. Nov. 7; sp. Parents.

FLICKINGER, EVA SUSANNA, dr. Georg Flickinger and w. Eva; b. Oct. 11; bap. Dec. 6; sp. Martin Mueckli and w. Anna Catharina.

SPED, HANS GEORG, s. Johannes Sped and w. Anna Maria; b. Nov. 22; bap. Dec. 6; sp. Hans Georg Shed and Anna Barbara Burckhalder.

SEGER, MARIA SUSANNA, dr. Christian Seger and w. Maria Susanna; b. in the beginning of Oct.; bap. Dec. 6; sp. Stephan Baille[55] and Anna Maria Shaefer.

RECORDS OF EGYPT REFORMED CHURCH.

MILLER, EVA CATHARINA, dr. Sebastian Miller and w. Catharina; b. Nov. 21; bap. Dec. 27; sp. Jacob Flickinger and w. Maria Elisabeth.

NEUHARDT, FRIDERICH, s. Michael Neuhardt and w. Maria Barbara; b. Dec. 19; bap. Dec. 27; sp. Friederich Neuhardt and w. Apollonia.

1773.

RAUCH, JOHANNES, s. Peter Rauch and w. Margreth; b. Jan. 14; bap. Feb. 14; sp. Johann Theobald Herzog and Eva Catharina Saeger.

STOECKEL, PETER, s. Peter Stoeckel and w. Anna Elisabetha; b. Nov. 8, 1772; bap. Jan. 20; sp. Peter Burghalder and w. Eva Catharina.

MUECKLI, JOHANN PETER, s. Jacob Mueckli and w. Susanna; b. Jan. 17; bap. April 11; sp. Christian Miller and w. Magdalena.

MILLER, BARBARA, dr. Philip Miller and w. Catharina; b. Aug. 26, 1772; bap. April 11; sp. Parents.

LEIBINGUT, MARIA SUSANNA, dr. Christian Leibinguth and w. Maria Magdalena; b. April 12; bap. May 9; sp. Samuel Plessli and Elisabeth Hauesli.

DESCHLER, DAVID, s. Peter Deschler and w. Magdalena; b. April 8; bap. May 23; sp. Jacob Mueckli and w. Susanna.

GRAF, MARIA BARBARA, dr. Georg Graf and w. Barbara; b. April 30; bap. May 31; sp. Peter Kohler and Barbara, wife of Jacob Kohler.

KELCHNER, ELISABETH, dr. Michel Kelchner and w. Elisabeth; b. July 15; bap. Aug. 8; sp. Christophel Schneider and w. Anna Elisabeth.

KERN, SUSANNA, dr. Christoph Kern and w. Catharina Elisabeth; b. Aug. 9; bap. Sept. 5; sp. Jacob Kern and w. Margreth.

HOFFMANN, MICHAEL, s. John Hoffmann and w. Maria Catharina; b. Sept. 4; bap. Oct. 17; sp. Michael Hoffmann and w. Apollonia.

HARTMAN, ISAAC, s. Jacob Hartman and w. Maria Margreth; b. Sept. 18; bap. Oct. 17; sp. Peter Sigfried and w. Eva Elisabeth.

WUESS, JOHAN JACOB, s. Georg Wuess and w. Anna Maria; b. Oct. 9; bap. Oct. 17; sp. Jacob Kern and Maria Barbara Burghalder.

DESCHLER, DAVID, s. Adam Deschler[56] and w. Catharina; b. Sept. 17; bap. Oct. 17; sp. David Deschler and w. Susanna, David Kern and Susanna Baillet.

KERN, JOSEPH, s. Peter Kern and w. Catharina; b. Oct. 18; bap. Dec. 12; sp. Peter Deschler and w. Maria Magdalena.

MUECKLI, SUSANNA, dr. Hans Martin Mueckli and w. Catharina; b. Oct. 19; bap. Dec. 12; sp. Hans Jacob Mueckli and w. Susianna.

1774.

ROEDER, Maria Susanna, dr. Martin Roeder and w. Catharina; b. Nov. 10, 1773; bap. Jan. 23, 1774; sp. Joh. Adam Trachsel and Susanna Baillet.

VOITURIN, JOHANES, s. Abraham Voiturin and w. Margreth; b. Jan. 9; bap. Jan 23; sp. Joh. Peter Trachsel and Eva Catharina Saeger.

MILLER, JOHANNES, s. Jacob Miller and w. Elisabeth; b. Oct. 17, 1773; bap. Feb. 20, 1774; sp. Peter Kohler and w. Juliana.

KOHLER, ANNA MARGRETHA, dr. Jacob Kohler and w. Maria Barbara; b. Jan. 17; bap. Feb. 20; sp. Schoolmaster Johann Carl Shribeler and w. Anna Margreth.

TREISBACH, SUSANNA, dr. Johannes Treisbach and w. Elisabeth; b. Feb. 20; bap. March 6; sp. Susanna, daughter of Adam Treisbach.

SHICK, JOHANNES, s. Georg Emmerich Shick and w. Maria Margreth; b. Feb. 2; bap. Mar. 7; sp. Ulrich Hauser and w. Barbara

REISWIG, MARIA SUSANNA, dr. Johannes Reiswig and w. Catharina Margreth; b. Feb. 16; bap. Mar. 7; sp. Conrad Reiswig and Susanna Roth.

N. B. These three children were baptized on the other side of the Lehigh, the first in Allen, and the others in Moor Township.

THORMEYER, MARIA MAGDALENA, dr. Andreas Thormeyer and w. Catharina; b. April 1; bap. April 8; sp. Nicolaus Voiturin and Anna Maria Shreiber, widow.

SPED, JOHANNES, s. Johannes Sped and w. Anna Maria; b. Feb. 15; bap. April 10; sp. Lorenz Ruch and w. Charlotte.

HECK, JOHANNES, s. Andreas Heck and w. Barbara; b. Sept. 3, 1773; bap. April 23; sp. Jacob Shreiber and w. Catharina Elisabeth.

KERN, JOH. MICHAEL, s. Jacob Kern and w. Maria Margreth; b. Feb. 21; bap. April 23; sp. Michael Neuhard, the younger, and w. Maria Barbara.

MILLER, ANNA ELISABETH, dr. Sebastian Miller and w. Catharina; b. May 1; bap. May 23; sp. Georg Jacob Miller and Anna Elisabeth Herzog.

NEUHARD, CATHARINA ELISABETH, dr. Friedrich Neuhard[57] and w. Apolionia; b. May 9; bap. May 23; sp. Jost Dreisbach, Maria Barbara Neuhard, Catharina Elisabeth Miller.

SAEGER, ANNA MARIA, dr. Samuel Saeger[58] and w. Eva; b. June 24; bap. July 24; sp. Adam Kuntz and Eva Catharina Saeger.

BERGER, MARIA ELISABETH, dr. Conrad Berger and w. Elisabeth; b. May 11; bap. Aug. 21; sp. Henrich Beil and w. Marie Elisabeth.

ROTH, JOH. PHILIP, s. Joh. Philip Roth and w. Catharina; b. July 26; bap. Aug. 21; sp. Georg Graf and w. Barbara.

RAUCH, SUSANNA, dr. Peter Rauch and w. Anna Margreth; b. Aug. 4; bap. Sept. 4; sp. Johannes Grob and Anna Maria Leisinring.

GRAF, SOLOMON, s. Martin Graf[59] and w. Anna Barbara; b. Aug. 14; bap. Sept. 18; sp. Peter Stoeckli and w. Elisabeth.

NITSCHMAN, JOHANNES, s. Johannes Nitschman and w. Maria Margreth; b. Aug. 21; bap. Sept. 18; sp. Johannes Geringer and w. Maria Elisabeth.

SHAEFER, MARIE CATHARINA, dr. Dewald Shaefer and w. Magdalena; b. Sept. 7; bap. Oct. 2; sp. Adam Kuntz and Eva Catharina Saeger.

FLICKINGER, MARIA EVA, dr. Peter Flickinger and w. Maria Barbara; b. Sept. 21; bap. Oct. 15; sp. Georg Flickinger and w. Maria Eva.

NEUHARD, JOHANNES, s. Michel Neuhard, the younger, and w. Maria Barbara; b. Sept. 29; bap. Oct. 15; sp. Martin Meyer and Anna Maria Leisinring.

SEMM, MARIA MAGDALENA, dr. Georg Semm and w. Margreth; b. Sept. 22; bap. Oct. 16; sp. Peter Neuhard and w. Maria Magdalena.

WUESS, ELISABETH, dr. Georg Wuess and w. Anna Maria; b. Oct. 24; bap. Nov. 6; sp. Michael Kelchner and w. Elisabeth.

LEIBINGUTH, JOHANNES, s. Christian Leibinguth and w. Magdalena; b. Oct. 23; bap. Dec. 4; sp. Johannes Moritz and w. Magdalena.

RUCH, CATHARINA, dr. Lorentz Ruch[61] and w. Charlotte; b. Oct. 30; bap. Dec. 4; sp. Philip Knaus and Catharina Ruch.

FLICKINGER, MARIA MAGDALENA, dr. Georg Flickinger and w. Eva; b. Nov. 8; bap. Dec. 4; sp. Peter Flickinger and w. Barbara.

1775.

SAEGER, JOH. JACOB, s. Christian Saeger[62] and w. Susanna; b. Oct. 29, 1774; bap. Jan. 1, 1775; sp. Jacob Stoeckel and Anna Barbara Saeger.

MUECKLI, HENRICH, s. Joh. Jacob Mueckli and w. Susanna; b. Dec. 11, 1774; bap. Jan. 29, 1775; sp. Joh. Martin Mueckli and w. Catharina.

PFEIFFER, JOHANN NICOLAUS, s. Henrich Pfeiffer and w. Barbara; b. Jan. 8; bap. Jan. 29; sp. Joh. Nicolaus Meyer[63] and Christina Mosgenung.

MARX, JOHAN PETER, s. Joh. Nicklaus Marx and w. Eva; b. Jan. 15; bap. Jan. 29; sp. Joh. Peter Trachsel and Barbara Maurer.

HOFMAN, GEORG JACOB, s. Engelbert Hofman and wife; b. Jan. 6; bap. Feb. 26; sp. Joachim Hauesli and w. Margreth.

KERN, ELISABETH, dr. Christoph Kern and w. Catharina; b. Jan. 7; bap. Feb. 26; sp. Johannes Grob and Dorothea Ott.

FLICKINGER, JOHANN GOERG, s. Jacob Flickinger and w. Maria Elisabeth; b. Feb. 4; Mar. 26; sp. Johann Georg Sies and w. Maria Magdalena.

WEST, MARIA ELISABETH, dr. Georg West and w. Maria Elisabeth; b. March 3; bap. March 26; sp. Friderich West, Gertrude Stoeri.

SHREIBER, SUSANNA, dr. Jacob Shreiber and w. Elisabeth; b. Feb. 4; bap. April 17; sp. Peter Kern and w. Catharina.

RINKER, MARIA EVA, dr. Michel Rinker and w. Margreth; b. Feb. 25; bap. April 29; sp. Georg Flickinger and w. Maria Eva.

SHEURER, ADAM, s. Adam Sheurer and w. Anna Elisabeth; b. May 5; bap. May 21; sp. Theobald Hertzog and Louise Lutter.

MEYER, JOH. JACOB, s. Stephanus Meyer; b. ———; bap. May 21; sp ———Hartman, ——— Schneider.

RECORDS OF EGYPT REFORMED CHURCH.

DESCHLER, CATHARINA, dr. Peter Deschler and w. Magdalena; b. April 19; bap. May 28; sp. Peter Burckhalder and w. Eva Catharina.

ZERFASS, MARIE ELISABETH, dr. Adam Zerfass and w. Marie Elisabeth; b. June 12; bap. July 23; sp. Johannes Nitschman and w. Margreth.

HOMS, ANNA BARBARA, dr. J. Georg Homs and w. Anna Barbara; b. July 17; bap. Aug. 27; sp. John Hofmann and w. Catharina.

SEYP, WILHELM, s. Wilhelm Seyp and w. Susanna; b. July 23; bap. Aug. 27; sp. Antoni Shaefer and w. Catharina.

MEYER, BARBARA, dr. Peter Meyer and w. Catharina; b. Aug. 17; bap. Sept. 24; sp. Michael Neuhard and w. Barbara.

HARTMAN, DANIEL, s. Jacob Hartman and w. Margreth; b. Aug. 20; bap. Sept. 24; sp. Jacob Shumacher and Elisabeth Schneider.

MARX, JOHANNES, s. Conrad Marx and w. Margreth; b. Aug. 22; bap. Sept. 24; sp. Johannes Moritz and Barbara, wife of Michael Neuhard, the elder.

DESCHLER, MARIA SUSANNA, dr. Adam Deschler and w. Maria Catharina; b. Sept. 4; bap. Sept. 24; sp. Peter Mueckli, Eva Baillet.

NEUHARD, JOH. PETER, s. Friedrich Neuhard and w. Apollonia; b. Sept. 9; bap. Sept. 24; sp. Peter Neuhard and w. Magdalena.

BURGHALDER, ADAM, s. Peter Burghalder and w. Eva Catharina; b. Sept. 16; bap. Sept. 24; sp. Schoolmaster Joh. Carl Shribeler and w. Maria Margreth.

MUECKLI, DANIEL and ANNA MARGARETHA, twins, ch. Joh. Martin Mueckli and w. Catharina; b. Oct. 19; bap. Nov. 27; sp. Nicolaus Marx and Elisabeth, w. of Peter Stoeckel, Schoolmaster Joh. Carl Snribeler and w. Anna Margreth.

1776.

KERN, JULIANA, dr. Peter Kern and w. Catharina; b. Dec. 19, 1775; bap. Feb. 11, 1776; sp. Georg Shreiber and w. Juliana.

GRAF, JOHANN GEORG, s. Martin Graf and w. Anna Barbara; b. Feb. 14; bap. March 10; sp. Nicolaus Saeger and Anna Margreth Siegfried.

MILLER, JOH. JACOB, s. Sebastian Miller and w. Catharina; b. April 3; bap. April 21; sp. Nicolaus Saeger and Magdalena Herzog.

MICHEL, HENRICH, s. Johannes Michael and w. Catharina; b. May 18; bap. June 9; sp. Daniel Kern, Maria Elisabeth Frey.

MICKLI, DANIEL, s. Jacob Mickli and w. Susanna; b. May 29; bap. July 7; sp. Peter Mickli and Maria Barbara Burghalder.

FRANTZ, JOH. GEORG, s. Jacob Frantz and w. Margreth; b. June 12; bap. July 7; sp. Georg Koehler and w. Maria Elisabeth.

VOITURIN, DANIEL, s. Abraham Voiturin and w. Margreth; b. June 28; bap. July 21; sp. Abraham Voiturin and Catharina Trachsel.

KUNTZ, WILHELM, s. Daniel Kuntz and w. Christina; b. June 11; bap. Aug. 4; sp. Wilhelm Schneider and Catharina Hartman.

FLICKINGER, MARGARETA, dr. Peter Flickinger and w. Maria Barbara; b. Sept. 15; bap. Oct. 26; sp. Christian Bertsch and Margaretha Thiel.

NEUHARD, JULIANA, dr. Michel Neuhard and w. Barbara; b. Sept. 23, bap. Oct. 26; sp. Georg Jacob Kuntz and Juliana Seiberling.

NEUHARD, MARIA BARBARA, dr. Peter Neuhard and w. Magdalena; b. Sept. 25; bap. Oct. 27; sp. Friedrich Neuhard and w. Appollonia.

LEIBINGUTH, ELISABETH, dr. Christian Leibinguth and w. Maria Magdalena; b. Nov. 5; bap. Nov. 24; sp. Christian Bertsch and Elisabeth Haucsli.

FUHR, CATHARINA ELISABETH, dr. Johannes Fuhr and w. Maria Margreth; b. Dec. 6; bap. Dec. 12; died Dec. 13; s. Catharina Elisabeth Shad.

SAEGER, MARIE CHARLOTTE, dr. Samuel Saeger and w. Anna Eva; b. Oct. 30; bap. Dec. 22; sp. Lorentz Ruch and w. Charlotte.

KERN, JOHANNES, s. Christoph Kern and w. Catharina; b. Nov. 22; bap. Dec. 22; sp. Georg Koehler and w. Elisabeth.

1777.

RAUCH, CATHARINA, dr. Peter Rauch and w. Anna Margreth; b. Nov. 10, 1776; bap. Feb. 2, 1777; sp. Christian Saeger and w. Maria Susanna.

SHEURER, PETER, s. J. Adam Sheurer and w. Catharina Elisabeth; b. Jan. 30; bap. Feb. 2; sp. Michael Ringer and Anna Maria Herzog.

GROB, JOHANNES, s. Johannes Grob[64] and w. Anna Maria; b. Jan. 12; bap. Mar. 2; sp. Conrad Leisenring[65] and w. Sibylla.

FLICKINGER, JOH. JACOB, s. Joh. Georg Flickinger and w. Anna Eva; b. Jan. 31; bap. Mar. 29; sp. Joh. Jacob Flickinger, Catharina Keiper.

NEUHARD, JOH. FRIDERICH, s. Friedrich Neuhard and w. Appollonia; b. Apr. 1; bap. Apr. 20; sp. Georg Jacob Miller and Margreth Kuntz.

RUCH, MARIA SUSANNA, dr. Lorentz Ruch and w. Charlotte; b. Mar. 11; bap. May 4; sp. Nicolaus Saeger and Margaretha Saeger.

MEYER, ELISABETH, dr. Peter Meyer and w. Catharina; b. Mar. 2; bap. May 4; sp. Martin Meyer and Eva Catharina Kern.

MARX, MARGARETHA, dr. Conrad Marx and w. Margaretha; b. Apr. 6; bap. May 4; sp. Michael Neuhard and w. Maria Barbara.

HERTZOG, DANIEL, s. Theobald Hertzog and w. Catharina; b. Apr. 20; bap. May 4; sp. Adam Trachsel and Magdalena Hertzog.

MUECKLI, CATHARINA, dr. Joh. Martin Mueckli and w. Catharina; b. Mar. 30; bap. May 18; sp. Peter Mueckli and Margaretha Stoeckel.

SHREIBER, SUSANNA, dr. Jacob Shreiber and w. Elisabeth; b. July 14; bap. Aug. 24; sp. Christoph Kern and w. Catharina.

GRAF, MAGDALENA, dr. Martin Graf and w. Barbara; b. July 9; bap. Sept. 7; sp. Jacob Flickinger and w. Maria Elisabeth.

SEIP, GEORG JACOB, s. Wilhelm Seip and w. Susanna; b. Aug. 4; bap. Sept. 21; sp. Georg Goldner and w. Gertrude.

KERN, JOH. PETER, s. Peter Kern and w. Catharina; b. Sept. 15; bap. Oct. 26; sp. Joh. Peter Burghalder and Catharina Deshler.

NEUHARD, ELISABETH, dr. Peter Neuhard and w. Magdalena; b. Nov. 20; bap. Nov. 23; sp. Peter Kohler and Anna Elisabeth Peter.

1778.

OTT, MARIA MAGDALENA, dr. Bejamin Ott and w. Magdalena; b. Dec. 24, 1777; bap. Jan. 25, 1778; sp. Abraham Jund Sept. 1; bap. Oct. 15; sp. Peter Beil and w. Christina.

LEHIGH COUNTY—1734-1834.   25

ZERFASS, JOS. GEORG. s. J. Adam Zerfass and w. Maria Elisabeth; b. Jan. 15; bap. Jan. 25; sp. J. Georg Flickinger and w. Anna Eva.
GROB, JOSEPH, s. Johannes Grob and w. Anna Maria; b. Feb. 19; bap. Mar. 22; sp. Henrich Grob and Elisabeth Leisering.
PETER. JOH. DANIEL. s. Casper Peter and w. Elisabeth; b. Mar. 29; bap. Apr. 18; sp. Johannes Moritz and w. Magdalena.
MUECKLI, MAGDALENA, Ir. J. Jacob Mueckli and w. Susanna; b. Mar. 1; bap. Apr. 19; sp. Andreas Miller and w. Anna Elisabeth.
NEUHARD, MICHAEL, s. Fridrich Neuhard and w. Apollonia; b. July 11; bap. Sept. 6; sp. Michel Neuhard, the elder, and w. Barbara.
KOHLER, JOH. JACOB. s. Jacob Kohler and w. Barbara; b. Aug. 13; bap. Sept. 6; sp. Georg Koehler and w. Maria Elisabeth.
HOFMANN, BARBARA, dr. Engelbert Hofmann and w. Magdalena; b. July 14; bap. Sept. 6; sp. Michel Neuhard, the younger, and w. Barbara.
SHWANDER, HENRICH, s. Jacob Shwander and w. Barbara; b. Sept. 2; bap. Oct. 3; sp. Johannes Shad and Maria Margretha Gerster.
KNOER, EVA CATHARINA, dr. Leonhard Knoer and 'w. Susanna; b. Aug. 13; bap. Oct. 4; sp. John Balliet and Eva Catharina Kern.
DESHLER, MAGDALENA, dr. Adam Deshler and w. Maria Catharina; b. Sept. 28; bap. Oct. 4; sp. Peter Deshler and w. Magdalena.
MEYER, JOHANNES, s. Peter Meyer and w. Catharina; b. Oct. 15; bap. Nov. 29; sp. Peter Kern and w. Catharina.
MILLER, SUSANNA, dr. Sebastian Miller and w. Catharina; b. Oct. 19; bap. Nov. 29; sp. Andreas Siegfried and w. Anna Elisabeth.
HERTZOG, CATHARINA, dr. Theobald Hertzog and w. Catharina; b. Nov. 4; bap. Nov. 29; sp. Nicolaus Hertzog and w. Maria Cathar'na.
MARCK, DANIEL, s. Nicolaus Marck and w. Eva; b. Dec. 12; bap. Dec. 25; sp. Daniel Shneider and Eva Balliet.
MUECKLI, JULIANA, dr. Joh. Martin Mueckli and w. Catharina; b. Nov. 19; bap. Dec. 25; sp. Henrich Stoeckel and Catharina Mueckli.

KERN, MAGDALENA, dr. Christoph Kern and w. Catharina; b. Dec. 1; bap. Dec. 25; sp. Jacob Kern and Eva Catharina Shreiber.

1779.

MARCK, MARIA MAGDALENA, dr. Conrad Marck and w. Margaretha; b. Dec. 6, 1778; bap. Jan. 10, 1779; sp. Casper Peter and w. Maria Elisabeth.

NEUHARD, PETER, s. Michael Neuhard, the younger, and w. Maria Barbara; b. Dec. 23, 1778; bap. Jan. 10, 1779; sp. Peter Meyer and w. Catharina.

HARTMAN, ANDREAS, s. Jacob Hartman and w. Margreth; b. Feb. 12; bap. Apr. 2; sp. Andreas Knoer and Catharina Mueckli.

SIEGFRIED, MARIA BARBARA, dr. Andreas Siegfried and w. Anna Elisabeth; b. Feb. 21; bap. Apr. 2; sp. Martin Graf and w. Maria Barbara.

FLICKINGER, MARIA ELISABETH, dr. Jacob Flickinger and w. Maria Elisabeth; b. Mar. 23; bap. Apr. 24; sp. Martin Graf and w. Anna Barbara

NEUHARD, MARIA MARGRETH, dr. Peter Neuhard and w. Catharina; b. Sept. 2; bap. Oct. 3; sp. Georg Kuntz, Juliana Miller.

MEYER, MAGDALENA, dr. Peter Meyer and w. Catharina; b. Oct. 26; bap. Dec. 5; sp. Conrad Marck and w. Margreth.

KOHLER, MARIA ELISABETH, dr. Jacob Kohler and w Maria Barbara; b. Dec. 16; bap. Dec. 19; sp. Georg Graf and w. Barbara.

1780.

KERN, Jonas, s. Peter Kern and w. Catharina; b. Dec. 30, 1779; bap. Feb. 27, 1780; sp. Adam Deshler and w. Maria Catharina.

SHREIBER, JACOB, s. Jacob Shreiber and w. Elisabeth; b. Jan. 3; bap. Feb. 27; sp. Peter Deshler and w. Magdalena.

FLICKINGER, JOHANNES, s. Georg Flickinger and w. Anna Eva; b. Feb. 15; bap. Mar. 24; sp. Johannes Keiper and Catharina Homs.

FLICKINGER, MARIA MAGDALENA, dr. Peter Flickinger and wife; b. Mar. 5; bap. Apr. 19; sp. Georg Flickinger and w. Anna Eva

PETER, GOTTFRIED, s. Casper Peter and w. Elisabeth; b. Mar. 21; bap. Apr. 30; sp. Gottfried Laure and w. Susanna.

LEHIGH COUNTY—1734-1834. 27

NEUHARD, MARIA SALOME, dr. Fridrich Neuhard and w. Apollonia; b. Mar. 24; bap. May 15; sp. Jacob Miller, Eva Catharina Kern.

HARTMAN, CATHARINA, dr. Joh. Dietrich Hartman and w. Elisabeth; b. Apr. 15; bap. May 15; sp. Abraham Hartman, Catharina Mueckli.

MUECKLI, DANIEL, s. Joh. Jacob Mueckli and w. Susanna; b. May 7; bap. June 11; sp. Joh. Adam Miller and Maria Catharina, wife of John Hofmann.

LAURE, WILHELM, s. Wilhelm Laure and w. Margreth; b. July 21; bap. Aug. 22; sp. Johannes Rockel and w. Catharina.

BURGHALDER, HENRICH, s. Joh. Peter Burghalder[66] and w. Dorothea; b. Aug. 23; bap. Oct. 28; sp. Henrich Stoeckel, Eva Catharina Kern.

GRAF, PETER, s. Martin Graf and w. Maria Barbara; b. Sept. 25; bap. Oct. 28; sp. Peter Siegfried and Eva Catharina Graf.

KERN, JOH. PETER, s. Christoph Kern and w. Catharina; b. Sept. 21; bap. Oct. 29; sp. Peter Kern and w. Catharina.

MILLER, PETER, s. Sebastian Miller and w. Catharina; b. Oct. 5; bap. Nov. 26; sp. Peter Shneck and w. Magdalena.

MUECKLI, JOH. JACOB, s. Joh. Martin Mueckli and w. Catharina; b. Oct. 11; bap. Nov. 26; sp. Jacob Stoeckel and w. Eva Catharina.

TRACHSEL, NICOLAUS, s. Adam Trachsel and w. Anna Maria; b. Oct. 29; bap. Nov. 26; sp. Joh. Niclaus Trachsel and Barbara, w. of Michael Neuhard.

ILLEGITIMATE, CONRAD, s. Maria Margreth Gerster; b. Dec. 29, 1779; bap. Nov. 26, 1780; sp. Conrad Schneider and Sybilla, wife of Conrad Leisenring.

STOECKEL, MARIA SUSANNA, dr. Jacob Stoeckel and w. Eva Catharina; b. Oct. 11; bap. Nov. 26; sp. Joh. Martin Mueckli and w. Catharina.

MARTIN, JOH. JACOB, s. Joh. Adam Martin and w. Margreth; b. Nov. 21; bap. Dec. 7; sp. Jacob Gut, Magdalena Burghalder.

ROTH, JOH. JACOB, s. Joh. Philip Roth and w. Catharina; b. Oct. 30; bap. Dec. 24; sp. Jacob Kohler and w. Maria Elisabeth.

SIGFRIED, PETER, s. Andreas Sigfried and w. Elisabeth; b. Nov. 11; bap. Dec. 24; sp. Peter Kern and w. Catharina.

1781.

KOHLER, JOH. PETER, s. Peter Kohler and w. Juliana; b. Dec. 18, 1780; bap. Jan. 13; sp. Georg Koehler and Eva, wife of John Miller.

SHWANDER, FRIDERICH, s. Jacob Shwander and w. Barbara; b. Dec. 29, 1780; bap. Jan. 28; sp. Friderich Shwander and w. Catharina.

MARCK, MARIA BARBARA, dr. Conrad Marck and w. Margreth; b. Feb. 2; bap. Mar. 24; sp. Martin Meyer, Maria Barbara Marck.

NEUHARD, MARIA SALOME, dr. Michel Neuhard and w. Barbara; b. Mar. 11; bap. Apr. 22; sp. Fridrich Neuhard and w. Apollonia.

DESHLER, JACOB, s. Peter Deshler and w. Magdalena; b. Mar. 30; bap. May 6; sp. Jacob Shreiber and w. Elisabeth.

DESHLER, MARIA SUSANNA, dr. Adam Deshler and w. Maria Catharina; b. May 7; bap. June 3; sp. Johannes Baer and w. Susanna.

KOHLER, EVA MARIA, dr. Jacob Kohler and w. Maria Elisabeth; b. May 31; bap. July 8; sp. Conrad Shneider and wife.

HARTMAN, JOSEPH, s. Jacob Hartman and w. Margreth; b. ———; bap. Aug. 19; sp. Daniel Shwartz and wife.

MEYER, JACOB, s. Peter Meyer and w. Catharina; b. June 23; bap. Sept. 2; sp. Jacob Kern and w. Gertrude.

FRANTZ, SUSANNA MARGRETH, dr. Jacob Frantz and w. Margreth; b. Oct. 6; bap. Nov. 18; sp. Niclaus Voiturin and w. Margreth; Elisabeth, wife of Samuel Kestin.

1782.

KERN, JONATHAN, s. Jacob Kern and w. Gertrude; b. Nov. 11, 1781; bap. Jan. 1; sp. Georg Kern, Catharina Albrecht.

SAEGER, MARIA SUSANNA, dr. Nicolaus Saeger and w. Eva; b. Nov. 20, 1781; bap. Jan. 1; sp. Jacob Stoeckel and w. Eva Catharina.

HARTMAN, ELISABETH, dr. Johann Diedrich Hartman nad w. Elisabeth; b. Dec. 17, 1781; bap. Jan. 27; sp. Lorentz Ruch and w. Charlotte.

TRACHSEL, PETER, s. Adam Trachsel and w. Anna Maria; b. Dec. 30, 1781; bap. Jan. 27; sp. Henrich Stoeckel and Maria Barbara Trachsel.

HARTMAN, MAGDALENA, dr. Jacob Hartman, the younger, and w. Eva; b. Dec. 21, 1781; bap. Feb. 24; sp. Johannes Meyer and Eva Hartman.

BALLIET, MAGDALENA, dr. John Balliet and w. Catharina; b. Jan. 5; bap. Feb. 24; sp. Jacob Mueckli and w. Susanna.

LAURI, JOH. DANIEL, s. Wilhelm Lauri and w. Maria Margreth; b. Feb. 9; bap. Feb. 24; sp. Casper Peter and w. Elisabeth.

FREY, PETER, s. Leonhard Frey and w. Catharina; b. ———; bap. see in Schlosser's Church record; sp. Peter Frey.

FUHR, ANNA MARIA, dr. Johannes Fuhr and w. Maria Margreth; b. Apr. 16; bap. Apr. 19; sp. Andreas Siegfried and w. Anna Elisabeth.

BURGHALDER, MAGDALENA, dr. Peter Burghalder and w. Dorothea; Apr. 1; bap. May 12; sp. Stephan Balliet and w. Magdalena.

HELLMANN, ELISABETH, dr. Christian Hellman and w. Rosina; b. May 25; bap. Aug. 11; sp. Paul Knaus[67] and w. Catharina.

MUECKLI, HENRICH, s. Jacob Mueckli and w. Susanna; b. July 10; bap. Aug. 11; sp. Peter Mueckli and w. Eva.

FLICKINGER, JOH. GEORG, s. Georg Flickinger and w. Anna Eva; b. Aug. 3; bap. Sept. 8; sp. Adam Kerfass and w. Maria Elisabeth.

SHREIBER, ELISABETH, dr. Jacob Shreiber and w. Elisabeth; b. Sept. 7; bap. Nov. 3; sp. Jacob Kern and w. Margreth.

MILLER, CATHARINA, dr. Sebastian Miller and w. Catharina; b. Sept. 27; bap. Nov. 3; sp. Nicolaus Hertzog and w. Catharina.

KERN, CATHARINA, dr. Christoph Kern and w. Catharina; b. Oct. 29; bap. Dec. 1; sp. Adam Deshler and w. Maria Catharina.

1783.

STOECKEL, EVA CATHARINA, dr. Jacob Stoeckel[68] and w. Eva Catharina; b. Dec. 12, 1782; bap. Jan. 26; sp. Henrich Stoeckel and Christina Saeger.

LAURE, ELISABETH, dr. Gottfried Laure and w. Susanna; b. Dec. 30, 1782; bap. Jan. 26; sp. Casper Peter and w. Elisabeth.

MEYER, PETER, s. Peter Meyer and w. Catharina; b. Dec. 30, 1782; bap. Feb. 23; sp. Johannes Kern, Eva Shreiber,

KOHLER, MARIA CATHARINA, dr. Jacob Kohler and w. Maria Elisabeth; b. Jan. 31; bap. Feb. 26; sp. Leonhard Frey and w. Catharina.

MARCK, CATHARINA, dr. Conrad Marck and w. Margreth; b. Feb. 10; bap. Apr. 20; sp. Peter Meyer and w. Catharina.

SIGFRIED, DANIEL, s. Andreas Sigfried and w. Elisabeth; b. Mar. 8; bap. Apr. 20: sp. Sebastian Miller and w. Catharina.

NEUHARD, Conrad, s. Fridrich Neuhard and w. Apollonia; b. Mar. 15; bap. Apr. 20; sp. Conrad Greiter and w. Regina.

HERTZOG, PETER, s. Theobald Hertzog and w. Catharina; b. Mar. 16: bap, Apr. 20: sp. Adam Sheurer and w. Catharina Elisabeth.

HARTMAN, SOLOMON, s. Joh. Dider Hartman and w. Elisabeth; b. May 21; bap. June 15; sp. Conrad Ruch, Elisabeth Kleder.

REMELLI, GEORG, s. Georg Remelli and w. Elisabeth; b. July 20; bap. July 26; sp. Georg Koehler and w. Maria Elisabeth.

NEUHARD, JOH. JACOB, s. David Neuhard and w. Eva Catharina; b. June 22; bap. Aug. 10; sp. Johann Jacob Buchmann, Magdalena Neuhard.

DESHLER, CATHARINA, dr. Adam Deshler and w. Maria Catharina; b. July 29; bap. Sept. 20; sp. Peter Shreiber and Catharina Kern.

RINGER, JOHANNES, s. Michel Ringer, Jun'r, and w. Catharina; b. Aug. 24; bap. Sept. 21; sp. Johannes Peter and w. Margreth.

RUCH LORENTZ, s. Henrich Ruch and wife; b. ———; bap. Sept. 21; sp. Lorentz Ruch and w. Charlotte.

SOHN, JOH. JACOB, s. Jacob Sohn and w. Albertina; b. Oct. 6; bap. Oct. 12; sp. Jacob Laub and w. Catharina.

JOHNSON, Maria Barbara dr. Thomas Johnson and wife; b. ———; bap. Nov. 16; sp. Johannes Shantz and Margretha Haag.

RUCH, HANNA, dr. Lorentz Ruch and w. Charlotte; b. Oct. 12; bap. Nov. 16; sp. Christian Saeger and w. Susanna.

MILLER, ELISABETH. dr. Michael Miller and w. Eva; b. Oct. 27; bap. Dec. 14; sp. Jacob Hartman, Jun'r, and w. Eva.

1784.

BURGHALDER, PETER, s. Peter Burghalder and w. Dorothea; b. Jan. 7; bap. Feb 8; sp. Peter Deshler and w. Magdalena.

HELLMAN, GEORG JACOB, s. Christian Hellman and w. Rosina; b. Dec. 23, 1783; bap. Mar. 7; sp. Michel Neuhard, Jun. and wife.

HAAG, CATHRINA, dr. Jacob Haag and w. Elisabeth; b. Dec. 26, 1783; bap. Mar. 7; sp. Conrad Haag and Catharina Fischer.

BAERTSCH, JOHANNES, s. John Baertsch and w. Catharina; b. Jan. 17; bap. Mar. 7; sp. Christian Seger and w. Maria Susanna.

FENSTERMACHER, PHILIP, s. Christian Fenstermacher and w. Barbara; b. Nov. 20, 1783; bap. Apr. 4; sp. Philip Faust[69] and w. Barbara.

MEYER, CATHARINA, dr. Johannes Meyer and w. Eva; b. Mar. 4; bap. Apr. 4; sp. Georg Jacob Miller, Rosina Meyer.

BALLIET, JOHANNES, s. Johannes Balliet and w. Catharina; b. Mar. 15; bap. Apr. 4; sp. Peter Shreiber, Susanna Mueckli.

SHWARTZ, MARGARETHA, dr. Jacob Shwartz and w. Christina; b. Jan. 1; bap. Apr. 18; sp. Johannes Meyer and w. Catharina.

SHWARTZ, MARIA EVA, dr. Daniel Shwartz and w. Anna Elisabeth; b. Jan. 24; bap. May 20; sp. Conrad Shneider and w. Maria Eva.

MUECKLI, MARIA BARBARA, dr. Joh. Martin Mueckli and w. Catharina; b. Mar. 27; bap. May 20; sp. Johannes Stoeckel, Elisabeth Klein.

KERN, SALOME, dr. Peter and w. Catherina; b. Apr. 11; bap. May 20; sp. Peter Burghalder and w. Eva Catharina.

TRACHSEL, CHRISTIAN, s. Adam Trachsel and w. Anna Maria; b. May 1; bap. May 20; sp. Christian Drachsel and Sibilla Veronica Hecker.

FISCHER, SUSANNA, dr. Georg. Fischer and w. Anna Maria; b. June 20; bap. July 4; sp. Nicolaus Hertzog and w. Maria Catharina.

MUECKLI, JOSEPH, s. Jacob Mueckli and w. Susanna; b. May 26; bap. July 11; sp. Peter Shreiber and Barbara Miller.

MILLER, JOHANNES, s. Sebastian Miller and w. Catharina; b. July 22; bap. Aug. 1; sp. Georg Flickinger and w. Eva.

MEYER, PETER, s. Jacob Meyer and w. Elisabeth; b. July 7; bap. Aug. 1; sp. Michel Neuhard, Jun., and w. Barbara.

RECORDS OF EGYPT REFORMED CHURCH.

MEYER. MARIA MAGDALENA, dr. Martin Meyer and w. Margreth; b. Aug. 13; bap Sept. 19; sp. Johannes Moritz and Barbara w. of Michel Neuhard.
HARTMAN, EVA CATHARINA, dr. Jacob Hartman and w. Eva Catharina; b. Sept. 30; bap. Oct. 23; sp. Christian Hartman, Margreth Meyer
MEYER, CATHARINA, dr. Peter Meyer and w. Catharina; b. Oct. 24; bap. Nov. 9; sp. Daniel Kern and w. Magdalena.
FUHR, MARIA MARGRETH, dr. Johannes Fuhr and w. Maria Margreth; b. Aug. 30; bap. Dec. 19; sp. Lorentz Ruch and w. Charlotte.

1785.

LAURE, Elisabeth, dr. Wilhelm Laure and w. Margreth; b. Jan. 6; bap. Jan. 30; sp. J. Peter Rockel and Elisabeth Remelli.
HARTMAN, MARIA DOROTHEA, dr. Georg Hartman and w. Elisabeth; b. Jan. 12; bap. Feb. 27; sp. Michael Miller and w. Maria Eva.
KERN, JACOB, s. Christoph Kern and w. Catharina; b. Jan. 15; bap. Feb. 27; sp. Jacob Geiger and w. Eva Catharina.
STOECKEL, ABRAHAM, s. Jacob Stoeckel and w. Eva Catharina; b. Jan. 12; bap. Feb. 27; sp. Nicolaus Seger and w. Eva.
NEUHARD, PETER, s. David Neuhard and w. Eva Catharina; b. Feb. 14; bap. Mar. 10; sp. Peter Kohler and w. Juliana.
KNAPENBERGER, SOLOMON, s. Philip Knapenberger and w. Margreth; b. Feb. 24; bap. Mar. 26; sp. Caspar Ritter and w. Ottilia.
SIEGFRIED, ELISABETH, dr. Andreas Siegfried and w. Elisabeth; b. Jan. 4; bap. Mar. 27; sp. Margreth Heller, a born Siegfried.
KERN, JESSE, s. Daniel Kern and w. Magdalena; b. Feb. 1; bap. Mar. 27; sp. Johannes Kern and Margreth Kleder.
HARTMAN, JACOB, s. J. Dider Hartman and w. Elisabeth; b. Feb. 12; bap. Mar. 27; sp. Jacob Hartman and w. Margreth.
MEYER, MARGARETHA, dr. Johannes Meyer and w. Eva; b. Mar. 15; bap. Mar. 27; sp. Martin Ritter and w. Margreth.
GRAF, MARIA BARARA, dr. Martin Graf and w. Barbara; b. Mar. 3; bap. Mar 27; sp. Georg Graf and w. Barbara.
FLICKENGER, DANIEL, s. Georg Flickenger and w. Eva; b. Apr. 7; bap. May 8; sp. Sebastian Miller and w. Catharina.

NEUHARD, MARIA MAGDALENA, dr. Fridrich Neuhard and w. Appolonia; b. Apr. 16; bap. May 8; sp. Christian Hellmann and w. Rosina.
GROB, HENRICH, s. Johannes Grob and w. Maria; b. Apr. 26; bap. May 29; sp. Conrad Leisering and w. Catharina.
SHREIBER, DANIEL, s. Jacob Schreiber and w. Elisabeth: b. June 4; bap. July 24; sp. Christoph Kern and w. Catharina.
SAEGER, JOHANNES, s. Nicolaus Saeger and w. Eva; b. June 10; bap. July 24; sp. Martin Graf and w. Barbara.
KOHLER, BENJAMIN, s. Jacob Kohler and w. Maria Elisabeth; b. Aug. 21; bap. Sept. 18; sp. Peter Kohler, Esq., and w. Juliana.
DODERER, MARIA EVA, dr. Solomon Doderer and w. Catharina; b. June 20; bap. Sept. 18; sp. Jacob Hartman, jun'r. and w. Maria.
STOECKEL, PETER, s. Henrich Stoeckel and w. Maria; b. Aug. 27; bap. Sept. 18; sp. Jacob Stoeckel and Hanna, w. of Michel Shreider.
RUCH, GEORG HENRICH, s. Henrich Ruch and wife; b. Sept. 2; bap. Oct. 16; sp. Georg Meyer, Maria Ruch.
MILLER, JONAS, s. Georg Miller and w. Rosina; b. Oct. 1; bap. Oct. 27; sp. Christian Hartman, Margreth Meyer.
MEYER, JOHANNES, s. Jacob Meyer and w. Elisabeth; b. Nov. 16; bap. Dec. 18; sp. Johannes Moritz and w. Magdalena.

1786.

BURGHALDER, SALOME, dr. Peter Burghalder and w Dorothea; b. Dec. 7, 1785; bap. Jan. 8; sp. Peter Burghalder, Sen. and w. Eva Catharina.
MEYER, SALOME, dr. Martin Meyer[70] and w. Margreth; b. Dec. 18, 1785; bap. Jan. 29; sp. Henrich Stoeckel and w. Maria.
GEIGER, SUSANNA, dr. Jacob Geiger and w. Eva Catharina; b. Dec. 30, 1785; bap. Feb. 5; sp. Peter Shreiber and Susanna Kern.
HOERDLI, CATHARINA, dr. Robert Hoardli and w. Elisabeth; b. Jan. 16; bap. Feb. 13 ;sp. Jon. Martin Mueckli and w. Catharina.
MUSGENUNG, JACOB, s. David Musgenung and w. Anna Maria; b. Jan. 29; bap. Apr. 2; sp. Michel Zoellner and Margreth Meyer.
MILLER, JOHANNES, s. Michel Miller and w. Maria Eva; b. Feb. 20; bap. Apr. 2; sp. Johannes Miller and Margreth Zerfass.

34   RECORDS OF EGYPT REFORMED CHURCH.

HARTMAN, ESTHER, dr. Georg Hartman and w. Elisabeth; b. Mar. 1; bap. Apr. 2; sp. Jacob Stoeckel and w. Eva Catharina.

DESHLER, SALOME, dr. Adam Deshler and w. Maria Catharina; b. Mar. 8; bap. Apr. 2; sp. Paul Balliet and Susanna Kern.

SIEGFRIED, CATHARINA, dr. Andreas Siegfried and w. Elisabeth; b. Jan. 26; bap. Apr. 8; sp. Theobald Hertzog and w. Catharina.

MILLER, JONATHAN, s. Sebastian Miller and w. Catharina; b. Apr. 10; bap. Apr. 30; sp. Georg Fischer and w. Anna Maria.

HAUER, EVA CATHARINA, dr. Andreas Hauer and w. Catharina; b. Feb. 12; bap. May 25; sp. Jacob Hauer, Eva Cathrina Shreiber.

FUCHS, HENRICH, s. Andreas Fuchs and w. Eva; b. May 14; bap. June 18; sp. Henrich Stemmler and Catharina Helfrich.

FAUST, ABRAHAM, s. Henrich Faust and w. Catharina; b. Apr. 24; bap. June 18; sp. Andreas Hering, Magdalena Kelchner.

SHAD, JONAS, s. Johannes Shad and w. Elisabeth; b. May 20; bap. June 10, sp. Christian Seger and w. Susanna.

RUCH, ELISABETH, dr. Lorentz Ruch and w. Charlotte; b. May 21; bap. June 18; sp. Johannes Stoeckel and Elisabeth Knauss.

BUERI, MARIA CATHARINA, dr. Henrich Bueri and w. Maria Salome; b. June 28; bap. Aug. 13; sp. Georg Adam Blank, Catharina Kolb.

FISCHER, SUSANNA, dr. Jacob Fischer and w. Elisabeth; b. July 3; bap. Aug. 13; sp. Georg Shmoll, Catharina Klein

KERN, PETER, s. Peter Kern and w. Catharina; b. July 10; bap. Aug. 13; sp. Peter Meyer and w. Catharina.

NEUHARD, PETER, s. Peter Neuhard and w. Catharina; b. Sept. 7; bap. Oct. 8; sp. Friedrich Neuhard and w. Apollonia.

MEYER, SARAH, dr. Peter Meyer and w. Catharina; b. Sept. 20; bap. Oct. 8; sp. Jacob Kern and w. Maria Margreth.

TRAXEL, HANNA, dr. Adam Traxel and w. Anna Maria; b. Oct. 5; bap. Nov. 4; sp. Michael Neuhard, Sen., Catharina, wife of Nicolaus Traxel.

LEISENRING, EVA CATHARINA, dr. Conrad Leisenring[72] and w. Catharina; b. Oct. 3; bap. Nov. 5; sp. Philip Shantz, Catharina Pfeiffer.

SOHN, CATHARINA, dr. Jacob Sohn and w. Albertina; b. Nov. 20; bap. Dec. 3; sp. Ambrosius Remelly, Catharina Fliokinger.

1787.

KERN, SARA, dr. Christoph Kern and w Catharina; b. Dec. 1, 1786; bap. Jan. 7; sp. Peter Deshler and w. Magdalena.

HERTZOG, JOHANNES, s. Theobald Hertzog and w. Catharina; b. Dec. 10, 1786; bap. Jan. 7; sp. Paul Balliet and Catharina Saeger.

RINKER, EVA, dr. Michel Rinker, jun'r. and w. Catharina; b. Dec. 9; 1786; bap. Feb. 4; sp. Georg Rinker and Elisabeth Ritter.

MUECKLI, SARA, dr. Jacob Mueckli and w. Susanna; b. Nov. 27, 1786; bap. Feb. 4; sp. Johann Martin Mueckli and w. Cathrina.

HARTMAN, SARA, dr. Jacob Hartman and w. Eva; b. Jan. 7; bap. Mar. 4; sp. Abraham Hartman, Susanna Mueckli.

KNAPENBERGER, JONATHAN, s. Philip Knapenberger and w. Margreth; b. Jan. 24; bap. Mar. 4; sp. Adam Knapenberger, Elisabeth Kolb.

MEYER, EVA, dr. John Meyer and w. Eva; b. Feb. 22; bap. Mar. 4; sp. Georg Adam Blank, Margreth Meyer.

SHEURER, MARIA MAGDALENA, dr. Adam Sheurer and w. Cath. Elisabeth; b. Jan. 25; bap. Mar. 11; sp. Joh. Peter Shneck and w. Magdalena.

MILLER, SALOME, dr. Georg Jacob Miller and w. Barbara; b. Feb. 7; bap. Apr. 1; sp. Jacob Miller and w. Elisabeth.

HELFRICH, CATHARINA, dr. Johannes Helfrich and w. Magdalena; b. Feb. 8; bap. Apr. 1; sp. Georg Adam Blank, Catharina Margreth Hauck.

HARTMAN, MARIA MAGDALENA, dr. J. Dietrich Hartman and w. Elisabeth; b. Feb. 11; bap. Apr. 1; sp. Johannes Hofmann and Maria Ruch.

SIGFRIED, SOLOMON, s. Andreas Sigfried and w. Elisabeth; b. Mar. 19; Apr. 14; sp. Nicolaus Hertzog and w. Catharina.

SHAD, GEORG, s. Georg Shad and w. Salome; b. Mar. 13; bap. Apr. 14; sp. Jacob Miller and w. Maria Elisabeth.

HECKER, ANNA MARIA, dr. Adam Hecker and w. Catharina; b. Jan. 10; bap. May 13; sp. John Nickel Traxel and w. Catharina.

MEYER, DANIEL, s. Jacob Meyer and w. Elisabeth; b. July 26; bap. Aug 19; sp. Peter Stein and Margretha Neuhardt.

KOHLER, ABRAHAM, s. Jacob Kohler and w. Maria Elisabeth; b. Aug. 8; bap. Sep. 16; sp. Jacob Stoeckel and w. Eva Catharina.

NEUHARD, MARIA CATHARINA, dr. Friedrich Neuhard and w. Appollonia; b. Aug. 3; bap. Sept. 16; sp. Paul Knaus and w. Catharina.

KOCHER, STEPHANUS, s. Johannes Kocher and w. Catharina; b. Aug. 19; bap. Sept. 16; sp. Stephan Balliet and Elisabeth Ritter.

NEUHARD, DANIEL, s. David Neuhard and w. Eva Catharina; b. Sept. 3; bap. Sept. 16; sp. Daniel Buchman, Magdalena Neuhard.

STOECKEL, SALOME, dr. Johannes Stoeckel and w. Magdalena; b. Sept. 22; bap. Nov. 10; sp. Johann Martin Mueckli and w. Catharina.

GANGENWEHR, CARL, s. Georg Gangenwehr[73] and w. Christina; b. July 20; bap. Nov. 11; sp. Jacob Wotering, Sibilla Gangenwer.

GROB, JONAS,[74] s. Johannes Grob and w. Anna Maria; b. Nov. 4; bap. Dec. 9; sp. Peter Leisenring, Sybilla Pfeiffer.

BUERI, JACOB, s. Henrich Bueri and w. Maria Salome; b. Nov. 9; bap. Dec. 26; sp. J. Jacob Mueckli and w. Susanna.

1788.

MEYER, SUSANNA, dr. Peter Meyer and w. Catharina; b. Dec. 10, 1787; bap. Jan. 13; sp. Christoph Kern and w. Catharina.

KOCH, JONAS, s. J. Georg Koch and w. Elisabeth; b. Oct. 23, 1787; bap. Feb. 10; sp. Adam Traxel and w. Anna Maria.

BURGHALDER, MAGDALENA, dr. Peter Burghalder and w. Dorothea; b. Jan. 10; bap. Feb. 10; sp. Stephan Balliet and w. Magdalena.

HARTMAN, BENJAMIN, s. Georg Hartman and w. Elisabeth; b. Jan. 11; bap. Feb. 10; sp. Georg Shmoll and Catharina Hofman.

DUSSINGER, MARIA MAGDALENA, dr. Johannes Dussinger and w. Margreth; b. Jan. 14; bap. Feb. 10; sp. Stephen Meyer and w. Juliana.

HARTMAN, JACOB, s. Johannes Hartman and w. Elisabeth; b. Jan. 5; bap. Mar. 9; sp. Jacob Hartman and w. Margreth.

FISCHER, JOH. GEORG, s. Peter Fischer and w. Eva; b. Jan. 18; bap. Mar. 9; sp. Georg Flickinger and w. Eva.

MEYER, DANIEL, s. Martin Meyer and w. Margreth; b. Jan. 24; bap. Mar. 9; sp. Conrad Marck and w. Margreth.

BALLIET, ABRAHAM, s. Johannes Balliet and w. Barbara; b. Dec. 19, 1786; bap. Mar. 30, 1788; sp. (Rev.) Abraham Blumer and w. Susanna.

RUCH, ELISABETH, dr. Henrich Ruch and w. Elisabeth; b. Jan. 25; bap. Mar. 30; sp. Johannes Shad and w. Elisabeth.

FAUST, JOHANNES, s. Henrich Faust and w. Catharina; b. Feb. 17; bap. May 10; sp. Fridrich Bueri, Hanna Hering.

MILLER, SALOME, dr. Sebastian Miller and w. Catharina; b. May 1; bap. June 1; sp. Peter Miller and Catharina Flickinger.

HARTMAN, SALOME, dr. Christian Hartman and w. Magdalena; b. May 30; bap. June 29; sp. J. Jacob Mueckli and w. Susanna.

HECK, CHRISTIAN, s. Henrich Heck and w. Elisabeth; b. June 6, bap. June 29; sp. Christian Shwartz and w. Elisabeth.

STOFLET, SUSANNA, dr. John Stoflet and w. Eva; b. June 8; bap. July 27; sp. Ludwig Stoflet, Susanna Kern.

SHAD, PETER, s. Georg Shad and w. Salome; b. June 27; bap. Aug. 3; sp. Peter Neuhard and w. Catharina.

KOCHER, SALOME, dr. Johannes Kocher and w. Catharina; b. July 27; bap. Aug. 24; sp. Johannes Georg and w. Anna Elisabeth.

ARNER, EVA CATHARINA, dr. Jacob Arner and w. Margreth; b. July 27; bap. Aug. 24; sp. Nicolaus Seger and w. Eva.

HARTMAN, SARA, dr. J. Dider Hartman and w. Elisabeth; b. July 18; bap. Sept. 2; sp. Christian Shwartz and w. Elisabeth.

FLICKINGER, EVA, dr. Georg Flickinger and w. Eva; b. Aug. 6; bap. Sept. 21; sp. Ludwig Keiper and w. Caththina.

DESHLER, SARA, dr. Peter Deshler and w. Magdalena; b. Aug. 23; bap. Sept. 21; sp. Adam Deshler and w. Maria Catharina.

DESHLER, ELISABETH, dr. George Deshler and Susanna Mueckli; b. Aug. 31; bap. Sept. 21; sp. Jacob Mueckli and w. Susanna.

FISCHER, JOH. CHRISTIAN, s. Leonhard Fischer and w. Barbara; b. Oct. 5; bap. Oct. 14; sp. Maria Magdalena, wife of Johannes Moritz.

MEYER, MARIA MAGDALENA, dr. Andreas Meyer and w. Martha; b. Sept. 4; bap. Oct. 19; sp. William Meyer and Christina Remelly.

TRAXEL, JOHANNES, s. Peter Traxel and w. Sibilla Veronica; b. Oct. 4 ; bap. Oct. 19; sp. Johann Nickel Traxel and w. Catharina.

HOERDLI, ELISABETH, dr. Robert Hoerdli and w. Elisabeth; b. Dec. 4; bap. Dec. 28; sp. Christian Mueckli, Barbara Neuhard.

KERN, JOSEPH, s. Christoph Kern and w. Catharina; b. Dec. 10; bap. Dec. 28; sp. Peter Meyer and w. Catharina.

NEUHARD, DANIEL, s. Michel Neuhard, Jun'r and w. Barbara; b. Dec. 17; bap. Dec. 28; sp. Martin Meyer and w. Margreth.

1789.

KELCHNER PETER, s. Christoph Kelchner and w. Barbara; b. Jan. 9; bap. Jan. 18; sp. Georg Flickinger and w. Eva.

KERN, DANIEL, s. Peter Kern and w. Catharina; b. Dec. 29, 1788; bap. Jan. 18; sp. Christoph Kern and w. Catharina.

STOECKEL, SOLOMON, s. Henrich Stoeckel and w. Maria; b. Dec. 13, 1788; bap. Jan. 18; sp. Peter Sneider, Magdalena Mueckli.

WOTRING, ELISABETH, dr. Jacob Wotring and w. Magdalena; b. Dec. 25, 1788; bap. Feb. 15; sp. William Wotring, Susanna Saeger.

RITTENHAUS, MARIA SALOME, dr. Jacob Rittenhaus and w. Maria Salome; b. Dec. 20, 1788; bap. Feb. 15; sp. Michel Deubert and Margreth, wife of John Kern.

SOHN, MARGRETHA, dr. Jacob Sohn and w. Albertina; b. Jan. 19; bap. Feb. 15; sp. Conrad Miller and w. Margreth.

MILLER, JOHANNES, s. Conrad Miller and w. Margreth; b. Feb. 23; bap. Mar. 14; sp. Peter Traxel and w. Sibilla Veronica.

SIEGFRIED, JOHANNES, s. Andreas Siegfried and w. Elisabeth; b. Feb. 8; bap. Mar. 15; sp. Georg Fischer and w. Anna Maria.

STOECKEL, JOHN JACOB, s. Jacob Stoeckel and w. Eva Catharina; b. Mar. 21; bap. Apr. 25; sp. J. Jacob Saeger, Susanna Mueckli.

SHAD, JOHANNES, s. John Shad and w. Elisabeth; b. Mar. 15; bap. Apr. 26; sp. Daniel Kern and w. Magdalena.

DESHLER, ELISABETH, dr. Adam Deshler and w. Maria Catharina; b. Apr. 25; bap. May 10; sp. Peter Burghalder and w. Eva Catharina.

MUECKLI, MAGDALENA, dr. J. Jacob Mueckli, Jun'r and w. Eva Catharina; b. Apr. 11; bap. May 21; sp. J. Jacob Mueckli, Sen'r, and w. Susanna.

MEYER, MAGDALENA, dr. Jacob Meyer and w. Elisabeth; b. Apr. 18; bap. May 21; sp. Conrad Miller and w. Margreth.

HARTMAN, JACOB, s. Jacob Hartman and w. Eva; b. May 16; bap. June 7; sp. Jacob Hartman, Sen'r, and w. Margreth.

MEYER, JOSEPH, s. Peter Meyer and w. Catharina; b. May 4; bap. June 7; sp. Peter Burghalder,, Jun'r, and w. Dorothea.

GRAF, STEPHANUS, s. Martin Graf and w. Barbara; b. May. 1; bap. June 14; sp. Stephanus Balliet and w. Magdalena.

RUCH, WILHELM, s. Henrich Ruch and w. Elisabeth; b. June 9; bap. July 26; sp. Henrich Ruch.

RUCH, SALOME, dr. Heinrich Ruch and w. Elisabeth; b. June 9; bap. July 26; sp. Jacob Arner and w. Margreth.

FENSTERMACHER, MAGDALENA, dr. Dewald Fenstermacher and w. Catharina; b. July 21; bap. Sept. 20; sp. Conrad Shneider and w. Eva.

MERTZ, ESTHER, dr. Henrich Mertz and w. Elisabeth; b. July 14; bap. Sept. 30; sp. Christian Shwartz and w. Elisabeth.

RUEB, CATHARINA, dr. Isaac Rueb and w. Catharina; b. May 5; bap. Sept. 27; sp. Johannes Mufli and w. Barbara.

NEUHARD, MARIA SALOME, dr. David Neuhard and w. Eva Catharina; b. Aug. 7; bap. Sept. 27; sp. Peter Mufli and Maria Salome Bueri.

GROB, JOHANNES, s. Henrich Grob75 and w. Margreth; b. Aug. 15; bap. Sept. 27; sp. Johannes Grob and w. Anna Maria.

KOHLER, DANIEL, s. Jacob Kohler and w. Maria Elisabeth; b. Sept. 5; bap. Sept. 25; sp. Jacob Strein and w. Maria Barbara.

SHANTZ, HANNA, dr John Shantz and w. Magdalena; b. Sept. 5; bap. Sept. 27; sp. Peter Kohler and w. Juliana.

HARTMAN, SARA, dr. Johannes Hartman and w. Elisabeth; b. Sept. 12; bap. Oct. 25; sp. Christian Hartman and w. Magdalena.

JEHL, JULIANA, dr. Andreas Jehl and w. Margreth; b. Sept. 17; bap. Oct. 25; sp. Johannes Seger and Juliana Pelz.

HECK, JOHANNES, s. Henrich Heck and w. Elisabeth; b. Sept. 16; bap. Nov. 22; sp. Christian Hartman and w. Magdalena.

SAEGER, SALOME, dr. Nicolaus Saeger and w. Eva; b. Dec. 5 ;bap. Dec. 25; sp. Christian Saeger and w. Susanna.

1790.

STOECKEL, DANIEL, s. John Stoeckel and w. Magdalena; b. Nov. 25, 1789; bap. Jan. 1; sp. Jacob Stoeckel and w. Eva Catharina.

FISCHER, JACOB, s. Leonhard Fischer and w. Barbara; b. Dec. 21, 1789; bap. Jan. 24; sp. Jacob Miller and w. Maria.

ARNER, SUSANNA, dr. Jacob Arner and w. Margreth; b. Feb. 18; bap. Mar. 28; sp. Johannes Baer and w. Susanna.

BURGHALDER, DANIEL, s. Peter Burghalder and w. Dorothea; b. Mar. 25; bap. Mar. 28; sp. Peter Meyer and w. Catharina.

FAUST, MARIA CATHARINA, dr. Henrich Faust and w. Catharina; b. Feb. 14; bap. May 9; sp. Jacob Hering and w. Catharina.

FISCHER, JACOB, s. Jacob Fischer and w. Elisabeth; b. May 8; bap. May 24; sp. Peter Leisenring and Magdalena Mueckli.

SHAD, SALOME, dr. Georg Shad and w. Salome; b. Apr. 29; bap. June 27; sp. Peter Miller, Anna Maria Sped.

SHNECK, MAGDALENA, dr. Jacob Shneck and w. Magdalena; b. Apr. 26; bap. June 27; sp. Casper Ritter and w. Ottilia.

DEUBERT, MARIA EVA, dr. G. Adam Deubert and w. Maria Eva; b. May 19; bap. June 27; sp. Michael Deubert and Daniel Shneider's widow.

HARTMAN, ABRAHAM, s. Christian Hartman and w. Magdalena; b. May 23; bap. June 27; sp. Abraham Hartman, Susanna Kostard.

MILLER, JACOB, s. Sebastian Miller and w. Catharina; b. July 17; bap. Aug. 22; sp. Petter Fischer and w. Elisabeth.

NEUHARD, SALOME, dr. Peter Neuhard and w. Catharina; b. Aug. 1; bap. Aug. 22; sp. Peter Miller, Catharina Elisabeth Neuhard.

WALB, MARIA CATHARINA, dr. John Walb and w. Margreth; b. Aug. 17; bap. Sept. 19; sp. Jost Walb and w. Maria Catharina.

SOHN, DANIEL, s. Jacob Sohn and w. Albertina; b. Aug. 18; bap. Sept. 19; sp. Georg Flickinger and w. Eva.

FISCHER, ELISABETH, dr. Georg Fischer and w. Anna Maria; b. Aug. 29; bap. Sept. 19; sp. Georg Rinker and w. Elisabeth.

MEYER, CONRAD, s. Jacob Meyer and w. Elisabeth; b. Sept. 12; bap. Oct. 16; sp. Conrad Marck and w. Margreth.

STOFFLET, MAGDALENA, dr. Ludwig Stofflet and w. Susanna; b. Sept. 25; bap. Oct. 16; sp. Jacob Mueckli. Junr. and w. Eva Catharina.

SHEUER, JOH. GEORG, s. Adam Sheurer and w. Catharina Elisabeth; b. Sept. 14; bap. Oct. 17; sp. Georg Shad and w. Salome.

FEIGNER, JACOB, s. John Feigner and w. Catharina; b. Sept. 24; bap. Oct. 17; sp. Jacob Kendel, Susanna Flickinger.

LEISENRING, PETER, s. Conrad Leisenring and w. Catharina; b. Oct. 3; bap. Nov. 14; sp. Peter Leisenring, Elisabeth Zerfass.

KELCHNER, ELISABETH, dr. Stoffel Kelchner and w. Barbara; b. Oct. 7; bap. Nov. 14; sp. Michel Kelchner and w. Elisabeth.

MILLER, EVA CATHARINA, dr. Georg Miller and w. Salome; b. Oct. 10; bap. Nov. 14; sp. Johannes Keck, Eva Neuhard.

MEYER, JOH. GEORG, s. Peter Meyer and w. Catharina; b. Oct. 5; bap. Nov. 14; sp. Georg Kern and w. Barbara.

MUECKLI, SARA, dr. Jacob Mueckli, Jun'r, and w. Eva Catharina; b. Dec. 5; bap. Dec. 21; sp. John Balliet and w. Catharina.

1791.

SHAD, LORENZ, s. Johannes Shad and w. Elisabeth; b. Dec. 10, 1790; bap. Jan. 23, 1791; sp. Lorentz Ruch and w. Charlotte.

FREY, SUSANNA, dr. Martin Frey and w. Sibilla; b. Jan. 9; bap. Jan. 23; sp. Anna Maria, widow of Jacob Frey.

FENSTERMACHER, JOHANNES, s. Dewald Fenstermacher and w. Catharina; b. Jan. 19; bap. Feb. 20; sp. Johannes Fenstermacher, Elisabeth Feigner.

HECK, PETER, s. Henrich Heck and w. Elisabeth; b. Dec. 20, 1790; bap. Feb. 20; sp. Peter Burghalder, Jun'r and w. Dorothea.

BRETZ, ANNA MARGRETH, dr. Philip Bretz and w. Margreth; b. Mar. 11; bap. Mar. 17; sp. Christian Saeger and w. Susanna.

SIEGFRIED, SALOME, dr. Andreas Siegfried and w. Anna Elisabeth; b. Feb. 3; bap. Mar. 20; sp. Adam Sheurer and w. Catharina Elisabeth.

RECORDS OF EGYPT REFORMED CHURCH.

HERTZOG, MARIA MAGDALENA, dr. Theobald Hertzog and w. Catharina; b. Feb. 26; bap. Mar. 20; sp. Adam Traxel and w. Anna Maria.

RUCH, JOSEPH, s. Henrich Ruch and w. Elisabeth; b Mar. 20; bap. Apr. 17; sp. Adam Sheurer and w. Catharina.

MILLER, SUSANNA, dr. Jacob Miller and w. Maria; b. Mar. 11; bap. Apr. 17; sp. Johannes Moritz and w. Magdalena.

EHRENHARD, JACOB, s. John Ehrenhard and w. Margreth; b. Apr. 17; bap. Apr. 18; sp. Nicolaus Saeger, Jun'r, and w. Eva.

BUERI, ELISABETH, dr. Henrich Bueri and w. Salome; b. Apr. 8; bap. May 29; sp. Friedrich Neuhard and w. Apollonia.

KOCHER, PETER, s. John Kocher and w. Catharina; b. May 15; bap. June 13; sp. Peter Kocher and Magdalena Ritter.

HECKER, ADAM, s. Jost Wilhelm Hecker76 and w. Regina; b. June 2; bap. June 19; sp. Adam Traxel and w. Maria.

HARTMAN, ESTHER, dr. Jacob Hartman and w. Eva; b. July 15; bap. Aug. 14; sp. Henrich Bueri and w. Salome.

SHANTZ, ELISABETH, dr. John Shantz and w. Magdalena; b. Aug. 12; bap. Sept 11; sp. Jacob Flickinger and w. Maria Elisabeth.

RUCH, JOH. HENRICH, s. Lorentz Ruch and w. Charlotte; b. Oct. 1; bap. Oct. 8; sp. Henrich Bueri and w. Salome.

NEUHARD, MARIA MARGRETH, dr. David Neuhard and w. Eva Catharina; b. Aug. 27; bap. Oct. 9; sp. Wilhelm Laure and w. Margreth.

JEHL, MARIA ELISABETH, dr. Jacob Jehl and w. Anna Margreth; b. Oct. 4; bap. Dec. 4; sp. Wilhelm Walb and Margreth, widow of John Walb.

KERN, THOMAS, s. Peter Kern and w. Catharina; b. Oct. 31; bap. Dec. 4; sp. Joh. Martin Mueckli and w. Catharina.

1792.

KERN, DANIEL, s. Daniel Kern and w. Magdalena; b. Dec. 2, 1791; bap. Jan. 8; sp. Johannes Mueckli and Susanna Kern.

HARTMAN, PETER, s. John Hartman and w. Elisabeth; b. Dec. 13, 1791; bap. Feb. 19; sp. Carl Peter Hartman, Magdalena Bueri.

GROB, JONAS, s. Henrich Grob and w. Margreth; b. Jan. 3; bap. Feb. 19; sp. Conrad Leisering and w. Catharina.

KERN, DANIEL, s. Christoph Kern and w. Catharina; b. Jan. 16; bap. Feb. 19; sp. Jacob Shreiber and w. Catharina Elisabeth.

KERN, JOSEPH, s. Nicolaus Kern and w. Catharina; b. Jan. 18; bap. Feb. 19; sp. Jacob Kern and w. Margreth.

GROB, TOBIAS,77 s. Johannes Grob and w. Anna Maria; b. Jan. 29 ; bap. Mar. 18; sp. Schoolmaster Jacob Strein and w. Maria Barbara.

SHAD, MAGDALENA, dr. Georg and w. Salome; b. Jan. 28; bap. Mar. 25; sp. Adam Sheurer and w. Catharina.

FENSTERMACHER, SALOME, dr. Dewald Fenstermacher and w. Catharina; b. Mar. 19; bap. Apr. 6; sp. Christian Bertsch and k. Juliana.

FISCHER, PETER, s. Leonhard Fischer and w. Barbara; b. Mar. 26; bap. May 13; sp. Peter Neuhard and Christina Klein.

SAEGER, MARIA MAGDALENA, dr. Nicolaus Saeger and w. Eva; b. Apr. 18; bap. Mar. 17; sp. Nicolaus Wotring and w. Margretha

HECK, ELISABETH, dr. Henrich Heck and w. Elisabeth; b. May 8; bap. May 27; sp. John Hoffmann, Jun'r, and Barbara Meyer.

STOECKEL, PETER, s. John Stoeckel and w. Magdalena; b. June 12; bap. July 15; sp. Michael Neuhard and w. Barbara.

BURGHALDER, JOSEPH, s. Peter Burghalder and w. Dorothea; b. May 25; bap. July 15; sp. Nicolaus Saeger and w. Eva.

HARTMAN, ELISABETH, dr. Georg Hartman and w. Elisabeth; b. May 21; bap. Aug. 12; sp. Christian Shwartz and w. Elisabeth.

NEUHARD, MAGDALENA, dr. Michael Neuhard and w. Elisabeth; b. July 16; bap. Aug. 31; sp. Michael Neuhard and w. Barbara.

FEIGNER, JOHANNES, s. Johannes Feigner and w. Catharina; b. July 22; bap. Sept. 9; sp. Johannes Hofmann and Maria Hefelfinger.

FISCHER, JOHANNES, s. Georg Fischer and w. Anna Maria; b. July 24; bap. Sept. 9; sp. Adam Sheurer and w. Catharina.

MUECKLI, ELISABETH, dr. Christian Mueckli and w. Elisabeth; b. Aug. 13; bap. Oct. 6; sp. John Jacob Mueckli and w. Susanna.

HARTMAN, JOSEPH, s. Christian Hartman and w. Magdalena; b. Aug. 26; bap. Oct. 6; sp. Jacob Shreiber and w. Elisabeth.

MILLER, MARIA MAGDALENA, dr. Michael Miller and w. Eva; b. Sept. 8; bap. Oct. 6; sp. Jacob Philip Faust and w. Barbara.

SAEGER, DANIEL, s. Johannes Saeger[79] and w. Magdalena; b. Aug. 29; bap. Oct. 6; sp. Johannes Ritter and Elisabeth Saeger.

GLOECKNER, SUSANNA, dr. Nicolaus Gloeckner and w. Barbara; b. July 25; bap. Oct. 7; sp. Gottfried Lauri and w. Susanna.

ILLEGITIMATE, MICHAEL, s. Michael Zoellner and Cathrina Flickinger; b. Oct. 25, 1791; bap. Oct. 15, 1792; sp. Jacob Flickinger and w. Maria Elisabeth.

TRAXEL, PETER, s. Peter Traxel and w. Sibilla Veronica; b. Sept. 25; bap. Nov. 4; sp. Jost Wilhelm Hecker and w. Regina.

SHEURER, JOSEPH, s. Adam Sheurer and w. Catharina; b. Oct. 10; bap. Nov. 18; sp. Andreas Siegfried and w. Maria Elisabeth.

THOMAS, PETER, s. Conrad Thomas and w. Elisabeth; b. Dec. 6; bap. Dec. 25; sp. Peter Neuhard and w. Catharina.

STOFFLET, MARIA, d. John Stofflet and w. Eva; b. Nov. 22; bap. Dec. 25; sp. Jonas Hecker and Maria Stofflet.

HAUSER, NICOLAUS, s. Georg Hauser and w. Elisabeth; b. Dec. 16; bap. Dec. 25; sp. Nicolaus Kern and w. Catharina.

1793.

KOCHER, DANIEL, s. John Kocher and w. Catharina; b. Nov. 15, 1792; bap. Jan. 6; sp. Joseph Balliet and w. Margreth.

MEYER, MARIA MAGDALENA, dr. Georg Meyer and w. Maria; b. Jan. 13; bap. Mar. 3; sp. Jost Meyer and w. Maria.

FENSTERMACHER, ELISABETH, dr. Jacob Fenstermacher and w. Margreth; b. Jan. 20; bap. Mar. 3; sp. Johannes Fenstermacher and w. Elisabeth.

' SIEGFRIED, JOH. ANDREAS, s. Andreas Siegfried and w. Anna Elisabeth; b. Jan. 4; bap. Mar. 3; sp. Andreas Rueb and w. Eva.

KELCHNER, SUSANNA, dr. Christoph Kelchner and w Barbara; b Jan. 5; bap. Mar. 3; sp. Peter Kelchner, Susanna Flickinger.

MILLER, BARBARA, dr. Jacob Miller and w. Maria; b.
Feb. 3; bap. Mar. 3; sp. Leonhard Fischer and w. Barbara.
HORNUNG, SALOME, dr. Johannes Hornung and w. Elisabeth; b. Feb. 24; bap. Mar. 6; sp. Samuel Wotring, Barbara Remelli.
NEUHARD, JONAS, s. Michael Neuhard and w. Barbara; b. Mar. 12; bap. Mar. 29; sp. Johannes Moritz and w. Magdalena;
LEISENRING, JOHANNES, s. Conrad Leisenring and w. Catharina; b. Feb. 7; bap. Mar. 29; sp. Henrich Grob and w. Margreth.
MEYER, GOTTFRIED, s. Jacob Meyer and w. Elisabeth; b. Feb. 18; bap. Mar. 29; sp. Gottfried Lauri and w. Susanna.
KOHLER, JOHANNES, s. Jacob Kohler and w. Maria Elisabeth; b. Feb. 21; bap. Mar. 29; sp. Michael Frey and w. Barbara.
SHAD, CATHARINA, dr. Johannes Shad and w. Elisabeth b. Feb. 27; bap. Mar. 29; sp. Isaac Herzog and w. Margreth.
FREY, MARIA ELISABETH, dr. Martin Frey and w. Sybilla; b. Feb. 7; bap. Mar. 29; sp. Jacob Kohler and w. Maria Elisabeth.
TRAXEL, JONAS, s. Adam Traxel and w. Anna Maria; b. Mar. 26; bap. Apr. 13; sp. Jonas Hecker and Maria Stoffiet.
LINDEMAN, CATHARINA ELISABETH, dr. Jacob Lindeman and w. Eva; b. Feb. 5; bap. Apr. 14; sp. Philip Odenwaelder and w. Catharina.
HARTMAN, DANIEL, s. Abraham Hartman and w. Barbara; b. Mar. 27; bap. May 9; sp. Jacob Hartman and w. Eva.
SHMOLL, CATHARINA, dr. Georg Shmoll[80] and w. Susanna; b. Mar. 13; bap. May 9; sp. Georg Koehler and w. Maria Elisabeth.
SHAD, SUSANNA, dr. Georg Shad and w. Salome; b. Apr. 14; bap. June 2; sp. Nicolaus Antoni and w. Maria Elisabeth.
SOHN, ELISABETH, dr. Jacob Sohn and w. Albertina; b. May 29; bap. June 23; sp. Jacob Frantz and w. Margreth.
DODERER, ELISABETH, dr. Solomon Doderer and w. Catharina Elisabeth; b. Apr. 23; bap. June 23; sp. Christian Swartz and w. Elisabeth.
MENSCH, ADAM, s. Adam Mensch and w. Margreth; b. Mar. 12, 1792; bap. June 23, 1793; sp. Adam Zerfass and w Maria Elisabeth.

MEYER, DOROTHEA, dr. Peter Meyer and w. Catharina; b. July 31; bap. Sept. 15; sp. Martin Meyer and w. Margreth.

KERN, PETER, s. Nicklaus Kern and w. Catharina; b. Sept. 20; bap. Oct. 12; sp. Peter Meyer and w. Catharina.

HARTMAN, ELISABETH, dr. Jacob Hartman and w. Eva; b. Sept. 9; bap. Oct. 12; sp. John Hofmann and w. Catharina.

HECKER, ELISABETH, dr. Jost Wilhelm Hecker and w. Regina; b. Oct. 15; bap. Nov. 10; sp. John Stofflet and w. Eva.

WILLIAMSON, JACOB, s. Samuel Williamson and w. Elisabeth; b. Oct. 6; bap. Nov. 10; sp. Peter Burghalder, Sen'r, and w. Eva Catharina.

HECKER, DANIEL, s. Jonas Hecker and w. Magdalena; b. Nov. 29; bap. Dec. 26; sp. Adam Traxel and w. Anna Maria.

1794

HARTMAN, ELISABETH, dr. Johannes Hartman and w. Elisabeth; b. Nov. 9, 1793; bap. Jan. 5; sp. Henrich Bueri and w. Salome.

FUHR, JOSEPH, s. Johannes Fuhr and w. Juliana; b. Feb. 6; bap. Feb. 9; sp. Peter Miller and Elisabeth Sigli.

WILLAUER, MARIA, dr. Joseph Willauer and w. Margreth; b. Feb. 23; bap. Mar. 5; sp. Margretha, Jacob Hartmann's widow.

NEUHARD, SALOME, dr. Michael Neuhard, Jun'r, and w Elisabeth; b. Jan. 19; bap. Mar. 9; sp. Peter Neuhard, Juliana Neuhard.

REMELI, JONAS, s. Johannes Remeli and w. Catharina; b. Mar. 24, bap. Apr. 6; sp. Conrad Laubach, Anna Maria Remeli.

ANTONI, JACOB, s. Philip Antoni and w. Elisabeth; b. Feb. 17; bap. May 3; sp. Jacob Mueckli and w. Catharina.

MUECKLI, JACOB, s. Jacob Mueckli and w. Catharina; b. Mar. 27; bap. May 3; sp. Jacob Shreiber and w. Elisabeth.

FISCHER, ELISABETH, dr. Leonhard Fischer and w. Barbara; b. Mar. 8; bap. Apr. 3; sp. John Neuhard, Elisabeth Neuhard.

BERENTZ, MAGDALENA, dr. Georg Berentz and w. Margreth; b. Apr. 9; bap. May 3; sp. Friedrich Neuhard, Magdalena Fischer.

BURGHALDER, CATHARINA, dr. Peter Burghalder and w. Dorothea; b. Apr. 8; bap. May 3; sp. Jacob Stoeckel and w. Eva Catharina.

LEHIGH COUNTY—1734-1834. 47

STREIN, MARIA BARBARA, dr. Schoolmaster Jacob Strein and w. Maria Barbara; b. July 26; bap. Aug. 6; sp. Jacob Kohler and w. Maria Elisabeth.

KOCHER, CATHARINA, dr. John Kocher and w. Catharina; b. July 15;·bap. Aug. 24; sp. Peter Kocher and w. Elisabeth.

MUECKLI, SALOME, dr. Christian Mueckli and w. Elisabeth; b. June 25; bap. Sept. 21; sp. Peter Mueckli and Magdalena Bueri.

HORNUNG,˜SALOME, s. Johannes Hornung and w. Elisabeth; b. Oct.˜ 9; bap. Oct. 19; sp.˚ Abraham Zerfass, Maria Remelli.

SHMOLL, PETER, s. Georg Shmoll and w. Susanna; b. Oct. 1; bap. Nov. 16; sp. Peter Kohler, Maria Levan.

GROB, SARAH,[81] dr. Johannes Grob and w. Maria; b. Oct. 12; bap. Nov. 16; sp. Peter Shwager and w. Elisabeth.[82]

GROB, ELISABETH, dr. Henrich Grob and w. Margreth; b. Oct. 20; bap. Dec. 14; sp. Peter Shwager and w. Elisabeth.

HERTZOG, ADAM, s. Theobald Hertzog and w. Catharina; b. Nov. 18; bap. Dec. 26; sp. Adam Sheurer, Maria Krum.

KELCHNER, JOHANNES, s. Christoph Kelchner and w. Barbara; b. Nov. 21; bap. Dec. 26; sp. Peter Roth and Magdalena Flickinger.

HAUSER, ELISABETH, dr. J. Georg Hauser and w. Elisabeth; b. Dec. 13; bap. Dec. 26; sp. Jacob Shreiber and w. Elisabeth.

NAUMANN, MICHAEL, s. Michael Neumann and w Anna Maria ;b. Dec. 5; bap. Dec. 28; sp. Nicklaus Gloecker and w. Barbara.

1795.

MILLER, JONAS, s. Jacob Miler and w. Anna Maria; b. Dec. 31, 1794; bap. Feb. 22; sp. Antony Fischer, Juliana Neuhard.

GLOECKNER, JOHANNES, s. Nicklaus Gloeckner and w. Barbara; b. Jan. 24; bap. Feb. 22; sp. John Balliet and w. Catharina.

NEUHARD, CATHARINA, dr. Friedrich Neuhard and w. Elisabeth; b. Feb. 1; bap. Mar. 22; sp. Peter Neuhard and Juliana Neuhard.

JEHL, CATHARINA ELISABETHA, dr. Jacob Jehl and w. Margreth; b. Jan. 25; bap. Apr. 6; sp. Henrich Helfrich and Eva Rincker.

SOHN, MARIA BARBARA, dr. Jacob Sohn and w. Albertina; b. Feb. 28; bap. Apr 6; sp. Maria Barbara, wife of Samuel Wotring.

RECORDS OF EGYPT REFORMED CHURCH.

TRAXEL, CATHARINA, dr. Peter Traxel and w. Sybilla; b. Mar. 6; bap. Apr. 6; sp. Niclaus Balliet and Sarah Koch.

DRAXEL, SALOME, dr. John Draxel and w. Catharina; b. May 2; bap. May 24; sp. Peter Draxel, Sen'r, and w. Anna Maria.

LAURI, CATHARINA, dr. Gottfried Lauri and w. Susanna; b. Apr. 29; bap. June 14; sp. Georg Flickinger and w. Eva.

SIEGFRIED, JOSEPH, s. Andreas Siegfried and w. Anna Elisabeth; b. June 16; bap. Apr. 9; sp. Peter Sheurer, Magdalena Graf.

MEYER, ELISABETH, dr. Jacob Meyer and w. Elisabeth; b. July 1; bap. Aug. 9; sp. Friedrich Neuhard and w. Elisabeth.

KERN, ANNA, dr. Nicolaus Kern and w. Catharina; b. July 19; bap. Sept. 6; sp. Nicolaus Saeger and w. Magdalena.

DINCKY, PETER, s. Jacob Dincky and w. Susanna; b. July 4; bap Sept. 6; sp. Nicolaus Wotring and w. Margreth.

MUSIC, CATHARINA, dr. David Music[83] and w. Elisabeth; b. Aug. 4: bap. Sept. 27; sp. Georg Henrich, Catharina Music.

FISCHER, PETER, s. Georg Fischer and w. Anna Maria; b. Aug. 30; bap. Oct. 4; sp. Gottfried Lauri and w. Susanna.

RITTER, DANIEL, s. John Ritter and w. Anna Maria; b. Sept. 5; bap. Oct. 4; sp. Peter Hefelfinger, Catharina Ritter.

MILLER, SUSANNA, dr. Peter Miller and w. Christina; b. Sept. 13; bap. Oct. 4; sp. Johannes Miller and Susanna Deubert.

FENSTERMACHER, ELISABETH, dr. Dewald Fenstermacher and w. Catharina; b. Nov. 4; bap. Dec. 27; sp. Johannes Shad and w. Elisabeth.

HECKER, WILHELM, s. Jonas Hecker and w. Magdalena; b. Nov. 21; bap. Dec. 27; sp. Jacob Saeger and w. Margreth.

BUERI, PETER, s. David Bueri[84] and w. Susanna; b. Dec. 2; bap. Dec. 27; sp. Jacob Stoeckel and w. Eva Catharina.

1796.

FRACK, CATHARINA, dr. Jacob Frack and w. Barbara; b. Sept. 14, 1795; bap. Jan. 24; sp. Jacob Mueckli and w. Eva Catharina.

RITTER, JOHN, s. Andreas Ritter and w. Susanna; b. Jan. 13; bap. Jan. 24; sp. John Miller, Catharina Ritter.

KOHLER, ISAAC, s. Jacob Kohler and w. Maria Elisabeth; b. Jan. 24; bap. Feb. 3; sp. Jacob Strein, Schoolmaster, and w. Maria Barbara.

BUERI, SALOME, dr. Fridrich Bueri and w. Salome; b. Jan. 3; bap. Feb. 21; sp. Philip Faust and w. Barbara.

FISCHER, HENRICH, s. Leonhard Fischer and w. Barbara; b. Mar. 27; bap. May 3; sp. Henrich Haas and Juliana Neuhard, his wife.

ANTON, MARIA ELISABETH, dr. Philip Anton and w. Elisabeth; b. Apr. 17; bap. May 15; sp. Jacob Kohler and w. Maria Elisabeth.

BURGHALDER, ELISABETH, dr. Peter Burghalder and w. Dorothea; b. Apr. 10; bap. May 15; sp. Elisabeth, widow of Peter Stoeckel.

LINS, JOHANNES, s. Martin Lins and w. Elisabeth; b. May 22; bap. May 29; sp. Friedrich Burger and w. Margreth.

SHAD, ANNA MARIA, dr. Georg Shad and w. Salome; b. May 3; bap. June 5; sp John Miller and w. Anna Maria.

MUECKLI, JOHN, s. Peter Mueckli and w. Salome; b. Apr. 5; bap. June 12; sp. John Balliet and w. Catharina.

KOCHER, GEORG, s. John Kocher and w. Catharina; b. Apr. 30; bap. June 12; sp. Jacob Miller and w. Elisabeth.

MEYER, HANNA, dr. John Nicolaus Meyer and w. Anna Maria; b. Apr. 28; bap. July 10; sp. Philip Loehr and w. Eva.

SHAD, HENRICH, s. Johannes Shad and w. Elisabeth; b. May 30; bap. July 10; sp. Adam Draxel and w. Maria.

HOFMANN, PETER, s. John Hofmann and w. Barbara; b. May 30; bap. July 10; sp. Peter Meyer and w. Catharina.

————, JACOB, s. Catharina Hartman; b. July 4; bap July 14; sp. Jacob Hartman and w. Eva.

GUT, MAGDALENA. dr. Friedrich Gut and w. Sophia; b. June 23; bap. July 31; sp. Magdalena, wife of Stephan Balliet.

NEUHARD, SUSANNA, dr. Friedrich Neuhard and w. Appolonia; b. July 8; bap. Aug. 7; sp. Leonhard Fischer and w. Barbara.

SYMONDS, MAGDALENA, dr. Assah Symonds and w. Margreth; b. June 13; bap. Aug. 7; sp. Michael, son of Friedrich Neuhard.

SHANTZ, DANIEL and JOHN, sons of John Shantz and w. Magdalena; b. Aug. 26; bap. Aug. 31; sp. Jacob Flickinger and w. Maria Elisabeth.

RECORDS OF EGYPT REFORMED CHURCH.

SAEGER, SALOME, dr. Jacob Saeger and w. Margreth; b. Sept. 13; bap. Sept. 17; sp. Elisabeth, widow of Peter Stoeckel.

NEUHARD, JOHN, s. Michael Neuhard, Jun'r, and w. Elisabeth; b. Aug. 26; bap. Oct. 9; sp. John Stoeckel and w. Magdalena.

HAAS, ELISABETH, dr. Henrich Haas and w. Juliana; b. Sept. 1; bap. Oct. 9; sp. John Neuhard and Barbara Haas.

KELCHNER, GEORG, s. Christoph Kelchner and w. Maria Barbara; b. Sept. 26; bap. Nov. 5; sp. Georg Flickinger and w. Eva.

HARTMAN, JONAS, s. Jacob Hartman and w. Eva; b. Sept. 26; bap. Nov. 5; sp. Georg Hartman and w. Elisabeth.

DESHLER, JACOB, s. David Deshler[85] and w. Catharina; b. Nov. 6; bap. Dec. 4; sp. Peter Leisenring and w. Susanna.

1797.

RITTER, ELISABETH, dr. Andreas Ritter and w. Susanna; b. Apr. 30, 1792; bap. Jan. 1, 1797; sp. Assah Symonds and w. Margreth.

RITTER, ANNA, dr. Andreas Ritter and w. Susanna; b. Apr. 13, 1794; bap. Jan. 1, 1797; sp. Michael Neuhard, Jun'r, and w. Salome.

DRACHSEL, SUSANNA, dr. Peter Drachsel and w. Sibilla; b. Dec. 27, 1796; bap. Jan. 29; sp. Nicklaus Drachsel, Maria Stofflet.

MILLER, J. GEORG, s. John Miller and w. Anna Maria; b. Jan. 5; bap. Jan. 29; sp. Georg Sem and w. Margreth.

MILLER, ELISABETH, dr. Peter Miller and w. Christina; b. Jan. 24; bap. Jan. 29; sp. Jacob Miller and w. Rebecca Elisabeth.

VERBILGER, CATHARINA, dr. Henrich Verbilger and w. Catharina; b. Feb. 8; bap. Feb. 26; sp. Henrich Orsenbach and w. Catharina.

MEYER, JONAS, s. Jacob Meyer and w. Elisabeth; b Feb. 12; bap. Mar. 26; sp. Leonhard Fischer and w. Maria Barbara.

MILLER, JOHANNES, s. Jacob Miller and w. Maria; b. Feb. 15; bap. Mar. 26; sp. Jacob Flickinger and w. Maria Elisabeth.

HORNUNG, JOH. GEORG, s. Johannes Hornung and w. Elisabeth; b. Feb. 28; bap. Mar. 26; sp. Georg Remeli and w. Elisabeth.

MUECKLI, ANNA, dr. Jacob Mueckli and w. Eva Catharina; b. Mar. 12; bap. Apr. 22; sp. Christian Shwartz and w. Elisabeth.

HAUSER, MAGDALENA, dr. Georg Hauser and w. Elisabeth; b. Mar. 19; bap. Apr. 22; sp. Henrich Beil and Barbara Shreiber.

KERN, WILHELM, s. Nicklaus Kern and w. Catharina; b. Apr. 11; bap. May 21; sp. David Deshler and w. Catharina.

HARTMAN, ELISABETH, dr. Abraham Hartman and w. Barbara;[86] b. Dec. 20, 1796; bap. May 21; sp. Christian Shwartz and w. Elisabeth.

SIGFRID, ANNA, dr. Andreas Sigfrid and w. Anna Elisabeth; b. May 18; bap. June 18; sp. Adam Sheurer, Catharina Herzog.

BUERI, MARIA MAGDALENA, dr. Fridrich Bueri[87] and w. Salome; b. May. 6; bap. June 18; sp. Gottfried Knauss[88] and w. Anna Maria.

NEUHARD, CATHARINA, dr. Peter Neuhard and w. Catharina; b. June 21; bap. Aug. 13; sp. Georg Shad and w. Salome.

MUECKLI, PETER, s. Christian Mueckli and w. Elisabeth; b. July 17; bap. Aug. 13; sp. Friedrich Bueri and w. Salome.

HOFMANN, SUSANNA, dr. Peter Hofmann and w. Magdalena; b. Aug. 6; bap. Sept. 10; sp. Michael Neuhard, Barbara Hofmann.

NEUHARD, JONAS, s. Fridrich Neuhard and w. Elisabeth; b. Sept. 1; bap. Oct. 8; sp. G. Jacob Lautenschlaeger, Salome Neuhard.

GROB, SUSANNA, dr. Henrich Grob and w. Margreth; b. Sept. 1; bap. Nov. 4; sp. John Neuhard and w. Sarah.

FISCHER, JOH. FRIDRICH, s. Leonhard Fischer and w. Barbara; b. Aug. 31; bap. Nov. 5; sp. Fridrich Neuhard and w Appollonia.

FISCHER, MARIA BARBARA, dr. Leonhard Fischer and w. Barbara; b. Aug. 31; bap. Nov. 5; sp. Michael Neuhard and w. Barbara.

MILLER, JOHN GEORG, s. Michael Miller and w. Eva; b. Nov. 7; bap. Dec. 3; died Dec. 11; sp. Andreas Hauer and w. Catharina

BUERI, MARIA, MARGRETH, dr. David Bueri and w. Susanna; b. Nov. 10; bap. Dec. 26; sp. Henrich Bueri, Sen'r, and w. Salome

HECKER, JOSEPH, s. Jonas Hecker and w. Magdalena; b. Nov. 25; bap. Dec. 26; sp. John Nicolaus Drachsel, Susanna Stoeckel.

LEISENRING, LYDIA. dr. Peter Leisenring[89] and w. Susanna; b. Nov. 2; bap. Dec. 26; sp. John Grob and w. Maria.

KRATZER, MAGDALENA, dr. Daniel Kratzer and w. Anna Maria; b. Nov. 30; bap. Dec. 26; sp. G. Adam Blank and w. Magdalena.

1798.

MEYER, PETER, s. Martin Meyer and w. Margreth; b Dec. 22, 1797; bap. Jan. 27; sp. Peter Burghalder and w. Dorothea.

TRACHSEL, STEPHAN, s. Adam Trachsel and w. Maria; b. Dec. 29, 1798; bap. Jan. 28; sp. Stephan Balliet and w. Magdalena.

ANTONY, JOHN, s. Philip Antony and w. Elisabeth; b. Dec. 3, 1797; bap. Feb. 25; sp. Christian Mueckli and w. Elisabeth.

FRACK, TOBIAS, s. Jacob Frack and w. Barbara; b. Dec. 15, 1797; bap. Feb. 25; sp. Georg Hauser and w. Elisabeth.

MILLER, JOHN, s. John Miller and w. Anna Maria; b. Jan. 28; bap. Mar. 25; sp. Georg Shad and w. Salome.

HOFMANN, CATHARINA, dr. John Hofmann and w. Barbara; b. Mar. 8; bap. Mar. 25; sp. John Hofmann, Sen'r, and w. Catharina.

BURGHALDER, CARL, s. Peter Burghalder, Jun'r, and w. Dorothea; b. Feb. 26; bap. May 1; sp. Martin Meyer and w Margreth.

KOCHER, HENRICH, s. John Kocher and w. Catharina; b. Apr. 12; bap. May 20; sp. Gottfried Laure and w. Susanna.

NEUHARD, JONAS, s. John Neuhard and w. Sara; b. May 21; bap. June 17; sp. Michael Neuhard, Sen. and w. Barbara.

MILLER, PETER, s. Peter Miller and w. Christiana; b. May 26; bap. June 17; sp. Ambrosius Remely and w. Elisabeth Barbara.

HOFMANN, DANIEL, s. J. Georg Hofmann and w. Barbara; b. July 10; bap. July 15; sp. Michael Neuhard and Barbara Hofmann.

DESHLER, DAVID,[90] s. David Deshler and w. Catharina; b. Sept. 7; bap. Sept. 18; sp. Christian Deyli and w. Maria Catharina.

KELCHNER, CATHARINA, dr. Christoph Kelchner and w. Maria Barbara; b. Sept. 20; bap. Oct. 4; sp. Joseph Albrecht and w. Catharina.

LEHIGH COUNTY—1734-1834. 53

KERN, JACOB, s. Michael Kern and w. Maria Barbara; b. Oct. 3; bap. Nov. 3; sp. Peter Meyer and w. Catharina.

1799.

HARTMAN, CATHARINA, dr. Abraham Hartman and w. Barbara; b. Oct. 3, 1798; bap. Jan. 26; sp. Jacob Roth[91] and w. Catharina, a born Roth.
HARTMAN, LYDIA, or. Jacob Hartman and w. Eva; b. Oct. 13, 1798; bap. Jan. 26; sp. Jacob Bottner and w. Maria.
BOTTNER, MARIA, dr. Joseph Bottner and w. Maria; b. Dec. 31; 1798; bap. Jan. 26; sp. Jacob Hartman and w. Eva.
MUECKLI, MARIA SALOME, dr. Peter Mueckli and w. Salome; b. Dec. 24, 1798; bap. Jan. 26; sp. Henrich Bueri and w. Salome.
STOFFLET, JONAS, s. John Stofflet and w. Eva; b. Dec. 10, 1798; bap. Jan. 27; sp. Nicolaus Seager, Esq., and w. Maria.
GROB, DANIEL,[92] s. John Grob and w. Maria; b. Nov. 20, 1798; bap. Jan. 27; sp. Peter Leisenring and w. Susanna.
REMELi, J. PETER, s. Georg Remeli and w. Elisabeth; b. Feb. 15; bap. Feb. 24; sp. Jacob Gut and w. Catharina.
LOEHR, JACOB, s. Philip Loehr and w. Eva; b. Mar. 22; bap. Mar. 23; sp. Jacob Dorner and w. Elisabeth.
LOEHR, MARIA MAGDALENA, dr. Philip Loehr and w. Eva; b. Mar. 22; bap. Mar. 23; sp. Daniel Kern and w. Maria Magdalena.
MILLER, MARIA MARGARETHA, dr. Jacob Miller and w. Maria; b. Feb. 2; bap. Mar. 24; sp. Wilhelm Lauri and w. Margreth.
MEYER, LEA, dr. Georg Meyer and w. Anna Maria; b. Feb. 5; bap. Mar. 24; sp. Jacob Dorner, Jun'r, Hanna Ruch.
MICHEL, PETER, s. Ulrich Michel and w. Maria; b. Mar. 23; bap. May 11; sp. Georg Shad and w. Salome.
MUCEKLI, JOSEPH, s. Jacob Mueckli and w. Eva Catharina; b. Mar. 24; bap. May 11; sp. Peter Mueckli and w. Salome.
NEUHARD, PETER, s. Michael Neuhard, Jun'r, and w Elisabeth; b. Apr. 19; bap. May 11; sp. Peter Neuhard and w. Catharina.
KOHLER, JOSEPH, s. Jacob Kohler and w. Maria Elisabeth; b. May 19; bap. 22; sp. Peter Kohler and Susanna Stoeckel.
BUERI, JOSEPH, s. Fridrich Bueri and w. Salome; b. May 4; bap. June 16; sp. Henrich Bueri and w. Catharina.

LEISENRING, CATHARINA, dr. Peter Leisenring and w. Catharina; b. May 13; bap July 14; sp. David Deshler and w. Catharina.

SIEGFRIED, JONATHAN, dr. Andreas Siegfried and w. Anna Elisabeth; b. June 23; bap. Aug. 11; sp. John Hofmann, Jun. and w. Barbara.

MILLER, CATHARINA, dr. John Miller and w. Anna Maria; b. July 7; bap. Aug. 11; sp. Peter Neuhard and w. Catharina.

LESER, MAGDALENA, dr. John Leser and w. Catharina; b. July 4; bap. Aug. 11; sp. Henrich Burghalder and w. Barbara.

MILLER, SALOME, dr. Sebastian Miller and w. Maria Margreth; b. July 27; bap. Aug. 8; sp. Jacob Miller and w. Elisabeth.

SHAD, ABRAHAM, s. Johannes Shad and w. Elisabeth; b. Sept. 19; bap. Nov. 3, sp. Peter Ruch and Maria Barbara Kleder.

MUENICH, MAGDALENA, dr. Peter Muenich and w. Magdalena; b. Oct. 4; bap. Nov. 3; sp. Andreas Siegfried and w. Anna Elisabeth.

NEUHARD, CATHARINA, dr. Peter Neuhard and w. Maria Barbara; b. Oct. 16; bap. Nov. 3; sp. Lorentz Kester and Catharina Neuhard.

SHUMACHER, SUSANNA, dr. Fridrich Shumacher and w. Barbara; b. Oct. 16; bap. Nov. 3; sp. G. Jacob Lautenschlaeger and Susanna Esch.

MEYER, ELISABETH, dr. Martin Meyer and w. Margreth; b. Oct. 3; bap. Nov. 3; sp. Elisabeth, widow of Peter Stoeckel.

BUERI, LYDIA, dr. David Bueri and w. Susanna; b. Oct. 28; bap. Dec. 1; sp. Jonas Hecker and w. Magdalena.

DRAXEL, SOLOMON, s. Peter Drexel and w. Sybilla; b. Nov. 28; bap. Dec. 26; sp. Nicolaus Wotring, Maria Koch.

HASS, PETER, s, Henrich Haas and w. Juliana; b. Nov. 14; bap. Dec. 29; sp. Peter Neuhard, Margreth Haas.

KERN, DANIEL, s. J. Nicolaus Kern and w. Catharina; b. Nov. 15; bap. Dec. 29; sp. Peter Deshler, Jun'r, and w. Magdalena.

HAUSER, SALOME, dr. Georg Hauser and w. Elisabeth; b. Nov. 18; bap. Dec. 29; sp. Christian Shwartz and w. Elisabeth.

1800.

MILLER, MARIA BARBARA, dr. Peter Miller and w. Christina; b. Dec. 3, 1799; bap. Jan. 5, 1800; sp. John Deubert and w. Maria Barbara.

LEHIGH COUNTY—1734-1834.   b5

KOCHER, EVA, dr. John Kocher and w. Catharina; b. Jan. 24; bap. Jan. 30; died Jan. 31; sp. Georg Flickinger and w. Eva.

HOFMANN, LYDIA, dr. John Hofmann, Jun'r, and w. Barbara; b. Jan. 9; bap. Feb. 23; sp. John Nicolaus Kern and w. Catharina.

FISCHER, MAGDALENA, dr. Leonhard Fischer and w. Barbara; b. Jan. 13; bap. Feb. 23; sp. Peter Neuhard and Eva Lautenschlaeger.

NEUHARD, PETER, s. John Neuhard and w. Sara; b Jan. 20; bap. Feb. 23; died Aug. 21, 1801; sp. Michael, son of Friedrich Neuhard, Susanna Lautenschlaeger.

SAEGER, JOHN PETER, s. John Saeger and w. Magdalena; b. Feb. 5; bap. Mar. 8; sp. Nicolaus Saeger, Sen'r, and w. Barbara.

LEHANT, CARL, s. Solomon Lehant and w. Magdalena; b. Jan. 7; bap. Mar. 16; sp. J. Jacob Mueckli, Sen., and w. Susanna.

SHUMACHER, SALOME, dr. J. Henrich Shumacher and w. Christina Margreth; b. Feb. 28; bap. Mar. 18; sp. Jacob Baer, Jun'r, and w. Maria Elisabeth.

SHMOLL, CARL, s. Georg Shmoll and w. Susanna; b. Feb. 3; bap. Mar. 23; sp. Jacob Kohler and w. Maria Elisabeth.

BURGHALDER, ELISABETH, dr. Henrich Burghalder and w. Barbara; b. Mar. 5; bap. Apr. 3; sp. Peter Burghalder and w. Charlotte.

LEHR, CATHARINA, dr. William Lehr and w. Eva; b. Feb. 6; bap. Apr. 11; sp. Peter Meyer and w. Catharina.

FLICKINGER, GEORG, s. Jacob Flickinger and w. Catharina; b. Feb. 26; bap. Apr. 11; sp. Georg Flickinger and w. Eva.

NEUHARD, MICHAEL, s. Peter Neuhard and w. Catharina; b. Feb. 28; bap. Apr. 11; sp. Michael Neuhard, Sen. and w. Barbara.

GROB, SALOME, dr. Henrich Grob and w. Margreth; b. Mar. 3; Apr. 11; sp. Joseph Grob and Maria Elisabeth Flickinger.

KERN, LYDIA, dr. Michael Kern and w. Maria Barbara; b. Mar. 8; bap. Apr. 11; sp. John Hofmann, Jun., and w. Barbara.

KESTER, JOHN, s. Philip Kester and w. Polly; b. Feb. 8; bap. May 18; sp. Georg Shmoll and w. Susanna.

DORY, MARIA MAGDALENA, dr. Benjamin Dory and w. Magdalena; b. Mar. 9; bap. May 18; sp. Georg Zerfass and Susanna Wagenmann.

ANTHONI, SARA, dr. Philip Anthoni and w. Elisabeth; b. Mar. 22; bap. May 18; sp. Johannes Shad and w. Elisabeth.

SHEURER, CATHARINA, dr. Peter Sheurer and wife; b. May 28; bap. June 15; sp. Adam Sheurer and wife.

STOFFELT, WILLIAM, s. Ludwig Stoffelt and w. Susanna; b. Aug. 16, 1798; bap. June 23; sp. Parents.

SAEGER, PETER, s. Nicolaus Seager and w. Salome; b. June 6; bap. July 6; sp. Johannes Saeger[93] and w. Catharina, of Indian Land.

MILLER, MARIA SALOME, dr. Michael Miller and w. Eva; b. written in the church book of the Lutheran congregation; bap. July 13, 1800; sp. Heurich Bueri and w. Salome.

MUECKLI, CATHARINA, dr. Christian Mueckli and w. Elisabeth; b. May 8; bap. Aug. 10; sp. John Balliet and w. Catharina.

KUERSCHNER, MAGDALENA, dr. Jeremias Kuerschner and w. Margreth; b. July 2; bap. Sept. 7; sp. John Drachsel and w. Catharina.

KELCHNER, MARIA BARBARA, dr. Christoph Kelchner and w. Maria Barbara; b. July 10; bap. Sept. 7; sp. Georg Shmoll and w. Susanna.

SOHN, PETER, s. Jacob Sohn and w. Albertina; b. Oct. 26; bap. Nov. 30; sp. Jacob Meyer and w. Elisabeth.

SHUMACHER, WILHELM, s. Fridrich Shumacher and w. Barbara; b. Nov. 10; bap. Dec. 25; sp. Wilhelm Lauri and Magdalena Shumacher.

MUECKLI, HANNA, dr. Peter Mueckli and w. Salome; b. Oct. 16; bap. Dec. 25; sp. Solomon Lehant and w. Magdalena.

BUERI, HANNA, dr. Fridrich Bueri and w. Salome; b. Dec. 10; bap. Dec. 25; sp. David Bueri and w. Susanna.

1801.

MILLER, PETER, s. Sebastian Miller and w. Margreth; b. Dec. 16, 1800; bap. Jan. 25; sp. Peter Miller and w. Christina.

DRAXEL, CATHARINA, dr. John Draxel and w. Catharina; b. Jan. 15; bap. Feb. 15; sp. Jeremias Kuerschner and w. Margreth.

DREIN, JACOB, s. George Drein and w. Maria Barbara; b. Feb. 16; bap. Feb. 22; sp. Peter Kohler and Catharina Stoeckel.

DREIN, SUSANNA, dr. George Drein and w. Maria Barbara; b. Feb. 16; bap. Feb. 22; sp. John Theichmann[94] and w. Susanna.

DESHLER, MARIA, dr. David Deshler and w. Catharina; b. Apr. 4; bap. May 17; 3p. Nicolaus Kern and w. Catharina.

HECKER, JEREMIAS, s. Jonas Hecker and w. Magdalena; b. June 26; bap. July 26; by Rev. Dill; sp. Johannes Ritter and w. Maria.

HARTMAN, ABRAHAM, s. Abraham Hartman and w. Barbara; b. Feb. 20; bap. Aug. 9, by Rev. Abr. Blumer; sp. Michael Miller and w. Eva.

MILLER, CATHARINA, dr. Jacob Miller and w. Maria; b. Apr. 9; bap. Aug. 9, by Rev. Abr. Blumer; sp. Jacob Flickinger, Jun'r, and w. Catharina.

GRAFF, CATHARINA, dr. George Graff and w. Elisabetha; b. Aug. 20; bap, Sept. 20; by Rev. Casper Dill; sp. John Teichman and w Susanna.

The following children were baptized by J. Gobrecht, Reformed Minister:

ROTH, CATHARINA, dr. Peter Roth and w. Maria; b. Aug. 20; bap. Oct. 4; sp. Peter Kohler and w. Catharina.

BURKHALTER, ESTHER, dr. Henry Burkhalter and w. Barbara; b. Aug. 31; bap. Oct. 4; sp. Peter Burkhalter and w. Eva Catharina, grandparents.

HOFFMAN, JOEL, s. John Hoffman and w. Maria Barbara; b. Sept. 11; bap. Oct. 20; sp. Michael Kern and w. Maria Barbara.

SHAD, JONATHAN, s. Georg Shad and w. Salome; b. Aug. 30; bap. Nov. 1; sp. Sebastian Miller and w. Margareth.

FREYMANN, DANIEL, s. Abraham Freymann and w. Barbara; b. Nov. 21; bap. Nov. 24; sp. Wilhelm Laury and Magdalena Remely, both single.

1802.

HAUSSER, CATHARINA, dr. George Hausser and w. Elisabetha; b. Dec. 25, 1801; bap. Feb. 21; sp. David Deshler and w. Catharina.

MILLER, ANNA MARIA, dr. John Miller and w. Anna Maria; b. Dec. 27, 1801; bap. Feb. 21; sp. Jost Hecker and w. Regina.

NEUHARDT, ELISABETH, dr. Michael Neuhardt and w. Elisabeth; b. Nov. 13, 1801; bap. Jan. 5; sp. Peter Neuhardt and Catharina Zink.

BIERY, JOSEPH, s. David Biery and w. Susanna; b. Jan. 21; bap. Feb. 21; sp. Jacob Mueckly and w. Susanna.

LEVAN, JOHN, s. Solomon Levan and w. Magdalena; b. Oct. 16, 1801; bap. Feb. 21; sp. Johannes Balliet and w. Catharina.

BIERY, DANIEL, s. Friedrich Biery and w. Salome; b. Feb. 15; bap. Feb. 21; sp. Christian Mueckly and w. Elisabeth.

MUECKLY, JOSEPH, s. Peter Mueckly and w. Salome; b. Jan. 27; bap. Feb. 21; sp. Henrich Burkhalter and w. Barbara.

LOESER, ELISABETH, dr. Johannes Loeser and w. Catharina; b. Jan. 8; bap. Feb. 28; sp. Peter Ruch and Margretha Bigily.

SCHUMACHER, HENRICH, s. Friedrich Schumacher and w. Barbara; b. Feb. 15; bap. Mar. 21; sp. Henrich Schumacher and Elisabeth Lauri.

STECKEL, JOSEPH, s. Johannes Steckel and w. Magdalena; b. Mar. 27; bap. Apr. 13, sp. Peter Traxel and w. Sybilla Veronica.

NEUHARDT, ELISABETH, dr. Johannes Neuhardt and w. Sara; b. Mar. 17; bap. Apr. 17; sp. Georg Koch and w. Elisabeth.

ROTH, ANNA, dr. Philip Roth and w. Susanna; b. Jan. 31; bap. Apr. 18; sp. Parents.

HAAS, HENRICH, s. Henrich Haas and w. Juliana; b. Mar. 7; bap. Apr. 26; sp. Michael Neuhardt and w. Maria Barbara.

FISCHER, JOSEPH, s. Leonhard Fischer and w. Barbara; b. Apr. 11; bap. May 27; sp. Nicolaus Saeger, Esq., and w. Anna Maria.

ANTHONY, MARIA, Jr. Philip Anthony and w. Elisabeth; b. Mar. 18; bap. May 27; sp. Henrich Steckel and w. Maria.

KELCHNER, HANNA, dr. Christoph Kelchner and w. Maria Barbara; b. Feb. 13; bap. June 13; sp. Abraham Zerfass and w. Hanna.

DINKY, JONAS, s. Jacob Dinky and w. Susanna; b. Apr. 4; bap. June 29; sp. Nicolaus Wutring and w. Maria Margreth.

KOCHER, EVA, dr. Johannes Kocher and w. Catharina; b. May 30; bap. July 11; sp. Georg Flickinger and w. Eva.

KERN, MARIA, dr Nicolaus Kern and w. Catharina; b. May 23; bap. July 11; sp. Peter Kohler and w. Catharina.

MILLER, EVA, dr. Sebastian Miller and his deceased w. Maria Margretha; b. July 9; bap. July 18; sp. Georg Schad and w. Salome.

BUERY, JOSEPH, s. Abraham Buery and w. Salome; b. Aug. 8; bap. Sept. 12; sp. John Peter Burkhalter, Jun'r, and w. Charlotte.

MEYER, JOSEPH, s. Jacob Meyer and w. Elisabeth; b. Ang. 10; bap. Oct. 2; sp. Johannes Neuhardt and w. Sara.

RITTER, JOHN, s. Johannes Ritter and w. Maria; b. ———; bap. Oct. 31; sp. Henrich Hefelfinger and w. Susanna.

PRESTON, MAGDALENA, dr. James Preston and w. Catharina; o. Sept. 6; bap. Oct 31; sp. Catharina Deyly, the child's grandmother.

HECKMANN, JOHN, s. Georg Heckmann and w. Magdalena; b. Oct. 21; bap. Nov. 28; sp. Georg Flickinger and w. Eva.

GRAFF, CARL, s. George Graff and w. Elisabeth; b. Oct. 14; bap. Nov. 28; sp. Abraham Teichmann and Elisabeth Graff.

SIEGFIED, SUSANNA, dr. Peter Siegfried and w. Susanna; b. Nov. 5; bap. Dec. 13; sp. Michael Hoffman and Elisabeth Siegfried.

1803.

TRAXSEL, JOEL, s. Peter Traxsel and w. Sybilla Veronica; b. Nov. 27, 1802; bap. Jan. 1, 1803; sp. Peter Traxel, single.

DORY, JAN PETRUS, s. Benjamin Dory and w. Magdalena; b. Oct. 19, 1802; bap. Jan. 23, 1803; sp. Johannes Goebel and w Susanna.

FREYMANN, JOHANN GEORG, s. Abraham Freymann and w. Barbara; b. Feb. 27; bap. Mar. 4; sp. Johan Georg Franz and w. Catharina.

STECKEL, REGINA, dr. Jacob Steckel and w. Eva Catharina; b. Feb. 6; bap. Mar. 15; sp. Daniel Saeger and w. Margretha.

JUNDT, JOSEPH, s. Abraham Jundt and w. Elisabeth; b. Feb. 22; bap. Mar. 17; sp. Peter Meyer and w. Catharina.

KOHLER, JUDITH, dr. Peter Kohler[95] and w. Susanna; b. Feb. 1; bap. Mar. 20; sp. Jacob Kern and w. Maria Margreth.

KOHLER, ESTHER, dr. Peter Kohler[96] and w. Catharina; b. Mar. 7; bap. Mar. 23; sp. John Teichmann and w. Susanna.

ZERFASS, JOHN, s. George Zerfass and w. Susanna; b. Apr. 2; bap. Apr. 5; sp. Jacob Flickinger, Jun'r, and w. Catharina.

MUECKLY, MAGDALENA, dr. Christian Mueckly and w. Elisabeth; b. Feb. 19; bap. Apr. 11; sp. Jacob Mueckly, Jun'r, and w. Eva Catharina.

FRANZ, PETER, s. Georg Franz and w. Catharina; b. Apr. 28; bap. May 15; sp. Jacob Franz and w. Margreth.

GROB, LYDIA, dr. Henrich Grob and w. Margreth; b. Mar. 25; bap. Map 15; sp. Christian Hartman and w. Anna Maria.

HUBLER, MOSES, s. Abraham Hubler and w. Anna Margreth; b. Apr. 14; bap. May 23; sp. Daniel Schneider and w. Catharina.

STOFLET, HANNA, John Stoflet and w. Eva; b. May 31; bap. July 10; sp. Hanna Traxel, single.

SCHUMACHER, JACOB, s. Friedrich Schumacher and w. Barbara; b. Aug. 10; bap. Sept. 4; sp. Jacob Buchmann and w. Magdalena.

MAYER, PETER, s. Jacob Mayer and w. Christina; b. July 12; bap. Sept. 25; sp. Jacob Hubler and Sara Meyer.

BURKHALTER, CARL, s. Henrich Burkhalter and w. Barbara; b. Sept. 10; bap. Oct. 29; sp. John Teichmann and w. Susanna.

MILLER, JOHN, s. Sebastian Miller and w. Barbara; b. Aug. 20; bap. Oct. 30; sp. John Miller and w. Anna Maria.

STRAUS, CARL, s. Simon Straus and w. Elisabeth; b. Oct. 12; bap. Oct. 30; sp. Georg Ehret and w. Charlotte.

MILLER, LEONHARD, s. Jacob Miller and w. Anna Maria; b. Oct. 24; bap. Nov. 27; sp. Leonhard Miller and w. Magdalena.

SIEGFRIED, AARON, s. Peter Siegfried and w. Susanna; b. Nov. 12; bap. Dec. 22; sp. Elisabeth Siegfried, wife of Andreas Siegfried.

HECKER, CARL, s. Jonas Hecker and w. Magdalena; b. Nov. 10; bap. Dec. 25; sp. David Buery and w. Susanna.

MUECKLY, CARL, s. Peter Mueckly and w. Salome; b. Oct. 22; bap. Dec. 25; sp. Jacob Mueckly, Jun'r, and w. Eva Catharina.

BUERY, MARIA SALOME, dr. Abraham Buery and w. Salome; b. Nov. 15; bap. Dec. 25; sp. Henrich Buery and w. Maria Salome.

1804.

HOFFMAN, DINA, dr. John Hoffman and w. Maria Barbara; b. Dec. 10, 1803; bap. Jan. 7; sp. Abraham Yundt and w. Elisabeth.

KELCHNER, MICHAEL, s. Christoph Kelchner and w. Maria Barbara; b. Nov. 1, 1803; bap. Jan. 22; sp. Philip Roth and w. Susanna.

FLICKINGER, ADAM, s. Jacob Flickinger, Jun'r, and w. Catharina; b. Dec. 12, 1803; bap. Jan. 22; sp. Adam Heckmann and w. Maria.

LAUTENSCHLAEGER, JOSEPH, s. Jacob Lautenschlaeger and w. Eva; b. Nov. 26, 1803; bap. Jan. 22; sp. John Boryer, Margreth Lautenschlaeger.

LOESER, JOHN, s. John Loeser and w. Catharina; b. Jan. 30; bap. Feb. 3; sp. Peter Kohler and w. Catharina.

TRAXEL, ELIAS, s. Peter Traxel and w. Sybilla Veronica; b. Jan. 20; bap. Feb. 6; sp. Peter Wutring and w. Elisabeth.

MILLER, JOSEPH, s. John Miller and w. Anna Maria; b. Dec. 7, 1803; bap. Feb. 19; sp. Joseph Siegfried and w, Susanna.

ROTH, MAGDALENA, dr. Peter Roth and w. Maria; b. Jan. 11; bap. Feb. 19; sp. Adam Traxel and w. Maria.

MUECKLY, MAGDALENA, dr. Henrich Mueckly and w. Magdalena; b. Jan. 3; bap. Mar. 18; sp. Henrich Blumer[97] and w. Sara.

NEUHARDT, MAGDALENA, dr. Peter Neuhardt and w. Catharina; b. Jan. 23; bap. Mar. 18; sp. Jacob Franz and Magdalena Neuhardt.

GEORG, ANNA MARIA, dr. Philip Georg and wife; b. ———; bap. Apr. 14; sp. Johannes Schad and w. Elisabeth.

FREYMAN, CATHARINA, dr. Johannes Freyman and w. Magdalena; b. ———; bap. Apr. 14; sp. John Traxel and w. Catharina.

ROTH, REBECCA, dr. Philip Roth and w. Susanna; b. Feb. 28; bap. Apr. 14; sp. Parents.

FISCHER, CARL, s. Leonhardt Fischer and w. Barbara; b. Feb. 21; bap. Apr. 15; sp. Peter Neuhardt, Sen'r, and w. Catharina.

MILLER, GEORG, s. Peter Miller and w. Christina; b. Feb. 25; bap. Apr. 15; sp. Georg Schad and w. Salome.

HUSTON, CATHARINA, dr. William Huston and w. Catharina; b. Mar. 9; bap. Apr. 15; sp. Peter Hoffmann and w. Magdalena

DIEHL, ANNA, dr. John Diehl and w. Barbara; b. Jan. 14; bap. Apr. 18; sp. Andreas Siegfried and w. Elisabeth.

BRAUMILLER, GEORG, s. Friederich Braumiller and w. Barbara; b. Apr. 1; bap. May 13; sp. Georg Nolf and wife.

FRANZ, JOSEPH, s. Henrich Franz and w. Margreth; b. Apr. 7; bap. June 10; sp. Jacob Franz and Barbara Ritter.

NEUHARDT, MICHAEL, s. John Neuhardt and w. Sara; b. June 1; bap. July 8; sp. Michael Neuhardt and w. Maria.

DAUT, DANIEL, s. Daniel Daut and w. Maria; b. July 4; bap. Aug. 5; sp. John Daut and w. Elisabeth.

KERN, LEVI, s. Johann Nicolaus Kern and w. Catharina; b. June 28; bap. Aug. 5; sp. Jacob Steckel and w. Eva. Catharina.

SCHAD, LEA, dr. Georg Schad and w. Salome; b. June 29; bap. Aug. 26; sp. Georg Jacob Miller and w. Barbara.

ROTH, JOSEPH, s. Jacob Roth and w. Elisabeth; b. July 17; bap. Aug. 26; sp. J. Nicolaus Traxel and w. Maria.

SAEGER, ISAAC, s. Daniel Saeger and w. Margretha; b. July 31; bap. Sept. 2: sp. Nicolaus Saeger and w. Catharina.

BIERY, CATHARINA, dr. David Biery and w. Susanna; b. July 20; bap. Sept. 16; sp. Henrich Biery and w. Catharina.

BIERY, SALOME, dr. David Biery and w. Susanna; b. Juyl 20; bap. Sept. 16; sp. Friedrich Biery and w. Salome.

GRAF, ANNA, dr. George Graf and w. Elisabeth; b. Aug. 11; bap. Sept. 30; sp. Solomon Graf⁹⁵ and Catharina Teichmann.

KOHLER, WILLIAM, s. Peter Kohler and w. Catharina; b. Sept. 8; bap. Sept. 30; sp. Jacob Steckel and w. Eva Catharina.

YUNDT, RUFFINA, dr. Abraham Yundt and w. Elisabeth; b. Aug. 3; bap. Oct. 7; sp. Georg Yundt,[99] Sen'r, and w. Catharina.

RUCH, ELISABETH. dr. Peter Ruch[100] and w. Susanna; b. Oct. 14; bap. Oct. 15; died Oct. 17; sp. Elisabeth Meyer.

LEVAN, THOMAS, s. Solomon Levan and w. Magdalena; b. Sept. 20; bap. Nov. 25; sp. Abraham Levan and w. Magdalena.

BALLIET, ANNA, dr. Johannes Balliet, Jun'r, and w. Elisabeth; b. Oct. 26; bap. Nov. 25; sp. Jacob Mueckly, Jun'r, and w. Eva Catharina.

KOHLER, JOSEPH, s. Jacob Kohler, Jun'r, and w. Maria; b. Nov. 19; bap. Dec. 23; sp. Jacob Kohler, Sen'r, and w. Maria Elisabeth.

1805.

ANTHONY, WILLIAM, s. Philip Anthony and w. Elisabeth; b. Nov. 12, 1804; bap. Jan. 13; sp. Peter Ruch and w. Susanna.

MAYER, THOMAS, s. Jacob Mayer and w. Christina; b. Nov. 19, 1804; bap. Jan. 26; sp. Andreas Kratzer and w. Magdalena.

HECKMANN, DANIEL, s. Johann Georg Heckmann and w. Magdalena; b. Dec. 25, 1804; bap. Feb. 17; sp. Daniel Flickinger and Elisabeth Laury.

ZERFASS, GEORG, s. Abraham Zerfass and w. Hanna; b. Jan. 28; bap. Mar. 17; sp. Gottfried Knaus and w. Maria.

GEORG, JOSEPH, s. Philip Georg and w. Margreth; b. Jan| 8; bap. Mar. 17; sp. Jacob Gut and w. Catharina.

TRAXEL, MARIA, ?r. Johann Nicolaus Traxel and w. Maria; b. Feb. 11; bap. Mar. 17; sp. Adam Traxel and w. Maria.

MAYER, ANNA, dr. John Mayer and w. Magdalena; b. Feb. 5; bap. Apr. 6; sp. Lorentz Ruch and w. Charlotte.

HORN, MAGDALENA, dr. Jacob Horn and w. Elisabeth; b. Feb. 12; bap. Apr. 7; sp. John Peter Burkhalter and w. Charlotte.

HARTMAN, ELIAS, s. Jacob Hartman and w. Eva Catharina; b. Jan. 27; bap. Apr. 12; sp. Mother.

SIEGFRIED, JOHN, s Joseph Siegfried and w. Susanna; b. Jan. 15; bap. Apr. 14; sp. John Miller and w. Anna Maria.

ROCKEL, MARIA CATHARINA, dr. Melchior Rockel and w. Maria; b. Feb. 10; bap. Apr. 12; sp. Henrich Breisch and w. Catharina.

BRAUN, MARIA, dr. David Braun and w. Magdalena; b. Mar. 31; bap. Apr. 28; sp. John Hoffman, Sen'r, and w. Catharina.

BIERY, ANNA, dr. Abraham Biery and w. Salome; b. Apr. 29; bap. May. 19; sp. Henrich Burkhalter and w. Barbara.

RITTER, JONAS, s. Johannes Ritter and w. Maria; b. Apr. 18; bap. May 19; sp. Jonas Hecker and w. Magdalena.

ROTH, JOEL, s. Peter Roth and w. Maria; b. May 25; bap. July 2; sp. Henrich Franz and w. Margreth.

SCHEURER, LYDIA, dr. Nicolaus Scheurer and w. Susanna; b. June 28; bap. July 8; died July 19; sp. Peter Romig and w. Hanna.

LAURY, DAVID,[101] s. John Laury and w. Magdalena; b. June 1; bap. July 14; sp. Gottfried Laury and w. Susanna.

BRAUMILLER, DANIEL, s. Friedrich Braumiller and w. Barbara; b. Sept. 9; bap. Oct. 6; sp. Daniel Siegfried and w. Sara.

ZERFASS, PETER, s. George Zerfass and w. Susanna; b. Sept. 15; bap. Oct. 6; sp. Peter Neuhardt and w. Catharina.

SEIBEL, JONAS, s. Jacob Seibel and w. Sara; b. Oct. 9; bap. Oct. 15; sp. Jacob Hartman and w. Eva Catharina.

DORY, CATHARINA, dr. Benjamin Dory and w. Magdalena; b. Sept. 7; bap. Oct. 15; sp. Jacob Hartman and w. Eva Catharina.

SCHMOLL, SARA, dr. George Schmoll and w. Susanna; b. Sept. 19; bap. Oct. 17; died Oct. 20; sp. Maria Siegfried, widow of John Siegfried.

SCHEURER, MAGDALENA, dr. John Scheurer and w. Eva; b. Sept. 17; bap. Oct. 20; sp. Michael Hoffman and Magdalena Scheurer.

MILLER, JOSEPH, s. Abraham Miller and w. Susanna; b. Sept. 23; bap. Nov. 2; sp. David Biery and w. Susanna.

SCHREIBER, SALOME, dr. Jacob Schreiber[102] and w. Eva; b. Sept. 6; bap. Nov. 2; sp. Johannes Grob and w. Anna Maria.

MICHEL, ELISABETH dr. Ulrich Michel and w. Maria; b. ———; bap. Nov. 2; sp. Simon Strauss and w. Elisabeth.

SAEGER, SALOME, dr. Nicolaus Saeger and w. Catharina; b. Sept. 24; bap. Nov. 2; sp. Daniel Schneider and w. Catharina.

YUNG, ELISABETH, dr. John Yung and w. Maria; b. Oct. 7; bap. Nov. 5; sp. Maria Haas.

SIEGFRIED, AARON, s. Peter Siegfried and w. Susanna; b. Sept. 1; bap. Nov. 23; sp. Jacob Hubler and Catharina Moser.

SCHNERR, LEVI, s. Georg Schnerr and w. Magdalena; b. Oct. 19; bap. Dec. 1; sp. Jacob Schnerr ad w. Magdalena.

MILLER, SALOME, dr. Peter Miller and w. Christina; b: Oct. 4; bap. Dec. 1; sp. Joseph Siegfried and w. Susanna.

MUECKLY, ELISABETH, dr. Peter Mueckly and w. Salome; b. Oct. 2; bap. Dec. 1; sp. Peter Steckel and w. Elisabeth.

MILLER, SIMON, s. Jacob Miller and w. Anna Maria; b. Nov. 4; bap. Dec. 29; sp. Johannes Grob and w. Anna Maria.

1806.

SAEGER, NATHAN, s. Samuel Saeger and w. Barbara; b. Oct. 24, 1805; bap. Jan. 1; sp. Jacob Wutring and w. Magdalena.

NEUHARDT, JOSEPH, s. Peter Neuhardt and w. Catharina; b. Oct. 13, 1805; bap. Jan. 12; sp. Henrich Franz and w. Margreth.

SAEGER, ELISABETH, dr. Christian Saeger and w. Magdalena; b. Dec. 7, 1805; bap. Jan. 26; sp. Nicolaus Saeger and w. Catharina.

STRAUSS, CATHARINA, dr. Peter Strauss and w. Catherina; b. Dec. 7, 1805; bap. Jan. 26; sp. Jost Strauss an w. Elisabeth.

RUCH, WILLIAM, s. Peter Ruch and w. Susanna; b. Jan. 15; bap. Jan. 31; sp. Nicolaus Saeger and w. Magdalena.

YUNDT, ESTHER, dr. Abraham Yundt and w. Elisabeth; b. Dec, 30, 1805; bap. Feb. 1; sp. Jacob Mayer and w. Christina.

HOFFMANN, MARIA MAGDALENA, dr. Johannes Hoffmann and w. Barbara; b. Jan. 20; bap. Feb. 1; sp. Michael Hoffman and w. Magdalena.

GRAF, LOUISE, dr. Georg Graf and w. Elisabeth; b. Dec. 27, 1805; bap. Feb. 9; sp. Peter Butz and w. Susanna.

BURKHALTER, HENRICH, s. Peter Burkhalter, Jun'r, and w. Catharina; b. Nov. 25, 1805; bap. Feb. 15; sp. Henrich Burkhalter and w. Barbara.

HUBLER, RUEBEN, s. Jacob Hubler and w. Susanna; b. Feb. 13; bap. Feb. 15; died Mar. 5; sp. John Peter Burkhalter, Sen'r and w. Charlotte.

HUBLER, SALOME, dr. Jacob Hubler and w. Susanna; b. Feb. 13; bap. Feb. 15; died Mar. 24; sp. Abraham Biery and w. Salome.

MILLER, PETER, s. Johannes Miller and w. Anna Maria; b. Dec, 5, 1805; bap. Feb. 23; sp. Peter Neuhardt, Sen'r, and w. Catharina.

YEHL, ANNA, dr. Henrich Yehl and w. Magdalena; b. Dec. 19, 1805; bap. Feb.23; sp. Daniel Siegfried and Maria Fischer.

KELCHNER, MAGDALENA, dr. Christoph Kelchner and w. Maria Barbara; b. Dec. 11, 1805; bap .Mar. 23; sp. John Kelchner and Maria Elisabeth Flickinger.

MILLER, JOSEPH, s. Sebastian Miller and w. Barbara; b. Jan. 15; bap. Mar. 23; sp. Peter Neuhardt, Sen'r, and w Catharina.

FLICKINGER, ELISABETH, dr. Jacob Flickinger and w. Catharina, b. Jan. 22; bap. Mar. 23; sp. Henrich Heffelfinger and w. Susanna.

LAUTENSCHLAEGER, STEPHAN, s. Georg Jacob Lautenschlaeger and w. Eva; b. Feb. 8; bap. Apr. 4; sp. Adam Traxel and w. Maria.

FISCHER, JONAS, s. Leonhardt Fischer and w. Barbara; b. Jan. 30; bap. Apr. 4; sp. Jacob Kuns and Salome Steckel.

LOESER, CARL, s. John Loeser and w. Catharina; b. Feb. 9; bap. Apr. 4; sp. George Shaed and wk. Margreth.

KRATZER, PETER, s. Andreas Kratzer and w. Magdalena; b. Mar. 13; bap. May 25; sp. Peter Meyer, Sen'r, and w. Catharina.

FLICKINGER, MAGDALENA, dr. Georg Flickinger and w| Magdalena; b. May 9; bap. June 15; sp. Jacob Flickinger and w. Maria Elisabeth.

BURKHALTER, STEPHANUS, s. Henrich Burkhalter and w. Barbara; b. May 14; bap. July 13; sp. Martin Mayer and w. Margreth.

DESCHLER, JOHN, s. David Deschler and w. Catharina; b. July 19; bap. Aug. 10: sp. Peter Schreiber and w. Susanna.

STRAUSS, SARA, dr. Simon Strauss and w. Eisabeth; b. July 9; bap. Aug. 10; sp. Jost Strauss and w. Elisabeth.

BALLIET, JOHN, s. John Balliet, Jun'r, and w. Elisabeth; b. July 31; bap. Aug. 17; sp. John Balliet, Sen'r, and w. Catharina.

MUECKLY, ANNA, dr. Henrich Mueckly and w. Magdalena; b. July 22; bap. Aug. 17; sp. J. Peter Burkhalter, Sen'r, and w. Charlotte.

MUECKLY, SUSANNA CATHARINA, dr. Daniel Mueckly and w. Thamar; b. Oct. 29, 1802; bap. Aug. 17, 1806; sp. Jacob Mueckly, Sen'r, and w. Susanna.

HORN, LOUISE, dr. Jacob Horn and w. Elisabeth; b July 17; bap. Aug. 17; sp. Peter Wutring and w. Elisabeth.

ROTH, WILLIAM, s. Philip Roth and w. Susanna; b. July 22; bap. Sept. 7; sp. Parents.

TRAXEL, ELISABETH, dr. J. Nicolaus Traxel and w. Maria; b. Aug. 24; bap. Sept. 21; sp. David Heller and w. Elisabeth.

KERN, CATHARINA, dr. J. Nicolaus Kern and w. Catharina; b. Aug. 13; bap. Sept. 28; sp. Eva Catharina Geyer.

ILLEGITIMATE, ROBERT, s. Robert Nelson and Elisabeth Knapenberger; b. Aug. 19; bap. Sept. 28; sp. Henrich Burkhalter and w. Barbara.

MAYER, STEPHANUS, s. Jacob Mayer and w. Christina; b. Sept. 25; bap. Oct. 26; sp. Peter Mayer, Jun'r, and w. Catharina.

STECKEL, SALOME, dr. Peter Steckel and w. Elisabeth; b. Oct. 22; bap. Oct. 29; sp. Henrich Steckel and w. Maria.

SAEGER, EDWARD, s. Daniel Saeger and w. Margreth; 9. Oct. 6; bap. Nov. 16; sp. Daniel Schneider and w. Catharina.

MOHARTER, JACOB, s. Jacob Moharter and w. Margreth; b. Oct. 14; bap. Nov. 16; sp. Jacob Gut and w. Catharina.

MAYER, SALOME, dr. John Mayer and w. Magdalena; b. Sept. 27; bap. Nov. 29; sp. Abraham Jundt and w. Elisabeth.

HOFFMANN, MARIA ANNA, dr. Michael Hoffman and w. Maria Magdalena; b. Oct. 23; bap. Dec. 7; sp. Johannes Hoffmann, Sen'r, and w. Catharina.

SIECFRIED, PETER, s. Joseph Siegfried and w. Susanna; b. Nov. 2?; bap. Dec. 26; sp. Peter Neuhardt, Sen'r, and w Catharina.

HORNUNG, JOSEPH, s. Johannes Hornung and w. Elisabeth; b. Oct. 23; bap. Dec. 26; sp. Adam Traxel and w. Maria.

HECKER, JULIANA, dr. Jonas Hecker and w. Magdalena; b. Nov. 7; bap. Dec. 26; sp. Christian Traxel and w. Barbara.

NEUHARDT, JOSEPH, s. John Neuhardt and w. Sara; b. Nov. 20; bap. Dec. 26; sp. Nicholas Saeger, Esq. and w. Maria.

1807.

KOHLER, ANNA, dr. Jacob Kohler, Jun'r, and w. Maria; b. Nov. 25, 1806; bap. Jan. 11; sp. Peter Hoffman and w. Margreth.

ROTH, GEORG, s. Peter Roth and w. Maria; b. Dec. 23, 1806; oap Jan. 18; sp. Christoph Kelchner and w. Maria Barbara.

TRAXEL, HANNA, dr. Peter Traxel and w. Catharina; b. Jan. 16; bap. Feb. 15; sp. Adam Traxel and w. Maria.

LEVAN, LEWIS FERDINAND, s. Solomon Levan and w. Magdalena; b. Jan. 4; bap. Mar. 8; sp. Abraham Levan and w. Catharina.

THUREURN, JENNY, b. Jan. ——, 1793; bap. Mar. 8, 1807; sp. John Balliet and w. Catharina.

ROCKEL, JOHANN GEORG, s. Melchior Rockel and w. Anna Maria; b. Feb. 9; bap. Mar. 22; sp. Martin Meyer and w. Margreth.

FISCHER, PETER, s. Anthony Fischer and w. Barbara; b. Jan. 25; bap. Mar. 30; sp. Michael Neuhardt and w. Barbara.

TRAXEL, JULIANA, dr. Christian Traxel and w. Barbara; b. Mar. 12; bap. Apr. 5; sp. Adam Traxel and w. Maria.

SIEGFRIED, Anna Elisabeth, dr. Peter Siegfried and w. Susanna; b. Mar. 27; bap. Apr. 6; sp. Andreas Siegfried and w. Anna Elisabeth.

LAUTENSCHLAEGER, JONATHAN, s. Georg Lautenschlaeger and w. Eva; b. Mar. 8; bap. Apr. 12; sp. Peter Moll and w. Sa'me.

MEYER, WILHELM, s. Peter Meyer, Jun'r, and w. Catharina; b. Feb. 13; bap. Apr. 12; sp. Wilhelm Gangwehr and w. Elisabeth.

BIERY, MAGDALENA, dr. Abraham Biery and w. Salome; b. Apr. 4; Apr. 16; sp. Lorentz Ruch and w. Charlotte.

BUCHMANN, MAGDALENA, dr. Daniel Buchmann and w. Maria Barbara; b. Dec. 2. 1806; bap. May 5; sp. Jacob Kuns and Magdalena Buchmann.

SCHEURER, Anna, dr. Johann Jacob Scheurer and w. Maria Catharina; b. Apr. 23; bap. May 10; sp. Catharina Elisabeth Scheurer, the child's grandmother.

BURKHALTER, PETER, s. Peter Burkhalter and w. Catharina; b. Apr. 18; bap. May 18; sp. Johann Peter Burkhalter and w. Charlotte.

SCHREIBER, EDWARD, s. Jacob Schreiber and w. Eva; b. May 6; bap. May 31; sp. Jacob Mueckly, Jun'r, and w. Eva Catharina.

KOHLER, PETER, s. Peter Kohler and w. Catharina; b. Apr. 24; bap. May 31; sp. Peter Dorney and w. Catharina.

RUCH, DAVID, s. Peter Ruch and w. Susanna; b. June 23; bap. July 8; sp. Jacob Saeger and w. Margreth.

RITTER, JEREMIAS, s. Johannes Ritter and w. Maria; b. ———; bap. Aug. 23; sp. Henrich Hoffmann and w. Barbara.

ROTH, DAVID, s. Jacob Roth and w. Elisabeth; b. Aug 13; bap. Sept. 20; sp. Nicolaus Wutring. Sen'r, and w. Margreth.

GROB, ANNA, dr. Henrich Grob and w. Elisabeth; b. Aug. 26; bap. Oct. 17; sp. Georg Flickinger, Jun'r, and w. Magdalena.

NEUHARDT, SALOME, dr. Peter Neuhardt and w. Catharina; b. Sept. 9; bap. Nov. 15; sp. Johannes Kuns and Salme Neuhardt.

SIEGFRIED CARL, s. Daniel Siegfried and w. Susanna; b. Oct. 18; bap. Nov. 15; sp. Georg Scheurer and Catharina Siegfried.

SCHREIBER, MARIA, dr. Peter Schreiber and w. Susanna; b. Nov. 2; bap. Dec. 13; sp. David Deschler and w. Catharina.

1808.

MILLER, CHRISTINA, dr. Peter Miller and w. Christina b. Nov. 17, 1807; bap. Jan. 10; sp. Tobias Deubert and w. Christina.

MILLER, LYDIA, dr. John Miller and w. Anna Maria; b. Dec. 28, 1807; bap. Jan. 10; sp. Friedrich Neuhardt and w. Apollonia.

HOFFMANN, LEA, dr John Hoffmann and w. Barbara; b. Dec. 28, 1807; bap. Jan. 31; sp. Andreas Kratzer and w. Magdalena.

KELCHNER, JOSEPH, s. Christoph Kelchner and w. Maria Barbara; b. Nov. 7, 1807; bap. Feb. 7; sp. Jacob Flickinger and w. Catharina.

SCHAD, SALOME, dr. George Schad, Jun'r, and w. Magdalena; b. Jan. 15; bap. Feb. 21; sp. Georg Schad, Sen'r, and w. Salome.

MAYER, EDWARD, s. Joseph Mayer and w. Susanna; b. Feb. 7; bap. Mar. 6; sp. Abraham Biery and w. Salome.

HEMSING, SARA, dr. Daniel Hemsing and w. Margreth; b. Dec. 17, 1807; bap. Mar. 6; sp. Conrad Leisenring and w. Catharina.

BURKHALTER, MARIA SALOME, dr. Henrich Burkhalter and w. Barbara; b. Jan. 9; bap. Mar. 6; sp. Maria Salome Biery, the child's grandmother.

STECKEL, ANNA MARIA, dr. Solomon Steckel and w. Anna Maria; b. Jan. 19; bap. Mar. 6; sp. Henrich Steckel and w. Maria.

TRAXEL, ADAM, s. Nicolaus Traxel and w. Maria; b. Feb. 17; bap. Mar. 11; sp. Christian Traxel and w. Barbara.

MUECKLY, CHRISTINA, dr. Peter Mueckly and w. Salome; b. Feb. 17; bap. Mar. 22; sp. Catharina Biery, wife of Henrich Biery.

BIERY, SALOME, dr. Henrich Biery and w. Catharina; b. Dec. 29. 1807; bap. Mar. 22; sp. Maria Salome Biery, the child's grandmother.

GANGWEHR, DAVID, s. Thomas Gangwehr and w. Susanna; b. Jan. 28; bap. Mar. 26; sp. John Schad, Jun'r, and Sara Meyer.

GANGWEHR, JACOBUS, s. Wilhelm Gangwehr and w. Elisabeth; b. Feb. 23; bap. Apr. 2; sp. Daniel Meyer and Magdalena Rockel.

GRAFF, AUGUSTUS, s. Peter Graff and w. Elisabeth; b. Mar. 30; bap. Apr. 10; sp. Solomon Graff and w. Elisabeth.

STECKEL, JOHANN PETER, s. Peter Steckel and w. Elisabeth; b. Mar. 28; bap. Apr. 30; sp. John Steckel and w. Magdalena.

BAX, WILHELM, bap. Apr. 28, after previous instruction, aged 16 years.

HEMSING, MARGRETH, wife of Daniel Hemsing; bap. Apr. 28, after receiving instructions, aged 21 years.

HOFFMANN, SALOME. dr. Michael Hoffmann and w. Magdalena; b. Apr. 24; bap. May 22; sp. Catharina Elisabeth Scheurer, widow.

BIERY, MAGDALENA ,dr. David Biery and w. Susanna; b. Apr. 9; bap. May 29; sp. Jacob Saeger and w. Margreth.

FLICKINGER, ANNA, dr. Georg Flickinger, Jun'r, and w. Magdalena; b. Apr. 16; bap. May 29; sp. Johannes Semel and w. Maria.

LAUTENSCHLAEGER, JOSUA, s. Georg Jacob Lautenschlaeger and w. Eva; b. Mar. 20; bap. May 29; sp. Joseph Balliet and w. Margreth.

FRANZ, ABRAHAM, s. Henrich Franz and w. Margreth; b. May 18; bap. June 5; sp. Christian Traxel and w. Barbara.

DUERR, JOSEPH, s. Jacob Duerr and w. Maria; b. May 1; bap. June 26; sp. Jacob Kohler, Sen. and w. Maria Elisabeth.

MUECKLY, DEBORA, dr. Christian Mueckly and w. Elisabeth; b. May 31; bap. Aug. 11; died Sept. 2; sp. Charles Daeschler, Esq. and w. Catharina.

MUECKLY, SUSANNA, dr. Christian Mueckly and w. Elisabeth; b. May 31; bap. Aug. 11; died Aug. 22; sp. Peter Mueckly and w. Salome.

TRAXEL, SAMUEL, s. Christian Traxel and w. Barbara; b. July 22; bap. Aug. 21; sp. Johann Nicolaus Traxel and w. Maria.

STRAUS, SIMON, s. Simon Straus and w. Elisabeth; b. July 13; bap. Aug. 21; sp. George Ebret and w. Charlotte.

GEORG, SOLOMON, s. Henrich Georg and w. Magdalena; b. July 20; bap. Aug. 21; sp. George Teichman and Rosina Kaemmerer.

MEYER, GEORGE, s. Jacob Meyer and w. Christina; b. July 20; bap. Aug. 21; sp. George Spaet and w. Margreth.

MILLER, MARIA MAGDALENA, dr. Jacob Miller and w. Maria; b. May 2; bap. Aug. 22; sp. Peter Muselmann and w. Magdalena.

GOBRECHT, ESTHER, dr. John Gobrecht, V. D. M. and w. Hanna; b. May 31, 1806; bap. June 29, 1806; sp. Adam Traxel and w. Maria, grandparents.

GOBRECHT, SARA, dr. John Gobrecht, V. D. M. and w. Hanna; b. Feb. 25; 1808; bap. Apr. 3, 1808; sp. Jacob Stettler and w. Catharina.

GRAFF, ELISABETH, dr. George Graff and w. Elisabeth; b. July 4; bap. Aug. 28; sp. George Teichmann and Elisabeth Burger.

LEHIGH COUNTY—1734-1834.   71

HAAS, JOSEPH, s. Henrich Haas and w. Juliana; b. July 13; bap. Sept. 4; sp. Anton Fischer and w. Salme.

JANS, RUBEN, s. Wilhelm Jans and w. Christina; b. July 28; bap. Sept. 4; sp. Georg Faust and w. Catharina.

BIERY, ESTHER, dr. Jacob Biery and w. Salome; b. Aug. 22; bap. Sept. 11; sp. David Biery and w. Susanna.

STRAUSS, JOHANN PETER, s. Peter Strauss and w. Catharina; b. Aug. 21; bap. Oct. 16; sp. Friedrich Neuhardt, Sen. and w. Appolonia.

ROTH, SALOME, dr. Peter Roth and w. Maria; b. Oct. 29; bap. Nov. 13; sp. John Nicolaus Traxel and w. Maria.

HORN, SUSANNA, dr. Jacob Horn and w. Elisabeth; b. Nov. 5; bap. Dec. 5; sp. Susanna Balliet, wife of Stephen Balliet, Jun.

BURKHALTER, EDWARD, s. Peter Burkhalter and w. Catharina; b. Nov. 10; bap. Dec. 11; sp. Peter Ruch and w. Susanna.

BIERY, DELILA, dr. Abraham Biery and w. Salome; b. Oct. 7; bap. Dec. 11; sp. Peter Kohler and w. Catharina.

ILLEGITIMATE, JACOBUS, s. James Jameson and Catharina Siegfried; b. Nov. 7; bap. Dec. 11; sp. Solomon Siegfried, single.

KESTER, REGINA, dr. Wilhelm Kester and w. Salome; b. Sept. 25; bap. Dec. 14; sp. Jonathan Knapenburger and Catharina Neuhardt.

MEYER, PETER, s. John Meyer and w. Magdalena; b. Oct. 4; bap. Dec. 25; sp. Ulrich Michel and w. Maria.

MEYER, SALOME, dr. Peter Meyer, Jun. and w. Catharina; b. Oct. 15; bap. Dec. 25; sp. Adam Michel and Catharina Schad.

1809.

SCHREIBER, RUBEN, s. Daniel Schreiber and w. Barbara; b. Dec. 6, 1808; bap. Jan. 8; sp. Peter Ruch and w. Susanna.

KRATZER, SARA, dr. Andreas Kratzer and w. Magdalena; b. Nov. 10, 1808; bap. Jan. 8; sp. Jacob Meyer and w. Christina.

SIEGFRIED, HENRIETTE, dr. Peter Siegfried and w. Susanna; b. Jan. 13; bap. Jan. 22; sp. Peter Meyer, Jun. and w. Catharina.

FISCHER, JOSEPH, s. Anton Fischer and w. Salme; b. Dec. 18, 1808; bap. Feb. 5; sp. Adam Labach and w. Margreth.

KAEMMERER, MAGDALENA, dr. Georg Adam Kaemmerer and w. Susanna; b. Nov. 29, 1808; bap. Feb. 5; sp. Jacob Mueckly and w. Eva Catharina.

NEUHARDT, MARGRETH, dr. Peter Neuhardt and w. Catharina; b. Dec. 17, 1808; bap. Feb. 12; sp. Jacob Franz, Sen. and w. Margreth.

SIEGFRIED, DANIEL, a grown person; b. Dec. 20, 1767; bap. Feb. 27, 1809.

SIEGFRIED, SARA, dr. Joseph Siegfried and w. Susanna; b. Dec. 17, 1808; bap. Feb. 27; sp. Daniel Siegfried and w. Sara.

HEMSING, MARGRETH, dr. Daniel Hemsing and w. Margreth; b. Dec. 13, 1808; bap. Mar. 5; sp. Schoolmaster Henrich Hemsing and w. Margreth.

MUECKLY, EDWARD, s. Henrich Mueckly and w Magdalena; b. Dec. 17, 1808; bap. Mar. 26; sp. Peter Miller and w. Maria.

NEUHARDT, MARIA, dr. John Neuhardt and w. Sara; b. Mar. 23; bap. Apr. 30; sp. Daniel Neuhardt and Eva Koch.

KOHLER, JACOB, s. Jacob Kohler, Jun. and w. Maria; b. Apr. 22; bap. May 3; sp. Johannes Grob and w. Maria.

KOHLER, MARIA, dr. Jacob Kohler, Jun. and w. Maria; b. Apr. 22; bap. May 3; sp. Margreth Kretschmann, single.

MILLER, MARIA BARBARA, dr. Sebastian Miller and w. Maria Barbara; b. Apr. 10; bap. June 8; sp. Georg Fischer, Sen. and w. Anna Maria.

FLICKINGER, LYDIA, dr. Daniel Flickinger and w. Catharina; b. May 2; bap. June 25; sp. John Flickinger and w. Margreth.

KOHLER, AARON, s. Peter Kohler and w. Catharina; b. June 1; bap. July 9; sp. Abraham Steckel and Catharina Strieby.

FISCHER, NATHAN, s. George Fischer, Jun. and w. Maria; b. June 11; bap. July 23; sp. George Fischer, Sen. and w. Anna Maria.

DESHLER, DEBORA, dr. David Deshler and w. Catharina; b. June 17; bap. July 23; sp. John Teichmann and w. Susanna.

MEYER, HANNA, dr. Joseph Meyer and w. Susanna; b. June 13; bap. July 23; sp. Solomon Siegfried and w. Susanna.

STRAUS, REGINA, dr. Philip Straus and w. Salome; b. July 15; bap. Aug. 17; sp. Martin Meyer and w. Maria Margreth.

GROB, DANIEL, s. Henrich Grob and w. Elisabeth; b. July 26; bap. Aug. 20; sp. John Flickinger and w. Margreth.

TRAXEL, CARL, s. Peter Traxel and w. Christina; b. Aug. 10; bap. Sept. 17; sp. George Koch and Elisabeth Hecker.

NAAS, CHRISTIAN, s. Michael Naas and w. Christina; b. Mar. 24; bap. Oct. 2; sp. Christian Baertsch and w. Juliana.

FRANZ, SALOME, dr. Jacob Franz and w. Christina, of Quacake; b. Aug. 29, 1808; bap. Nov. 5; sp. Henrich Franz and w. Margreth.

FAUST, PAULUS, s. Jonas Faust and w. Susanna; b. Sept. 1; bap. Nov. 12; sp. Paulus Faust and w. Susanna.

SAEGER, STEPHANUS, s. Christian Saeger and w. Magdalena; b. Sept. 23; bap. Nov. 12; sp. Johannes Saeger and w. Magdalena.

TRAXEL, SARA, dr. Nicolaus Traxel and w. Maria; b. Oct. 25; bap. Nov. 12; sp. Anton Lautenschlaeger and Elisabeth Hecker.

DREISSBACH, JONAS, s. Michael Dreissbach and w. Susanna; b. Nov. 12; bap. Dec. 4; sp. Christian Baertsch and w. Juliana.

REMELY, LYDIA, dr. George Remely and w. Regina; b. Oct. 24; bap. Dec. 4; sp. Peter Schaefer and w. Lydia.

SCHAEFER, JAMES, s. Jacob Schaefer and w. Elisabeth; b. July 7; bap. Dec. 4; sp. George Remely and w. Regina.

STOFLET, ELISABETH, dr. John Stoflet and w. Eva; b. Sept. 3; bap. Dec. 9; sp. Margreth, wife of Nicolaus Wutring.

KERN, MANASSE, s. Nicolaus Kern and w. Catharina; b. Oct. 31; bap. Dec. 10; Peter Schreiber and w. Susanna.

HOFFMANN, MARIA MAGDALENA, dr. Michael Hoffmann and w. Magdalena; b. Nov. 20; bap. Dec. 10; sp. John Teichmann and w. Susanna.

GOBRECHT, RACHEL, dr. John Gobrecht, V. D. M. and w. Hanna; b. Nov. 27; bap. Dec. 24; sp. Stephan Balliet, Jun. and w. Susanna.

ILLEGITIMATE, DANIEL, s. Margreth Becker and Robert Baersteln; b. Nov. 15; bap. Dec. 25; sp. Daniel Flickinger and w. Catharina.

HECKER, PETER s. Jonas Hecker and w .Magdalena; b. Oct. 28; bap. Dec. 26; sp. Peter Traxel and w. Christina.

GANGWEHR, ANNA, dr. Wilhelm Gangwher and w. Elisabeth; b. Oct. 8; bap. Dec. 31; sp. George Spaet and w. Margreth.

1810

SAEGER, ABIGAIL, dr. Jacob Saeger and w. Margreth; b. Nov. 18, 1809; bap. Jan. 7; sp. Nicolaus Saeger, Esq. and w. Maria.

ROTH, CHRISTIAN, s. Jacob Roth and w. Elisabeth; b. Nov. 23, 1809; bap. Jan. 7; sp. Christian Traxel, Jun. and w. Barbara.

BIERY, DEBORA, dr. Henrich Biery and w. Catharina; b. Nov. 22, 1809; bap. Jan. 28; sp. Peter Mueckly and w. Salome.

RECORDS OF EGYPT REFORMED CHURCH.

LEVI, SARA, dr. Moses Levi and w. Maria; b. Oct. 25, 1809; bap. Jan. 28; sp. David Biery and w. Susanna.

BURKHALTER, DAVID, s. Henrich Burkhalter and w. Barbara; b. Dec. 14, 1809; bap. Feb. 4; sp. David Biery and w. Susanna.

GILBERT, CATHARINA, dr. Schoolmaster Adam Gilbert and w. Susanna; b. Jan. 23; bap. Feb. 4; sp. Daniel Steckel and Catharina Umbehauer.

GRAFF, SARA, dr. George Graff and w. Elisabeth; b. Jan. 7; bap. Feb. 11; sp. Peter Wutring and w. Elisabeth.

SCHEURER, JACOBUS, s. Johann Jacob Scheurer and w. Catharina; b. Dec. 28, 1809; bap. Feb. 11; sp. Solomon Scheurer and Susanna Schad.

BIEGY EDWARD, s. Jacob Biegy and w. Salome; b. Feb. 22; bap. Apr. 20; sp. Jacob Hartmann and Magdalena Schad.

MILLER, SUSANNA, dr. John Miller and w. Anna Maria; b. Feb. 18; bap. Apr. 20; sp. Peter Neuhardt and w. Catharina.

HEMSING, DANIEL, s. Daniel Hemsing and w. Margreth; b. Apr. 3; bap. Apr. 23; sp. Parents.

KRATZER, JOSEPH, s. Andreas Kratzer and w. Magdalena; b. Mar. 24; bap. May 12; sp. Martin Mayer and w. Margreth.

MEYER, DAVID, s. Peter Meyer, Jun. and w. Catharina; b. Mar. 19; bap. May 20; sp. George Spaed and w. Margreth.

TRAXEL, WILHELM, s. Christian Traxel and w. Barbara; b. May 2; bap. May 27; sp. Jonas Traxel and Maria Magdalena Horn.

KOHLER, ELIZA, dr. Benjamin Kohler and w. Catharina; b. Apr. 4; bap. May 27; sp. Peter Kohler and w. Catharina.

MEYER, DAVID, s. John Meyer and w. Magadalena; b. Feb. 21; bap. May 27; sp. Peter Meyer, Sen. and w. Catharina.

MEYER, MANASSE, s. Jacob Meyer and w. Christina; b. Mar. 20; bap. May 27; sp. John Gobrecht, V. D. M. and w. Hanna.

HAAS, DANIEL, s. Henrich Haas and w. Juliana; b. May 1; bap. June 24; sp. John Steckel and w. Magdalena.

MILLER, MICHAEL, s. Peter Miller and w. Christina; b. Apr. 25; bap. June 24; sp. Michael Neuhardt and w. Maria.

FLICKINGER, LYDIA, dr. Georg Flickinger and w. Magdalena; b. Apr. 23; bap. June 24; sp. Henrich Grob and w. Elisabeth.

SIEGFRIED, JULIANA, dr. Solomon Siegfried and w. Susanna; b. May. 13; bap. June 24; sp. George Spaed and w. Margretn.

BECKER, DANIEL, s. Friedrich Becker and w. Eva; b. June 25; bap. July 29; sp. Daniel Flickinger and w. Catharina.

LEHIGH COUNTY—1734-1834. 75

GRAFF, STEPHANUS, s. Peter Graff and w. Elisabeth; b. June 15; bap. July 29; sp. Stephanus Ballliet and w. Susanna.

MILLER, ELISABETH, dr. Jacob Miller and w. Maria; b.
———; bap. Aug. 5; sp. Abraham Zerfass and w. Hanna.

SCHMIDT, WILHELM, s. Wilhelm Schmidt and w. Catharina; b. July 4; bap. Aug. 5; sp. John Kelly and w. Elisabeth.

TORNER, STEPHANUS, s. Jacob Torner and w. Catharina; b. July 6; bap. Aug. 13; sp. Isaac Siegfried and Catharina Schmoll.

ROTH, DANIEL, s. Peter Roth and w. Maria; b. Aug. 9; bap. Sept. 2; sp. Ambros Remely and w. Elisabeth Barbara.

BIERY, DAVID, s. David Biery and w. Susanna; b. July 30; bap. Sept. 9; sp. Jacob Biery and w. Salome.

HOFFMANN, JOHN, s. John Hoffmann and w. Barbara; b. Aug. 22; bap. Sept. 9; sp. J. Gobrecht, V. D. M. and w. Hanna.

MEYER, CARL, s. Joseph Meyer and w. Susanna; b. July 22; bap. Sept. 9; sp. John Hoffmann and w. Barbara.

STECKEL, SOLOMON, s. Solomon Steckel and w. Anna Maria; b. Aug. 17; bap. Sept. 23; Peter Burkhalter and w. Catharina.

STECKEL, ESTHER, dr, Peter Steckel and w. Elisabeth; b. Sept. 17; bap. Sept. 23; sp. Henrich Burkhalter and w. Barbara.

WILLIAMS, PETER, s. John Williams and w. Maria; b. Aug. 11; bap. Sept. 28; sp. Simon Strauss and w. Elisabeth.

KELLY, JAMES, s. John Kelly and w. Elisabeth; b. Sept 1; bap. Sept. 28; sp. John Williams and w. Maria.

SCHREIBER, AARON, s. Daniel Schreiber and w. Barbara; b. Aug. 12; bap. Sept. 29; sp. Conrad Leisenring and w. Catharina.

SCHAD, DELILA, dr. Peter Schad and w. Magdalena; b. Aug. 17; bap. Sept. 30; sp. Georg Schad, Sen. and w. Salome.

STRAUSS, JOHANN PETER, s. Simon Strauss and w. Elisabeth; b. Aug. 24; bap. Oct. 28; sp. Georg Ehret and w. Charlotte.

SCHEURER, ELISABETH, dr. Nicolaus Scheurer and w. Susanna; b. Sept. 24; bap. Nov. 11; sp. Georg Fischer, Sen. and w. Anna Maria.

FRANZ, DANIEL, s. Henrich Franz and w. Margreth; b. Oct. 4; bap. Nov. 25; sp. Johannes Ritter and w. Maria.

BIERY, REUBEN, s. Abraham Biery and w. Salome; b. Oct. 19; bap. Nov. 25; sp. Simon Straus and w. Elisabeth.

1811.

FREYMANN, SALOME, dr. Michael Freymann and w. Elisabeth; b. July ——, 1808; bap. Feb. 2; sp. Elisabeth Steinberger, widow.

FREYMANN, ELISABETH, dr. Michael Freymann and w. Elisabeth; b. Nov. 30, 1810; bap. Feb. 2; sp. Johannes Kepp, Sen. and w. Susanna.

TRAXEL, ROBERT, s. Peter Traxel and w. Christina; b. Jan. 22; bap. Feb. 17; Nicolaus Traxel and w. Maria.

FLICKINGER, JOHN, s. Daniel Flickinger and w. Catharina; b. Dec. 28, 1810; bap. Feb. 17; sp. Henrich Heffelfinger and w. Susanna.

ILLEGITIMATE, BARBARA, dr. Daniel Kohler and Susanna Becker; b. Feb. 13; bap. Feb. 17; sp. Friedrich Becker and w. Eva.

BURKHALTER, SOLOMON, s. Peter Burkhalter and w. Catharina; b. Mar. 17; bap. Apr. 15; sp. Solomon Steckel and w. Anna Maria.

NEUHARDT, LYDIA, dr. Peter Neuhardt and w. Catharina; b. Apr. 14; bap. May 23; sp. John Miller and w. Anna Maria.

KOHLER, SOPHIANA, dr. Peter Kohler and w. Catharina; b. Apr. 7; bap. May 23; sp. Jacob Saeger and w. Margreth.

STRAUSS, JOHN, s. Philip Strauss and w. Salome; b. May 2; bap. June 2; sp. Henrich Breisch and w. Catharina.

BRAUN, ISAAC, s. Adam Braun and w. Margreth; b. May 28; bap. June 2; sp. John Steckel and w. Magdalena.

BIERY, WILLIAM, s. Jacob Biery and w. Salome; b. May 11; bap. June 9; sp. John Steckel and w. Magdalena.

FISCHER, SUSANNA, dr. Anton Fischer and w. Salome; b. Mar. 22; bap. June 9; sp. Henrich Haas and w. Juliana.

SIEGFRIED, CATHARINA, dr. Peter Siegfried and w. Susanna; b. May 16; bap. June 16; sp. Catharina Siegfried, single.

GOBRECHT, JULIANA, dr. John Gobrecht V. D. M. and w. Hanna; b. June 1; bap. June 30; sp. J. Nicolaus Traxel and w. Maria.

MICKLY, DEBORA, dr. Henrich Mickly and w. Magdalena; b. May 12; bap. July 14; sp. Daniel Burkhalter and Catharina Mickly.

KOHLER, CATHARINA, dr. Benjamin Kohler and w. Catharina; b. June 22; Aug. 4; sp. Peter Burkhalter, Jun. and w. Catharina.

BIEGY, PETER, s. John Biegy and w. Elisabeth; b. July 31; bap. Aug. 14; died Aug. 16; sp. Christian Schwarz and w. Elisabeth.

LAUTENSCHLAEGER, RUBEN, s. Anton Lautenschlaeger and w. Elisabeth; b. July 15; bap. Sept. 1; sp. Adam Traxel and w. Maria.
TRAXEL, CARL, s. Nicolaus Traxel and w. Maria; b. Sept. 6; bap. Oct. 13; sp. Peter Traxel and w. Christina.
JEHL, ELISABETH, dr. Andreas Jehl and w. Elisabeth; b. Sept. 23; bap. Oct. 19; sp Wilhelm Rinker and w. Juliana.
KOHLER, EUPHEMIA, dr. Jacob Kohler, Jun. and w. Maria; b. Aug. 27; bap. Oct. 26; sp. Georg Schnerr and w. Magdalena.
LARASCH, ELIZABETH, dr. Jacob Larasch and w. Sara; b. Oct. 10; bap. Nov. 24; sp. Georg Miller and Margreth Deubert.

1812.

MOHARTER, MAGDALENA, dr. Jacob Moharter and w. Margreth; b. Aug. 23, 1811; bap. Jan. 5; sp. Jacob Hartmann and w. Catharina.
BIERY, WILHELM, s. Henrich Biery and w. Catharina; b. Nov. 3, 1811; bap. Jan. 24; sp. Daniel Mayer and Catharina Amhaeuser.
WERZ, ELIZA, dr. John Werz and w. Magdalena; b. Dec. 10, 1811; bap. Feb. 2; sp. Anton Fischer and w. Salome.
BURKHALTER, DEBORA, dr. Henrich Burkhalter and w. Barbara; b. Dec. 19, 1811; bap. Feb. 2; sp. Peter Steckel and w. Elisabeth.
HOFFMANN, DEBORA, dr. Michael Hoffmann and w. Magdalena; b. Jan. 21; bap. Feb. 16; sp. Peter Scheurer and w. Catharina.
SIEGFRIED, ISAAC, s. Solomon Siegfried and w. Susanna; b. Nov. 27, 1811; bap. Feb. 23; sp. Andreas Siegfried and w. Anna Elisabeth.
MEYER, RUBEN, s. Peter Meyer, Jun. and w. Catharina; b. Jan. 19; bap. Mar. 15; sp. Philip Strauss and w. Salome.
MEYER, DEBORA, dr. Joseph Meyer and w. Susanna; b. Jan. 11; bap. Mar. 15; sp. John Meyer and Dorothea Meyer.
PETER, ELIZABETH, dr. Casper Peter and w. Catharina; b. Feb. 6; bap. Mar. 15; sp. Gottfried Peter and w. Elisabeth.
ROTH, ANNA ELISABETH, dr. Jacob Roth and w. Elisabeth; b. Feb. 14; bap. Apr. 2; sp. Anna Elisabeth, wife of David Heller.
MILLER, MATTHEUS, s. Sebastian Miller and w. Maria Barbara; b. Dec. 2, 1811; bap. Apr. 12; sp. Matthaeus Graeber and w. Elisabeth.

NEUHARDT, ABRAHAM, s. John Neuhardt and w. Sara; b. Mar. 16; bap. Apr. 12; sp. Peter Neuhardt, Sen. and w. Catharina.

ROSS, HANNA, dr. John Ross and w. Regina; b. Feb. 15; bap. Apr. 12; sp. Solomon Gruber and Magdalena Fenstermacher.

GANGWEHR, ABRAHAM, s. Charles Gangwehr and w. Maria Magdalena; b. Jan. 9; bap. May 10; sp. Michale Frack and w. Hanna.

KELCHNER, PAUL, s. Christoph Kelchner and w. Maria Barbara; b. Mar. 28; bap. May 10; sp. Jacob Flickinger and w. Catharina.

ROTH, JAMES, s. Peter Roth and w. Maria; b. Mar. 26; bap. May 10; sp. George Remely and w. Regina.

LEIBEGUTH, ALEXANDER, s. Georg Leibeguth and w. Anna; b. Feb. 18; bap. May 15; sp. Parents.

MUECKLY, SUSANNA, dr. Peter Mueckly and w. Salome; b. Mar. 28; bap. May 17; sp. Christian Mueckly and w. Elisabeth.

LAUTENSCHLAEGER, ELISABETH, dr. Jacob Lautenschlaeger and w. Eva; b. Feb. 9; bap. May 24; sp. Henrich Haas and w. Juliana.

GILBERT, RUBEN, s. Jacob Gilbert and w. Maria; b. Apr. 3; bap. May 24; sp. Casper Dick and w. Catharina.

GILBERT, SOPHIANA, dr. Jacob Gilbert and w. Maria; b. Apr. 3; bap. May 24; sp. John Lautenschlaeger and w. Margreth.

SCHMIDT, SALME, dr. Wilhelm Schmidt and w. Catharina; b. Mar. 1; bap. May 24; sp. Michale Biegy and Salme Lenz.

MEYER, JONAS, s. Georg Meyer and w. Anna Maria; b. June 5; bap. June 10; sp. Samuel Saeger and w. Barbara.

MICKLY, ELISABETH, dr. Joseph Mickly and w. Estehr; b. May 12; bap. July 12; sp. Parents.

BIEGY, JOHN, s. John Biegy and w. Elisabeth; b. July 20; bap. Aug. 2; died ———; sp. John Paul and w. Esther.

FLICKINGER, SALME, dr. Georg Flickinger and w. Magdalena; b. June 5; bap. Aug. 2; sp. Magdalena Schneck, Peter Schneck's widow.

MEYER, WILHELM, s Daniel Meyer and w. Susanna; b. July 26; bap. Aug. 5; died Aug. 12; sp. Gottfried Laury and w. Susanna.

TRAXEL, MARGRETHA, dr. Christian Traxel and w. Barbara; b. Aug. 9; bap. Aug. 23; sp. Margreth Deuber, single.

STRAUSS, RUBEN, s. Simon Strauss and w. Elisabeth; b. July 11; bap. Aug. 30; sp. Peter Ruch and w. Susanna.

LEHIGH COUNTY—1734-1834. 79

FRANZ, JOHN, s. Peter Franz and w. Salme; b. Aug. 1; bap. Aug. 30; sp. Johannes Schad and w. Elisabeth.
MEYER, CATHARINA, dr. Jacob Meyer and w. Christina; b. July 2; bap. Aug. 30; sp. George Heninger and w. Catharina.
LEVI, MARIA ANNA, dr. Moses Levi and w. Maria; b. Sept. 13; bap. Sept. 19; died Sept. 20; sp. Catharina Biery, wife of Henrich Biery.
KOHLER, MANASSE, s. Benjamin Kohler and w. Catharina; b. Aug. 22; bap. Sept. 27; sp. Jacob Kohler, Sen. and w. Maria Elisabeth.
HAAS, JOHN, s. Henrich Haas and w. Juliana; b. Sept. 16; bap. Sept. 27; sp. Johannes Metzger and w. Maria.
STECKEL, HENRICH, s. Peter Steckel and w. Elisabeth; b. Oct. 6; bap. Oct. 25; sp. Solomon Steckel and w. Anna Maria.
SCHEURER, SALME, dr. Jacob Scheurer and w. Catharina; b. Sept. 10; bap. Oct. 25; sp. Peter Scheurer and w. Catharina.
SCHMIDT, CARL, s. Daniel Schmidt and w. Catharina; b. Oct. 28; bap. Nov. 21; sp. John Miller and w. Anna Maria.
HARTMANN, LUCIANA, dr. Jacob Hartmann and w. Catharina; b. Nov. 1; bap. Nov. 22; sp George Huettel and Salme Gut.
BIEBER, JULIANA, dr. John Bieber and w. Magdalena; b. Sept. 10; bap. Nov. 22; sp. Christoph Freymann and w. Eva.
PAUL, RUBEN, s. John Paul and w. Esther; b. Oct. 5; bap. Dec. 20; sp. John Biegy and w. Elisabeth.

1813.

SCHREIBER, APOLLONIA, dr. Daniel Sscheiber and w. Barbara; Oct. 29, 1812; bap. Jan. 1; sp. Peter Schreiber and w. Susanna.
BURKHALTER, WILHELM, s. Daniel Burkhalter and w. Catharina; b. Oct. 15, 1812; bap. Jan. 17; sp. parents.
BURKHALTER, ANNA MARIA, dr. Peter Burkhalter and w. Catharina; b. Dec. 11, 1812; bap. Jan. 17; sp. Peter Steckel and w. Elisabeth.
BIERY, ELISABETH, dr. Abraham Biery and w. Salome; b. Dec. 20, 1812; bap. Jan. 26; sp. Isaac Hermany and w. Catharina.
BECKER, ELISABETH, dr. Friedrich Becker and w. Eva; b. Jan. 16; bap. Feb. 15; died Mar. 8; sp. Henrich Heffelfinger and w. Susanna.
ILLEGITIMATE, DANIEL, s. James Jameson and Catharina Siegfried; b. Dec. 17, 1812; bap. Feb. 16; sp. Susanna, Peter Siegfried's wife.

RECORDS OF EGYPT REFORMED CHURCH.

MEYER, JAMES, s. Peter Meyer and w. Margreth; b. Jan. 18; bap. Feb. 21; sp. John Neuhardt and w. Sara.

EISENHARDT, ELIZA, dr. George Eisenhardt and w. Elisabeth; b. Feb. 8; bap. Feb. 25; sp. Christian Traxel and w. Barbara.

BIEGY, CATHARINA, dr. Michael Biegy and w. Salome; b. Jan. 25; bap. Feb. 28; sp. Jacob Hirsch and w. Catharina.

GILBERT, ESTHER, dr. Schoolmaster Adam Gilbert and w. Susanna; b. Feb. 25; bap. Mar. 9; sp. J. Gobrecht and w. Hanna.

FRANZ, HENRICH, s. Henrich Franz and w. Margreth; b. Feb. 22; bap. Mar. 14; sp. Henrich Ritter and w. Elisabeth.

SCHEURER, GEORGE, s. Nicolaus Scheurer and w. Susanna; b. Jan. 21; bap. Mar. 14; sp. George Scheurer and w. Elisabeth.

MEYER, WILHELM, s. Joseph Meyer and w. Susanna; b. Feb. 2; bap. Apr. 11; sp. Jacob Meyer, Jun. and w. Christina.

TRAXEL, CATHARINA, dr. Nicolaus Traxel and w. Maria; b. Mar. 26; bap. Apr. 25; sp. J. Gobrecht, V. D. M. and w. Hanna.

HAESE, SAMUEL, bap. Apr. 21, after previous instruction, in the 15th year of his age.

FISCHER, JAMES, s. Jacob Fischer and w. Barbara; b. Apr. 10; bap. May 12; sp. George Fischer, Sen. and w. Maria.

BIERY, STEPHAN, s. David Biery and w. Susanna; b. Mar. 28; bap. May 16; sp. Peter Mickly and w. Salome.

KRATZER, DAVID, s. Andreas Kratzer and w. Magdalena; b. Mar. 14; bap. May 16; sp. David Biery and w. Susanna.

DICK, ELISABETH, dr. Casper Dick and w. Catharina; b. May 8; bap. May 27; sp. Anton Lautenschlaeger and w. Elisabeth.

STRAUSS, MAGDALENA, dr. Philip Strauss and w. Salome; b. Apr. 1; bap. May 27; sp. Daniel Meyer and w. Magdalena.

SAEGER, MARIA, dr. Jacob Saeger and w. Margreth; b. May 3; bap. June 20; sp. Peter Kohler and w. Catharina.

MILLER, JACOB, s. Peter Miller and w. Christina; b. June 9; bap. June 27; sp. Georg Miller and Catharina Neuhardt.

GOBRECHT, SOPHIA, dr. John Gobrecht, V. D. M. and w. Hanna; b. June 4; bap. June 27; sp. Peter Traxel and w. Christina.

STECKEL, WILHELM, s. Solomon Steckel and w. Maria; b. June 4; bap. July 4; sp. Peter Steckel and w. Elisabeth.

TRAXEL, EDWARD, s. Peter Traxel and w. Christina; b. June 6; bap. July 4; sp. Anton Lautenschlaeger and w. Elisabeth.

ILLEGITIMATE, SALME, dr. John Schreiber and Magdalena Meyer; b. July 1, 1811; bap. July 26, 1813; sp. Elisabeth, wife of Jacob Meyer.

LOBACH, ABRAHAM, s. Peter Lobach and w. Magdalena; b. June 7; bap. Aug. 1; sp. Abraham Lerch and Catharina Nagel.

HOFFMANN, MANASSE, s. John Hoffmann and w. Barbara; b. July 1; bap. Aug. 1; sp. Jacob Meyer, Jun. and w. Christina.

MILLER, ABRAHAM, s. Jacob Miller and w. Maria; b. June 26; bap. Aug. 29; sp. Nicholas Saeger, Esq. and w. Maria.

SCHNECK, RUBEN, s. John Schneck and w. Magdalena; b. Aug. 2; bap. Aug. 29; sp. John Schneck and Magdalena Schneck.

MUECKLY, WILHELM, s. Henrich Mueckly and w. Magdalena; b. June 30; bap. Sept. 5; sp. Daniel Meyer and w. Magdalena.

BIERY, HANNA, dr. Henrich Biery and w. Catharina; b. Sept. 15; bap. Oct. 2; sp. David Biery and w. Susanna.

MEYER, ELIZABETH, dr. Daniel Meyer and w. Susanna; b. Sept. 18; bap. Oct. 13; sp. Jacob Meyer, Sen. and w. Elisabeth.

MEYER, CARL, s. Peter Meyer, Jun. and w. Catharina; b. Aug. 30; bap. Oct. 23; sp. Jacob Saeger and w. Margreth.

BIEGY, SALOME, dr. John Biegy and w. Elizabeth; b. Sept. 5; bap. Oct. 24; sp. Jacob Biegy and w. Anna Maria.

BAX, WILHELM, s. Wilhelm Bax and w. Magdalena; b. Sept. 25; bap. Nov. 21; sp. J. Nicolaus Kern and w. Catharina.

SIEGFRIED, PETER, s. Peter Siegfried and w. Susanna; b. Oct. 14; bap. Nov. 28; sp. Andreas Siegfried and w. Elisabeth.

FRAEHN, MAGDALENA, dr. John Fraehn and w. Christina; b. July 31; bap. Nov. 28; sp. Charles Gangwehr and w. Magdalena.

HOFFMANN, STEPHANUS, s. Michael Hoffmann and w. Magdalena; b. Nov. 5; bap Nov. 28; sp. J. Jacob Scheurer and w. Catharina.

KOHLER, JOSUA, s. Peter Kohler and w. Catharina; b. Oct. 8; bap. Dec. 5; sp. Jacob Steckel and w. Maria.

1814.

HARTMANN, CARL, s. Jacob Hartmann and w. Catharina; b. Dec. 11, 1813; bap. Jan. 9; sp. Georg Huettel, grandfather of the child.

RINKER, WILLIAM, s. Wilhelm Rinker and w. Eva; b. Dec. 21, 1813; bap. Jan. 7; sp. Nicholas Saeger and w. Catharina.

GROB, STEPHAN, s. Henrich Grob and w. Barbara; b. Jan. 1; bap. Feb. 13; sp. Conrad Leisenring and w. Catharina

PETER, CATHARINA, dr. Gottfried Peter and w. Elisabeth; b. Jan. 21; bap. Feb. 13; sp. John Peter and w. Elisabeth.

MEYER, WILHELM, s. Peter Meyer and w. Margreth; b. Jan. 24; bap. Feb. 27; sp. George Dinky and w. Susanna.

FISCHER, MAGDALENA, dr. George Fischer, Jun. and w. Maria; b. Dec. 21, 1813; bap. Mar. 3; sp. Michael Hoffmann and w. Magdalena.

MOHARTER, SALOME, dr. Jacob Moharter and w. Margreth; b. Jan. 24; bap. Mar. 13; sp. Peter Scheurer and w. Catharina.

SOHN, JACOB, s. Daniel Sohn and w. Maria; b. Mar. 11; bap. Mar. 23; sp. Jacob Sohn and w. Albertina.

LAURY, ADAM, s. Daniel Laury and w. Catharina; b. Mar. 27; bap. Apr. 9; sp. Martin Semmel and w. Catharina.

KOHLER, MARGRETH, dr. Jacob Kohler and w. Maria; b. Feb. 28; bap. Apr. 9; sp. Susanna, wife of Peter Kohler.

LARASCH, SALOME, dr. Jacob Larasch and w. Sara; b. Feb. 21; bap. Apr. 10; sp. Margreth, widow of Lorenz Miller.

ROTH, MARGRETH, dr. Jacob Roth and w. Elisabeth; b. Apr. 2; bap. Apr. 24; sp. Henrich Franz and w. Margreth.

NEUHARDT, REGINA, dr. Peter Neuhardt and w. Catharina; b. Feb. 23; bap. May 19; sp. Peter Strauss and w. Catharina.

SIEGFRIED, MARIA MAGDALENA, dr. Solomon Siegfried and w. Susanna; b. Mar. 24; bap. May 19; sp. Peter Muennich and w. Magdalena.

SAHM, MARIA, dr. Johannes Sahm and w. Susanna; b. Apr. 7; bap. May 19; sp. Jacob Braun and w. Margreth.

KOHLER, LUCAS, s. Benjamin Kohler and w. Catharina; b. Mar. 3; bap. May 19; sp. Jacob Scheurer and w. Catharina.

MEYER, PAUL, s. Jacob Meyer and w. Christina; b. Apr. 8; bap. May 19; sp. Daniel Meyer and w. Magdalena.

MEYER, WILHELM, s. John Meyer and w. Eva; b. May 4; bap. May 29; sp. Georg Adam Deuber and w. Eva.

MEYER, PETER, s. Joseph Meyer and w. Susanna; b. May 7; bap. June 25; sp. Peter Meyer, Jun. and w. Catharina.

SAEGER, SALANDA, dr. Joseph Saeger and w. Magdalena; b. May 30; bap. July 17; sp. Nicolaus Saeger Sen. and w. Magdalena, grandparents.

BURKHALTER, GEORGE, s. Peter Burkhalter and w. Catharina; b. June 17; bap. Juy 31; sp. George Kern and w. Salome.

HORN, ESTHER, dr. Jacob Horn and w. Elisabeth; b. Apr. 28; bap. Aug. 7; sp. Catharina Loeser, wife of John Loeser.

STRAUSS, ELISABETH, dr. Simon Strauss and w. Elisabeth; b. Aug. 21; bap. Sept. 5; sp. parents.
ILLEGITIMATE, FRIEDRICH, s. Friedrich Stricker and Elisabeth Sohn; b. Aug. 20; bap. Sept. 18; sp. Daniel Sohn and w. Maria.
NEUHARDT, RUBEN, s. Jonas Neuhardt and w. Eva; b. Sept. 13; bap. Sept. 25; sp. Johannes Saeger and w. Magdalena.
LAUTENSCHLAEGER, SARA, dr. Anton Lautenschlaeger and w. Elisabeth; b. Aug. 30; bap. Oct. 2; sp. Jonas Traxel and w. Sara.
FLICKINGER, RUBEN, s. Georg Flickinger and w. Magdalena; b. Aug. 31; bap. Oct. 22; sp. Martin Semmel and w. Catharina.
YUNDT, HENRICH, s. Abraham Yundt and w. Elisabeth; b. Sept. 23; bap. Oct. 22; sp. Henrich Steckel and w. Maria.
LEH, DANIEL, s. Henrich Leh and w. Susanna; b. July 27; bap. Oct. 23; sp. Nicholas Saeger, Esq. and w. Maria.
NEUHARDT, LYDIA, dr, John Neuhardt and w. Sara; b. Sept. 27; bap. Oct. 23; sp. J. Gobrecht, V. D. M. and w. Hanna.
KELCHNER, JULIANA, dr. Peter Kelchner and w. Magdalena; b. Oct. 8; bap. Oct. 30; sp. Christoph Kelchner and w. Maria Barbara.
BURKHALTER, NATHAN, s. Daniel Burkhalter and w. Catharina; b. Oct. 10; bap. Nov. 20; sp. Peter Mueckly and w. Salome.
RITTER, DANIEL, s. Henrich Ritter and w. Elisabeth; b. Oct. 27; bap. Nov. 20; sp. Johannes Ritter and w. Maria.
CHRISTEIN, SOLOMON, s. John Christein and w. Salome; b. Sept. 22; bap. Nov. 20; sp. George Remely and w. Regina.
FAUST, DAVID, s. Jonas Faust and w. Susanna; b. Oct. 27; bap. Dec. 18; sp. John Paul and w. Esther.
STECKEL, DEBORA, dr. Peter Steckel and w. Elisabeth; b. Nov. 3; bap. Dec. 18; sp. Joseph Burkhalter and w. Barbara.
BOX, LUDWIG, s. Wilhelm Box and w. Magdalena; b. Nov. 21; bap. Dec. 25; sp. Peter Kohler and w. Catharina.

1815.

HUETTEL, CATHARINA FRIEDERICA, dr. George Huettel and w. Maria; b. Dec. 18, 1814; bap. Jan. 8; sp. Jacob Hartmann and w. Catharina.
GANGWEHR, MAGDALENA, dr. Wilhelm Gangwehr and w. Elisabeth; b. Nov. 27, 1814; bap. Jan. 8; sp. Thomas Gangwehr and w. Susanna.
MILLER, HENRICH, s. Jacob Miller and w. Maria; b. Oct. 21, 1814; bap. Jan. 15; sp. Adam Schneck and w. Susanna.

STRAUS, DAVID, s. Philip Straus and w. Salome; b. Jan. 2; bap. Feb. 12; sp. Peter Schreiber and w. Susanna.

MEYER, DAVID, s. Peter Meyer and w. Margreth; b. Feb. 7; bap. Mar. 19; sp. George Teichmann and w. Susanna.

TRAXEL, LYDIA dr. Nicolaus Traxel and w. Maria; b. Feb. 27; bap. Apr. 2; sp. Solomon Scheurer and w. Catharina.

ILLEGITIMATE DANIEL, s. Daniel Steckel and Catharina Neuhard; b. Dec. 22, 1814; bap. Apr. 11; sp. John Neuhardt and w. Sara.

TRAXEL, ISABELLA, dr. Jonas Traxel and w. Sara; b. Mar. 22; bap. Apr. 16; sp. Stephan Traxel and Catharina Geiger.

SAEGER, RUBEN, s. Daniel Saeger and w. Barbara; b. Mar. 15; bap. May 14; sp. Nicolaus Saeger, Esq. and w. Maria.

QUEER, EVA ELIZABETH, dr. Daniel Queeer and w. Eva; b. Nov. 21, 1814; bap. June 4; sp. John Walter and Elizabeth Biegy.

MILLER, WILLIAM, s. George Miller and w. Susanna; b. June 29; bap. July 10; sp. Christoph. Kelchner and w. Maria Barbara.

GILBERT, SUSANNA, dr. Schoolmaster Adam Gilbert and w. Susanna; b. July 13; bap. July 30; sp. J. Nicolaus Traxel and w. Maria.

SAEGER, TILGHMAN, s. Samuel Saeger and w. Barbara; b. July 11; bap. Aug. 13; sp. J. Nicolaus Kern and w. Catharina.

FRANZ, LYDIA, dr. Henrich Franz and w. Margreth; b. July 29; bap. Aug. 27; sp. Peter Neubardt and w. Catharina.

SCHAD, RUBEN, s. Lorenz Schad and w. Magdalena; b. July 22; bap. Aug. 27; sp. Adam Labach and w. Maria Margreth.

HECKER, MARIA MAGDALENA, dr. Jonas Hecker and w. Maria Magdalena; b. July 22; bap. Sept. 24; sp. Nicolaus Saeger and w. Catharina.

KOHLER, ANNA LEVINA, dr. Peter Kohler and w. Catharina; b. Aug. 18; bap. Oct. 22; sp. Nicolaus Kern and w. Catharina.

KOHLER, DEBORA, dr. Daniel Kohler and w. Magdalena; b. Oct. 13; bap. Nov. 19; sp. Jacob Kohler, Sen. and w. Maria Elisabeth.

MEYER, LYDIA, dr. Conrad Meyer and w. Elisabeth; b. Oct. 1; bap. Nov. 19; sp. Jacob Hartmann and w. Catharina.

MEYER, MARIA, dr. John Meyer and w. Eva; b. Nov. 11; bap. Nov. 22; sp. J. Nicolaus Traxel and w. Maria.

BECKER, SUSANNA, dr. Friedrich Becker and w. Eva; b. Nov. 5; bap. Dec. 9; sp. Henrich Leh and Susanna Becker.

MEYER ELIZA, dr. Peter Meyer and w. Catharina; b. Oct. 6; bap. Dec. 17; sp. John Steckel and w. Magdalena.
RINKER, JONAS, s. Georg Rinker and w. Maria; b. Dec. 6; bap. Dec. 26; sp. John Stoflet and w. Eva.

1816.

KOHLER, LUCIANA, dr. Benjamin Kohler and w. Catharina; b. Dec. 21, 1815; bap. Jan. 14; sp. Ahraham Kohler and Elisabeth Burkhalter.
SCHEURER, HANNA, dr. Nicolaus Scheurer and w. Susanna; b. Dec. 11, 1815; bap. Jan. 28; sp. Michael Frack and w. Hanna.
GRAFF, MARIA, dr. Peter Graff and w. Elisabeth; b. Jan. 1; bap. Feb. 4; sp. Elisabeth, widow of Georg Graff.
KOHLER, LUCIANA, dr. Jacob Kohler and w. Maria; b. Nov. 30, 1815; bap. Feb. 11; sp. Peter Kohler and w. Catharina.
JACOBI, LUCIANA, dr. Jacob Jacobi and w. Maria; b. Jan. 15; bap. Feb. 11; sp. John Teichmann and w. Susanna.
WOTRING, ELISABETH, dr. Peter Wotring and w. Elisabeth; b. Dec. 29, 1815; bap. Feb. 11; sp. George Scheurer and w. Elisabeth.
SIEGFRIED, SALOME, dr. Solomon Siegfried and w. Susanna; b. Feb. 5; bap. Feb. 18; sp. Peter Siegfried and w. Susanna.
SIEGFRIED, MAGDALENA, dr. Peter Siegfried and w. Susanna; b. Dec. 25, 1815; bap. Feb. 18; sp. Joseph Siegfried and Elisabeth Kelly.
BIEGY, SARA, dr. Michael Biegy and w. Salome; b. Jan. 19; bap. Feb. 25; sp. Jacob Biegy and w. Maria, grandparents.
NEUHARDT, ELIZA, dr. Jonas Neuhardt and w. Catharina; b. Jan. 22; bap. Feb. 25; sp. George Dinky and w. Susanna.
BURKHALTER, JOSEPH, s. Peter Burkhalter and w. Catharina; b. Feb. 8; bap. Apr. 2; sp. Daniel Burkhalter and w. Catharina.
SAHM, JOHANNES JACOB, s. Johannes Sahm and w. Susanna; b. Feb. 24; bap. Apr. 7; sp. Jacob Braun and w. Margreth.
CHRISTEIN, ELIZABETH, dr. John Christein and w. Salome; b. Mar. 13; bap. Apr. 24; sp. Elisabeth Hornung, widow.
MEYER, SOLOMON, s. Casper Meyer and w. Barbara; b. Apr. 12; bap. Apr. 28; sp. Nicolaus Traxel and w. Maria.
BURKHALTER, DANIEL, s. Daniel Burkhalter and w. Catharina; b. Mar. 23; bap. May 4; sp. Peter Steckel and w. Elisabeth.

STECKEL, CATHARINA, dr. Peter Steckel and w. Elisabeth; b. Mar. 24; bap. May 4; sp. Daniel Burkhalter and w. Catharina.

LARASCH, LUCIANA, dr. Jacob Larasch and w. Sara; b. Mar. 19; bap. May 5; sp. John Burger and w. Elisabeth.

GANGWEHR, ELIZABETH, dr. Charles Gangwehr and w. Magdalena; b. Apr. 2; bap. May 8; sp. Michael Fenstermacher and Elisabeth Gruber.

BRAUN, LYDIA, dr. Adam Braun and w. Margreth; b. Apr. 2; bap. May 14; sp. Salome Biery, widow.

WRIGHT, LUCIANA, dr. George Wright and w. Magdalena; b. May 2; bap. May 19; sp. Henrich Franz and w. Margreth.

KRATZER, WILHELM, s. Andreas Kratzer and w. Magdalena; b. Apr. 1; bap. June 9; sp. Joseph Meyer and w. Susanna.

MEYER, SALOME, dr. Jacob Meyer and w. Christina; b. Apr. 29; bap. June 9; sp. Jacob Biery and w. Salome.

YOHE, JONAS, s. John Yohe and w. Catharina; b. July 17; bap. Aug. 25; sp. Jonathan Faust and w. Susanna.

GOBRECHT, ELIZABETH, dr. John Gobrecht, V. D. M. and w. Hanna; b. Aug. 19; bap. Sept. 1; sp. Jonas Traxel and w. Sara.

ZERFASS, SUSANNA, dr. Henrich Zerfass and w. Susanna; b. Aug. 11; bap. Sept. 22; sp. Peter Kester and Salome Ritter.

KERN, HENRIETTE, dr. Joseph Kern and w. Hanna; b. Sept. 6; bap. Oct. 19; sp. Nicolaus Kern and w. Catharina.

PAUL, THOMAS, s. John Paul and w. Esther; b. Aug. 31; bap. Oct. 27; sp. Philip Faust and w. Barbara.

PAUL, HANNA, dr. John Paul and w. Esther; b. Aug. 31; bap. Oct. 27; sp. Henrich Beil and w. Hanna.

ROTH, SOLOMON, s. Jacob Roth and w. Elisabeth; b. Oct. 13; bap. Nov. 4; sp. Solomon Scheurer and w. Catharina.

SAEGER, ABIGAIL, dr. Joseph Saeger and w. Magdalena; b. Oct. 28; bap. Nov. 7; sp. Nicolaus Saeger and w. Magdalena.

STRAUSS, MARIA, dr. Simon Strauss and w. Elisabeth; b. Sept. 17; bap. Nov. 17; sp. Michael Frack and w. Hanna.

STECKEL, ELISABETH, dr. Daniel Steckel and w. Salome; b. Nov. 7; bap. Dec. 1; sp. John Steckel and w. Magdalena.

YUNDT, MATHILDA, dr. Abraham Yundt and w. Elisabeth; b. Nov. 7; bap. Dec. 3; sp. Peter Burkhalter and w. Catharina.

KERN, FLORIANA, dr. Peter Kern and w. Margreth; b. Nov. 6; bap. Dec. 15; sp. Nicolaus Kern and w. Catharina.

SIEGFRIED, THOMAS, s. Andreas Siegfried, Jun. and w. Magdalena; b. Nov. 11; bap. Dec. 22; sp. George Scheurer and w. Elisabeth.

1817.

WIDDES, MARIA ANNA, dr. Isaac Widdes and w. Rebecca; b. Dec. 21, 1816; bap. Jan. 1; sp. John Miller and w. Anna Maria.

MEYER, SUSANNA, dr. Joseph Meyer and w. Susannna; b. Nov. 30, 1816; bap. Jan. 12 ;sp. Peter Hoffmann and w. Susanna.

MEYER, ABIGAIL, dr. Peter Meyer and w. Margreth; b. Dec. 16, 1816; bap. Jan. 12; sp. John Saeger and w. Catharina.

GANGWEHR, RUBEN, s. Wilhelm Gangwehr and w. Elisabeth; b. Nov. 17, 1816; bap. Jan. 19; sp. Lorenz Schad and w. Magdalena.

STECKEL, MARIA SALOME, dr. Peter Steckel and w. Elisabeth, a born Hartmann; b. Jan. 16; bap. Jan. 25; sp. Salome Biery, widow of Henrich Biery.

SAEGER, JOHN, s. Johann Jacob Saeger, deceased, and w. Barbara; b. Jan. 2; bap. Jan. 30; sp. John Teichmann and w. Susanna.

MEYER, CARL, s. Conrad Meyer and w. Elisabeth; b. Jan. 19; bap. Feb. 9; sp. Peter Meyer and w. Catharina, a born Gangwehr.

JACOBI, MAGDALENA, dr. Jacob Jacobi and w. Maria; b. Jan. 26; bap. Mar. 2; sp. Nicolaus Saeger and w. Magdalena.

FLICKINGER, DANIEL, s. Georg Flickinger and w. Magdalena; b. Jan. 15; bap. Mar. 9; sp. Michael Zoellner and w. Catharina.

GEORG, SALOME, dr. Henrich Georg. and w. Magdalena; b. Jan. 29; bap. Mar. 9; sp. Magdalena, widow of Michael Hoffmann.

SCHREIBER, MARIA, dr. Jacob Schreiber and w. Eva; b. Dec. 21, 1816; bap. Mar. 9; sp. Conrad Leisenring, Sen. and w. Catharina.

JEHL, CATHARINA, dr. Peter Jehl and w. Susanna; b. Feb. 19; bap. Mar. 11; sp. Wilhelm Rinker and w. Juliana.

GRAFF, ELISABETH, dr. Peter Graff and w. Elisabeth; b. Jan. 16; bap. Mar. 19; sp. Elisabeth Graff, single.

YUNDT, CARL, s. John Yundt and w. Hanna; b. Feb. 25; bap. Mar. 30; sp. Daniel Siegfried, Jun. and w. Catharina.

BIERY SUSANNA, dr. David Biery and w. Susanna; b. Apr. 3; bap. Apr. 5; sp. Jonas Faust and w. Susanna.

RECORDS OF EGYPT REFORMED CHURCH.

BIERY, ELIZA, dr. Peter Biery and w. Anna Maria; b. Mar. 14; bap. Apr. 5; sp. Peter Mickly and w. Salome.

KELCHNER, ISABELLA, dr. John Kelchner and w. Magdalena; b. Jan. 30; bap. Apr. 13; sp. George Miller and w. Susanna.

TRAXEL, ANNA SUSANNA, dr.' Nicolaus Traxel and w. Maria; b. May 2; bap. May 12; sp. David Heller, Sen. and w. Elisabeth.

BERNDT, THOMAS, s. Tobias Berndt and w. Elisabeth; b. Apr. 9; bap. May 15; sp. Tobias Wasser and w. Magdalena.

SCHAEFER, LOUISE FRIDERICA, dr. Daniel Schaefer and w. Anna Maria; b. Jan. 17; bap. May 16; sp. parents.

LEVI, NATHAN, s. Moses Levi and w. Maria; b. May 27; bap. May 30; sp. Jacob Biegy, Sen. and w. Anna Maria.

RINKER, JEREMIAS, s. George Rinker and w. Maria; b. Apr. 25; bap. June 1; sp. Wilhelm Rinker and w. Juliana.

DESCHLER, CATHARINA, dr. David Deschler and w. Catharina; b. May 7; bap. June 1; sp. J. Gobrecht, V.D.M. and w. Hanna.

FISCHER, MARIA ANNA, dr. George Fischer, Jun. and w. Maria; b. June 3; bap. July 20; sp. Henrich Leh and Elisabeth Happel.

BIEGILY, ESTHER, dr. Jacob Biegely and w. Maria; b. Apr. 12; bap. July 20; sp. Susanna, widow of Adam Hecker.

BURGER, MOSES, s. Samuel Burger and w. Hanna; b. July 19; bap. July 22; sp. Peter Schmoll and w. Salome.

KOHLER, HENRIETTE, dr. Benjamin Kohler and w. Catharina; b. May 13; bap. July 27; sp. Daniel Kohler and w. Magdalena.

PETER, GOTTFRIED, s. Gottfried Peter and w. Elisabeth; b. Aug. 4; bap. Aug. 24; sp. Daniel Ritter and Elisabeth Meyer.

SCHAD, DEBORA, dr. Lorenz Schad and w. Magdalena; b. July 27; bap. Aug. 24; sp. Henrich Schad and Catharina Labach.

REIT, AARON, s. George Reit and w. Magdalena; b. Aug. 11; bap. Sept. 21; sp. Daniel Saeger and w. Susanna.

GILBERT, DAVID, s. Schoolmaster Adam Gilbert and w. Susanna; b. Sept. 23; bap. Oct. 12; sp. Peter Traxel and w. Christina.

MEYER, ELIAS, s. George Meyer and w. Margreth; b. Aug. 13; bap. Oct. 18; sp. Peter Hoffmann and w. Susanna.

SAHM, SUSANNA, dr. Johannes Sahm and w. Susanna; b. Sept. 5; bap. Oct. 18; sp. Peter Schreiber and w. Susanna.

KERN, SALOME ANNA, dr. Joseph Kern and w. Hanna; b. Sept. 17; bap. Oct. 18; sp. George Kern and w. Salome.
DIEHL, JOHN, s. Abraham Diehl and w. Salome; b. Sept. 24; bap. Oct. 19; sp. Daniel Meyer and w. Magdalena.
ROSS, ELIZA, dr. John Ross and w. Catharina; b. Aug. 14; bap. Oct. 26; sp. Johann Adam Kolb and w. Susanna.
MEYER, CATHARINA. dr. John Meyer and w. Eva; b. Oct. 9; bap. Nov. 2; sp. Jonas Meyer and Catharina Miller.
RINKER, ELISABETH, dr. Daniel Rinker and w. Salome; b. Nov. 8; bap. Nov. 18; sp. Henrich Franz and w. Margreth.
STECKEL, JAMES, s. Daniel Steckel and w. Salome; b. Oct. 20; bap. Nov. 23; sp. Henrich Haas and w. Juliana.
BIERY, ELIZA, dr. Peter Biegy and w. Charlotte; b. Oct. 10; bap. Nov. 30; sp. Friedrich Gut and w. Susanna.
NEUHARDT, LEVINA, dr. Jonas Neuhardt and w. Catharina; b. Nov. 12; bap. Dec. 7; sp. Peter Lautenschlaeger and Elisabeth Haas.
STRAUSS, SALOME, dr. Philip Strauss and w. Salome; b. Nov. 4; bap. Dec. 21; sp. John Meyer and Lydia Hoffmann.
SAEGER, MARIA, dr. Samuel Saeger and w. Barbara; b. Nov. 22; bap. Dec. 25; sp. Solomon Knaus and w. Maria.

1818.

FLICK, JULIANA, dr. Paul Flick and w. Maria Margreth; b. July 15, 1817; bap. Jan. 11; sp. John Steckel and w. Magdalena.
MEYER, REBECCA, dr. Peter Meyer and w. Catharina; b. Nov. 4, 1817; bap. Jan. 19; sp. George Meyer and w. Margreth.
SCHEURER, TILGHMAN, s. Jonas Scheurer and w. Dorothea; b. Dec. 23, 1817; bap. Jan. 25; sp. Peter Scheurer and w. Catharina.
RITTER, DANIEL, s. Daniel Ritter and w. Elisabeth; b. Jan. 15; bap. Jan. 27; sp. Jacob Meyer and w. Elisabeth.
ABBOT, WILLIAM, s. William Abbot and w. Catharina; b. Jan. 18; bap. Feb. 7; sp. John Hausknecht and w. Maria.
BURKHALTER, CATHARINA, dr. Peter Burkhalter and w. Catharina; b. Nov. 27, 1817; bap. Feb. 8; sp. Daniel Meyer and w. Magdalena.
STECKEL, ELISABETH, dr. Peter Steckel and w. Elisabeth, a born Biery; b. Dec. 14, 1917; bap. Feb. 8; sp. Peter Kern and w. Margreth.
MEYER, ELIZA, dr. Henrich Meyer and w. Elisabeth; b. Jan. 15; bap. Feb. 15; sp. Conrad Meyer and w. Elisabeth.
NEUHARDT, OWEN, s. John Neuhardt and w. Sara; b. Jan. 20; bap. Mar. 1; sp. Peter Neuhardt and w. Catharina.

RECORDS OF EGYPT REFORMED CHURCH.

KIEFER, WILLIAM, s. John Kiefer and w. Susanna; b. Feb. 5; bap. Mar. 8; sp. Henrich Grob Sen. and w. Elisabeth.

BURKHALTER, HANNA, dr. Daniel Burkhalter and w. Catharina; b. Feb. 26; bap. May 2; sp. Joseph Kern and w. Hanna.

SCHEURER, PAULUS, s. Nicolaus Scheurer and w. Susanna; b. Apr. 15; bap. May 10; sp. Peter Wotring and w. Elisabeth.

BREISCH, CARL, s. Jacob Breisch and w. Barbara; b. Apr. 13; bap. May 18; sp. John Teichmann and w. Susanna.

SIEGFRIED, WILHELM, s. Andreas Siegfried and w. Magdalena; b. Mar. 27; bap. May. 24; sp. John Roth and w. Catharina.

MICKLY, STEPHANUS, s. Henrich Mickly and w. Magdalena; b. Mar. 24; bap. May 31; sp. Joseph Burkhalter and w. Barbara.

BOGGS, STEPHANUS, s. Benjamin Boggs and w. Elisabeth; b. Mar. 22; bap. May 31; sp. Henrich Mickly and w. Magdalena.

WOTRING, JOHN, s. Peter Wotring and w. Elisabeth; b. May 14; bap. June 14; sp. J.Gobrecht, V. D. M. and w. Hanna.

KERN, OWEN, s. Peter Kern and w. Margreth; b. May 12; bap. June 28; sp. David Biery and w. Susanna.

MEYER, JONAS, s. Joseph Meyer and w. Susanna; b. July 2; bap. Aug. 23; sp. Jonas Traxel and w. Sara.

KOHLER, EPHRAIM, s. Daniel Kohler and w. Magdalena; b. July 7; bap. Aug. 23; sp. Nicolaus Hensinger and w. Elisabeth.

TRAXEL, EDWARD, s. Jonathan Traxel and w. Elisabeth; b. Aug. 23; bap. Aug. 27; sp. John Bieber and w. Magdalena.

TRAXEL, LEVINA, dr. John Traxel and w. Salome; b. Aug. 9; bap. Aug. 30; sp. Peter Mickly, Sen. and w. Salome.

MICKLY, ANNA LEVINA, dr. Jacob Mickly and w. Anna; b. Sept. 2; bap. Sept. 13; sp. Jacob Mickly, Sen. and w. Eva Catharina.

HOFFMANN, MAGDALENA, dr. Peter Hoffmann and w. Susanna; b. Sept. 2; bap. Sept. 14; sp. Henrich Georg and w. Magdalena.

BERNDT, JAMES, s. Tobias Berndt and w. Elisabeth; b. Aug. 28; bap. Sept. 17; sp. Simon Straus and w. Elisabeth.

LEH, RUBEN, s. Henrich Leh, Sen. and w. Susanna; b. May 5; bap. Sept. 20; sp. John Koch and w. Magdalena.

GRAFF, PETER, s. Peter Graff and w. Elisabeth; b. Aug. 18; bap. Oct. 10; sp. Paul Balliet.

ROTH, JOHN, s. John Roth and w. Catharina; b. Sept. 17; bap. Oct. 17; sp. Andreas Siegfried, Jun. and w. Magdalena.

LARASCH, HANNA, dr. Jacob Larasch and w. Sarah; b. Sept. 21; bap. Oct. 18; sp. Joseph Kern and w. Hanna.

MEYER, CARL, s. Daniel Meyer and w. Susanna; b. Oct. 7; bap. Oct. 19; sp. Peter Lautenschaeger and Barbara Laury.

SAEGER, ELI JOSEPH, s. Joseph Saeger and w. Magdalena; b. Nov. 2; bap. Nov. 8; sp. Joseph Siegfried and w. Elisabeth.

GLOECKNER, ELIZABETH, dr. Solomon Gloeckner and w. Catharina; b. Oct. 4; bap. Nov. 13; sp. Philip Weber and w. Elisabeth.

YUNDT, ESTHER, dr. Jonas Yundt and w. Lydia; b. Sept. 30; bap. Nov. 15; sp. Jacob Biery and w. Salome.

RINKER, JAMES, s. George Rinker and w. Maria; b. Oct. 13; bap. Nov. 15; sp. Daniel Rinker and w. Salome.

SCHAAL, MARIA, dr. Michael Schaal and w. Elizabeth; b. Oct. 24; Nov. 29; sp. Joseph Siegfriedt and w. Elisabeth.

STRAUS, THOMAS, s. Simon Straus, deceased, and w. Elisabeth; b. Nov. 8; bap. Dec. 13; sp. Daniel Schreiber and w. Barbara.

RINKER, RUBEN, s. Daniel Rinker and w. Salome; b. Dec. 2; bap. Dec. 25; sp. George Remely and w. Regina.

1819.

REIT, STEPHANUS, s. George Reit and w. Magdalena; b. Dec. 6, 1818; bap. Jan. 1; sp. Jonathan Traxel and w. Elisabeth.

BIERY, ELI, s. Peter Biery and w. Magdalena; b. Nov. 30, 1818; bap. Jan. 10; sp. David Biery and w. Susanna, grandparents.

OBLINGER, CATHARINA, dr. Nicolaus Oblinger and w. Salome; b. Apr. 21, 1818; bap. Jan. 10; sp. Jacob Buchmann and w. Magdalena.

YEHL, JOHN, s. John Yehl and w. Maria; b. Jan. 3; bap. Jan. 13; died; sp. Henrich Beyer and w. Susanna.

YEHL, SAMUEL, s. John Yehl and w. Maria; b. Jan. 3; bap. Jan. 13; died; sp. Christian Traxed and w. Barbara

GEORG, MAGDALENA, dr. Henrich Georg and w. Magdalena; b. Jan. 10; bap. Feb. 14; sp. Jonas Kaemmerer and Magdalena Georg.

BURKHALTER, ELISABETH, dr. Henrich Burkhalter and w. Barbara; b. Jan. 22; bap. Feb. 25; sp. Daniel Burkhalter and w. Catharina.

BURKHALTER, ELISABETH, dr. Peter Burkhalter and w. Catharina; b. Jan. 27; bap. Feb. 25; died Feb. 28; sp. Jacob Diery and w. Salome.

SCHMIDT, SAMUEL, s. Daniel Schmidt and w. Catharina; b. Dec. 27, 1818; bap. Feb. 27; sp. Peter Neuhardt and w. Catharina.

KOHLER, FLORIANA, dr. Benjamin Kohler and w. Catharina; b. Jan. 13; bap. Mar. 3; sp. Henrich Haes and w. Eva.

MEYER, LUCIANA, dr. George Meyer and w. Margreth; b. Dec. 28, 1818; map. Mar. 7; sp. John Hoffman and w. Barbara.

TAYLOR, SEM, s. William Taylor and w. Sarah; b. Oct. 4, 1807; bap. Mar. 16; sp. Daniel Siegfried, Sen. and w. Sarah.

TRAXEL, DRUSILLA, dr. Peter Traxel and w. Christina; b. Mar. 2; bap. Mar. 28; sp. Solomon Scheurer and w. Catharina.

KERN, MAGDALENA, dr. Joseph Kern and w. Hannah; b. Feb. 16; bap. Apr. 4; sp. Joseph Saeger and w. Magdalena.

RITTER, WILHELM, s. Daniel Ritter and w. Elisabeth; b. Feb. 26; bap. Apr. 4; sp. Gottfried Peter and w. Elisabeth.

MEYER, ELISABETH, dr. John Meyer and w. Eva; b Mar. 31; bap. Apr. 18; sp. Jacob Meyer and w. Elisabeth, grandparents.

BOGGS, CARL, s. Benjamin Boggs and w. Elisabeth; b. Mar. 8; bap. May 2; sp. David Thimm and widow Magdalena Hoffmann.

WASSER, THOMAS, s. Tobias Wasser and w. Magdalena; b Apr. 4; bap. May 2; sp. Jacob Schreiber and w. Eva.

ZOELLNER, ELIAS, s. Michael Zoellner and w. Catharina; b. Feb. 27; bap. May 7; sp. Jonas Yehl and Maria Elisabeth Flickinger.

NEUHARDT, ELISABETH, dr. Jonas Neuhardt, Jun. and w. Magdalena; b. Apr. 26; bap. May 23; sp. John Metzger and w. Maria.

KIEFER, DANIEL, s. John Kiefer and w. Susanna; b. May 14; bap. May 26; sp. Susanna, wife of John Teichmann.

SCHAD, ESTHER, dr. John Schad and w. Maria; b. May 6; bap. May 30; sp. John Baertsch and w. Susanna.

ILLEGITIMATE, JOSEPH, s. Joseph Meyer and Christina, Jacob Meyer's widow; b. Apr. 25; bap. June 13; sp. Henrich Straus and Catharina Andrea.

FLICKINGER, CATHARINA, dr. Georg Flickinger and w. Magdalena; b. May 5; bap. June 27; sp. Peter Remely and Salome Yehl.

SCHNECK, ELIZA, dr. John Schneck and w. Magdalena; b. May. 26; bap. June 27; sp. Peter Schneider and w. Hanna.
GILBERT, ANNA LEVINA, dr. Schoolmaster Adam Gilbert and w. Susanna; b. July 5; bap. July 25; sp. Peter Kohler and w. Catharina.
MILLER, LEVINA, dr. Wilhelm Miller and w. Maria; b. July 22; bap. Aug. 1; sp. Margreth Paul, single.
STECKEL, LEVINA, dr. Daniel Steckel and w. Salome; b. June 21; bap. Aug. 15; sp. Daniel Neuhardt and w. Barbara.
ROTH, DANIEL, s. Jacob Roth and w. Elisabeth; b. Aug. 17; bap. Sept. 15; sp. Daniel Saeger and w. Susanna.
KOCH, EPHRAIM, s. Tobias Koch and w. Lydia; b. Aug. 8; bap. Sept. 19; sp. Jonathan Traxel and w. Elisabeth.
STRAUSS, SIMON, s. Philip Strauss and w. Salome; b. Aug. 26; bap. Oct. 16; sp. Adam Braun and w. Anna Margreth.
LEH, WILHELM, s. Samuel Leh and w. Magdalena; b. Sept. 2; bap. Oct. 17; sp. Henrich Leh and w. Catharina.
SCHREIBER, MARIA, dr. Daniel Schreiber and w. Barbara; b. Oct. 11; bap. Nov. 11; sp. Conrad Beil and w. Maria.
MUEHLHAUSEN, SUSANNA, dr. Heinrich Muehlhausen and w. Anna Kunigunda; b. Oct. 7; bap. Nov. 14; sp. John Kiefer and w. Susanna.
HAEUSE, ELISABETH, dr. Samuel Haeuse and w. Anna; b. Oct. 29; bap. Nov. 14; sp. Peter Steckel and w. Elisabeth.
BAERTSCH, ELIZA, dr. John Baertsch and w. Susanna; b. Oct. 11; bap. Nov. 29; sp. Catharina Gut, the child's grandmother.
SCHEURER, ELIZA, dr. David Scheurer and w. Elisabeth; b. Oct. 25; bap. Dec. 5; sp. Solomon Scheurer and w. Catharina.
PETER, WILHELM, s. Gottfried Peter and w. Elisabeth; b. Nov. 17; bap. Dec. 12; sp. Daniel Peter and w. Catharina.
STECKEL, ELI, s. Solomon Steckel and w. Anna Maria; b. Nov. 21; bap. Dec. 12; sp. Jonas Traxel and w. Sarah.
MICKLY, THOMAS, s. Peter Mickly and w. Anna; b. Dec. 16; bap. Dec. 19; sp. Paul Balliet and w. Elisabeth.
OSMUN, PAUL, s. Samuel Osmun and w. Magdalena; b. Nov. 25; bap. Dec. 19; sp. Abraham Miller and w. Susanna.
SCHAD, MARIA, ANNA, dr. Lorenz Schad and w. Magdalena; b. Jan. 1; bap. Jan. 23; sp. George Dinky and w. Susanna.
PAUL, ELISABETH, dr. John Paul and w. Esther; b. Dec. 27,1819; bap. Feb. 12; sp. Parents.
SCHEURER, ELI, s. Jonas Scheurer and w. Dorothea; b. Dec. 24, 1819; bap. Feb. 17; sp. John Hoffmann and w. Barbara.

REIT, WILLIAM, s. George Reit and w. Magdalena; b. Jan. 28; bap. Feb. 20; sp. Daniel Rinker and w. Salome.

WOTRING, PETER, s. Peter Wotring and w. Elisabeth, now dead; b. Feb. 19; bap. Feb. 27; died Mar. 11; sp. Samuel Wotring and w. Eva.

MEYER, SIMON, s. Peter Meyer, Jun. and w. Catharina; b Dec. 22, 1819; bap. Mar. 5; sp. Jonas Traxel and w. Sarah.

MEYER, MAGDALENA, dr. Joseph Meyer and w. Susanna; b. Jan. 30; bap. Mar. 15; sp. Abraham Roth and w. Barbara.

KIEFER, ELIZA, dr. John Kiefer and w. Susanna; b. Apr. 10; bap. May 11; sp. Henrich Meyer and w. Elisabeth.

MICKLY, THOMAS, s. Henrich Mickly and w. Magdalena; b Apr. 5; bap. May 28; sp. Carl Burkhalter and Magdalena Mickly.

RITTER, WILLIAM, s. Johannes Ritter and w. Sarah; b. May. 8; bap. June 3; sp. Henrich Grob and w. Elisabeth.

RITTER, CATHARINA, dr. Johannes Ritter and w. Sarah; b. May 8; bap. June 3; sp. Gottfried Peter and w. Elisabeth.

KELCHNER, LEVINA, dr. Peter Kelchner and w. Magdalena; b. May 26; bap. June 11; sp. Jacob Fenstermacher and Barbara Kelchner.

LEH, STEPHAN, s. Henrich Leh, Jun. and w. Catharina; b. June 3; bap. June 18; sp. Henrich Leh, Sen. and w. Susanna.

TRAXEL, MILTON, s. Jonathan Traxel and w. Elisabeth; b. June 17; bap. July 2; sp. John Traxel and w. Salome.

FLICK, MARIA MARGRETHA, dr. Paul Flick and w. Maria Margretha; b. May 25; bap. July 8; sp. Henrich Leh, Sen. and w. Susanna.

ILLEGITIMATE, WILLIAM, s. Jacob Siegfried and Magdalena Feldhoff; b. Jan. 23; bap. July 8; sp. Paul Flick and w. Maria Margreth.

SIEGFRIED, RUBEN, s. Andreas Siegfried and w. Magdalena; b. May 22; bap. July 9; sp. Friedrich Gut and w. Susanna.

YUNDT, MARIA ANNA, dr. Jonas Yundt and w. Lydia; b. May 26; bap. July 23; sp. George Kern and w. Salome.

STECKEL, THOMAS, s. Peter Steckel and w. Elisabeth; b June 25; bap. July 23; sp. David Biery and w. Susanna.

KOHLER, MARIA, dr. Peter Kohler and w. Catharina; b. June 15; bap. July 30; sp. Wilhelm Beck and w. Elisabeth.

GEORG, LYDIA, dr. Henrich Georg and w. Magdalena; b. July 4; bap. July 30; sp. Georg Adam Kaemmerer and w. Susanna.

LEHIGH COUNTY—1734-1834. 95

HARZEL, SAMUEL, s. George Harxel and w. Anna Maria;
b. July 7; bap. Aug. 2; sp. Georg Bibelheimer and w. Anna
Margreth.

SCOTLAN, ANDREAS, s. John Scotlan and w. Maria; b.
Apr. 11; bap. Sept. 6; sp. Peter Meyer, Jun. and w. Catharina.

KOHLER, DOROTHEA, dr. Benjamin Kohler and w. Catharina; b. July 26; bap. Sept. 17; sp. Georg Adam Kaemmerer and w. Susanna.

STECKEL, MARIA, dr. Daniel Steckel and w. Salome; b.
Sept. 9; bap. Oct. 14; sp. Peter Steckel and w. Elisabeth, a born Hartmann.

NEUHARDT, WILHELM, s. Jonas Neuhardt and w. Catharina; b. Sep t.24; bap. Oct. 15; sp. John Neuhardt and w. Sarah, grandparents.

ROTH, PAUL, s. John Roth, Jun. and w. Catharina; b. Sept.
28; bap. Oct. 21; sp. Jonas Traxel and w. Sarah.

RINKER, MARIA ANNA, dr. Daniel Rinker and w. Salome;
b. Oct. 11; bap. Nov. 5; sp. George Reit and w. Magdalena.

ILLEGITIMATE, twin ch. of Joseph Klenberg and Elisabeth Franz; b. Aug. 11; bap. Nov. 5; Carl, sp. Daniel Rinker and w. Salome; Eliza, sp. Beorge Reit and w. Magdalena.

STOFLET, CATHERINA, dr. Jonas Stoflet and w. Margreth; b. Oct. 26; bap. Nov. 8; sp. Nicolaus Saeger and w. Catharina, grandparents.

KERN, WILLIAM, s. Joseph Kern and w. Hanna; b. Oct.
8; bap. Nov. 20; sp. Daniel Burkhalter and w. Catharina.

KERN, MARIA, dr. Peter Kern and w. Margreth; b. Oct.
14; bap. Nov. 12; sp. George Kern and w. Salome.

MICKLY, MARIA, dr. Jacob Mickly, Jun. and w. Anna;
b. Oct. 23; bap. Nov. 19; sp. Catharina, widow of Nicolaus Kern.

KICHEL, LEVINA, dr. John Kichel and w. Catharina; b.
Aug. 18; bap. Nov. 19; sp. Parents.

SCHEURER, ERWINE, s. Nicolaus Scheurer and w.
Susanna; b. Oct. 19; bap. Nov. 26; sp. Friedrich Handwerk and w. Catharina.

RINKFR, SALOME, dt. George Rinker and w. Maria; b.
Oct. 28; bap. Dec. 10; sp. Samuel Schneider and w. Salome.

MEYER, JOEL, s. Peter Meyer and w. Margreth; b. Oct. 31;
bap. Dec. 10; sp. Conrad Meyer and w. Elisabeth.

TRAXEL, JOSEPH, s. J. Nicolaus Traxel and w. Maria; b.
Nov. 27; bap. Dec. 31; sp. Jonas Traxel and w. Sarah.

96 RECORDS OF EGYPT REFORMED CHURCH.

1821.

BOGGS, SUSANNA, dr. Benjamin Boggs and w. Elisabeth; b. Oct. 25, 1820; bap. Jan. 1; sp. John Teichmann and w. Susanna.

BURKHALTER, JOSEPH, s. Joseph Burkhalter and w. Barbara; b. Nov. 6, 1820; bap. Jan. 12; sp. Daniel Burkhalter and w. Catharina.

TRAXEL, THOMAS, s. John Traxel and w. Salome; b. Dec. 22, 1820; bap. Jan. 14; sp. Henrich Mickly and w. Magdalena.

YOHE, SARAH, dr. John Yohe and w. Catharina; b. Dec. 13, 1820; bap. Jan. 14; sp. Abraham Miller and w. Susanna.

LEIBENGUTH, HANNA, dr. Georg Leibenguth and w. Catharina; b. 3 weks before Christmas, 1819; bap. Jan. 16; sp. Abraham Roth and w. Barbara.

HOFFMANN, DANIEL, s. Peter Hoffmann and w. Susanna; b. Dec. 23, 1820; bap. Feb. 1; sp. John Hoffmann and w. Barbara.

GUT, ABIGAIL, dr. Friedhich Gut and w. Susanna; b. Jan. 8, bap. Feb. 4; sp. Peter Ruch and w. Susanna.

BIERY, MARIA, dr. Joseph Biery and w. Salome; b. Jan. 24; bap. Feb. 11; sp. Peter Biery and w. Anna Maria.

MICKLY, ANNA, dr. Joseph Mickly and w. Catharina; b. Jan. 27; bap. Feb. 11; sp. John Traxel and w. Salome.

RINKER, ESTHER, dr. William Rinker and w. Juliana; b. Jan. 12; bap. Mar. 2; sp. George Scheurer, Esq. and w. Elisabeth.

FRANZ, MARIA ANNA, dr. Jacob Franz and w. Salome; b. Jan. 10; bap. Mar. 11; sp. Henrich Franz and w. Margreth, grandparents.

BURKHALTER, THOMAS, s. Carl Burkhalter and w. Magdalena; b. Jan. 20; bap. Mar. 18; sp. Michael Biegy and w. Susanna.

LEH, MARIA ANNA, dr. Samuel Leh and w. Magdalena; b. Feb. 22; bap. Apr. 1; sp. Henrich Leh, Sen. and w. Susanna.

HAUSKNECHT, SALLY ANNA, dr. Daniel Hausknecht and w. Gertraut; b. Feb. 4; bap. Apr. 1; sp. David Bibelheimer and Sarah Hausknecht.

GILBERT, MARIA, dr. Schoolmaster Adam Gilbert and w. Catharina; b. Mar. 8; bap. Apr. 1; sp. Gottfried Peter and w. Elisabeth.

MUEHLHAUSEN, ELISABETH, dr. Henrich Muehlhausen and w. Anna Kunigunda; b. Mar. 18; bap. Apr. 29; sp. Jonas Scheurer and w. Dorothea.

REIT, MAGDALENA, dr. George Reit and w. Magdalena; b. Apr. 26; bap. May 27; sp. Jacob Franz, Jun. and w. Salome.
GREULING, HANNA, dr. George Greuling and w. Elisabeth; b. May 6; bap. May 27; sp. Peter Traxel and w. Christina.
MEYER, LEVINA, dr. Conrad Meyer and w. Elisabeth; b. Apr. 2; bap. May 27; sp. Peter Meyer and w. Margreth.
LAUTENSCHLAEGER, ELIZABETH, dr. Anton Lautenschlaeger and w. Elisabeth; b. Apr. 21; bap. May 27; sp. Nicolaus Traxel and w. Maria.
SIEDER, LEVINA, dr. John Sieder and w. Catharina; b. May 4; bap. June 3; sp. George Acker and Elisabeth Derr.
SCHMIDT, SALLY ANN, dr. Daniel Schmidt and w. Catharina; b. Mar. 20; bap. June 10; sp. Daniel Acker and w. Christina.
KRATZER, ELIZA, dr. Andreas Kratzer and w. Magdalena; b. May 25; bap. July 5; sp. Joseph Lang and w. Lydia.
HECKER, STEPHEN, s. Daniel Hecker and w. Elisabeth; b. July 9; bap. July 10; sp. Henrich Haas and w. Juliana, grandparents.
WASSER, CATHARINA, dr. Tobias Wasser and w. Magdalena; b. June 7; bap. July 22; sp. Tobias Berndt and w. Elisabeth.
BIBELHEIMER, GEORGE, s. George Bibelheimer and w. Maria Margreth; b. —— 28; bap. July 26; sp. Georg Adam Kaemmerer and w. Susanna.
KOHLER, TILGHMAN, s. Daniel Kohler and w. Magdalena; b. July 5; bap. Aug. 19; sp. J. Jacob Scheurer and w. Catharina.
SCHAD, MARIA, dr. John Schad, Jun. and w. Maria; b. July 16; bap. Aug. 19; sp. Carl Gangwehr and w. Magdalena.
KOCH, JOSEPH, s. Jacob Koch and w. Catharina; b. July 23; bap. Sept. 16; sp. George Koch and w. Anna Maria, grandparents.
SCHAD, MARGRETHA, dr. Lorenz Schad and w. Magdalena; b. Aug. 6; bap. Sept. 23; sp. Adam Koch and w. Margreth.
GROB, EDMUND, s. Daniel Grob and w. Catharina; b. Aug. 27; bap. Sept. 30; sp. George Teichmann and w. Susanna.
TRAXEL, AMANDUS, s. Jonathan Traxel and w. Eliza; b. Aug. 25; bap. Sept. 30; sp. Jacob Scheurer and w. Catharina.
BECKER, JONATHAN, s. Friedrich Becker and w. Eva; b. Sept. 5; bap. Oct. 14; sp. Jacob Saeger and Elisabeth Peter.

BURKHALTER, ELI, s. Daniel Burkhalter and w. Catharina; b. Sept. 16; bap. Nov. 11; sp. John Traxel and w. Salome.

KIEFER, DANIEL, s. John Kiefer and w. Susanna; b. Oct. 26; bap. Dec. 9; sp. Henrich Ritter and w. Elisabeth.

YUNDT, MAGDALENA, dr. John Yundt, Jun. and w. Anna; b. Sept. 18; bap. Dec. 29; sp. Daniel Meyer and w. Magdalena.

1822.

ISTMANN, DANIEL, s. Daniel Istmann and w. Sophia; b. Nov. 23, 1821; bap. Jan. 1; sp. Christoph Kelchner and w. Maria Barbara.

MEYER, SARAH, dr. George Meyer and w. Margretha; b. Oct. 9, 1821; bap. Jan. 1; sp. Jacob Biery and w. Salome.

MEYER, LUCINDA, dr. Peter Meyer and w. Catharina; b. Dec. 10, 1821; bap. Jan. 1; sp. Barbara Hoffmann, widow of John Hoffmann.

MEYER, ANGELINE, dr. Jonas Meyer and w. Susanna; b. Dec. 15, 1821; bap. Jan. 6; sp. Johann Ritter and w. Sarah.

BIEGY, NATHAN, s. Peter Riegy and w. Charlotta; b. Nov. 23, 1821; bap. Jan. 20; sp. Paul Balliet and w. Elisabeth.

LABACH, JOSUA, s. Chrsitian Labach and w. Elisabeth; b. Oct. 8, 1821; bap. Jan. 29; sp. David Kaemmerer and w. Anna.

GEORG, WILHELM, s. Henrich Georg and w. Magdalena; b. Jan. 11; bap. 10; sp. Friedrich Kaemmerer, grandfather.

OSMUN, RUBEN, s. Samuel Osmun and w. Magdalena; b. Jan. 6; bap. Feb. 10; sp. Jonas Faust and w. Susanna.

BURKHALTER, RUBEN, s. Henrich Burkhalter and w. Barbara; b. Dec. 18, 1821; bap. Feb. 13; sp. Jacob Biery and w. Salome.

BURKHALTER, MARIA, dr. Henrich Burkhalter and w. Barbara; b. Dec. 18, 1821; bap. Feb. 13; sp. Joseph Burkhalter and w. Barbara.

RITTER, ESTHER, dr. Daniel Ritter and w. Elisabeth; b. Feb. 8; bap. Feb. 22; sp. Jonas Meyer and w. Susanna.

GRAFF, CAROLINA, dr. Peter Graff and w. Elisabeth; b. Jan. 16; bap. Feb. 24; sp. Johannes Georg and w. Susanna.

SCHEURER, CATHARINA, dr. Jonas Scheurer and w. Dorothea; b. Jan. 24; bap. Mar. 3; sp. Catharina Scheurer, widow, the child's grandmother.

MICKLY, MARIA, dr. Henrich Mickly and w. Magdalena; b. Feb. 4; bap. Mar. 10; sp. Joseph Mickly and w. Catharina.

HECKER, ROBERT, s. William Hecker and w. Catharina; b. Mar. 14; bap. Mar. 24; sp. J. Nicolaus Traxel and w. Maria.

SCHOLL, JACOB, s. Dr. Henrich Scholl and w. Regina; b. Mar. 15; bap. Mar. 28; sp. Peter Kohler and w. Catharina.

BIEGYLY, WILLIAM, s. Jacob Biegyly and w. Anna Maria; b. Oct. 27, 1821; bap. Mar. 31; sp. Anton Lautenschlaeger and w. Elisabeth.

RINKER, ABIGAIL, dr. Daniel Rinker and w. Salome; b. Mar. 6; bap. Mar. 31; sp. George Rinker and w. Maria.

GRUBER, SOLOMON, s. Nicolaus Gruber and w. Susanna; b. Feb. 11; bap. Mar. 31; sp. Peter Daniel and w. Catharina.

STECKEL, CARL, s. Peter Steckel and w. Elisabeth; b. Mar. 6; bap. Apr. 7; sp. Peter Schneider and w. Maria.

KERN, ELI, s. Joseph Kern and w. Hanna; b. Feb. 16; bap. Apr. 7; sp. Joseph Mickly and w. Catharina.

KOHLER, MARIA, dr. Isaac Kohler and w. Catharina; b. Feb. 28; bap. Apr. 7; sp. Daniel Kohler and w. Magdalena.

KOHLER, RUBEN, s. Joseph Kohler and w. Elisabeth; b. Mar. 24; bap. Apr. 27; sp. J Jacob Scheurer and w. Catharina.

SCHEURER, MARIANE, dr. David Scheurer and w. Elisabeth; b. Apr. 4; bap. Apr. 27; sp. Catharina Scheurer, widow, the child's grandmother.

PETER, MATHILDA, dr. John Peter and w. Susanna; b. Apr. 17; bap. May 26; sp. Michael Frack and w. Hanna.

LENZ, ESTHER, dr. Stephan Lenz and w. Catharina; b. Apr. 25; bap. May 26; sp. Wilhelm Lenz and w. Magdalena.

MUEHLHAUSEN, HENRICH, s. Henrich Muehlhausen and w. Anna Kunigunda; b. May 5; bap. June 23; sp. George Greuling and w. Elisabeth.

SCHREIBER, THERESIA, dr. Daniel Schreiber and w. Barbara; b. May 13; bap. June 23; sp. Daniel Leisenring and w. Anna.

STECKEL, ELI, s. Daniel Steckel and w. Salome; b. Apr. 24; bap. June 23; sp. Christian Weber and w. Elisabeth.

SIEGFRIED, CAROLINE, dr. Isaac Siegfried and w. Catharina; b. June 16; bap. July 21; sp. Joseph Siegfried and w. Elisabeth.

SCHAD, WILLIAM, s. Henrich Schad and w. Magdalena; b ———; bap. July 21; sp. Jonathan Knaus and w. Elizabeth, grandparents.

WALTER, SOLOMON, s. John Walter and w. Elisabeth; b. July 20; bap. Aug. 4; sp. Solomon Scheurer and w. Catharina.

BIEGY, SOPHIA, dr. Michael Biegy and w. Susanna; b. Aug. 7; bap. Sept. 1; sp. Samuel Helfrich and w. Anne.

PAUL, ANNA, dr. John Paul and w. Esther; b. Aug. 24; bap. Sept. 22; sp. Parents.

EISENHARDT, SARAH ANNE, dr. George Eisenhardt and w. Elisabeth; b. Sept. 9; bap. Oct. 13; sp. John Kelchner and w. Maria.

MILLER, THOMAS, s. George Miller and w. Magdalena; b. Sept. 13; bap. Oct. 13; sp. Peter Neuhardt and w. Catharina, grandparents.

SCHREIBER, ELIZA JULIANA, dr. Jacob Schreiber and w. Eva; b. July 15; bap. Oct. 16; sp. Juliana Schreiber, widow of George Schreiber.

FLICK, SARA, dr. Paul Flick and w. Margreth; b. Sept. 28; bap. Oct. 18; sp. Maria Siegfried, widow of John Siegfried.

NEUHARDT, JACOBUS, s. Jonas Neuhardt and w. Catharina; b. Sept. 25; bap. Oct. 20; sp. Peter Miller and w. Christina, grandparents.

YOHE, MARIA, dr. John Yohe and w. Catharina; b. Sept. 23; bap. Oct. 21; sp. Parents.

MATTHEUS, ANNA CAROLINE, dr. Dr. Samuel Mattheus and w. Esther; b. Oct. 1; bap. Oct. 27; sp. Peter Kohler and w. Catharina, grandparents.

TRAXEL, NICOLAUS, s. J. Nicolaus Traxel and w. Maria; b. Sept. 28; bap. Nov. 3; sp. George Schourer, Dsy. and w. Elisabeth.

ROTH, MAGDALENA, dr. John Roth and w. Catharina; b. Oct. 4; bap. Nov. 10; sp. Andreas Siegfried and w. Anna Elisabeth, grandparents.

LEH, CARL, s. Henrich Leh and w. Catharina; b. Oct. 19; bap. Nov. 10; sp. Leonhardt Larasch and Susanna Leh.

MEYER, CARL, s. Abraham Meyer and w. Magdalena; b. Nov. 10; bap. Dec. 5; sp. Daniel Roth and Salome Braun.

TRAXEL, OWEN, s. John Traxel and w. Salome; b. Nov. 8; bap. Dec. 8; sp. Jacob Biery and w. Salome.

STECKEL, MARIA, dr. Solomon Steckel and w. Anna Maria; b. Nov. 16; bap. Dec. 8; sp. Eva Catharina Traxel, widow, the child's grandmother.

FEHLER, WILLIAM, s. George Fehler and w. Elisabeth; b. Oct. 31; bap. Dec. 15; sp. Joseph Mickly and w. Catharina.

RITTER, JOSEPH, s. Johannes Ritter and w. Sarah; b. Nov. 21; bap. Dec. 17; sp. Martin Semmel and w. Catharina.

GROB, CARL GEORG, s. Daniel Grob and w. Catharina; b. Nov. 8; bap. Dec. 22; sp. Tobias Grob and Elisabeth Graff.

REIT, ESTHER, dr. George Reit and w. Magdalena; b. Dec. 8; bap. Dec. 29; sp. George Franz and w. Catharina.

LEHIGH COUNTY—1734-1834. 101

1823.

KERN, DAVID, s. Peter Kern and w. Margretha; b. Nov. 15, 1822; bap. Jan. 3; sp. Jacob Mickly, Jun. and w. Anne.

FRANZ, SARAH, dr. Jacob Franz and w. Salome; b. Dec. 14, 1822; bap. Jan. 5; sp. Johannes Ritter and w. Sarah.

ILLEGITIMATE, SARAH ANNE, dr. George Keck and Catharina Biery; b. Nov. 21, 1822; bap. Jan. 12; sp. Peter Biery and w. Anna Maria.

DESCHLER, JACOB GRIMM, s. James Deschler and w. Elizabeth; b. Dec. 21, 1822; bap. Jan. 21; sp. Anna Maria, formerly Mr. Buskirch's, now Weber's widow, the child's greatgrandmother.

HECKMANN, ELIZABETH, dr. George Heckman and w. Polly; b. Oct. 30, 1822; bap. Feb. 2; sp. John Rothrock and w. Polly.

SCHMIDT, STEPHANUS, s. John Schmidt and w. Hannah; b. Dec. 26, 1822; bap. Feb. 3; sp. John Stoflet and w. Eva, grandparents.

MICKLY, CARL, s. Joseph Mickly and w. Catharina; b. Jan. 4; bap. Feb. 9; sp. Peter Mickly and w. Anna.

LANG, STEPHAN, s. Joseph Lang and w. Lydia; b. Feb. 5; bap. Feb. 21; sp. Peter Hoffmann and w. Susanna.

GRUBER, WILLIAM, s. Jacob Gruber and w. Elisabeth; b. Jan. 29; bap. Mar. 2; sp. Michael Frack and w. Hanna.

CONFER, LEVINA, dr. Henrich Confer and w. Elisabeth; b. Feb. 23; bap. Mar. 2; sp. Johannes Schoenebruch and w. Eva.

LAUTENSCHLAEGER, CAROLINE, dr, Peter Lautenschlaeger and w. Susanna; b. Feb. 1; bap. Mar. 2; sp. Abraham Gross and w. Barbara, grandparents.

BURKHALTER, ERWINE, s. Charles Burkhalter and w. Magdalena; b. Jan. 7; bap. Mar. 9; sp. Peter Mickly and w. Anna.

STOFLET, MARIA MAGDALENA, dr. Jonas Stoflet and w. Margreth; b. Feb. 13; bap. Mar. 13; sp. Johannes Stoflet and Eva, the child's grandparents.

RINGER, JOHN, s. George Ringer and w. Maria; b. Feb. 15; bap. Mar. 23; sp. Christian Traxel and w. Magdalena.

GREULING, MARIA, dr. George Greuling and w. Elisabeth; b Mar. 3; bap. Mar. 30; sp. William Hecker and w. Catharina.

PETER, VIOLETTA, dr. John Peter and w. Susanna; b. Mar. 26; bap. Apr. 4; sp. Thomas Gangwehr and w. Susanna.

LEH, SARAH, dr. Samuel Leh and w. Magdalena; b. Mar. 15; bap. Apr. 13; sp. George Remely and w. Regina.

GILBERT, JULIANA, dr. Schoolmaster Adam Gilbert and w. Catharina; b. Mar. 3; bap. May 18; sp. John Rinker and w. Elisabeth.

GANGWEHR, MARIA, dr. William Gangwehr and w. Elisabeth; b. Mar. 22; bap. May 19; sp. Henrich Reichel and w. Christina.

RITTER, CARL, s. Daniel Ritter and w. Elisabeth; b. Apr. 2; bap. May 19; sp. Peter Meyer and w. Margreth.

BURKHALTER, LEVINA, dr. Jooseph Burkhalter and w. Barbara; b. Apr. 15; bap. May 19; sp. Peter Steckel and w. Elisabeth.

HECKER, DANIEL, s. Daniel Hecker and w. Elisabeth; b. Apr. 26; bap. May 19; sp. Jonas Hecker and w. Magdalena, grandparents.

DUBS, ROBERT, s. Solomon Dubs and w. Catharina; b. Mar. 27; bap. May 25; sp. Peter Kohler and w. Catharina.

SCHEURER, THOMAS, s. Jonas Scheurer and w. Dorothea; b. June 11; bap. July 5; sp. J. Jacob Scheurer and w. Catharina.

MEYER, MARIA, dr. John Meyer and w. Magdalena; b. June 23; bap. July 5; sp. Maria Barbara Hoffmann, widow of J. Hoffmann.

HOFFMAN, RUBEN, s. Peter Hoffman and w. Susanna; b June 18; bap. July 20; sp. John Georg and Lea Hoffmann.

MEYER, RUBEN, s. Conrad Meyer and w. Elisabeth; b. May 30; bap. July 20; sp. Daniel Saeger and w. Susanna.

MICKLY, REBECCA, dr. Jacob Mickly, Jun. and w. Anna; b. June 19; bap. July 27; sp. Daniel Meyer and w. Magdalena.

KOHLER, WILLIAM, s. Isaac Kohler and w. Catharina; b. July 8; bap. Aug. 1; sp. Parents.

GUT, HORACE, s. Friedrich Gut and w. Susanna; b. July 3; bap. Aug. 3; sp. Michael Frack and w. Hanna.

REICHEL, WILLIAM, s. Henrich Reichel and w. Christina; b. June 5; bap. Aug. 3; sp. Samuel Saeger and w. Barbara.

ISTMANN, DAVID, s. Daniel Istmann and w. Sophia; b. May 20; bap. Aug. 10; sp. Henrich Muehlhausen and w. Anna Kunigunda.

SCHREIBER, ELIZABETH AMANDA MELVINA, dr. Peter Schreiber and w. Susanna; b. June 10; bap. Aug. 18; sp. J. Gobrecht, V. D. M. and w. Elizabeth.

BERNDT, FRANKLIN, s. Tobias Berndt and w. Elisabeth; b. July 22; bap. Aug. 24; sp. Daniel Schreiber and w. Barbara.

SCHAD, HANNA, dr. Lorenz Schad and w. Magdalena; b. Aug. 21; bap. Sept. 27; sp. John Schad and w. Maria.

BIERY, MATHILDA, dr. Joseph Biery and w. Salome; b. July 25; bap. Oct. 11; sp. David Biery and w. Susanna, grandparents.

RINGER, SARAH ANNA, dr. William Ringer and w. Juliana; b. Aug. 27; bap. Oct. 12; sp. Christian Traxel and w. Magdalena.

ROTH, MARIA, dr. John Roth and w. Catharina; b. Oct. 8; bap. Nov. 9; sp. Abraham Meyer and w. Magdalena.

TRAXEL, SOPHIA, dr. Jonathan Traxel and w. Elizabeth; b. Oct. 9; bap. Nov. 23; sp. Stephan Wotring and Elisabeth Franz.

EBERHARDT, NATHAN, s. David Eberhardt and w. Elisabeth; b. Nov. 12; bap. Dec. 14; sp. Peter Eberhard and w. Magdalena, grandparents.

SCHMOLL, SIMON, s. Peter Schmoll and w. Sarah; b. Oct. 31; bap. Dec. 21; sp. Johannes Ritter and w. Sarah.

MUSSELLMANN, THOMAS, s. Michael Musselmann and w. Salome; b. Nov. 27; bap. Dec. 26; sp. Jonas Musselmann and w Elisabeth.

1824.

BIEGY, ESTHER, dr. John Biegy and w. Elisabeth; b. Oct. 5, 1823; bap. Jan. 11; sp. Peter Biery and w. Anna Maria.

HERMANY, OWEN, s. Abraham Hermany and w. Maria Magdalena; b. Nov. 19, 1823; bap. Jan. 19; sp. Jacob Albert and w. Esther.

STECKEL, ALEXANDER, s. Daniel Steckel and w. Salome; b. Dec. 6, 1823; bap. Feb. 1; sp. Joseph Steckel and w. Maria.

LABACH, CARL, s. Christian Labach and w. Elisabeth; b. Oct. 3, 1823; bap. Feb. 19; sp. Peter Lautenschlaeber and w. Susanna.

ZOELLNER, TILLERA, dr. Michael Zoellner and w. Catharina; b. Dec. 25, 1823; bap. Feb. 29; sp. John Scheurer and w. Eva.

BIEGILY, THOMAS, s. Jacob Biegily and w. Maria; b. Dec. 13, 1823; bap. Feb. 29; sp. Wilhelm Remely and w. Magdalena.

STECKEL, JOSEPH, s. Peter Steckel and w. Elisabeth; b. Jan. 21; bap. Feb. 29; sp. Joseph Saeger and w. Magdalena.

RINKER, PAULUS, s. Daniel Rinker and w. Salome; b. Feb. 12; bap. Mar. 3; died Mar. 28; sp. Jacob Franz and w. Salome.

SCHAD, SARAH ANNA, dr. Henrich Schad and w. Magdalena; b. Feb. 21; bap. Mar. 13; died Mar 31; sp. Lorenz Schad and w. Magdalena.

GROB, EPHRAIM, s. Daniel Grob and w. Catharina; b. Feb. 22; bap. Mar. 14; sp. Solomon Graff and w. Elisabeth.

WASSER, ELI, s. Tobias Wasser and w. Magdalena; b. Feb. 11; bap. Mar. 28; sp. Peter Mickly, Jun. and w. Anna.

BURKHALTER, CHRISTINA, dr. Henrich Burkhalter and w. Barbara; b. Feb. 15; bap. Mar. 28; sp. Solomon Steckel and w. Maria.

BURKHALTER, MARIA, dr. Daniel Burkhalter and w. Catharina; b. Jan. 15; bap. Mar. 28; sp. John Kichel and w. Catharina.

MEYER, CHRISTINA, dr. Peter Meyer and w. Catharina, a born Gangwehr; b. Feb. 12; bap. Apr. 4; sp. Peter Hoffmann and w. Susanna.

SCHAD, CAROLINE, dr. John Schad, Jun. and w. Maria; b. Mar. 20; bap. Apr. 24; sp. Christian Baertsch and Susanna Frack.

MILLER, ELIZABETH, dr. George Miller and w. Magdalena; b. Mar. 27; bap. May. 9; sp. Joseph Miller and Salome Neuhardt.

SCHREIBER, HORACE, s. Adam Schreiber and w. Elisabeth; b. Apr. 16; bap. May 9; sp. Peter Schreiber and Anna Scheurer.

BIEGY, MONROD, s. Peter Blegy and w. Charlotte; b. Apr. 8; bap. May 9; sp. Samuel Helfrich and w. Anna Maria.

MATTHEUS, MAHLON, s. Dr. Samuel Mattheus and w. Esther; b. Apr. 18; bap. May 31; sp. John Teichmann and w. Susanna.

KOCK, DAVID, s. Jacob Koch and w. Catharina; b. Apr. 14; bap. June 7; sp. Friedrich App and w. Barbara.

BIEGE, JACKSON, s. Michael Biege and w. Susanna; b. June 26; bap. Aug. 1; sp. Michael Ritter and w. Margreth.

SCHAD, OWEN, s. Abraham Schad and w. Susanna; b. June 29; bap. Aug. 1; sp. Abraham Jacob and w. Elisabeth.

WERZ, CAROLINE, dr. Peter Werz and w. Maria; b. June 18; bap. Aug. 4; sp. Philip Weber and w. Elisabeth, grandparents.

MEYER, THOMAS, s. Jonas Meyer and w. Susanna; b. July 7; bap. Aug. 8; sp. Peter Meyer and w. Margretha.

SCHREIBER, CHRISTIANA, dr. Daniel Schreiber and w. Barbara; b. June 10; bap. Aug. 15; sp. Solomon Traxel and w. Salome.

KOHLER, JOSUA, s. Daniel Kohler and w. Magdalena; b. Aug. 3; bap. Sept. 12; sp. Peter Kohler and w. Catharina.

LEHIGH COUNTY—1734-1834. 105

BUTZ, JOHANN PETER, s. Thomas Butz and w. Elisabeth; b. Aug. 15; bap. Sept. 19; sp. Abraham Butz and w. Esther, grandparents.

LEH, MARIA, dr. Henrich Leh and w. Catharina; b. Sept. 2; bap. Sept. 26; sp. J. Nicolaus Traxel and w. Maria.

SCHEURER, AMANDUS, s. David Scheurer and w. Elisabeth; b. Sept. 28; bap. Oct. 4; sp. John Loeser, single.

MUEHLHAUSEN, DAVID, s. Henrich Muehlhausen and w. Anna Kunigunda; b. June 28; bap. Oct. 9; sp. Parents.

MEYER, JESSE, s. Conrad Meyer and w. Elisabeth; b. Aug. 26; bap. Oct. 10; sp. Gottfried Peter and w. Elisabeth.

MICKLY, SUSANNA, dr. Henrich Mickly and w. Magdalena; b. Aug. 18; bap. Oct. 17; sp. Georg Adam Kaemmerer and w. Susanna.

BAERTSCH, SARAH ANNE, dr. John Baertsch and w. Susanna; b. Oct. 3; bap. Oct. 23; sp. Jacob Gruber and w. Elisabeth.

KREGLI, DANIEL, s. John Kregli and w. Margreth; b. June 10; bap. Oct. 29; sp. Henrich Franz and w. Margreth.

GRUBER, SUSANNA EMILIA, dr. Nicolaus Gruber and w. Susanna; b. Sept. 14; bap. Nov. 1; sp. Susanna Kester.

NEUHARDT, MARIANNA, dr. Michael Neuhardt and w. Magdalena; b. Sept. 10; bap. Nov. 7; sp. Jonas Neuhardt and w. Magdalena.

REIT, SOPHIETTE, dr. George Reit and w. Magdalena; b. Oct. 8; bap. Nov. 14; sp. Peter Remely and Elisabeth Franz.

LEH, ESTHER, dr. Samuel Leh and w. Magdalena; b. Oct. 16; bap. Nov. 17; sp. Charles Scheurer and Salome Roth.

SOHN, APOLLONIA, dr. Jacob Sohn, Jun. and w. Elisabeth; b. Nov. 5; bap. Nov. 27; sp. Jacob Sohn, Sen. and w. Albertina.

MEYER, LYDIA, dr. Abraham Meyer and w. Magdalena; b. Sept. 29; bap. Dec. 5; sp. Jonas Traxel and w. Sarah.

PAUL, ELI, s. John Paul and w. Esther; b. Oct. 21; bap. Dec. 12; sp. Peter Biery and w. Anna Maria.

MICKLY, WILLIAM, s. Joseph Mickly and w. Catharina; b. Nov. 17; bap. Dec. 12; sp. Peter Mickly and w. Salome, grandparents.

TRAXEL, PAUL, s. Christian Traxel and w. Magdalena; b. Nov. 30; bap. Dec. 12; sp. George Ringer and w. Maria.

1825.

LARASCH, JACOB ETTWINE, s. Jacob Larasch and w. Sarah; b. Nov. 24, 1824; bap. Jan. 2; sp. Leonard Larasch and Salome Roth.

KERN, SARAH, dr. Peter Kern and w. Margretha; b. Dec. 10, 1824; bap. Jan. 28; sp. Joseph Biery and w. Salome.

MAERZ, SABINA, dr. Jonas Maerz and w. Salome; b. Dec. 22, 1824; bap. Jan. 30; sp. Conrad Knerr and w. Maria.

GREULING, CATHARINA, dr. George Greuling and w. Elisabeth; b. Nov. 27, 1824; bap. Jan. 30; sp. Samuel Klein and Catharina Hecker.

STOFLET, SUSANNA, dr. Jonas Stoflet and w. Margretha; b. Dec. 19, 1824; bap. Jan. 30; sp. Peter Traxel and w. Christina.

NEUHARDT, AARON, s. Peter Neuhardt, Jun. and w. Susanna; b. Jan. 13; bap. Feb. 3; sp. Peter Neuhardt, Sen. and w. Catharina.

MICKLY, FRANCISCA, dr. Jacob Mickly, Jun. and w. Anna; b. Dec. 19, 1824; bap. Feb. 6; sp. George Kern and w. Salome.

LAURY, SUSANNA ANNA, dr. Jacob Laury and w. Susanna; b. Jan. 5; bap. Feb. 13; sp. Jonathan Wisser and Lydia Miller.

RINKER, JOSEPH, s. Daniel Rinker and w. Salome; b. Feb. 20; bap. Feb. 24; died Feb. 25; sp. Samuel Schneider and w. Salome.

MEYER, MARIA, dr. George Meyer and w. Margreth; b. Feb. 2; bap. Feb. 27; sp. Peter Meyer and w. Catharina.

STECKEL, AEGIDIUS, s. Daniel Steckel and w. Salome; b. Jan. 18; bap. Feb. 27; sp. Nicolaus Traxel and w. Maria.

NEUHARDT, WILLIAM, s. Michael Neuhardt and w. Salome; b. Feb. 6; bap. Mar. 5; sp. George Kuns and w. Catharina.

SCHEURER, GEORGE LA FAYETTE, s. Jonas Scheurer and w. Dorothea; b. Dec. 10, 1824; bap. Mar. 6; sp. George Scheurer, Esq. and w. Elisabeth.

TRAXEL, WILLIAM, s. John Traxel and w. Salome; b. Feb. 13; bap. Mar. 7; sp. Parents.

GUTH, SOPHIA, dr. Friedrich Guth and w. Susanna; b. Jan. 13; bap. Mar. 27; sp. Peter bjegy and w. Charlotte.

MILLER, DAVID, b. July 12, 1805; bap. Apr. 6, after previous instruction.

GRUBER, ELIZA ANNE, dr. Jacob Gruber and w. Elisabeth; b. Apr. 8; bap. Apr. 19; sp. John Baertsch and w. Susanna.

HECKMANN, SALLY ANNE, dr. George Heckmann and w. Magdalena; b. Jan. 29; bap. May. 21; sp. Kelchner and w. Magdalena.

RITTER, SARAH, dr. Daniel Ritter and w. Elisabeth; b. Apr. 18; bap. May 22; sp. John Ritter and Magdalena Saeger.

GEORG, HENRICH, s. John Georg and w. Sarah; b. Apr. 22; bap. May 22; sp. Henrich Rici and w. Barbara.

GROB, EDWIN, s. Henrich Grob and w. Barbara; b. Apr. 10; bap. May. 23; sp. Schoolmaster Theodore Storb and w. Sarah.

GEORG, OWEN, s. John Georg and w. Lea; b. Apr. 24; bap. May. 29; sp. Joseph Lang and w. Lydia.

FRANZ, ESTHER, dr. Jacob Franz and w. Salome; b. May 28; bap. June 12; sp. Daniel Ringer and w. Salome.

LAUTENSCHLAEGER, MARIA, dr. Anton Lautenschlaeger and w. Elisabeth; b. May 12; bap. June 12; sp. Peter Traxel and w. Christina.

BEUTELMANN, ELIAS, s. Valentin Beutelmann and w. Maria; b. Apr. 16; bap. June 17; sp. Peter Ruch and w. Susanna.

SCHMOLL, CATHARINA, dr. Peter Schmoll and w. Salome; b. May 28; bap. July 17; sp. Jacob Ritter and w. Magdalena, grandparents.

SAEGER, MARIA, dr. Joseph Saeger and w. Magdalena; b. June 26; bap. Aug. 14; sp. Jacob Mickly, Jun'r, and w. Anne.

DESCHLER, ANNE CAROLINE, dr. James Deschler and w. Eliza; b. July 18; bap. Sept. 5; sp. Peter Grimm and w. Dina, grandparents.

KERN, CHRISTINA, dr. Joseph Kern and w. Hanna; b. July 25; bap. Sept. 18; sp. Peter Beil and w. Christina.

RITTER, CHARLES, s. Henrich Ritter and w. Elisabeth; b. Oct. 19; bap. Nov. 6; sp. Gottfried Peter and w. Elisabeth.

SCHAD, LUCIANA, dr. John Schad and w. Maria; b. Oct. 11; bap. Nov. 6; sp. Henrich Schad and w. Magdalena.

KOHLER, HORACE, s. Isaac Kohler and w. Catharina; b. Oct. 6; bap. Nov. 13; sp. J. Jacob Scheurer and w. Catharina.

STAPP, MARY, dr. Jacob Stapp and w. Anne; b. Oct. 23; bap. Nov. 20; sp. George Sieger and w. Elisabeth.

SCHAD, DAVID, s. Lorenz Schad and w. Magdalena; b. Oct. 10; bap. Nov. 20; sp. Abraham Schad and w. Susanna.

BRAUN, JULIANA, dr. Daniel Braun and w. Salome; b. Nov. 7; bap. Dec. 4; sp. Stephen Ringer and Margreth Braun.

HOFFMANN, EMILIA, dr. Peter Hoffmann and w. Susanna; b. Dec. 12; bap. Dec. 27; sp. Joel Hoffmann and w. Lydia.

FEHLER, CAROLINE, dr. George Fehler and w. Elisabeth; b. Nov. 18; bap. Dec. 27; sp. Henrich Georg and w. Magdalena.

1826.

ROTH, JOSIA, s. Jacob Roth, Jun'r, and w. Anna; b. Nov. 21, 1825; bap. Jan. 1; sp. Jacob Roth, Sen'r, and w. Catharina, grandparents.

BIERY, CAROLINE, dr. Joseph Biery and w. Salome; b. Sept. 29, 1825; bap. Jan. 8; sp. Abraham Miller and w. Susanna.

BOGGS, OZIAS, s. William Boggs and w. Susanna; b. Oct. 31, 1825; bap. Jan. 8; sp. George Kern and w. Salome.

KREGLI, MATHILDA, dr. Andreas Kregli and w. Susanna; b. Dec. 24, 1825; bap. Jan. 19; sp. Albertina Sohn, the child's grandmother.

ROTH, SARAH, dr. John Roth and w. Catharina; m. Dec. 31, 1825; bap. Feb. 5; sp. Joseph Freymann and Sarah Braun.

RINGER, SARAH, dr. Daniel Ringer and w. Salome; b. Jan. 25; bap. Feb. 19; sp. Joseph Franz and Salome Roth.

SCHAD, EDWIN, s. Abraham Schad and w. Susanna; b. Feb. 1; bap. Feb. 26; sp. Lorenz Schad and w. Magdalena.

STECKEL, CLARISSA, dr. Peter Steckel and w. Elisabeth; b. Jan. 4; bap. Feb. 26; sp. Jacob Biery and w. Salome.

MILLER, Daniel Miller and w. Susanna are parents of the following nine children, all baptized on Feb. 26, 1826:

ELISABETH, b. Sept. 28, 1801; sp. Catharina, Peter Koechlein's wife.

SUSANNA, b. June 4, 1803; sp. John Rothrock and w. Maria Magdalena.

JACOB, b. May 10, 1807; sp. Christoph Kelchner and w. Maria Barbara.

DANIEL, b. March 27, 1809; sp. Daniel Kohler and w. Magdalena.

JOSEPH, b. in Oct. 1811; sp. Gottfried Peter and w. Elisabeth.

ABRAHAM, b. in June, 1814; sp. John Teichmann and w. Susanna.

SAMUEL, b. Oct. 30, 1818; sp. Solomon Steckel and w. Maria.

EDWARD, b. Apr. 24, 1821; sp. Daniel Saeger and w. Susanna.

LEHIGH COUNTY—1734-1834.

CATHARINA, b. May 15, 1823; sp. George Kleppinger and w. Anna Maria.
MUSSELMANN, AARON, s. Michael Musselmann and w. Salome; b. Jan. 17; bap. Mar. 17; sp. Parents.
TRAXEL, EMILIA, dr. John Traxel and w. Salome; b. Mar. 7; bap. Mar. 31; sp. Joel Braun and w. Elisabeth.
SCHEURER, CAROLINE, dr. David Scheurer and w. Elisabeth; b. Mar. 18; bap. Apr. 16; sp. J. Jacob Scheurer and w. Catharina.
GOBRECHT, MARIA ADELINE ROSA, dr. John Gobrecht, V. D. M. and w. Elisabeth; b. Mar. 25; bap. Apr. 20; sp. David Deschler and w. Catharina.
BURKHALTER, SARAH, dr. Daniel Burkhalter and w. Catharina; b. Mar. 26; bap. Apr. 29; sp. George Fehler and w. Elisabeth.
MEYER, JACOB ETTWINE, s. Conrad Meyer and w. Elisabeth; b. Mar. 4; bap. Apr. 30; sp. John Neuhardt and w. Sarah.
MILLER, CAROLINE, dr. George Miller and w. Magdalena; b. Apr. 5; bap. May 21; sp. Peter Neuhardt, Jun'r. and w. Susanna.
BURKHALTER, RUBEN, s. Charles Burkhalter and w. Magdalena; b. May 9; bap. June 18; sp. George Kern and w. Salome.
MILLER, STEPHAN, s. Charles Miller and w. Sarah; b. Apr. 15; bap. July 16; sp. Daniel Xander and w. Susanna.
MILLER, CATHARINA, dr. Joseph Miller and w. Maria b. June 10; bap. July 16; sp. Henrich Ritter and w. Elisabeth, grandparents.
HERMANY, SAMUEL, s. Abraham Hermany and w. Maria; b. June 8; bap. July 23; sp. Samuel Helfrich and w. Anna.
BUTZ, THOMAS FRANKLIN, s. Thomas Butz and w. Elisabeth; b. July 25; bap. Sept. 10; sp. Henrich Beil and w. Hanna, grandparents.
GANGWEHR, MOSES, s. Charles Gangwehr and w. Magdalena; b. July 30; bap. Sept. 15; sp. John Baertsch and w. Susanna.
MEYER, ADELINE, dr. Peter Meyer and w. Catharina; b. Aug. 24; bap. Oct. 7; sp. Jacob Biery and w. Salome.
BURKHALTER, REBECCA, dr. Henry Burkhalter and w. Barbara; b. Aug. 8; bap. Oct. 7; sp. Peter Kohler and w. Catharina.
ZOELLNER, WILLIAM, s. Michael Zoellner and w. Catharina; b. Aug. 5; bap. Oct. 8; sp. Gottfried Peter and w. Elisabeth.

NEUHARDT, SUSANNA, dr. Peter Neuhardt, Jun'r, and w. Susanna; b. Sept. 6; bap. Oct. 8; sp. Daniel Saeger, Esq. and w. Susanna.

SCHREIBER, PETER, s. Daniel Schreiber and w. Barbara; b. Aug. 27; bap. Oct. 15; sp. John Schwartz and w. Elisabeth.

MICKLY, DAVID, s. Joseph Mickly and w. Catharina; b. Sept. 1; bap. Oct. 15; sp. Peter Beil and w. Christina.

MICKLY, EPHRAIM, s. Jacob Mickly and w. Anna; b. Aug. 18; bap. Oct. 15; sp. Peter Kern and w. Margreth.

MICKLY, JAMES, s. Henrich Mickly and w. Magdalena; b. Aug. 30; bap. Oct. 15; sp. Joseph Mickly and w. Catharina.

RENDSHEIMER, REBECCA, dr. Jacob Rendsheimer and w. Margreth; b. Sept. 13; bap. Oct. 15; sp. David Eberhardt and w. Elisabeth.

KOCH, ELI, s. Jacob Koch and w. Catharina; b. Aug. 21; bap. Oct. 15; sp. Daniel Steckel and w. Salome.

RITTER, ELISABETH, dr. Daniel Ritter and w. Elisabeth; b. Sept. 28; bap. Nov. 5; sp. John Ritter and w. Salome, grandparents.

BIEGY, ELISABETH, dr. John Biery and w. Elisabeth; b. Sept. 26; bap. Nov. 5; sp. David Eberhardt and w. Elisabeth.

LANG, WILHELMINE, dr. Joseph Lang and w. Lydia; b. Oct. 20; bap. Nov. 12; sp. Maria Barbara Hoffmann, grandmother.

GREILING, GEORGE, s. George Greiling and w. Elisabeth; b. Oct. 29; bap. Dec. 3; sp. Solomon Steckel and w. Anna Maria.

SCHEURER, MOSES, s. Jonas Scheurer and w. Dorothea; b. Oct. 14; bap. Dec. 3; sp. George Kaemmerer and Anne Scheurer.

ROTH, ELIZA, dr. George Roth and w. Elisabeth; b. Nov. 5; bap. Dec. 3; sp. Georg Franz and w. Catharina, grandparents.

SCHNEIDER, ELIZA, dr. Henrich Schneider and w. Margreth; b. Nov. 8; bap. Dec. 10; sp. Abraham Miller and w. Susanna.

MEYER, EMILIA, dr. John Meyer and w. Magdalena; b. Oct. 7; bap. Dec. 10; sp. Peter Hoffmann and w. Susanna.

SCHAD, BENJAMIN HENRY, s. Henrich Schad and w. Magdalena; b. Dec. 9; bap. Dec. 31; sp. Abraham Schad and w. Susanna.

MEYER, SUSANNA, dr. Jonas Meyer and w. Susanna; b. Nov. 12; bap. Dec. 31; sp. Jacob Franz and w. Salome.

1827.

MICKLY, ABRAHAM TILGHAM, s. Peter Mickly and w. Anna; b. Nov. 2, 1826; bap. Jan. 7; sp. Esther, widow of Abraham Butz, grandmother.

LEH, HORACE, s. Henrich Leh and w. Catharina; b. Dec. 17, 1826; bap. Jan. 9; sp. George Roth and w. Elisabeth.

STOFLET, CAROLINE, dr. Jonas Stoflet and w. Margreth; b. Nov. 25, 1826; bap. Jan. 14; sp. John Schmidt and w. Hanna.

GEORG, ISABELLA, dr. Henrich Georg and w. Magdalena; b. Feb. 6; bap. Mar. 4; sp. Dewalt Maerz and w. Catharina.

SIEGFRIED, ELIZA, dr. Joseph Siegfried and w. Magdalena; b. Jan. 11; bap. Mar. 4; sp. Henrich Mickly and w. Magdalena, grandparents.

SCHEERER, MARIANDA, dr. John Scheerer and w. Hanna; b. Feb. 3; bap. Mar. 25; sp. John Beisel and w. Elisabeth.

SCHMOLL, LEVI, s. Charles Schmoll and w. Salome; b. Feb. 21; bap. Mar. 25; sp. John Metzger and w. Maria.

PAUL, MARIA, dr. John Paul and w. Esther; b. Dec. 11, 1826; bap. Mar. 25; sp. Maria Derr, wife of Jacob Derr.

STECKEL, SALLY ANNE, dr. Daniel Steckel and w. Salome; b. Feb. 15; bap. Mar. 25; sp. John Leser and Salome Steckel.

GRUBER, RUBEN, s. Jacob Gruber and w. Elisabeth; b. Mar. 15; bap. Apr. 8; sp. John Schadt and w. Maria.

RITTER, MARIANNE, dr. John Ritter, Jun'r, and w. Elisabeth; b. Mar. 18; bap. Apr. 22; sp. Gottfried Peter and w. Elisabeth, grandparents.

GROB, ELIZA, dr. Henrich Grob, Jun'r, and w. Barbara; b. Mar. 9; bap. Apr. 22; sp. Daniel Schneider and w. Elisabeth.

HOFFMANN, JOSIA, s. Joel Hoffmann and w. Lydia; b. Apr. 12; bap. May 27; sp. Joseph Lang and w. Lydia.

STECKEL, EPHRAIM, s. Joseph Steckel and w. Maria; b. Apr. 12; bap. June 3; sp. Daniel Steckel and w. Salome.

KERN, PETER, s. Peter Kern and w. Margreth; b. Feb. 11; bap. June 4; sp. Peter Steckel and w. Elisabeth.

BRAUN, EMILIA, dr. Joel Braun and w. Elisabeth; b. Apr. 12; bap. June 4; sp. John Minnich and w. Susanna.

BLOS, CAROLINE, dr. Jonas Blos and w. Catharina; b. May 15; bap. June 17; sp. Daniel Saeger, Esq. and w. Susanna.

BURKHALTER, STEPHAN, s. Daniel Burkhalter and w. Catharina; b. June 8; bap. July 15; sp. Stephan Burkhalter and Esther Biery.

BAERTSCH, DANIEL, s. Daniel Baertsch and w. Catharina; b. Apr. 9; bap. July 15; sp. Jacob Baertsch and w. Barbara.

FRANZ, LYDIA, dr. Jacob Franz and w. Salome; b. June 29; bap. July 21; sp. Peter Neuhardt, Sen'r, and w. Catharina.

STECKEL, COLETTE, dr. Solomon Steckel and w. Anna Maria; b. June 24; bap. Aug. 12; sp. Jacob Schreiber and w. Eva.

MEYER, MARY, dr. Abraham Meyer and w. Magdalena; b. June 17; bap. Aug. 19; sp. Daniel Meyer and w. Magdalena.

MINNICH, ADELINA, dr. Michael Minnich and w. Maria; b. July 13; bap. Aug. 19; sp. Magdalena Braun, the child's grandmother.

NEUHARDT, SALLY ANNE, dr. Michael Neuhardt and w. Sarah; b. Aug. 11; bap. Sept. 9; sp. Catharina Neuhardt, the child's grandmother.

FEHLER, GEORGE, s. George Fehler and w. Elisabeth; b. July 7; bap. Sept. 16; sp. Parents.

SPAENGLER, CAROLINE, dr. George Spaengler and w. Catharina; b. Aug. 20; bap. Sept. 16; sp. John Hut and w. Lydia.

SCHAD, MAGDALENA, dr. John Schad and w. Maria; b. Aug. 29; bap. Oct. 14; sp. Jacob Gruber and w. Elisabeth.

SCHMIDT, CARL, s. Jacob Schmidt and w. Catharina; b. Aug. 21; bap. Nov. 11; sp. George Spaengler and w. Catharina.

RINGER, CATHARINA, dr. Daniel Ringer and w. Salome; b. Sept. 30; bap. Nov. 18; sp. Christian Traxel and w. Magdalena.

MILLER, WILLIAM, s. Peter Miller and w. Catharina; b. Oct. 20; bap. Dec. 2; sp. Joseph Borger and Lydia Bachmann.

WOTRING, RUBEN, s. Cain Wotring and w. Maria Anna; b. Oct. 4; bap. Dec. 2; sp. Nathan Saeger and Catharina Kern.

1828.

BOGGS, JAMES, s. William Boggs and w. Susanna; b. Nov. 1, 1827; bap. Nov. 3; sp. Peter Kern and w. Margretha.

HOFFMANN, SOLOMON, s. Peter Hoffmann and w. Susanna; b. Jan. 3;bap. Feb. 3; sp. Solomon Steckel and w. Anna Maria.

FREYMANN, WILLIAM TILGHMAN, s. Joseph Freymann and w. Salome; b. Dec. 21, 1827; bap. Feb. 3; sp. Jonas Traxel and w. Sarah.

LABACH, STEPHANUS, s. Christian Labach and w. Elisabeth; b. Dec. 18, 1827; bap. Feb. 8; sp. George Remely and w. Regina.

MEYER, WILLIAM, s. Conrad Meyer and w. Elisabeth; b. Jan. 1; bap. Feb. 24; sp. Jonas Meyer and w. Susanna.

KELCHNER, ANNA EMILIA, dr. Michael Kelchner and w. Anne; b. Mar. 5; bap. Mar. 17; sp. Peter Kohler and w. Susanna.

SCHNERR, WILLIAM, s. Peter Schnerr and w. Anna; b. Feb. 9; bap. Mar. 25; sp. Magdalena Schnerr, George Schnerr's widow, the child's grandmother.

MEYER, SOPHIANA, dr. John Meyer and w. Hanna; b. Feb. 25; bap. Mar. 26; sp. Daniel Frack and w. Magdalena.

GEORG, HELENA, dr. Abraham Georg and w. Catharina; b. Mar. 12; bap. Mar. 30; sp. John Georg and w. Eva.

STECKEL, REBECCA, dr. Peter Steckel and w. Elisabeth; b. Mar. 20; bap. Apr. 19; sp. George Kern and w. Salome.

MEYER, ABRAHAM, s. Peter Meyer and w. Catharina; b. Mar. 3; bap. Apr. 19; sp. Abraham Hermany and w. Magdalena.

BAERTSCH, CAROLINE, dr. Jacob Baertsch and w. Barbara; b. Feb. 29; bap. Apr. 19; sp. John Baertsch and w. Susanna.

MEYER, GIDEON, s. George Meyer and w. Margretha; b. Feb. 24; bap. Apr. 19; sp. Jacob Roth and w. Anne.

STECKEL, HENRIETTE, dr. Abraham Steckel and w. Elisabeth; b. Mar. 3; bap. Apr. 20; sp. John Teichmann and w. Susanna.

SCHAAD, SOPHIANA, dr. Abraham Schaad and w. Susanna; b. Apr. 30; bap. May 25; sp. Henrich Schaad and w. Magdalena.

BUTZ, ELIZA ANNE, dr. Thomas Butz and w. Elisabeth; b. May 3; bap. May 25; sp. Peter Mickly, Jun'r, and w. Anne.

MEYER, ELISABETH, dr. Jonas Meyer and w. Susanna; b. Mar. 3; bap. May 25; sp. Conrad Meyer and w. Elisabeth.

SCHAD, MOSES, s. Lorenz Schad and w. Magdalena; b. Mar. 22; bap. June 8; sp. Henrich Franz and w. Catharina.

RECORDS OF EGYPT REFORMED CHURCH.

ROTH, ELIZA MELVINA, dr. Jacob Roth and w. Anne; b. May 17; bap. June 14; sp. Peter Ruch and w. Susanna.

TRAXEL, JOHN, s. Chrietian Traxel and w. Magdalena; b. May 24; bap. July 6; sp. Samuel Schneider and w. Salome.

KOHLER, CARL, s. Daniel Kohler and w. Magdalena; b. May 17; bap. July 13; sp. George Weida and w. Elisabeth.

DESCHLER, WALTER JOHN, s. John Deschler and w. Anne; b. June 12; bap. July 20; sp. Peter Schanz and Debora Deschler.

FRANZ, ELI, s. Joseph Franz and w. Salome; b. June 23; bap. Aug. 3; sp. Henrich Franz and w. Margretha, grandparents.

GILBERT, CAROLINE, dr. Jacob Gilbert and w. Maria; b. Apr. 20; bap. Aug. 3; sp. Schoolmaster Adam Gilbert and w. Catharina.

REIT, BENJAMIN, s. Daniel Reit and w. Susanna; b. Mar. 10; bap. Aug. 10; sp. Jacob Koch and w. Catharina.

REIT, GEORGE, s. George Reit and w. Magdalena; b. May 29; bap. Aug. 10; sp. Peter Neuhardt, Sen. and w. Catharina.

SCHEERER, CLARISSA, dr. John Scheerer and w. Hannah; b. May 27; bap. Sept. 7; sp. Abraham Hartmann and w. Catharina.

GEORG, MARIA ANNA, dr. John Georg and w. Lea; b. Aug. 20; bap. Sept. 11; died Sept. 13; sp. Solomon Georg and Marianne Hoffmann.

ROTH, WILLIAM, s. George Roth and w. Elisabeth; b. Aug. 28; bap. Sept. 11; sp. Joseph Franz and w. Salome.

SCHEURER, OWEN, s. John Scheurer and w. Catharina; b. Aug. 24; bap. Sept. 14; sp. Solomon Kaemmerer and w. Magdalena.

FRANZ, JACOB, s. Jacob Franz and w. Salome; b. Oct. 17; bap. Oct. 29; sp. William Franz, single.

FRACK, ELEONORA, dr. Daniel Frack and w. Maria; b. Oct. 26; bap. Nov. 16; sp. Charles Traxel and w. Susanna.

MICKLY, JAMES WILLIAM, s. Jacob Mickly, Jun'r, and w. Anna; b. Sept. 28; bap. Dec. 7; sp. Jacob Mickly, Sen'r, and w. Eva Catharina, grandparents.

GANGWEHR, ABRAHAM, s. William Gangwehr and w. Elisabeth; b. Sept. 25; bap. Dec. 14; sp. Abraham Hermany and w. Magdalena.

1829.

MILLER, JAMES, s. Peter Miller and w. Lydia; b. Nov. 17, 1828; bap. Jan. 1; sp. Peter Anewalt and w. Elisabeth.

MILLER, SUSANNA, dr. Joseph Miller and w. Magdalena; b. Dec. 15, 1828; bap. Jan. 17; sp. Jeremias Ritter and Susanna Ritter.

SCHEURER, MARIA, dr. David Scheurer and w. Elisabeth; b. Dec. 23, 1828; bap. Jan. 18; sp. Nicolaus Traxel and w. Maria.

BIEGYLY, ADAM, s. Jacob Biegyly and w. Maria; b Nov. 7, 1828; bap. Jan. 25; sp. Peter Leisenring and w. Margreth.

ZOELLNER, ANNA CAROLINA, dr. Michael Zoellner and w. Catharina; b. Oct. 16, 1828; bap. Feb. 11; sp. George Frey and w. Magdalena.

MILLER, CATHARINA dr, George Miller and w. Magdalena; b. Dec. 11, 1828; bap. Feb. 15; sp. Daniel Saeger, Esq., and w. Susanna.

GANGWEHR, SUSANNA, dr. Charles Gangwehr and w. Magdalena; b. Dec. 9, 1828; bap. Feb. 24; sp. Joel Braun and w. Elisabeth.

KOHLER, CARL, s. Isaac Kohler and w. Catharina; b. Feb. 12; bap. Mar. 22; sp. Jacob Biery and w. Salome.

STECKEL, CAROLINE, dr. Daniel Steckel and w. Elisabeth; b. Feb. 20; bap. Mar. 22; sp. Henrich Franz and w. Margreth, grandparents.

FEHLER, ELIZA, dr. George Fehler and w. Elisabeth; b. Dec. 1, 1828; bap. Mar. 29; sp. Jonas Musselmann and w. Elisabeth.

MICKLY, ELIZA AMANDA, dr. Joseph Mickly and w. Catharina; b. Sept. 30, 1828; bap. Mar. 29; sp. Peter Mickly and w. Salome, grandparents.

GEORG, THOMAS, s. John Georg and w. Sarah; b. Feb. 2; bap. Apr. 5; sp. Samuel Saeger and w. Barbara.

STECKEL, EMILIA, dr. Joseph Steckel and w. Maria; b. Mar. 11; bap. Apr. 19; sp. Christian Labach and w. Elisabeth.

HECKMANN, CHRISTINA, dr. George Heckmann and w. Magdalena; b. Feb. 14; bap. Apr. 19; sp. John Metzger and w. Magdalena.

STRAUS, CLARISSA, dr. Philip Straus and w. Magdalena; b. Feb. 8; bap. Apr. 19; sp. Peter Straus and w. Clara Catharina.

MINNICH, EDWIN, s. Michael Minnich and w. Maria; b. Mar. 18; bap. Apr. 19; sp. Joseph Borger and Hanna Braun.

KERN, HENRIETTE, dr. Peter Kern and w. Margreth; b. Mar. 4; bap. Apr. 19; sp. Lewis Schmidt and w. Salome.

WOTRING, JONATHAN FRANKLIN, s. Cain Wotring and w. Mary Anne; b. Feb. 26; bap. Apr. 19; sp. Thomas Kern and w. Salome.

HOFFMANN, MARIA ANNA, dr. Joel Hoffmann and w. Lydia; b. Mar. 21; bap. Apr. 26; sp. Peter Hoffmann and w. Susanna.

GRUBER, SOPHIANA, dr. Jacob Gruber and w. Elisabeth; b. Apr. 13; bap. May 2; sp. Abraham Schad and w. Susanna.

SCHREIBER, DAVID, s. Daniel Schreiber and w. Barbara; b. Mar. 11; May 17; sp. Dewalt Burger and w. Lydia.

LANG, EDMUND, s. Joseph Lang and w. Lydia; b. Apr. 19; bap. May 24; sp. Solomon Georg and Susanna Mickly.

STOFLET, DEBORAH, dr. Jonas Stoflet and w. Margretha; b. Apr. 8; bap. June 7; sp. Solomon Kuns and w. Salome.

NEUHARDT, LEVINA, dr. Michael Neuhardt and w. Magdalena; b. Apr. 18; bap. June 8; sp. Joseph Neuhardt and Magdalena Neuhardt.

TRAXEL, EDMUND, s. Jonathan Traxel and w. Elisabeth; b. May 22; bap. June 28; sp. John Baertsch and w. Susanna.

ROTH, SALOME, dr. Charles Roth and w. Elisabeth; b. May 29; bap. July 5; sp. Joseph Roth and Hannah Roth.

BLOS, PETER, s. Jonas Blos and w. Catharina; b. June 13; bap. July 23; sp. Peter Lautenschlaeger and w. Susanna.

WASSER, EDWARD, s. Tobias Wasser and w. Magdalena; b. May 26; bap. Aug. 9; sp. James Deschler and w. Elisabeth.

NEUHARDT, RUBEN, s. Michael Neuhardt and w. Sarah; b. June 30; bap. Apg. 9; sp. Peter Neuhardt and w. Catharina.

RINGER, SUSANNA, dr. William Ringer and w. Juliana; b. July 21; bap. Aug. 23; sp. Henrich Wotring and w. Maria Barbara.

LEH, ELI, s. Henrich Leh and w. Catharina; b. Aug. 9; bap. Aug. 30; sp. Samuel Leh and w. Magdalena.

MAYER, ABIGAIL, dr Peter Mayer and w. Catharina; b. Aug. 2; bap. Sept. 6; sp. Daniel Frack and w. Maria.

EBERHARDT, MARY ANNE, dr. David Eberhardt and w. Elisabeth; b. July 27; bap. Sept. 13; sp. John Neuhardt and w. Sarah, grandparents.

MEYER, ABRAHAM, s. Abraham Meyer and w. Magdalena; b. July 5; bap. Sept. 13; sp. Johannes Schoenebruch and w. Eva.

BURKHALTER, PETER, s. Daniel Burkhalter and w. Catharina; b. Aug. 20; bap. Oct. 3; sp. Solomon Steckel and w. Anna Maria.

LEHIGH COUNTY—1734-1834. 117

RITTER, MARIANNE, dr. Henrich Ritter and w. Elisabeth; b. Sept. 13; bap. Oct. 9; sp. Henrich Franz and w. Margretha.
SCHUMACHER, LUCIANA, dr. Daniel Schumacher and w. Esther; b. Aug. 20; bap. Oct. 10; sp. Abraham Yundt and w. Elisabeth.
SCHAD, FRANKLIN, s. John Schad and w. Maria; b. Oct. 6; bap. Nov. 1; sp. Jonas Traxel and w. Sarah.
MUSSELMANN, ELI, s. Michael Musselmann and w. Salome; b. Oct. 3; bap. Nov. 1; sp. Martin Semmel and w. Catharina.
KREILING, RUBEN, s. George Kreiling and w. Elisabeth; b. Sept. 12; bap. Nov. 1; sp. James Deschler and w. Elisabeth.
FITZGERALD, SALLY ANNE, dr. Thomas Fitzgerald and w. Susanna; b. Oct. 30, 1828; bap. Nov. 1; sp. Jacob Mickly, Jun'r, and w. Anne.
FREYMANN, FRANZ JOSEPH, s. Joseph Freymann and w. Salome; b. Sept. 22; oap. Nov. 8; sp. Adam Braun and w. Margreth.
PREIS, CHARLES, s. John Preis and w. Regina; b. Sept. 25; bap. Nov. 22; sp. Parents.
MEYER, ELI, s. Jonas Meyer and w. Susanna; b. Nov. 3; bap. Dec. 20; sp. George Miller and w. Magdalena.

1830.

SCHEURER, MARIA, dr. William Scheurer and w. Lydia; b. Dec. 3, 1829; bap. Jan. 2; sp. Stephanus Schlosser and Elisabeth Scheurer.
BAERTSCH, THOMAS, s. John Baertsch and w. Susanna; b. Nov. 28, 1829; bap. Jan. 10; sp. Peter Romig, Sen'r, and w. Hanna.
MEYER, EMILIA, dr. Conrad Meyer and w. Elisabeth; b. Nov. 29, 1829; bap. Jan. 24; sp. Daniel Ritter and w. Elisabeth.
BOGGS, OWEN, s. William Boggs and w. Susanna; b. Nov. 2, 1829; bap. Jan. 24; sp. Jacob Schreiber and w. Eva.
RHOADS, ERASTUS DANIEL, s. Daniel Rhoads and w. Hanna; b. Jan. 18; bap. Jan. 28; sp. Daniel Leisenring and w. Anne.
FRANZ, MENTOR, s. Joseph Franz and w. Salome; b. Jan. 16; bap. Feb. 28; sp. Daniel Ringer and w. Salome.

ALLANDER, HENRICH, s. Jacob Allander and w. Magdanena; b. Dec. 25, 1829; bap. Mar. 14; sp. Abraham Schad and w. Susanna.

LABACH, JESSE, s. Christian Labach and w. Elisabeth; b. Jan. 24; bap. Mar. 21; sp. Joseph Steckel and w. Maria.

DUBS, HARRISON WEINBERT, s. Solomon Dubs and w. Catharina; b. Nov. 13, 1829; bap. Mar. 21; sp. Conrad Leisenring and w. Lydia.

STECKEL, ESTHER, dr. Daniel Steckel and w. Elisabeth; b. Mar. 5; bap. Apr. 9; sp. Jacob Franz and w. Salome.

SOHN, ELISABETH, dr. Daniel Sohn and w. Magdalena; b. Mar. 6; bap. Apr. 23; sp. Elisabeth Sohn.

TRAXEL, LEANDA, dr. John Traxel and w. Salome; b. Mar. 7; bap. May 2; sp. Daniel Burkhalter and w. Catharina.

TRAXEL, ELEONORA, dr. John Traxel and w. Salome; b. Mar. 7; bap. May 2; sp. Peter Steckel and w. Elisabeth.

REIT, MOSES, s. George Reit and w. Magdalena; b. Mar. 31; bap. May 16; sp. Joseph Franz and w. Salome.

KOHLER, EDMUND, s. Daniel Kohler and w. Magdalena; b. Mar. 10; bap. May 16; sp. Daniel Peter and w. Rebecca.

FRANZ, RUBEN, s. William Franz and w. Salome; b. Apr. 16; bap. May 16; sp. Gottfried Peter and w. Elisabeth, grandparents.

MUSCHLITZ, SOPHIANA, dr. Peter Muschlitz and w. Catharina; b. Feb. 1; bap. May 16; sp. Jacob Stapp and w. Christina, grandparents .

HOFFMAN, JAMES WASHINGTON, s. Peter Hoffmann and w. Susanna; b. Apr. 17; bap. May 23; sp. Daniel Meyer and w. Magdalena.

GEORG, DIANA, dr. John Georg and w. Lea; b. May 6; bap. May 23; sp. Peter Meyer and w. Catharina.

KAEMMERER, DANIEL, s. Jacob Kaemmerer and w. Dorothea; b. Apr. 10; bap. May 23; sp. Jonas Traxel and w. Sarah.

SCHAD, LENORA, dr. Lorenz Schad and w. Magdalena; b. Apr. 29; bap. June 13; sp. John Strauss and w. Lydia.

BUTZ, NATHAN, s. Thomas Butz and w. Elisabeth; b. Apr. 21; bap. June 20; sp. Tobias Wasser and w. Magdalena.

RENDSHEIMER, JOSEPH, s. Jacob Rendsheimer and w. Margreth; b. Feb. 27; bap. June 20; sp. Peter Eberhardt and w. Magdalena.

SCHEURER, MARIANNE, dr. John Scheurer, Jun'r, and w Catharina; b. May 16; bap. June 20; sp. John Scheurer, Sen'r, and w. Elisabeth.

MILLER, HARRISON WALTER, s. Peter Miller and w. Catharina; b. Feb. 26; bap. June 20; sp. Jacob Roth and w. Anne.

SCHAD, ESTHER, dr. Henrich Schad and w. Magdalena; b. June 10; bap. July 4; sp. Ruben Knaus and Esther Eisenhardt.

DESCHLER, ANNA LEVINA, dr. John Deschler and w. Anne; b. May 2; bap. July 11; sp. Edward Mickly and Mary I. Hall.

MICKLY, EDWIN, s. Jacob Mickly and w. Anne; b. Apr. 20; bap. July 18; sp. Esther Butz, widow of Abraham Butz.

FENSTERMACHER, CAROLINE, dr. Abraham Fenstermacher and w. Maria; b. June 13; bap. July 18; sp. Jonas Traxel and w. Sarah.

RITTER, CHRISTINA MESSINA, dr. Jeremias Ritter and w. Hannah; b. June 24; bap. Aug. 1; sp. Peter Traxel and w. Christina, grandparents.

SCHEURER, DAVID, s. David Scheurer and w. Elisabeth; b. June 2; bap. Aug. 1; sp. Joseph Steckel and w. Maria.

GILBERT, MELVINA, dr. Jacob Gilbert and w. Maria; b. July 11; bap. Aug. 4; sp. Dr. William Kohler and Maria Kern.

LEH, JAMES, s. Samuel Leh and w. Magdalena; b. June 18; bap. Aug. 8; sp. James Roth and Lydia Remely.

SCHUMACHER, ADAM, s. Daniel Schumacher and w. Esther; b. Aug. 26; bap. Aug. 27; sp. Henrich McLaughlin and w. Lea.

STECKEL, DAVID, s. Peter Steckel and w. Elisabeth; b. Aug. 6; bap. Sept. 12; sp. Peter Mickly, Sen'r, and w. Salome.

TRAXEL, WILLIAM HENRY, s. John Traxel and w. Anna Maria; b. Aug. 28; bap. Sept. 19; sp. Peter Traxel, Sen'r, and w. Magdalena.

MICKLY, ANNE CAROLINE, dr. Charles Mickly and w. Jedda; b. Aug. 21; bap. Oct. 10; sp. Parents.

ROTH, CATHARINA, dr. George Roth and w. Elisabeth; b. Sept. 10; bap. Oct. 17; sp. Henry Leh and w. Catharina.

STECKEL, MARIA, dr. Joseph Steckel and w. Maria; b. Aug. 14; bap. Oct. 17; sp. Maria Traxel, the child's grandmother.

LANE, MARY MARGRETH, dr. Matthias Lane and w. Susanna; b. Aug. 25; bap. Oct. 31; sp. Margreth Leyenberger, widow of Jacob Leyenberger, the child's grandmother.

FISCHER, WILLIAM, s. Peter Fischer and w. Elisabeth; b. Oct. 10; bap. Nov. 7; sp. George Fischer and w. Maria, grandparents.

STRAUSS, MARIANNE, dr. Philip Strauss and w. Mag-

RECORDS OF EGYPT REFORMED CHURCH.

dalena; b. Sept. 23; bap. Nov. 17; sp. Peter Strauss, Jun'r, and Elisabeth Scheurer.

ILLEGITIMATE, TILGHMAN, s. William Dean and Susanna Ritter; b. Oct. 24; bap. Dec. 1; sp. Jacob Fischer and w. Barbara.

HOFFMANN, RUBEN, s. Joel Hoffmann and w. Lydia; b. Nov. 3; bap. Dec. 5; sp. George Kaemmerer and w. Anna.

MILLER, ESTHER, dr. Peter Miller and w. Judith; b. Nov. 5; bap. Dec. 5; sp. Joseph Biery and w. Salome.

SCHAD, THOMAS, s. Abraham Schad and w. Susanna; b. Nov. 18; bap. Dec. 12; sp. Michael Frack, Sen'r, and w. Hanna.

SIEGFRIED, ELISABETH, dr. Joseph Siegfried and w. Elisabeth; b. Sept. 25; bap. Dec. 25; sp. Joseph Saeger and w. Magdalena.

CAREY, DANIEL, s. Benjamin Carey and w. Susanna; b. Oct. 15; bap. Dec. 26; sp. Daniel Saeger, Esq., and w. Susanna.

GRUBER, DAVID, s. Jacob Gruber and w. Elisabeth; b. Oct. 29; bap. Dec. 26; sp. Philip Fenstermacher and w. Margretha.

HECKMANN, MELINDA, dr. George Heckmann and w. Maria; b. Aug. 28; bap. Dec. 26; sp. Jonas Stoflet and w. Margretha.

BAKER, PHILENA, dr. Joseph Baker and w. Elisabeth; b. Mar. 1; bap. Dec. 26; sp. The mother.

1831.

KOHLER, JAMES, s. Isaac Kohler and w. Catharina; b. Dec. 1, 1830; bap. Jan. 24; sp. William Biery and Esther Braun.

SAUERWEIN, WILLIAM, s. Charles Sauerwein and w. Elisabeth; b. Dec. 24, 1830; bap. Jan. 29; sp. Nicolaus Scheurer and w. Susanna, grandparents.

FRANZ, WILLIAM, s. Joseph Franz and w. Salome; b. Feb. 10; bap. Feb. 14; sp. George Roth and w. Elisabeth.

BORGER, PETER DANIEL, s. Josehp Borger and w. Lydia; b. Jan. 26; bap. Feb. 15; sp. Jacob Roth and w. Anne.

1093 baptized by Rev. John Gobrecht. Record continued by Joseph S. Dubs, V. D. M.

STICHLER, MARIA CATHARINA, dr. Jacob Stichler and w. Eva; b. July 10; bap. Aug. 28; sp. Peter Miller and w. Maria.

MORAN, MATHILDA SOPHIA CATHARINA, dr. Dr. P. Moran and w. Esther; b. Aug. 4; bap. Aug. 28; sp. William Wetherhold and w. Sophia.

LEHIGH COUNTY—1734-1834. 121

FITZGERALD, MARY, dr. Thomas Fitzgerald and w. Susanna; b. Aug. 20; bap. Sept. 1; sp. Edward Schreiber and Abigail Schreiber, single.
KRAILING, SARAH, dr. George Krailing and w. Elisabeth; b. Aug. 10; bap. Oct. 2; sp. Jonas Traxel and w. Sarah.
FRANTZ, SALLY ANNA, dr. William Frantz and w. Salome; b. Sept. 10; bap. Oct. 30; sp. Henrich Frantz and w. Margretha, grandparents.
BIERY, SUSANNA, dr. Joseph Biery and w. Salome; b. Aug. 21; bap. Nov. 6; sp. Jacob Biery and w. Salome.
WETHERBOLD, HENRY WILLIAM, s. William Wetherbold and w. Sophia; b. Oct. 3; bap. Nov. 13; sp. Peter Kohler and w. Catharina, grandparents.
BURKHALTER, SUSAN, dr. Daniel Burkhalter and w. Catharina; b. Nov. 14; bap. Nov. 27; sp. Solomon Steckel, Jun'r, and Debora Burkhalter.
BURKHALTER, KITTY ANN, dr. Daniel Burkhalter and w. Catharina; sp. Mar. 14; bap. Nov. 27; sp. Edward Mickly and Polly Kohler.
WASSER, ELIZA ANN, dr. Tobias Wasser and w. Magdalena; b. Oct. 5; bap. Nov. 27; sp. John Metzgar and w. Polly.
LANG, SARAH ANNE, dr. Joseph Lang and w. Lydia; b. Oct. 15; bap. Nov. 27; sp. Joel Hoffmann and w. Lydia.
MEIER, ELIZA, dr. Abraham Meier and w. Magdalena; b. Sept. 16; bap. Dec. 4; sp. Henrich Roth and w. Maria.
BRAUN, EPHRAIM, s. Joel Braun and w. Elisabeth; b. Oct. 9; bap. Dec. 4; sp. Carl Gangwehr and w. Magdalena.
LEIENBERGER, CARL, s. Peter Leienberger and w. Elisabeth; b. Oct. 9; bap. Nov. 11; sp. Peter Leienberger and w. Susanna.
BLOOS, JOEL, s. Jonas Bloos and w. Catharina; b. Nov. 12; bap. Dec. 25; sp. William Remely and wife.
HOFFMANN, CARL LUDWIG, s. Peter Hoffmann and w. Susanna; b. Nov. 21; bap. Dec. 25; sp. Solomon Georg and Sarah Maier.
BORGER, JOHN JACOB, s. Philip Borger and wife; b Dec. 11; bap. Dec. 26; sp. Jacob Bartsch and w. Barbara.

1832.

HISKY, CAROLINA, dr. Henry Hisky and w. Eva; b. Dec. 22, 1831; bap. Jan. 22; sp. Solomon Steckel and w. Anna Maria.

NEWHARD, MARY ANN, dr. Michael Newhard and w. Sarah; b. Dec. 11, 1831; bap. Jan. 24; sp. Joseph Newhard and w. Maria.

MILLER, ELIZA, dr. Peter Miller and w. Judith; b. Dec. 23, 1831; bap. Jan. 29; sp. Peter Biery and w. Anna Maria.

ROTH, ANNA MARIA ELISABETH, dr. John Roth and w. Anna Maria; b. Dec. 7, 1831; bap. Feb. 3; sp. Jacob Roth and w. Anna.

FENSTERMACHER, EMILIA ROSINA, dr. Abraham Fenstermacher and w. Maria; b. Dec. 27, 1831; bap. Feb. 12; sp. John Fenstermacher and w. Rosina, grandparents.

LABACH, EDWARD CHRISTIAN, s. Catharian Labach and w. Elisabeth; b. Dec. 24, 1831; bap. Feb. 19; sp. Dr. William Kohler and w. Maria.

LEH, HENRY WILLIAM, s. Henrich Leh and w. Catharina; b. Jan. 16; bap. Feb. 19; sp. James Roth and Sarah Leh.

RITTER, SARAH ANNE, dr. Jeremias Ritter and w. Hannah; b. Jan. 29; bap. Feb. 19; sp. Jonas Traxel and w. Sarah.

FREY, DENNIS, s. Michael Frey and w. Susanna; b. Jan. 22; bap. Feb. 19; sp. Daniel Frey and w. Anna Maria.

SOHN, JESSE, s. Jacob Sohn and w. Elisabeth, b. Feb. 19; bap. Mar. 2, sp. Jesse Brechan and Hannah Sheirer.

BROWN, ELISABETH, dr. Paul Brown and w. Maria; b. Jan. 19; bap. Mar. 4; sp. Adam Brown and w. Margretha, grandparents.

ZOELLNER, TILGHMAN, s. Michael Zoellner and w. Catharina; b. Dec. 18, 1831; bap. Mar. 16; sp. Daniel Miller and w. Catharina.

McLACHLEN, CHRISTIANNA, dr. Anthony W. McLachlen and w. Lea; b. Dec. 27, 1831; bap. Mar. 25; sp. Daniel Schumacher and w. Catharina.

MICKLY, CATHARINA ANNA, dr. Jacob Mickly and w. Anna; b. Jan. 29; bap. Mar. 25; sp. Catharina Kern.

MEIER, RUBEN, s. Henry Meier and w. Elisabeth; b. Feb. 5; bap. Mar. 28; sp. John Biege and w. Elisabeth.

SCHAD, MARIA, dr. Henry Schad and w. Maria; b. Mar. 8; bap. Apr. 1; sp. Michael Frack and w. Anna.

KOHLER, EPHRAIM, s. Issac Kohler and w. Catharina; b. Mar. 24; bap. Apr. 11; sp. Daniel Kohler and w. Magdalena.

NEWHARD, EDWIN, s. Michael Newhard and w. Magdalena; b. Jan. 14; bap. Apr. 15; sp. Peter Newhard and w. Susanna.

KERN, ADELINA, dr. James Kern and w. Mawdalena; b. Feb. 19 ; bap. Apr. 15; sp. Daniel Saeger, Esq, and w. Susanna.

MICKLY, FRANKLIN PETER, s. Peter Mickly and w. Anna; b. Mar. 1; bap. Apr. 22; sp. Peter Traxel, Jun'r, and w. Elisabeth.

BREISCH, JOSEPH, s. Jacob Breisch and w. Barbara; b. Mar. 26; bap. May 13; sp. Joseph Saeger and w. Magdalena.

RUCH, WILLIAM HENRY, s. Peter Ruch and w. Susan; b. Apr. 5; bap. May 13; sp. Ruben Meier and Anna Frack.

BOGGS, CHARLES, s. William Boggs and w. Susanna; b. Feb. 11; bap. May 13; sp. John Hecker and w. Maria.

LAROSCH, HEINRICH, s. Jacob Larosch and w. Sarah; b. Apr. 1; bap. May 13; sp. Jacob Frack and w. Elisabeth.

RINGER, CAROLINA, dr. William Ringer and w. Julia; b. Mar. 19; bap. May 27; sp. Joseph Miller and w. Polly.

TRAXEL, SALLY ANN, dr. Adam Traxel and w. Lydia; b. June 5; bap. June 7; sp. Jonas Traxel and w. Sarah.

STECKEL, RUBEN, s. Daniel Steckel and w. Elisabeth; b. May 5; bap. June 10; sp. Solomon Steckel and w. Anna Maria.

BORGER, ANNA MARIA, dr. Joseph Borger and w. Lydia; b. Apr. 4; bap. June 10; sp. George E. Dodendorf and w. Lydia.

DESHLER, ELISABETH ANNA, dr. James Deshler and w. Elisabeth; b. Apr. 29; bap. June 10; sp. Joseph Saeger and w. Magdalena.

HOFFMANN, DAVID. s. Joel Hoffmann and w. Lydia; b. May 13; bap. June 17; sp. John Georg and w. Lea.

GRUBER, CAROLINA, dr. Jacob Gruber and w. Elisabeth; b. Apr. 26; bap. June 24; sp. Henrich Schad and w. Maria.

MEIER, CATHARINA, dr. Daniel Meier and w. Susanna; b. May 29; bap. July 8; sp. David Laury and w. Polly.

LORASH, SARAH ANN, dr. Leonhard Lorash and w. Sophia Ann; b. June 2; bap. July 8; sp. Dr. Wm. Kohler and w. Maria.

FRANTZ, HENRICH BENJAMIN, s. Abraham Frantz and w. Polly; b. July 18; bap. Aug. 5; sp. Benjamin Breinig and w. Esther.

FRANTZ, THOMAS, s. Joseph Frantz and w. Salome; b. June 30; bap. Aug. 17; sp. Jacob Frantz and w. Salome.

BERTSCH, DANIEL, s. John Bertsch and w. Susanna; b. July 28; bap. Aug. 19; sp. Joel Braun and w. Elisabeth.

SCHAD, SUSANNA, dr. Lorentz Schad and w. Magdalena; b. May 12; bap. Aug. 19; sp. Peter Ruch and w. Susanna.

ALLENTER, WILLIAM, s. Jacob Allenter and w. Maria; b. July 9; bap. Aug. 26; sp. William Boyer and w. Elisabeth.

FEHLER, LOUISA, dr Georg Fehler and w. Elisabeth; b. Apr. 8; bap. Sept. 9; sp. Parents.

MILLER, SARAH ANN, dr. John Miller and w. Sarah; b. Aug. 5; bap. Sept. 23; sp. Peter Newhard and w. Catharina, grandparents.

FRACK, SAMUEL, s. Daniel Frack and w. Maria Magdalena; b. July 22; bap. Sept. 23; sp. Michael Frack and w. Anna, grandparents.

MARX, URIAH LEWIS, s. Gideon Marx and w. Hetty; b. Aug. 20; bap. Sept. 30; sp. John Wenner and w. Polly.

SCHUMACHER, LUCINDA, dr. Daniel Schumacher and w. Catharina; b. Aug. 3; bap. Sept. 30; sp. John Metzger and w. Polly.

EISENBROWN, WILLIAM JONAS, s. Daniel Eisenbrown, Schoolmaster, and w. Charlotta Barbara; b. Oct. 12; bap. Oct. 19; sp. Jonas Traxel and w. Sarah.

YEHL, TILGHMAN, s. Jacob Yehl and w. Magdalena; b. Sept. 5; bap. Oct. 28; sp. Daniel Zerfass and w. Christina.

GREENAWALD, DANIEL, s. Thomas Greenawald and w. Catharina; b. Sept. 17; bap. Oct. 28; sp. John Newhard and Magdalena Mertz.

STECKEL, EDWARD, s. Joseph Steckel and w. Mary; b. Aug. 30; bap. Oct. 28; sp. Edward Kohler and Elisabeth Traxel.

TRAXEL, EMMELINA, dr. John Traxel and w. Anna Maria; b. Oct. 6; bap. Oct. 28; sp. Solomon Steckel and w. Anna Maria, grandparents.

WETHERHOLD, ALFRED PETER, s. William Wetherhold and w. Sophia; b. Sept. 29; bap. Nov. 2; sp. Peter Kohler, Jun'r, and Hetty Biery.

KEMMERER, JOSHUA, s. Jacob Kemmerer and w. Dorothea; b. Sept. 24; bap. Nov. 4; sp. Henry Schneider and w. Margaretha.

RENTZHEIMER, FRANKLIN, s. Jacob Rentzheimer and w. Margaretha; b. Aug. 9; bap. Nov. 4; sp. Daniel Meier and w. Magdalena.

TRAXEL, RUFUS, s. John Traxel and w. Salome; b. Oct. 11; bap. Nov. 20; sp. Jesse Feber and w. Sarah.

LEH, SAMUEL, s. Samuel Leh and w. Magdalena; b. Oct. 26; bap. Nov. 25; sp. Peter Remely and w. Hannah.

MINNICH, RUEBEN, s. Michael Minich and w. Maria; b. Oct. 17; bap. Nov. 25; sp. Isaac Braun and Sarah Minnich.

ZERFASS, CLORAI, dr. John Zerfass and w. Sarah; b. Oct. 14; bap. Dec. 7; sp. Clorai Musselmann.

FREYMAN, DEBORA, dr. Joseph Freyman and w. Salome; b. Nov. 12; bap. Dec. 15; sp. Joel Braun and w. Elisabeth.

LANE, SALLY ANN, dr. Mathias Lane and w. Susan; b. Sept. 29; bap. Dec. 23; sp. Peter Leinberger and w. Elisabeth.

HARDLY, JOHN CARL, s. David Hardly and w. Eliza; b. June 17, 1830; bap. Dec. 25; sp. John Georg and Rebecca Meier.

HARDLY, THOMAS PETER, s. David Hardly and w. Eliza; b. July 23; bap. Dec. 25; sp. Peter Hoffmann and w. Susanna.

HECKER, ADELINA, dr. Charles Hecker and w. Catharina; b. Oct. 5; bap. Dec. 25; sp. David Georg and Rebecca Hecker.

MICKLY, CARL MATHIAS, s. Carl Mickly and w. Jetta; b. Nov. 17; bap. Dec. 25; sp. Peter Mickly and w. Susan, grandparents.

SAUERWEIN, MARIA ANNA, dr. William Sauerwein and w. Sarah; b. Dec. 3; bap. Dec. 25; sp. Thomas Knappenberger and w. Sarah.

1833.

ASMAN, TILGHMAN, s. John Asman and w. Eliza; b. Dec. 9, 1832; bap. Jan. 6; sp. John Straus and w. Eva.

TRAXEL, ABRAHAM, s. Jonathan Traxel and w. Elisabeth; b. Dec. 31, 1832; bap. Feb. 3; sp. Abraham Schad and w. Susanna.

KOHLER, MARIA, dr. Joseph Kohler and w. Maria; b. Dec. 3, 1832; bap. Feb. 5; sp. Maria Kohler, grandmother.

SAEGER, MATHILDA, dr. Daniel Saeger, Esq., and w. Susanna; b. Dec. 1, 1832; bap. Feb. 17; sp. George Ricker and w. Judith.

KOHLER, SARAH ANN, dr. Daniel Kohler and w. Magdalena; b. Dec. 29, 1832; bap. Feb. 17; sp. Dr. Wm. Kohler and w. Maria.

LEINBERGER, DEBORA, dr. Peter Leinberger and w. Susanna; b. Dec. 27, 1832; bap. Feb. 17; sp. Peter Leinberger and w. Elisabeth.

MEIER, ELEMINA, dr. Peter Meier and w. Catharina; b. Jan. 11; bap. Feb. 24; sp. Stephen Graff and Maria Ruch.

KNAPPENBERGER, ABRAHAM, s. Thomas Knappenberger and w. Salome; b. Jan. 31; bap. Mar. 17; sp. John Sheurer and w. Catharina.

MILLER, RUEBEN, s. George Miller and w. Magdalena; b. Jan. 23; bap. Mar. 24; sp. Charles Leaser and Margaretha Newhard.

OTTERSON, MARY ANN, dr. John Otterson and w. Lydia; b. Mar. 6; bap. Apr. 12; sp. Conrad Meier and w. Elisabeth.

LEVAN, ABRAHAM, s. Peter Levan and Mary Jones; b. May 3, 1813; bap. Apr. 12; sp. Joseph Saeger and wife.

SIEGFRIED, CAROLINA, dr. Joseph Siegfried and w. Elisabeth; b. Feb. 19; bap. Apr. 14; sp. David Ruch and w. Maria.

KEMMERER, SARAH CATHARINA, dr. Solomon Kemmerer and w. Magdalena; b. Feb. 25; bap. Apr. 14; sp. Reuben Scheurer and Sarah Kemmerer.

FEBER, AMANDES, dr. Jesse Feber and w. Sarah; b. Mar. 13; bap. Apr. 28; sp. David Meier and Lydia Mickly.

WOODRING, LEWIS DAVID, s. Cain Woodring and w. Margaret; b. Mar. 30; bap. May 12; sp. David Laury and w. Maria.

SCHAAD, CAROLINA, dr. John Schaad and w. Maria; b. Apr. 8; bap. May 19; sp. John Traxel and w. Elisabeth.

NEWHARD, TILGHMAN, s. Peter Newhard and w. Susanna; b. Apr. 23; bap. June 9; sp. George Miller and w. Magdalena.

GEORG, THOMAS FRANKLIN, s. John Georg and w Lea; b. May 3; bap. June 16; sp. Joel Hoffmann and w. Lydia.

BAKER, EILZA ANN, dr. Joseph Baker and w. Elisabeth; b. Jan. 26; bap. June 25; sp. George Heckmann and w. Maria Margaretha.

HOFFMAN, SARAH ANNA ELISABETHA, dr. Peter Hoffman and w. Sarah Ann; b. May 20; bap. July 7; sp. Charles Goranflo and w. Hannah.

STECKEL, AMOS, s. Daniel Steckel and w. Elisabeth; b. July 20; bap. Aug. 4; sp. Charles Leaser and w. Margaretha.

HISKY, EDWIN, s. Henry Hisky and w. Eva; b. July 9; bap. Aug. 4; sp. Benjamin Breinig and w. Hetty.

HOFFMAN, ELI, s. Peter Hoffman and w. Susanna; b. July 9; bap. Aug. 4; sp. Joseph Lang and w. Lydia.

BORGER, ELIAS, s. Philip Borger and w. Salome; b. July 24; bap. Aug. 4; sp. George Meier and w. Margaretha.

BERTSCH, JOSHUA, s. Jacob Bertsch and w. Barbara; b. July 18; bap. Aug. 4; sp. Daniel App and w. Elisabeth.

KIEFER, ANNA SUSANNA. dr. John Kiefer and w. Susanna; b. Aug. 15; bap. Sept. 28; sp. Christian Traxel and w. Elisabeth.

BEISEL, SARAH ANN, dr. Jacob Beisel and w. Sarah; b. Aug. 17; bap. Sept. 29; sp. Jesse Fever and w. Sarah.

LEINBERGER, DIANA, dr. Peter Leinberger and w. Elisabeth; b. Aug. 8; bap. Sept. 29; sp. John Anewalt and w. Catharina.

HAGENBUCH, ELISABETH SUSANNA, dr. Stephen Hagenbuch and w. Polly; b. July 25; bap. Oct. 7; sp. Peter Schreiber and w. Susanna, grandparents.

NEWHARD, EZRA, s. Jonas Newhard and w. Catharina; b. Sept. 17; bap. Oct. 13; sp. George Miller and w. Lydia.

KERN, HENRY JOSEPH, s. Peter Kern and w. Margretha; b. Aug. 23; bap. Oct. 27; sp. Joseph Albrecht and w. Catharina.

WELSH, FEYANNA, dr. Charles Welsh and w. Margaretha; b. Sept. 12; bap. Oct. 27; sp. Theobald Mertz and wife, grandparents.

BROWN, SAMUEL ADAM, S Paul Brown and w. Maria; b. Oct. 20; bap. Nov. 3; sp. George Koch and w. Maria.

KOHLER, WILLIAM HENRY MICHAEL, s. Dr. William Kohler and w. Mary; b. Sept. 10; bap. Nov. 7; sp. Michael Kern and w. Elisabeth, grandparents.

KOHLER, JAMES ALFRED PETER, s. Dr. William Kohler and w. Mary; b. Sept. 10; bap. Nov. 7; sp. Peter Kohler and w. Catharina, grandparents.

RITTER, WILLIAM GEORGE, s. Henry Ritter and w. Anna; b. Sept. 28; bap. Nov. 24; sp. George Kern and w. Salome.

STECKEL, SALLY ANN, dr. Peter Steckel and w. Elisabeth; b. Oct. 23; bap. Nov. 24; spj. William Wetherhold and w. Sophia Ann.

MILLER, LOUISA, dr. Peter Miller and w. Judith; b. Oct. 21; bap. Nov. 29; sp. Henry Frack and w. Delila.

BIERY, WILLIAM JOSEPH, s. Joseph Biery and w. Salome; b. Oct. 5; bap. Dec. 1; sp. William H. Blumer and Susan Biery.

LORASH, JAMES WILLIAM, s. Leonhard Lorash and w. Sophianna; b. Nov. 9; bap. Dec. 12; sp. Jacob Lorash and w. Sarah.

GRAFF, MARY ANN, dr. Stephen Graff and w. Polly; b. Dec. 12; bap. Dec. 13; sp. Peter Ruch and w. Lucy Ann.

GEORG, KITTY ANN, dr. Solomon Georg and w. Abby; b. Nov. 7; bap. Dec. 22; sp. Georg Adam Newhard and w. Margaretha, grandparents.

BREISH, CAROLINA, dr. Jacob Breish and w. Barbara; b. Oct. 6; bap. Dec. 22; sp. Joseph Mertz and w. Elisabeth.

SCHEURER, ALFRED, s. David Scheurer and w. Elisabeth; b. Nov. 23; bap. Dec. 22; sp. Charles Leaser and w. Margaretha.

GINNERT, ANNA MATHILDA, dr. John Ginnert and w. Elisabeth; b. May 20; bap. Dec. 25; sp. Daniel Siegfried and w. Catharina.

SCHAD, MARIA, dr. Abraham Schad and w. Susanna; b. Nov. 10; bap. Dec. 29; sp. Henry Frack and w. Delila.

MEIER, HETTY, dr. Abraham Meier and w. Magdalena; b. Nov. 10; bap. Dec. 29; sp. Parents.

NAGEL, GUTILIA, dr. Joseph Nagel and w. Salome; b. Dec. 2; bap. Dec. 29; sp. John Biege and w. Elisabeth, grandparents.

BIEGE, JUDITH, dr. John Biege and w. Elisabeth; b. Oct. 11; bap. Dec. 29; sp. Peter Miller and w. Judith.

1834.

BIERY, HENRY, s. Joseph Biery and w. Polly; b Dec. 13, 1833; bap. Jan. 5; sp. Henry Frack and w. Delila.

RUCH, MARIA, dr. Peter Ruch and w. Lucianna; b. Dec. 17, 1833; bap. Jan. 19; sp. Solomon Steckel, Jun'r, and Isabella Traxel.

RUCH, SALLY ANN, dr. William Ruch and w. Lydia; b. Dec. 23, 1833; bap. Jan. 19; sp. Peter Ruch and w. Susan, grandparents.

GORANFLO, HENRY WILLIAM ALFRED, s. Charles Goranflo and w. Hanna; b. Dec. 4, 1833; bap. Jan. 19; sp. Reuben Shoch and Eliza Helfrich.

FISHER, CATHARINA, dr. James Fisher and w. Polly; b. Dec. 14, 1833, bap. Jan. 19; sp. Jacob Fisher and w. Barbara, grandparents.

HOFFMAN, ELIZA ANN, dr. Joel Hoffman and w. Lydia; b. Dec. 18, 1833; bap. Jan. 26; sp. George Meier and w. Margaretha.

MEIER, KITTY ANN, dr. Thomas Meier and w. Susan; b. Nov. 21, 1833; bap. Jan. 26; sp. Joel Hoffmann and w. Lydia.

SCHEURER, GEORG ADAM, s. John Scheurer and w. Catharina; b. Dec. 21, 1833; bap. Jan. 26; sp. George Adam Kemmerer and w. Maria Susanna, grandparents.

MARX, MARIA, dr. Gideon Marx and w. Esther; b. Jan. 17; bap. Feb. 2; sp. Catharina Eisenhardt, grandmother.

SCHNERR, LEVI, s. Thomas Schnerr and w. Lydia; b. Nov. 9, 1833; bap. Feb. 16; sp. Peter Hoffman and w. Magdalena.

ANTON, SUSANNA, dr. John Anton and w. Susanna; b. Jan. 1; bap. Feb. 16; sp. John Knerr and Lydia Laury.

FRANTZ, MARGARETHA, dr. Abraham Frantz and w. Polly; b. Jan. 10; bap. Feb. 16; sp. Henrich Frantz and w. Margaretha, grandparents.

WHITE, MARY, dr. George White and w. Hetty; b. Jan. 6; bap. Feb. 23; sp. Joel Braun and w. Elisabetha.

BURKHALTER, HENRICH PETER, s. David Burkhalter and w. Mary Anna; b. Jan. 18; bap. Feb. 23; sp. William Burkhalter and Debora Burkhalter.

MEIER, ABBY, dr. Conrad Meier and w. Elisabeth; b. Jan. 22; bap. Mar. 16; sp. Peter Lautenschlaeger and w. Susanna.

SCHAD, MONROE, s. Henry Schad and w. Maria; b. Mar. 8; bap. Mar. 23; sp. Henry Frantz and w. Catharina.

SCHAAD, JOSIAH, s. Lorentz Schaad and w. Magdalena; b. Feb. 16; bap. Mar. 23; sp. Gideon Marx and w. Esther.

STOFLET, NATHAN, s. Jonas Stoflet and w. Margaretha; b. Jan. 8; bap. Mar. 28; sp. Parents.

MEIER, REBECCA, dr. Jonas Meier and w. Susanna; b. Feb. 16; bap. Mar. 28; sp. Peter Lautenschlaeger and w. Susanna.

REIS, PETER MICHAEL, s. Daniel Reis and w. Sophia; b. Nov. 5, 1833; bap. Apr. 13; sp. John Teichman.

CANKE, ANNA MARIA, dr. James Canke and w. Catharina; b. Jan. 24; bap. Apr. 13; sp. Daniel Siegfried and w. Elisabeth.

BIERY, HETTY, dr. David Biery and w. Marianna; b. Mar. 3; bap. Apr. 22; sp. Parents.

TRAXEL, SAMUEL PETER, s. Adam Traxel and w. Lydia; b. Mar. 21; bap. May 8; sp. Peter Traxel and w. Magdalena, grandparents.

FREYMAN, GIDEON, s. Joseph Freyman and w. Salome; b. Apr. 20; bap. May 18; sp. Christopher Freyman and w Maria Eva, grandparents.

REIT, LEANDA, dr. George Reit and w. Polly; b. Apr. 11; bap. May 19; sp. Joseph Kohler and w. Polly.

McLACHLY, MARIA MARGARETHA, dr. Anton McLachly and w. Lea; b. Mar. 11; bap. May 26; sp. Philip Fenstermacher and w. Margaretha.

KEMMERER, ELIZA ANNA, dr. George Kemmerer and w. Anna; b. May 13; bap. May 31; sp. Charles Colver and w. Magdalena.

BUCHMAN, WILHELMINA, dr. Dewald Buchman and w. Anna Maria; b. May 3; bap. June 8; sp. Henrich Bahl and Wilhelmina Ringeiser.

KIRSCHNER, SUSANNA, dr. Daniel Kirschner and w. Lea; b. May 10; bap. June 8; sp. Abraham Schad and w. Susanna.

BIEGE, JOSEPH HENRY, s. Joseph Biege and w. Rebecca; b. May 14; bap. June 15; sp. John Hecker and w. Maria, grandparents.

RITTER, LOUISE CAROLINA, dr. Jeremiah Ritter and w. Hanna; b. May 27; bap. June 22; sp. Jacob Frantz and w. Sarah.

QUEER, ANGELINA, dr. Jonas Queer and w. Mary; b. Nov. 8, 1833; bap. June 24; sp. Rebecca Owen.

ALBRECHT, CATHARINA HANNA, dr. Joseph Albrecht, deceased, and w. Catharina; b. May 30; bap. July 28; sp. Peter Kern and w. Margaretha.

GUTH, JOHANNES, Friedrich Guth and w. Lydia; b Jan. 2; bap. July 28; sp. Daniel Siegfried and w. Catharina.

KOHLER, LEANNA, dr. Isaac Kohler and w. Catharina; b. June 31; bap. Aug. 31; sp. George Kemmerer and w. Anna.

KERN, SUSANNA, dr. James Kern and w. Maria; b. July 13; bap. Aug. 31; sp. Jonas Meier and w. Susanna.

ZERFASS, SUSANNA, dr. John Zerfass and w. Sarah; b. Aug. 27; bap. Sept. 5; sp. Jacob Vehl and w. Magdalena.

MILLER, MARY ANNA, dr. George Miller, Sen'r, and w. Magdalena; b. July 11; bap. Sept. 14; sp. George Miller, Jun'r, and w. Lydia.

KEHL, SARAH ANN, dr. Benjamin Kehl and w. Susanna; b. Aug. 22; bap. Sept. 27; sp. Daniel Wint and Hannah Rex.

STEIN, SARAH ANN, dr. Himan L. Stein and w. Julia Ann; b. Aug. 4; bap. Sept. 27; sp. Johannes Fenstermacher and w. Rosina, grandparents.

DESHLER, DAVID JAMES FRANKLIN, s. James Deshler and w. Elisabeth; b. Aug. 24; bap. Sept. 27; sp. Michael Biege and w. Lydia.

TRAXEL, ANNA MARIA, dr. John Traxel and w. Anna Maria; b. Sept. 10; bap. Oct. 5; sp. Peter Traxel, Jun'r, and Juliana Gobrecht.

KOHLER, EMILIE, dr. Joseph Kohler and w. Maria; b. Aug. 24; bap. Oct. 26; sp. Maria Saeger, grandmother.

BOX, SUSANNA CATHARINA, dr. William Box and w. Susanna; b. July 13; bap. Oct. 26; sp. James Deshler and w. Elisabeth.

MICKLY, ELIZA, dr. Jacob Mickly and w. Anna; b. July 19; bap. Oct. 26; sp. Peter Mickly and w. Anna.

TRAXEL, SALLY ANN, dr. John Traxel and w. Sally; b. Sept. 1; bap. Oct. 26; sp. John Lesar and Polly Traxel.

NEWHARD, JOHN HIRAM, s. Michael Newhard and w. Magdalena; b. Sept. 1; bap. Oct. 27; sp. Peter Zellner and w. Judith.

GRUBER, ROSINA EMILIA, dr. Jacob Gruber and w. Elisabeth; b. Aug. 28; bap. Nov. 2; sp. John Fenstermacher and w. Rosina.

FISHER, MARIA ANNA, dr. Peter Fisher and w. Elisabeth; b. Oct. 6; bap. Nov. 9; sp. Samuel Miller and Polly Iona.

SAUERWINE, NATHAN, s. Charles Sauerwine and w. Elisabeth; b. Oct. 1; bap. Nov. 9; sp. Ludwig Sauerwine and w. Christina, grandparents.

MILLER, REUBEN, s. John Miller and w. Sarah; b. Oct. 1; bap. Nov. 23; sp. Nathan Schifferstein and Rachel Newhard.

FRANTZ, SUSANNA, dr. Henry Frantz and w. Elisabeth; b. Oct. 31; bap. Nov. 23; sp. Daniel Steckel and w. Elisabeth.

SCHWAB, DANIEL, s. Jacob Schwab and w. Maria; b. Oct. 6; bap. Dec. 7; sp. Adam Schaeffer and w. Juliana.

NEWHARD, CARLOTTA LUCETTA, dr. Henry Newhard and w. Sarah; b. Nov. 14; bap. Dec. 21; sp. Solomon Steckel and w. Anna Maria.

SCHNECK, DAVID, s. John Schneck and w. Elisabeth; b. Nov. 20; bap. Dec. 21; sp. Edward Kohler and Julia Hecker.

BRUEGEL, JACOB, s. Michael Bruegel and w. Elisabeth; b. Nov. 7; bap. Dec. 25; sp. Jacob Schaeffer and Elisabeth Bachman.

SAUERWINE, HENRY WILLIAM, s. William Sauerwine and w. Sarah; b. Nov. 17; bap. Dec. 25; sp. Andrew Scheldon and w. Anna.

BEISEL, AARON JOSIAH, s. Jacob Beisel and w. Sarah; b. Nov. 19; bap. Dec. 25; sp. Joseph Heilman and Elisabeth Confer.

RITTER, REBECCA, dr. Daniel Ritter and w. Elisabeth; b. Nov. 28; bap. Dec. 25; sp. Daniel Meier and w. Magdalena.

SCHAAD, TILGHMAN, s. John Schaad and w. Maria; b. Dec. 1; bap. Dec. 28; sp. Charles Traxel and w. Susanna.

MARRIAGES.

Egypt.

Nov. 28, 1752. Samuel, son of Nicolaus Seeger, and Anna Eva, daughter of the deceased Fridrich Eberhard.

Heidelberg.

Dec. 12, 1752. Jacob Arnert, of Heidelberg, and Catharina, daughter of Henrich Knever, of Macunschi.[103]

Nov. 5, 1765. John Ruch, son of George Ruch, of Whitehall township, Northampton county, and Eva Fatzinger, daughter of George Fatzinger, of the same place.[104]

Nov. 12, 1771. Jacob Fohr, widower, of Allenstown, and Catharina, daughter of Martin Meyer.[105]

DEATHS.[106]

"Blessed are the dead which die in the Lord, for they rest from their labors and their works do follow them."

Egypt.

Abraham Wutring died Nov. 28, 1752. He was born July 11, 1700, lived in marriage 27 1-2 years and had sixteen children, of whom eight still live as long as God wills. His age was somewhat over 52 years.

Elisabeth, daughter of the deceased Henrich Roeder, of Heidelberg, died May 10, 1753, and was buried May 11th.

Christian Flickinger, single son of Ulrich Flickinger, of Whitehall township, was buried March 9, 1766; he died March 7th, in the twentieth year of his age.

Lucia Flickinger, wife of Ulrich Flickinger, died April 23, 1772, aged about seventy years, and was buried April 25th.

Anna Maria Weiss, daughter of Georg Weiss, died July 3, 1772, and was buried July 4th.

CONFIRMATIONS.[107]

List of the children permitted by me to come for the first time to the table of our Lord.

1753.

JOHANN ADAM, Jacob Bruecker's son.
JOHANN WILHELM, Abraham Wutring's son.
PETER, Ulrich Fleckinger's son.
PETER, Michael Behr's son.
JOHANN NICKEL FUCHS, servant with Peter Traxel.
CONRAD, Leonhard Schlosser's son.
JACOB, Ulrich Fleckinger's son.
JACOB, Jacob Meckli's son.
JOHANN GEORG, Jacob Schrieber's son.
LORENZ, Lorenz Guth's son.
CHRISTIAN, Peter Traxel's son.
JACOB, Daniel Roth's son.
GOTTFRIED, Gottfried Knaus' son.
NICOLAUS, Nicolaus Ramstet's son
MARIA MAGDALENA, Jacob Schrieber's daughter.
CATHARINA ELIZABETHA, Michael Hoffman's daughter.
CATHARINA ELIZABETHA, Georg Kern's daughter.
JULIANA MARGARETHA, Peter Traxel's daughter.
JULIANA MARGARETHA, Lorenz Guth's daughter.
ANNA BARBARA, Jacob Wirth's daughter.
CATHARINA BARBARA, Ulrich Flickinger's daughter.
MARIA EVA, Peter Miller's daughter.
ANNA MARGARETHA, Leonhard Schlosser's daughter.
EVA CATHARINA, Conrad Grumbach's daughter.
CHRISTINA MARGARETHA, Philip Leibenguth's daughter.
ELIZABETHA MARGARETHA, Michael Neuhard's daughter.
ELIZABETHA, Georg Wagenmacher's daughter.
MARIA CHRISTINA, Christian Schneyders daughter.
CATHARINA, Christian Schmid's daughter.
ELIZABETHA, Johan Deis Reg's (?) daughter.
ANNA MARIA, Johann Henrich Widerstein's daughter.

1754.

JOHANN HENRICH, Jacob Ferber's son.
PETER, Daniel Roth's son.
ANNA MARIA CATHARINA, Andreas Engelhard's daughter.
ANNA BARBARA, Abraham Woutring's daughter.

MEMORANDA.[10R]

N. B. ANNA MARGARETHA HEILMAN, on the 22nd of April, 1753, presented to the congregation at the Jordan a beautiful white altar-cloth. May God bless her in every way for this praiseworthy and Christian work.

When communion was held at Egypt, two shillings eight pence were held back. Jacob Kohler has the same in keeping.

Mr. Kohler also has 9 p.

I have also from the Jordan congregation one shilling one penny in keeping. Again, one shilling.

January 21, 1753, in the Heidelberg congregation, one shilling, 9 pence.

NOTES.

(In the translation of these records the spelling of the names has not been changed, except in cases where the vowel is modified, when a, o and u are written ae, oe and ue. C. R. R.)

1. Nothing without writing.
2. All for the glory of God and the salvation of our souls.
3. A Swiss of Zurich.
4. Peter Traxel emigrated from Switzerland and landed at Philadelphia with two sons, Peter and Daniel, Aug. 17, 1733 He settled at Egypt, but later removed a few miles westward and built a stone house in 1744, which still stands. He purchased a large tract of land, some of which is still owned by descendants.
5. Nicolaus Kern was one of the earliest settlers of Whitehall township. He afterwards removed to the present site of Slatington, where he died in 1747.
6. Daniel Roth was a native of Switzerland and arrived at Philadelphia Aug. 28, 1733. He settled two miles north of Allentown and died in the same hour in which this son was born, which was in April, 1737. The son, Peter, was reared among the Quakers, received a good education and changed the spelling of his name to Rhoads. He settled in Allentown in 1762 and was a member of the Constitutional Convention of July 15, 1776, a member of the Committee of Safety in 1776 and a member of the Assembly from 1777 to

1781. On Oct. 8, 1784, he was commissioned President Judge of the Courts of Northampton County by the Supreme Executive Council, was a member of the Constitutional Convention of 1790, and in 1791 was commissioned Associate Judge, which office he held until the erection of Lehigh County in 1812, when he was commissioned Senior Associate Judge in Lehigh County. He died in Allentown, Dec. 18, 1814. This entry is in the handwriting of Rev. Goetschius.

7. Abraham Wotring, formerly Voiturin, was born July 11, 1700, and arrived at Philadelphia on Sept. 28, 1733. He had sixteen children, of whom eight were living at the time of his death on Nov. 28, 1752, namely, Peter, Anna Margaretha, Anna Barbara, Magdalena, Elisabeth, William, Abraham and Eva. He was a delegate to the Coetus of the Reformed Church held in Philadelphia in 1747.

8. Ulrich Burghalter arrived at Philadelphia, Sept. 28, 1733, and settled upon one of the finest tracts of land in Whitehall township. He died in 1762, leaving one son, Peter, and six daughters.

9. Michael Hoffman landed at Philadelphia, Oct. 11, 1732, and settled on a tract of two hundred and fifty acres in Whitehall township. He died in 1786, leaving two sons, John and Michael, and four daughters, Maria Magdalena, Catharina Elisabetha, Juliana and Maria Barbara.

10. This is the last entry in the handwriting of Rev. Goetschius.

11. Nicolaus Saeger was born in Reichenbach, Bavaria, about 1694. He arrived at Philadelphia with his wife, Anna Barbara, and seven children on Sept. 28, 1733. He died in 1762. He had twelve children, of whom there survived him, Anna Mary, Anna Barbara, Samuel, Christian, Christina Barbara, Mary Margaret, John Nicholas, John Jacob, Anna Elisabeth and John. This and the two following entries are probably in Rev. Boehm's handwriting.

12. John Traxel arrived at Philadelphia on Aug. 20, 1737. He secured land in Whitehall township, but died a few years later.

13. Frederick Newhard was born in Zweibruecken in 1700. He arrived at Philadelphia with two brothers, Michael and George, on Sept. 26, 1737. He died Nov. 29, 1765, and is buried in Allentown. He had nine children. His son, Lorentz Newhard, died in Allentown on Aug. 1, 1817.

14 Lorentz Guth was a native of Zweibruecken and landed at Philadelphia on Sept. 19, 1738. He owned a large tract of land in Whitehall township and had six children, Juliana Mar-

garet, wife of Peter Kohler; Lorentz, Peter, Eva Barbara, wife of George Henry Mertz; Margaret, wife of Adam Dorney, and Adam Guth.

15. George Ruch was born in Zinzendorf, Alsace, in 1664, and died in Whitehall township in 1769, aged one hundred and four years and eleven months.

16. Ulrich Flickinger arrived at Philadelphia on Aug. 17, 1733. He died in 1792. His descendants removed from the county.

17. Michael Newhard was a brother of Frederick Newhard. He was born Feb. 9, 1713 and died March 10, 1793. His wife, Barbara Newhard, was born April 1, 1716 and died Sept. 12, 1792.

18. Peter Steckel purchased from Peter Traxel on May 20, 1768, a stone messuage and plantation of 410 acres, in Whitehall township, for fourteen hundred and twenty pounds sterling. The house, built in 1756, was until recently occupied by his descendants.

19. Adam Deshler was a prominent resident of Whitehall township and furnished the provincial troops with provisions in the French and Indian war. In 1760, he built a stone house which still stands. It was used as a military post during the Indian troubles of 1763, and was long called Fort Deshler. Adam Deshler died in 1781, leaving a widow, Appolonia, three sons and three daughters.

20. Peter Traxel, son of Peter Traxel, was born in January, 1724, and died Feb. 28, 1811. His wife Anna Maria Traxel, was born March 6, 1727 and died July 10, 1795. He was married May 19, 1747, and had seven sons and seven daughters.

21. Jacob Schreiber was a native of Niederbrunn, Alsace, and on April 28, 1733, married Anna Magdalena Roth. On the fourth of May following they sailed for America and arrived at Philadelphia on Aug. 28, 1733. He lived for a time in Skippack township, Montgomery county, but soon located four hundred acres of land along the Lehigh river in Whitehall township. The town of Coplay and a large cement plant are located on this land. He died about 1750, leaving a widow, two sons and one daughter.

22. Paul Balliet was born in Alsace in 1717 and arrived in Philadelphia on Sept. 11, 1738. He kept a tavern at Ballietsville for many years. He married Maria Magdalena Wotring, of Lorraine, France, and died March 19, 1777. He was a delegate to the Reformed Church Coetus held at Lancaster in 1767.

23. John Jacob Mickley landed at Philadelphia on Aug. 28, 1733, when, according to the ship's record, he was twenty-two

years old. In signing the oath of allegiance he wrote his name Muckli. He settled in Whitehall township, married Elizabeth Barbara Burghalter and died in August, 1769. Two of his children were killed by Indians on the memoriable Oct. 8, 1763.

24. Michael Ohl was a resident of Heidelberg township and was born June 26, 1729 and died July 4, 1804. He had three sons and seven daughters.

25. John Roth was an early settler along the Jordan creek in Whitehall township, where there is still standing a stone house built by him in 1775. He died in 1802, leaving a second wife surviving, and five children, Eva Catharina, John, Godfrey, George Jacob and Magdalena.

26. Godfrey Knauss was a resident of Whitehall township as early as 1750. He owned a large tract of land situated on the Jordan creek, two miles north of Allentown. Here he built in 1769 a substantial stone house, which is still in excellent condition. He died in 1777, when the house and that portion of the land south of the Jordan was purchased by Judge Peter Rhoads, by whom it was owned until his death in 1814, when his son John Rhoads became the owner and held it until 1837, when it passed into other hands. Upon the organization of Whitehall township in 1753, Godfrey Knauss was appointed constable. He was a delegate to the Coetus held at Easton in 1768. His first wife, Anna Eva, died about 1758, and he later married Regina Louisa, widow of John Reinhard Benny.

27. Felix Arner, a resident of Heidelberg township, was born Jan. 14, 1726, and died Feb. 20, 1776. His widow married Peter Anthony. Among Felix Arner's children were Salome, John, Felix, William and Dorothea.

28. Bernhard Jacob Rex, son of George Rex, was born April 5, 1724; married, May 16, 1746, Anna Elizabeth Arner, and died April 24, 1802. He had eleven children.

29. Elizabeth, wife of Martin Andreas, was a daughter of Abraham Wotring.

30. David Deshler was a son of Adam Deshler, of Whitehall township, and was one of the early settlers of Allentown, where he later owned a tan yard and bark mill. He was a member of the Provincial Conference of Committees held at Carpenter's Hall, Philadelphia, from June 18th to 25th, 1776, and on March 21, 1777, was appointed Sub Lieutenant for Northampton county. On June 3, 1777, he was appointed a Justice of the Peace and on Feb. 19, 1778, a Commissioner of Purchases for Northampton county. He died in 1796, leaving a widow, three sons and six daughters. He was quite wealthy

and bequeathed to his son George the tan yard and bark mill, to his wife, one thousand pounds, to his son David, if he married, one thousand pounds, and to each of his daughters, five hundred pounds.

31. Daniel Traxel was the second son of Peter Traxel, the emigrant, and arrived with his father at the age of nine years. He married Sophia Dotterer and later removed to Adams county.

32. Peter Kohler was the eldest son of Jacob Kohler, who was a native of Switzerland and the first settler at Egypt. Jacob Kohler was a man of great energy and built the first grist mill in the vicinity. Peter Kohler was born April 2, 1735. He was appointed one of the assessors for Northampton county in 1776; one of the persons to take subscriptions for the continental loan and one of the committee to collect clothing in 1777; a justice of the peace in 1779 and elected a member of the Assembly in 1780, 1781 and 1782. He died Sept. 27, 1793, leaving one son, Peter.

33. Lorent Guth, son of Lorent Guth, was born Jan. 21, 1743 and died Nov. 9, 1814. He was twice married and had fourteen children, eight sons and six daughters.

34. Maria Elizabeth Koehler was the eldest daughter of Jacob and Maria Elizabeth Kohler and was born May 17, 1733. She married, March 16, 1756, John George Koehler, and died July 25, 1825. They had no children. John George Koehler was born March 6, 1732, and died May 24, 1799.

35. John Snyder and wife with this child and two other children were killed by the Indians on Oct. 8, 1763. Two daughters were scalped but afterwards recovered.

This is the last entry in the first volume of the church record.

36. This entry is the first in the second volume of the church records, which contains the following inscription, "Church Book of the Congregation in Egypt begun in the year 1764, under the care of Rev. Daniel Gros, Reformed Minister." On the fly leaf is the following memorandum: "The Egypt Church. The Reformed congregation was founded Anno 1733. The first was a log church, built in 1764. The second was of stone, 40 by 50 feet, and was built in the year 1785. The third is of brick, 50 by 65 feet, and was built in 1851. It cost in money expended $7,383.00, and including the work cost about $11,000."

Then follows a memorandum by Rev. Gros to the effect that on Nov. 8, 1765, the alms money was counted in the presence of the Presbytery and the congregation, and after the deduction of

LEHIGH COUNTY—1734-1834.

the money paid out, two pounds, four shillings and eight pence were found remaining, which the then surveyor of alms, George Jacob Kern, handed to Jacob Mickle, the elder, alms surveyor for the year 1766.

On Dec. 17, 1766, the same procedure took place and Jacob Mickle paid the sum of one pound and six shillings to his successor, Johannes Schadt.

On the same date, at the same time, the church account was examined and no claims on the congregation were found up to date, but all debts were paid. Dated at Whitehall township, Northampton county, as above and signed by Adam Deshler, Michael Neihart and Rev. Gros.

Rev. Gros was pastor of Egypt congregation for five years, and the first baptismal entry by him was dated April 28, 1765.

37. Peter Burkhalter, son of Ulrich Burkhalter, was born in Switzerland, Dec. 2, 1731, and arrived at Philadelphia with his parents on Sept. 28, 1733. He was a member of the Constitutional Convention of 1776 and in November of the same year was elected a member of the Assembly, being the only member from that portion of Northampton county which now constitutes Lehigh county. He was re-elected in 1777, and again elected in 1784, 1785 and 1786. He died Oct. 22, 1805, and is buried at Egypt.

38. John Nicolaus Traxel had nine children, among whom were Adam, Peter, Magdalena, wife of John Horn, and Eva, wife of John Stofflet. He died in 1797.

39. John Jacob Mickly, son of John Jacob and Elizabeth Barbara Mickly, was born in 1734 and died in 1809. He married Susanna Margaret Miller and had ten children.

40. Jacob Kohler was a son of Jacob Kohler, and with his brother, Peter, inherited his father's land. He was twice married and had fifteen children. He died Nov. 1, 1830, in his ninety-first year.

41. Eva Catharina Miller was a daughter of Jacob Kohler and a sister to Peter and Jacob Kohler. She married John Miller and removed to Allentown, where he died in 1788. She subsequently married Judge Peter Rhoads, whose first wife was her sister, and died at Allentown, Sept. 2, 1825, in her seventy-ninth year.

42. Philip Jacob Schreiber was a son of John Jacob Schreiber and was born in Skippack township, Montgomery county on June 13, 1735. He married May 1, 1759, Catharina Elizabetha Kern, and died April 5, 1813. He had eleven children, five sons and six daughters. His farm of four hundred acres was one of the finest in the county and was beautifully situated on

the Lehigh river. During his life he ranked as one of the leading men of the community.

43. Peter Deshler was a son of Adam Deshler, Sr. and was born March 18, 1743 and died Sept. 28, 1800. He married Magdalena Mickley, daughter of Jacob Mickley.

44. Nicholas Wotring was born in Pistorf, Lorraine, in April, 1745, and died July 15, 1818.

45. Margaret Fox was a daughter of Jacob Kohler and married John Nicholas Fox, who later removed to Allentown and kept a tavern there for many years.

46. Magdalena Newhard was also a daughter of Jacob Kohler, Sr. She died in 1777. Her husband, Peter Newhard, married a second time and died Sept. 16, 1813.

47. Conrad Marck was born in 1745 and died in 1807. He was one of those actively concerned in the Fries Rebellion of 1799.

48. Philip Roth was married to Catharina Kohler, daughter of Jacob Kohler, Sr. and three sons, Peter, Philip and Jacob.

49. This is the first entry by Rev. Abraham Blumer.

50. Nicholas Marx was a shoemaker and lived near John Schneider, whose family were killed by the Indians on Oct. 8, 1763. Marks escaped and carried the news to Bethlehem.

51. George Graff was a son of Jacob Graff and was born in Killendorf, Lower Alsace, Germany, on Oct. 11, 1747. He arrived at Philadelphia with his parents, a brother and sister, on Oct. 16, 1754. On Oct. 8, 1763, he had a narrow escape from Indians who burned the home of Nicholas Marx, with whom he lived. He served as a captain in the Revolutionary War, then as Collector of Excise for Northampton county, Sheriff of Northampton county from 1787 to 1790, and Member of the Legislature from 1793 to 1796. He was Burgess of Allentown in 1814. He died in Allentown, Feb. 2, 1835, aged eighty-seven years. He married May 1, 1770, Barbara Kohler, daughter of Jacob Kohler, who was born Feb. 6, 1750, and died Feb. 8, 1826. Their children were, Barbara, wife of Peter Rhoads, Jr., Magdalena, wife of John Rhoads, Joseph, George, Sara, wife of Dr. Ferdinand Miller, Hanna, wife of Tobias Grob, Catharina and Anna, wife of Daniel Leisenring.

52. George Jacob Newhard was a son of Michael Newhard, and was born July 25, 1752. He married Anna Maria Kohler, daughter of Jacob Kohler, May 18, 1773. He removed to Allentown, where he followed the trade of a cabinetmaker. He died Sept. 18, 1835.

53. George Schreiber was a son of Jacob Schreiber and was born Dec. 6, 1739. He settled in Allentown in 1767 and kept a

store there many years. He married Barbara Deshler and died Nov. 6, 1800.

54. Peter Guth was a son of Lorentz Guth, Sr. and was born Feb. 7, 1746. He married Eva Catharina Lehr.

55. Stephen Balliet, son of Paul Balliet, was born in 1753. In Dec. 1776, he was a Lieut. Col. in the Revolutionary army, and in 1781, a colonel. In 1783 he was elected a member of the Supreme Executive Council for a term of three years, and in 1789 a member of the House of Representatives. In 1797, he was appointed revenue collector for the Second District of Pennsylvania. He married Magdalena Burkhalter and died August 4, 1821.

56. Adam Deshler was a son of Adam Deshler and was born Oct. 1, 1745, and died Feb. 24, 1790. He was a prosperous farmer of Whitehall township. He married Maria Catharina Balliet and had nine children.

57. Frederick Newhard, son of Michael Newhard, was born April 20, 1748, and died March 24, 1823. He married Apollonia Dreisbach, who was born Feb. 1, 1750, and died June 16, 1822.

58. Samuel Saeger, son of John Nicholas Saeger, was born in 1727 in Germany, and came to this country with his father in 1733. He married, Oct. 28, 1752, Anna Eva Eberhard.

59. Henry Beil, son of Balthazar and Elizabeth Beil, was born in Saucon township, Feb. 9, 1752. In 1773, he married Maria Elizabeth Edelman, who was born Jan. 1, 1754 and died March 20, 1838. He died in Allen township, Northampton county, Dec. 10, 1834.

60. Martin Graff, son of Jacob Graff and brother of Capt. George Graff, was born in Alsace in 1748. He settled in North Whitehall township, where he died in 1797, leaving a widow and seven children.

61. Lorentz Ruch, son of George Ruch, was born Nov. 14, 1744. He married, Nov. 5, 1769, Charlotte Barbara Knauss, daughter of George Knauss, and died Oct. 27, 1825. He owned a fine tract of 212 acres of land and was noted for his great strength. Philip Knaus, a sponsor, was a brother of Mrs. Ruch.

62. Christian Saeger, son of John Nicholas Saeger, was born Jan. 26, 1731, and died Nov. 30 1800. He married Maria Susanna Hann, who was born Feb. 6, 1736 and died Mar. 6, 1800. The children surviving were Nicholas, Jacob, Daniel, Magdalena, Catharina, Barbara, Christina and Margaret.

63. John Nicholas Meier was born Dec. 31, 1724 and died April 21, 1775, leaving a widow, Margaret, and five children, among whom were John, David and Margaret. His tombstone is the oldest legible one in Egypt churchyard, although there

are many buried there prior to 1775 whose tombstones have crumbled or are illegible.

64. John Grob, son of Henry Grob and wife Adelaide Hitz, was born Jan. 26, 1753. He married, March 12, 1776, Anna Maria, daughter of Conrad Leisenring. He died April 2, 1831, and is buried in Egypt churchyard.

65. Conrad Leisenring was born June 29, 1727, in Hildburghausen, Germany. He married Sibilla Veit in 1755 and in 1766 settled on a tract of land along the Lehigh river in Whitehall township. He died August 14, 1781, and is buried in Egypt churchyard. His children were Anna Maria, wife of John Grob, Elizabeth, wife of Jacob Herman, Conrad, John Sebastian, Eva Christina, wife of Henry Shettel, Andrew and Peter.

66. John Peter Burkhalter was a son of Peter Burkhalter and wife Eva Catharina. He married Dorothea Steckel and died in 1814.

67. Paul Knauss was a son of Godfrey Knauss, and resided in Allen township, where he followed the trade of a blacksmith. He was born April 13, 1747 and died Jan. 19, 1808. His wife, Catharina Griesemer was born April 12, 1754 and died Sept. 10, 1790. They are buried in the graveyard at the Kreidersville church.

68. Jacob Steckel, son of Peter Steckel, was born Nov. 1, 1753, and died June 15, 1836. He married, Jan. 16, 1780, Eva Catharina Saeger, who was born July 6, 1757 and died Jan. 7, 1815. They had five children, two sons and three daughters.

69. Philip Faust, son of Henry Faust, was born Oct. 1, 1760, in Greenville township, Berks county, and died July 12, 1832. The site of his farm is now included in the town of Catasauqua. His wife, Barbara, died Oct. 4, 1842.

70. Martin Meyer was born Aug. 3, 1755 and died Aug. 21, 1830. He married Margaret Steckel, daughter of Peter Steckel, who was born Nov. 12, 1759 and died Sept. 4, 1820.

71. Jacob Geiger was a clockmaker and died in 1798, leaving a widow and four children, Jacob, Catharina, Maria, wife of Solomon Steckel, and Sarah, wife of Jonas Traxel, who later removed to Cassel county, Md. His widow, Eva Catharina Kern, was born Jan. 13, 1760, married Adam Traxel, and died August 23, 1829.

72. Conrad Leisenring, son of Conrad and Sibilla Leisenring, was born Nov. 6, 1759 and died Feb. 10, 1824. He married, Oct. 7, 1783, Catharine Grob, who was born Aug. 31 1759, and died Sept. 11, 1828. He left surviving eight children, Daniel, Eva Catharina, wife of Jacob Schreiber, Barbara, wife of Daniel

Schreiber Peter, John, Conrad, Maria wife of Conrad Beil and Salome, wife of Solomon Troxell.

73. George Gangewere was born July 20, 1756, and died March 2, 1852, aged 95 years. He was a soldier in the Revolution.

74. Jonas Grubb removed from Lehigh county to Crawford county, and in 1839 settled near Quincy, Illinois. He married Sarah Wiser and died March 20, 1854. A son, George W. Grubb, is living in Liberty, Ill. Among the grandsons of Jonas Grubb are: Scott Wike, former Assistant Secretary of the Treasury, Jonathan Grubb, Professor of Latin in Lombard University, Galesburg, Ill., and Perry D. Grubb, formerly a member of the Missouri State Legislature.

75. Henry Grob, son of Henry Grob and wife Adelaide, was born July 14, 1762. His first wife, Margaret, was born Nov. 23, 1763, and died June 18, 1806.

76. Jost William Hecker was a son of Rev. John Egidius Hecker and died in March 1821. His wife, Regina, died in February, 1827.

77. Tobias Grubb was a gunsmith in Allentown, and married Sept. 11, 1813, Hanna Graff, daughter of Captain George Graff, who was born Oct. 14, 1783 and died Aug. 10, 1821. On Jan. 19, 1823, he married Elizabeth Graff, daughter of Martin Graff. He died in Crawford county, Pa., June 15, 1872. He had one daughter, Elizabeth, who married Jonathan Saeger, of Saegertown.

78. Christian Bertsch was born Aug. 17, 1753 and died July 8, 1819. His wife, Juliana, was born Sept. 12, 1758 and died Sept. 7, 1837. They are buried at Indianland church, Lehigh township, Northampton county.

79. John Saeger, son of Nicholas and Maria Barbara Saeger, and grandson of John Nicholas and Anna Barbara Saeger, was born Sept. 25, 1765 and died Aug. 10, 1830. He married Magdalena Ritter and had ten children.

80. George Smull was born in Germantown, Pa., July 22, 1764. He was adopted by George and Maria Elizabeth Koehler, of Egypt, and married June 22, 1792, Susanna Levan, who was born March 12, 1770 and died Aug. 18, 1826. He died Oct. 3, 1815. One of his descendants was the original compiler of Smull's Handbook.

81. Sarah Grob married Theodore Storb, an organist at Egypt church. The family removed to New Hanover, Montgomery county, where Mrs. Storb died Dec. 4, 1830, and is buried in the Lutheran church graveyard. A son, Albert Storb, resides in Pottstown.

144   RECORDS OF EGYPT REFORMED CHURCH.

82. Elizabeth Schwager, the eldest daughter of Henry and Adelaide Grob was born June 4, 1751 and died Jan. 26, 1835. Her husband, Peter Schwager, was born March 10, 1753 and died Nov. 23, 1827. They had no children.

83. David Music was a son of Samuel Music, who died in March, 1780 and his wife, Dorothea. Dorothea Music subsequently married Andrew Knedler.

84. David Biery was born in 1772 and died Jan. 7, 1827. He married Susanna Mickley, who was born Oct. 19, 1773 and died Nov. 21, 1872. Their children were: Peter, Joseph, David, Stephen Margaret, wife of Peter Kern, Lydia, wife of Jonas Yundt, Salome, wife of Ludwig Schmidt, Catharina, Magdalena, and Susanna, wife of William H. Blumer.

85. David Deshler, son of Adam and Maria Catharina Deshler, was born Sept. 17, 1778 and died March 19, 1827. He married Catharine Fogel, who was born May 27, 1777 and died Aug. 15, 1842.

86. Barbara Hartman was a daughter of Daniel and Catharina Margaret Roth and was born Aug. 16, 1771.

87. Frederick Biery was born April 22, 1770, in Berks county, and married, Aug. 4, 1795, Salome, daughter of Gottfried Knauss. Mrs. Biery was born March 16, 1773 and died Sept. 5, 1826. She had twelve children, six sons and six daughters. Frederick Biery married the second time, April 26, 1827, Catharine Frederick. He died Aug. 31, 1846.

88. Gottfried Knauss, son of Gottfried and Anna Eva Knauss, was born Jan. 15, 1742. He was a blacksmith and ring was born Feb. 28, 1770, and died Feb. 25, 1833. He Feb. 15, 1806. His wife, Anna Maria Griesemer, was born July 11, 1752 and died Sept 24, 1823.

89. Peter Leisenring, son of Conrad and Sibilla Leisenring was born Feb. 28, 1770, and died Feb. 25, 1833. He married Susanna Schad, who was born May 1, 1774, and died May 17, 1837. They are buried at Sunbury, Pa.

90. David Deshler, the second son of David and Catharina Deshler, was a surveyor and assisted in the government surveys of Kansas and Missouri. Later he became a merchant in St. Louis, and in Tuscumbia, Ala. He conceived the idea and successfully carried out the project of building a railroad from Tuscumbia to Decatur in 1834 or 1835, the first road west of the Alleghenies and probably the third in the United States. A son, David, was drowned while a student at West Point. James, his other son, graduated from West Point and became a brigadier general in the Confederate army. He was killed

at Chickamauga. David Deshler died at an advanced age in Georgia.

91. George Jacob Roth was a son of John and Sophia Dorothea Roth, and his wife Catharina, was a daughter of Daniel and Catharina Margaret Roth.

92. Daniel Grubb married Catharina Graff and removed to Crawford county, where he died May 31, 1883. Among his sons are Joseph Grubb, of Saegertown, Pa., and Stephen Grubb, of Cheney, Washington.

93. John Saeger of Lehigh township, Northampton county, was born May 3, 1743 and died Feb. 7, 1820. His wife, Anna Catharina, was born July 14, 1749 and died Oct. 18, 1809.

94. John Deichman was born Jan. 30, 1776 and died May 17, 1856. He married, Oct. 10, 1799, Maria Susanna Steckel, who was born Oct. 11, 1780 and died July 10, 1832.

95. Peter Kohler, son of Jacob Kohler, Jr. and wife Maria Barbara, was born June 18, 1768 and died May 24, 1848. He married in 1801, Susanna Kern, who was born Sept. 16, 1767 and died Nov. 2, 1846.

96. Peter Kohler, son of Peter and Juliana Margaret Kohler, was born Dec. 18, 1780 and died Jan. 23, 1871. He married, Sept. 3, 1801, Catharina Steckel, who was born Dec. 12, 1782, and died June 3, 1853.

97. Henry Blumer, son of Rev. Abraham Blumer, was born Oct. 18, 1778 and died Aug. 13, 1824. His wife, Sarah Mickley, was born Nov. 27, 1786 and died Jan. 25, 1859.

98. Solomon Graff, son of Martin Graff, married Elizabeth Snyder and removed to Crawford county, Pa., where he died in Meadville, on May 17, 1828.

99. George Yundt, son of Jacob Yundt, was born March 30, 1744 and died April 13, 1828. He was many years a justice of the peace. He marrier, March 26, 1771, Eva Catharina Knauss, who was born Aug. 15, 1750 and died April 22, 1818.

100. Peter Ruch, son of Lorenz Ruch, was born Feb. 28, 1779 and died Nov. 19, 1838. He was captain of a troop of cavalry from Whitehall township in the War of 1812. Subsequently he became active in militia organizations, rising to the rank of brigadier general of militia in 1821. He married, March 13, 1801, Susanna Schreiber, daughter of Philip Jacob Schreiber.

101. David Laury was a prominent citizen of North Whitehall township and held various commissions from captain to major general in the state militia organization. He was a member of the State Legislature and in 1868 was elected associate

judge of Lehigh county and re-elected in 1873. He died Sept. 28, 1883.

102. Jacob Schreiber was born Jan. 3, 1780 and died Dec. 25, 1865. His wife, Eve Catherine Leisenring, was born Oct. 3, 1786 and died May 31, 1866. This daughter, Salome, married Judge Jacob Dillinger.

103. These two entries of marriages in 1752 are in the handwriting of Rev. John Jacob Wissler. A special meeting of the Coetus of the Reformed Church was held in Philadelphia on this day, Dec. 12, 1752, to which Rev. Wissler sent his excuses, one of which was that he had an engagement to marry a couple.

104. This entry was made by Rev. J. Daniel Gros.

105. This marriage was performed by Rev. Abraham Blumer.

106. The first two entries of deaths were made by Rev Wissler, the third by Rev. Gros, and the last two by Rev. Blumer.

107. The names of the children confirmed were recorded by Rev. Wissler.

108. These memoranda were also written by Rev. Wissler.

INDEX

———, Jacob, 49
———, Maria Magdalena, 10
———, Catharina, 10
Abbot, Catharina, 89
Abbot, William, 89
Acker, Christina, 97
Acker, Daniel, 97
Acker, George, 97
Aeckert, Anna Margaretha, 10
Aeckert, Georg Nicolaus, 10
Aeckert, Joh. Georg, 10
Albert, Esther, 103
Albert, Jacob, 103
Albrecht, Catharina, 28, 52, 127, 130
Albrecht, Catharina Hanna, 130
Albrecht, Joseph, 52, 127, 130
Allander, Henrich, 118
Allander, Jacob, 118
Allander, Magdalena, 118
Alleman, Christian, 14
Alleman, Elisabetha Barbara, 14
Alleman, Jacob, 14
Allenter, Jacob, 124
Allenter, Maria, 124
Allenter, William, 124
Altmann, Maria Catharina, 10, 11
Altmann, Peter, 11
Amhaeuser, Catharina, 77
Andreas, Elisabetha, 11, 137
Andreas, Martin, 11, 137
Andreas, Wilhelm, 11
Anewalt, Catharina, 127
Anewalt, Elisabeth, 114
Anewalt, John, 127
Anewalt, Peter, 114
Anthoni, Elisabeth, 46, 56
Anthoni, Jacob, 46
Antoni, Maria Elisabeth, 45
Antoni, Nicolaus, 45
Anthoni, Philip, 46, 49
Anthoni, Sara, 56
Anthony, Elisabeth, 52, 58, 62,
Anthony, John, 51
Anthony, Maria, 58
Anthony, Peter, 137
Anthony, Philip, 51, 58, 62
Anthony, William, 62
Anton, Elisabeth, 49
Anton, John, 129
Anton, Maria Elisabeth, 49
Anton, Philip, 46, 49
Anton, Susanna, 129
App, Barbara, 104
App, Daniel, 127
App, Elisabeth, 127
App, Friedrich, 104
Arndt, Catharina Eva, 5
Arndt, Clementz, 5
Arndt, Maria, 5
Arner, Jacob, 40
Arner, (Jacob) Ulrich, 7
Arner, Anna Elizabeth, 137
Arner, Dorothea, 137
Arner, Eva Catharina, 37
Arner, Felix, 10, 137
Arner, Heinrich, 7
Arner, Jacob, 37, 39
Arner, Johannes, 12
Arner, John, 137
Arner, Margareth, 37, 39, 40
Arner, Margaretha, 12
Arner, Salome, 137

Arner, Susanna, 40
Arner, Ulrich, 12
Arner, William, 137
Arnert, Elisabetha, 10
Arnert, Felix, 10
Arnert, Jacob, 132
Asman, Tilghman, 125
Asman, Eliza, 125
Asman, John, 125
Bachman, Elisabeth, 131
Bachmann, Lydia, 112
Baehr, Appollonia, 15
Baer, Christoph, 10
Baer, Jacob, 55
Baer, Johannes, 28, 40
Baer, Maria Elisabeth, 55
Baer, Susanna, 28, 40
Baerstein, Daniel, 73
Baerstein, Robert, 73
Baertch, Johannes, 31
Baertch, John, 31
Baertsch, Barbara, 112, 113
Baertsch, Caroline, 113
Baertsch, Catharina, 31, 112
Baertsch, Christian, 72, 73, 104
Baertsch, Daniel, 112
Baertsch, Eliza, 93
Baertsch, Jacob, 112, 113
Baertsch, John, 92, 93, 105, 106, 109,
   113, 116, 117
Baertsch, Juliana, 72, 73
Baertsch, Sarah Anne, 105
Baertsch, Susanna, 92, 93, 105, 106,
   109, 113, 116, 117
Baertsch, Thomas, 117
Bahl, Henrich, 130
Baillet, Eva, 22
Baillet, Susanna, 18, 19
Baker, Elisabeth, 120, 126
Baker, Eliza Ann, 126
Baker, Joseph, 120, 126
Baker, Philena, 120
Baliet, Catharina, 13, 14
Baliet, Magdalena, 14
Baliet, Margreth, 70
Baliet, Maria Catharina, 14
Baliet, Paul, 15
Balliet, Abraham, 36
Balliet, Anna, 62
Balliet, Barbara, 36
Balliet, Catharina, 29, 31, 41, 47,
   49, 56, 58, 62, 66, 67, 93
Balliet, Elisabeth, 66, 98
Balliet, Eva, 25
Balliet, Johannes, 31, 36, 58, 62
Balliet, John, 25, 29, 41, 47, 49, 56,
   66, 67, Balliet, Joseph, 44, 70
Balliet, Magdalena, 29, 36, 39, 49, 52
Balliet, Margreth, 44
Balliet, Maria Catharina, 141
Balliet, Niclaus, 48
Balliet, Paul, 34, 35, 90, 93, 98,
   136, 141
Balliet, Stephan, 17, 29, 36, 49, 52,
   49, 73
Balliet, Stephanus, 39, 75
Balliet, Stephen, 71, 141
Balliet, Susanna, 71, 73, 75
Bartsch, Barbara, 121
Bartsch, Jacob, 121
Bax, Wilhelm, 69, 81
Beck, Anna Maria, 14

Beck, Elisabeth, 94
Beck, Peter, 14
Beck, Theobald, 14
Beck, Wilhelm, 94
Becker, Barbara, 76
Becker, Daniel, 73, 74
Becker, Elisabeth, 79
Becker, Eva, 74, 76, 79, 84, 97
Becker, Friedrich, 74, 76, 79, 84, 97,
Becker, Jonathan, 97
Becker, Margreth, 73
Becker, Susanna, 84
Becker, Susannah, 76
Behr, Michael, 133
Behr, Peter, 133
Beigy, Charlotte, 104
Beigy, Jacob, 74, 85
Beigy, Maria, 85
Beigy, Michael, 85
Beigy, Salome, 75, 85
Beil, Balthazar, 141
Beil, Christina, 24, 107, 110
Beil, Conrad, 93, 143
Beil, Elizabeth, 141
Beil, Hanna, 86, 109
Beil, Henrich, 20, 51, 86, 109
Beil, Henry, 141
Beil, Maria, 93
Beil, Marie Elisabeth, 20
Beil, Peter, 24, 107, 110
Beiry, Abraham, 71
Beiry, Anna Maria, 96, 103, 105
Beiry, David, 71
Beiry, Delila, 71
Beiry, Jacob, 71
Beiry, Joseph, 144
Beiry, Peter, 96
Beiry, Salome, 71, 96, 120
Beiry, Susanna, 71
Beisel, Aaron Josiah, 131
Beisel, Elisabeth, 111
Beisel, Jacob, 127, 131
Beisel, John, 111
Beisel, Sarah, 127, 131
Beisel, Sarah Ann, 127
Benny, John Reinhard, 137
Benny, Regina Louisa, 137
Benter, Catharina, 9
Benter, Jacob, 9
Berentz, Georg, 46
Berentz, Magdalena, 46
Berentz, Margreth, 46
Berger, Conrad, 20
Berger, Elisabeth, 20
Berger, Maria Elisabeth, 20
Berndt, Elisabeth, 88, 90, 97, 102
Berndt, Franklin, 102
Berndt, James, 90
Berndt, Thomas, 88
Berndt, Tobias, 88, 90, 97, 102
Berret, Johannes, 11
Bertsch, Barbara, 127
Bertsch, Christian, 23, 43, 143,
Bertsch, Christina, 23
Bertsch, Daniel, 123
Bertsch, Jacob, 127
Bertsch, Johannes, 5
Bertsch, John, 123
Bertsch, Joshua, 127
Bertsch, Juliana, 43, 143
Bertsch, Susanna, 123
Beuri, Elisabeth, 42
Beuri, Henrich, 42, 56
Beuri, Salome, 42
Beutelmann, Maria, 107
Beutelmann, Elias, 107
Beutelmann, Valentin, 107
Beyer, Henrich, 91

Beyer, Susanna, 91
Bibelheimer, Anna Margareth, 95
Bibelheimer, David, 96
Bibelheimer, Georg, 95
Bibelheimer, George, 97
Bibelheimer, Maria Margreth, 97
Bieber, John, 79, 90
Bieber, Julianna, 79
Bieber, Magdalena, 79, 90
Biege, Elisabeth, 122, 128
Biege, Jackson, 104
Biege, John, 122, 128
Biege, Joseph, 130
Biege, Joseph Henry, 130
Biege, Judith, 128
Biege, Lydia, 130
Biege, Michael, 130
Biege, Rebecca, 130
Biege, Susanna, 104
Biegily, Esther, 88
Biegily, Jacob, 88, 103
Biegily, Maria, 88, 103
Biegily, Thomas, 103
Biegy, Anna Maria, 81, 88
Biegy, Catharina, 80
Biegy, Charlotta, 98
Biegy, Charlotte, 106
Biegy, Edward, 74
Biegy, Elisabeth, 76, 78, 79, 81, 84, 103, 110
Biegy, Esther, 103
Biegy, Jacob, 81, 88
Biegy, John, 76, 78, 79, 81, 103
Biegy, Michael, 78, 80, 99
Biegy, Monroe, 104
Biegy, Nathan, 98
Biegy, Peter, 76, 98, 104, 106
Biegy, Salome, 80
Biegy, Sara, 81, 85
Biegy, Sophia, 99
Biegy, Susanna, 96, 99
Biegyly, Adam, 115
Biegyly, Anna Maria, 99
Biegyly, Jacob, 99, 115
Biegyly, Maria, 115
Biegyly, William, 98]
Biery, Abraham, 63, 65, 68, 69, 75, 79
Biery, Anna, 63
Biery, Anna Maria, 88, 101, 122
Biery, Caroline, 108
Biery, Catharina, 62, 69, 73, 79, 81, 77, 101, 144
Biery, Charlotte, 89
Biery, Daniel, 58
Biery, David, 57, 64, 65, 70, 74, 75, 80, 81, 87, 90, 91, 94, 103, 129, 144
Biery, Debora, 73
Biery, Eli, 91
Biery, Elisabeth, 79, 89, 110
Biery, Eliza, 88, 89
Biery, Esther, 71, 112
Biery, Friedrich, 58, 62
Biery, Frederick, 144
Biery, Hanna, 81
Biery, Henrich, 62, 69, 73, 77, 79, 81, 87
Biery, Henry, 128
Biery, Hetty, 124, 129
Biery, Jacob, 75, 76, 86, 91, 92, 98, 100, 108, 109, 115, 121
Biery, John, 110
Biery, Joseph, 57, 96, 103, 106, 108, 120, 121, 127, 128
Biery, Lydia,
Biery, Magdalena, 68, 70, 91, 144
Biery, Margaret, 144
Biery, Maria, 96

Biery, Maria Salome, 69
Biery, Marianna, 129
Biery, Mathilda, 103
Biery, Peter, 88, 89, 91, 101, 103, 105, 122, 144,
Biery, Polly, 128
Biery, Reuben, 75
Biery, Salome, 58, 62, 63, 68, 65, 69, 75, 76, 79, 86, 87, 91, 92, 98, 100, 103, 106, 108, 109, 115, 121, 127, 144
Biery, Sarah Anne, 101
Biery, Stephan, 80
Biery, Stephen, 144
Biery, Susan, 127
Biery, Susanna, 57, 62, 64, 70, 74, 75, 80, 81, 87, 90, 91, 94, 103, 121, 144
Biery, Wilhelm, 77
Biery, William, 76, 120
Biery, William Joseph, 127
Biggs, Charles, 123
Bigily, Margaretha, 58
Blank, G. Adam, 52
Blank, Georg Adam, 34, 35
Blank, Magdalena, 52
Bloos, Catharina, 121
Bloos, Joel, 121
Bloos, Jonas, 121
Blos, Caroline, 111
Blos, Catharina, 111, 116
Blos, Jonas, 111, 116
Blos, Peter, 116
Bloss, Anna Magdalena, 10
Bloss, Conrad, 10
Blumer, Abr., 57
Blumer, Abraham, 36, 140, 145, 146
Blumer, Henrich, 61
Blumer, Henry, 145
Blumer, Sara, 61
Blumer, Susanna, 36
Blumer, William H., 127, 144
Boehm, Rev.
Boggs, Benjamin, 90, 92, 95
Boggs, Carl, 92
Boggs, Elisabeth, 90, 92, 96
Boggs, James, 112
Boggs, Owen, 117
Boggs, Ozias, 108
Boggs, Stephanus, 90
Boggs, Susanna, 96, 108, 112, 117, 123
Boggs, William, 108, 112, 117, 123
Borger, Anna Maria, 123
Borger, Elias, 126
Borger, John Jacob, 121
Borger, Joseph, 112, 115, 120, 123
Borger, Lydia, 120, 123
Borger, Peter Daniel, 120
Borger, Philip, 121, 126
Borger, Salome, 126
Boryer, John, 61
Bottner, Jacob, 53
Bottner, Maria, 53
Box, Ludwig, 83
Box, Magdalena, 81, 83
Box, Susanna Catharina, 131
Box, Wilhelm, 83
Box, William, 131
Boyer, Elisabeth, 124
Boyer, William, 124
Braumiller, Barbara, 61, 63
Braumiller, Daniel, 63
Braumiller, Friederich, 61, 63
Braumiller, Georg, 61
Braun, Adam, 76, 86, 93, 117
Braun, Anna Margreth, 93
Braun, Daniel, 107
Braun, David, 63

Braun, Elisabeth, 109, 111, 115, 121, 123, 125, 129
Braun, Emilia, 111
Braun, Ephriam, 121
Braun, Esther, 120
Braun, Hanna, 115
Braun, Isaac, 76, 125
Braun, Jacob, 82, 111
Braun, Joel, 109, 111, 115, 121, 123, 125, 129
Braun, Juliana, 107
Braun, Lydia, 86
Braun, Magdalena, 63, 112
Braun, Margreth, 76, 82, 85, 86, 107, 117
Braun, Maria, 63
Braun, Salome, 100, 107
Braun, Sarah, 108
Brechan, Jesse, 122
Breinig, Benjamin, 123, 126
Breinig, Esther, 123
Breinig, Hetty, 126
Breisch, Barbara. 90, 123
Breisch, Carl, 90
Breisch, Catharina, 63, 76
Breisch, Henrich, 63, 76
Breisch, Jacob, 90, 123
Breisch, Joseph, 123
Breish, Barbara, 128
Breish, Carolina, 128
Breish, Jacob, 90, 128
Brengel, Anna Barbara, 9
Brengel, Christian, 5, 6, 7, 9
Brengel, Peter, 9
Bretz, Anna Margreth, 41
Bretz, Margreth, 41
Bretz, Philip, 41
Bricker, Anna Magdalena, 5
Bricker, Jacob, 5
Britenner, Anna Maria, 10
Britenner, Joseph, 10
Brown, Adam, 122
Brown, Elisabeth, 122
Brown, Margretha, 122
Brown, Maria, 122, 127
Brown, Paul, 122, 127
Brown, Samuel Adam, 127
Bruecker, Jacob, 133
Bruecker, Johann Adam, 133
Bruegel, Elisabeth, 131
Bruegel, Jacob, 131
Bruegel, Michael, 131
Buchman, Anna Maria, 130
Buchman, Daniel, 36
Buchman, Dewald, 130
Buchman, Jacob, 16
Buchman, Margretha, 13, 16
Buchman, Wilhelmina, 130
Buchmann, Daniel, 68
Buchmann, Jacob, 60, 91
Buchmann, Johann Jacob, 30
Buchmann, Magdalena, 60, 68, 91
Buchmann, Maria Barbara, 68
Box, Susanna, 131
Bueri, Jacob, 36
Bueri, Catharina, 53
Bueri, David, 51, 48, 49, 51, 56, 54, 58
Bueri, Fridrich, 37, 51, 56
Bueri, Friedrich, 51
Bueri, Hanna, 56
Bueri, Henrich, 34, 36, 46, 51, 53
Bueri, Joseph, 53
Bueri, Lydia, 54
Bueri, Magdalena, 42, 47, 51
Bueri, Maria Catharina, 34
Bueri, Maria Margreth, 51
Bueri, Maria Salome, 34, 39

Bueri, Maria Susanna, 36
Bueri, Peter, 49
Bueri, Salome, 46, 49, 51, 53, 56
Bueri, Susanna, 48, 51, 54, 56
Buery, Abraham, 59, 60
Buery, David, 60
Buery, Henrich, 60
Buery, Joseph, 59
Buery, Maria Salome, 60
Buery, Salome, 59, 60
Buery, Susanna, 60
Burckhalder, Eva Catharina, 22
Burckhalder, Peter, 22
Burckhalter, Anna Magdalena, 7
Burckhalter, Eva Catherina, 16
Burckhalter, Susanna, 16
Burckhalter, Ulrich, 9
Burckholder, Ann Barbara, 17
Burckholder, Maria Barbara, 16
Burckholder, Peter, 16
Burger, Dewalt, 116
Burger, Elisabeth, 70, 86
Burger, Friedrich, 49
Burger, Hanna, 88
Burger, John, 86
Burger, Lydia, 116
Burger, Margreth, 49
Burger, Moses, 88
Burger, Samuel, 88
Burghalder, Adam, 22
Burghalder, Barbara, 54, 55
Burghalder, Carl, 52
Burghalder, Catharina, 46
Burghalder, Charlotte, 55
Burghalder, Daniel 40
Burghalder, Dorothea, 27, 29, 30, 33, 36, 39, 40, 41, 43, 46, 49, 52
Burghalder, Elisabeth, 49, 55
Burghalder, Eva Catharina, 18, 22, 31, 33, 38, 46
Burghalder, Henrich, 27, 54, 55
Burghalder, Joh. Peter, 24, 27
Burghalder, Joseph, 43
Burghalder, Magdalena, 27, 29, 36
Burghalder, Maria Barbara, 18, 23
Burghalder, Peter, 18, 22, 29, 30, 31, 33, 36, 38, 39, 40, 41, 43, 46, 49, 51, 52, 55
Burghalder, Salome, 33
Burghalter, Anna Barbara, 5
Burghalter, Barbara, 5
Burghalter, Elisabeth Barbara, 137
Burghalter, Maria Barbel, 10
Burghalter, Peter, 65, 135
Burghalter, Ulrich, 5, 135
Burkhalter, Catharina, 68, 83
Burkhalter, Eva Catherina, 11
Burkhalter, Henrich, 66, 74
Burkhalter, Maria, 104
Burkhalter, Peter, 65
Burkhalter, Anna Maria, 79
Burkhalter, Barbara, 57, 58. 60, 63, 65, 66, 69, 74, 75, 77, 83, 90, 91, 96, 98, 102, 104, 109,
Burkhalter, Carl, 60, 94, 96
Burkhalter, Catharina, 65. 71, 75, 76, 79, 82, 85, 86, 89, 90, 01, 92, 95, 96, 98, 104,109, 112, 116, 118, 121
Burkhalter, Charles, 101, 109
Burkhalter, Charlotte, 59, 63, 65, 66, 68,
Burkhalter, Christina, 104
Burkhalter, Daniel, 76, 79, 83, 85, 86, 89, 91, 95, 96, 98, 104, 109, 112, 116, 118, 121
Burkhalter, David, 74, 129
Burkhalter, Debora, 77, 121, 129

Burkhalter, Edward, 71
Burkhalter, Eli, 98
Burkhalter, Elisabeth, 85, 91, 92
Burkhalter, Erwine, 101
Burkhalter, Esther, 57
Burkhalter, Eva Catharina, 13, 14, 57, 142
Burkhalter, George, 82
Burkhalter, Hanna, 90
Burkhalter, Henrich, 58, 60, 63, 66, 69, 75, 77, 91, 98, 104
Burkhalter, Henrich Peter, 129
Burkhalter, Henry, 57, 109
Burkhalter, J. Peter, 66
Burkhalter, Johann Peter, 68
Burkhalter, John Peter, 59, 63, 65, 142
Burkhalter, Joseph, 83, 85, 90, 96, 98, 102
Burkhalter, Kitty Ann, 121
Burkhalter, Levina, 102
Burkhalter, Magdalena, 13, 96, 101, 109, 141
Burkhalter, Maria, 98
Burkhalter, Maria Salome, 69
Burkhalter, Mary Anna, 129
Burkhalter, Nathan, 83
Burkhalter, Peter, 9, 13, 14, 57, 68, 71, 75, 76, 79, 82, 85, 86, 89, 92, 116, 139, 142
Burkhalter, Rebecca, 109
Burkhalter, Ruben, 98, 109
Burkhalter, Sarah, 109
Burkhalter, Solomon, 76
Burkhalter, Stephan, 112
Burkhalter, Stephanus, 66
Burkhalter, Susan, 121
Burkhalter, Thomas, 96
Burkhalter, Ulrich, 139
Burkhalter, Wilhelm, 79
Burkhalter, William, 129
Buskirch, Anna Maria, 101
Butz, Abraham, 105, 111, 119
Butz, Elisabeth, 105, 109, 113, 118
Butz, Eliza Jane, 113
Butz, Esther, 105, 111, 119
Butz, Johann Peter, 105
Butz, Nathan, 118
Butz, Peter, 65
Butz, Susanna, 65
Butz, Thomas, 105, 109, 113, 118
Butz, Thomas Franklin, 109
Canke, Anna Maria, 129
Canke, Catharina, 129
Canke, James, 129
Carey, Benjamin, 120
Carey, Daniel, 120
Carey, Susanna, 120
Christein, Elisabeth, 85
Christein, John, 83, 85
Christein, Salome, 83, 85
Christein, Solomon, 83
Colver, Charles, 130
Colver, Magdalena, 130
Confer, Elisabeth, 101, 131
Confer, Henrich, 101
Confer, Levina, 101
Daeschler, Charles, 70
Daeschler, Catharina, 70
Daniel, Catharina, 99
Daniel, Peter, 99
Daubenspeck, Anna Magdalena, 10
Daubenspeck, Jacob, 10
Daubenspeck, Juliana. 10
Daut, Daniel, 62
Daut, Elisabath, 62
Daut, John, 62
Daut, Maria, 62

Dean, Tilghman, 120
Dean, William, 120
Deichman, John, 145
Derr, Elisabeth, 97
Derr, Jacob, 111
Derr, Maria, 111
Deschler, Adam, 18, 22
Deschler, Anna Levina, 119
Deschler, Anne, 111, 119
Deschler, Anne Caroline, 107
Deschler, Catharina, 18, 22, 66, 68, 88. 109, 144
Deschler, David, 18, 66, 68, 88, 109
Deschler, Debora, 114
Deschler, Elisa, 117
Deschler, Elisabeth, 101, 116
Deschler, Eliza, 107
Deschler, Jacob Grimm, 101
Deschler, James, 101, 107, 116, 117,
Deschler, John, 66, 114, 119
Deschler, Magdalena, 18, 22
Deschler, Maria Magdalena, 19
Deschler, Maria Susanna, 22
Deschler, Peter, 18, 19, 22
Deschler, Susanna, 13, 18
Deschler, Walter John, 114
Deshler, Adam, 8 , 25, 26, 28, 29, 30, 34, 37, 38, 136, 137, 139, 140, 141,144
Deshler, Appolonia, 136
Deshler, Barbara, 141
Deshler, Catharina, 24, 30, 37, 50, 51, 52, 54, 57, 72
Deshler, David, 50, 51, 52, 54, 57, 72, 137, 144, 145
Deshler, David James Franklin, 130
Deshler, Debora, 72
Deshler, Elisabeth, 37, 38, 130, 131
Deshler, Elisabeth Anna, 123,
Deshler, George, 37, 137
Deshler, Jacob, 50
Deshler, James, 123, 130, 131, 144
Deshler, Magdalena, 25, 26, 28, 30, 35, 37, 54
Deshler, Maria, 57
Deshler, Maria Catharina, 25, 26, 28, 29, 30, 34, 38, 144
Deshler, Maria Susanna, 28
Deshler, Peter, 25, 26, 28, 30, 35, 37, 54, 140
Deshler, Salome, 34
Deshler, Sara, 37
Deuber, Eva, 82
Deuber, Georg Adam, 82
Deuber, Margreth, 78
Deubert, Christina, 68
Deubert, G. Adam, 40
Deubert, John, 54
Deubert, Margreth, 77
Deubert, Maria Barbara, 54
Deubert, Maria Eva, 40
Deubert, Michael, 40
Deubert, Michel, 38
Deubert, Susanna, 48
Deubert, Tobias, 68
Deyli, Christian, 52
Deyli, Catharina, 59
Deyli, Maria Catharina, 52
Dick, Casper, 78, 80
Dick, Catharina, 78
Dick, Elisabeth, 80
Diderer, Solomon, 45
Diehl, Abraham, 89
Diehl, Anna, 61
Diehl, Barbara, 61
Diehl, John, 61, 89
Diehl, Salome, 89
Dieter, Anna Maria, 11

Dieter, Elisabetha, 11
Dill, Rev., 57
Dillinger, Jacob, 146
Dincky, Jacob, 48
Dincky, Susanna, 48
Dinky, George, 82, 85, 93
Dinky, Jacob, 58
Dinky, Jonas, 58
Dinky, Peter, 48
Dinky, Susanna, 58, 82, 85, 93
Dodendorf, George E., 123
Dodendorf, Lydia, 123
Doderer, Catharina, 30
Doderer, Catharina, Elisabeth, 45
Doderer, Elisabeth, 45
Doderer, Maria Eva, 33
Doderer, Solomon, 33
Doeschler, Barbara, 14
Doeschler, Catharina, 14
Doeschler, David, 11
Doeschler, Joh. Adam, 7, 10
Doeschler, Johann Peter, 14
Doeschler, Magdalena, 13, 14
Doeschler, Peter, 13, 14
Dorner, Elisabeth, 53
Dorner, Jacob, 53
Dorney, Adam, 136
Dorney, Catharina, 68
Dorney, Peter, 68
Dorni, Daniel, 15
Dory, Benjamin, 56, 59, 64
Dory, Catharina, 64
Dory, Jan Petrus, 59
Dory, Magdalena, 56, 59, 64
Dory, Maria Magdalena, 56
Dotterer, Sophia, 138
Drachsel, Catharina, 13, 56
Drachsel, Christian, 31
Drachsel, John, 56
Drachsel, John Nicolaus, 51
Drachsel, Nicklaus, 50
Drachsel, Peter, 50
Drachsel, Susanna, 50
Draxel, Adam, 49
Draxel, Anna Maria, 48
Draxel, Catharina, 48, 56
Draxel, Johannes, 8
Draxel, John, 48, 56
Draxel, Magdalena, 8
Draxel, Maria, 49
Draxel, Peter, 48, 54
Draxel, Salome, 48
Draxel, Solomon, 54
Draxel, Sybilla, 54
Drein, Georg, 56, 57
Drein, Jacob, 56
Drein, Maria Barbara, 56, 57
Drein, Susanna, 57
Dreisbach, Apollonia, 141
Dreisbach, Jost, 20
Dreissbach, Jonas, 73
Dreissbach, Michael, 73
Dreissbach, Susanna, 73
Dubs, Catharina, 102, 118
Dubs, Harrison Weinbert, 118
Dubs, Joseph S., 120
Dubs, Robert, 102
Dubs, Solomon, 102, 118
Duerr, Jacob, 70
Duerr, Joseph, 70
Duerr, Maria, 70
Dussinger, Johannes, 36
Dussinger, Margretha, 36
Dussinger, Maria Magdalena, 36
Eberhard, Anna Eva, 8, 132, 141
Eberhard, Friedrich, 8, 132
Eberhard, Magdalena, 103
Eberhard, Peter, 103

Eberhardt, Catharina, 7
Eberhardt, David, 103, 110, 116
Eberhardt, Elisabeth, 103, 110, 116
Eberhardt, Friederich, 7
Eberhardt, Magdalena, 118
Eberhardt, Mary Anne, 116
Eberhardt, Nathan, 103
Eberhardt, Peter, 118
Eckert, Anna Margarethaa, 11
Eckert, Johann Georg, 11
Eckhert, Maria Christina, 11
Edelman, Maria Elizabeth, 141
Egender, Johannes, 5
Egender, Margaretha, 5
Ehrenhard, Jacob, 42
Ehrenhard, John, 42
Ehrenhard, Margreth, 42
Ehret, Charlotte, 60, 70, 75
Ehret, Georg, 60, 70, 75
Eisenbrown, Charlotta Barbara, 124
Eisenbrown, Daniel, 124
Eisenbrown, William Jonas, 124
Eisenhardt, Catharina, 129
Eisenhardt, Elisabeth, 80, 100
Eisenhardt, Eliza, 80
Eisenhardt, Esther, 119
Eisenhardt, George, 100
Eisenhardt, Sarah Anne, 100
Engelhard, Andreas, 133
Engelhard, Anna Maria Catharina, 133
Esch, Susanna, 54
Fatzinger, Eva, 132
Fatzinger, George, 132
Fatzinger, Valentin, 13, 14
Faust, Abraham, 34
Faust, Barbara, 31, 44, 49, 86, 142
Faust, Catharina, 34, 37, 40, 71
Faust, David, 83
Faust, Georg, 71
Faust, Henrich, 34, 37, 40
Faust, Henry, 142
Faust, Jacob Philip, 44
Faust, Johannes, 37
Faust, Jonas, 73, 83, 87, 98
Faust, Jonathan, 86
Faust, Maria Catharina, 40
Faust, Paulus, 73
Faust, Philip, 31, 49, 86, 142
Faust, Susanna, 73, 83, 86, 87, 98
Feber, Amandes, 126
Feber, Jesse, 124, 126
Feber, Sarah, 124, 126
Fehler, Caroline, 108
Fehler, Elisabeth, 100, 108, 109, 112, 115, 124
Fehler, Eliza, 115
Fehler, George, 100, 108, 109, 112, 115, 124
Fehler, Louisa, 124
Fehler, William, 100
Feichterr, Christoph, 10
Feigner, Catharina, 41, 43
Feigner, Elisabeth, 41
Feigner, Jacob, 41
Feigner, Johannes, 43
Feigner, John, 41
Feldhoff, Magdalena, 94
Feldhoff, William, 94
Fenstermacher, Abraham, 119, 122
Fenstermacher, Barbara, 31
Fenstermacher, Caroline, 119
Fenstermacher, Catharina, 39, 41, 43, 48
Fenstermacher, Christian, 31
Fenstermacher, Dewald, 39, 41, 43, 48
Fenstermacher, Elisabeth, 44, 48
Fenstermacher, Emilia Rosina, 122
Fenstermacher, Jacob, 44, 94

Fenstermacher, Johannes, 41, 44, 130
Fenstermacher, John, 122, 131
Fenstermacher, Magdalena, 39, 78
Fenstermacher, Margaretha, 120, 130
Fenstermacher, Margreth, 44
Fenstermacher, Maria, 119, 122
Fenstermacher, Michael, 86
Fenstermacher, Philip, 31. 120, 130
Fenstermacher, Rosina, 122, 130, 131
Fenstermacher, Salome, 43
Ferber, Jacob, 9, 133
Ferber, Johann Henrich, 133
Ferber, Susanna, 9
Fever, Jesse, 127
Fever, Sarah, 127
Filler, Catharina, 9
Filler, Maria Elisabeth, 9
Filler, Phillipp, 9
Fischer, Anna Maria, 31, 34, 38, 40, 43, 48, 72, 75
Fischer, Anthony, 67
Fischer, Anton, 71, 77
Fischer, Antony, 47
Fischer, Barbara, 37, 40, 43, 45, 46, 49, 51, 58, 61, 65, 67, 80, 120
Fischer, Carl, 61
Fischer, Catharina, 31
Fischer, Elisabeth, 34, 40, 46, 119
Fischer, Eva, 36
Fischer, Georg, 31, 34, 38, 40, 43, 48, 72, 75, 80, 82, 88, 119
Fischer, Henrich, 49
Fischer, Jacob, 34, 40, 80, 120
Fischer, James, 80
Fischer, Joh. Georg, 36
Fischer, Joh. Christian, 37
Fischer, Joh. Fridrich, 51
Fischer, Johannes, 43
Fischer, Jonas, 65
Fischer, Joseph, 58, 71
Fischer, Leonard, 37, 40, 43, 45, 46, 49, 50, 55, 58
Fischer, Leonhard, 49
Fischer, Leonhardt, 61, 65
Fischer, Magdalena, 46. 55, 82
Fischer, Maria, 65, 72, 80, 82, 88, 119
Fischer, Maria Anna, 88
Fischer, Maria Barbara, 50
Fischer, Nathan, 72
Fischer, Peter, 36, 40, 43, 48, 67, 119
Fischer, Salme, 71
Fischer, Salome, 76, 77
Fischer, Susanna, 31, 34, 76
Fischer, William, 119
Fisher, Anton, 76
Fisher, Barbara, 55, 128
Fisher, Catharina, 128
Fisher, Elisabeth, 131
Fisher, Jacob, 128
Fisher, James, 128
Fisher, Leonard, 51
Fisher, Maria Anna, 131
Fisher, Maria Barbara, 51
Fisher, Peter, 131
Fisher, Polly, 128
Fitzgerald, Mary, 121
Fitzgerald, Sally Anne, 117
Fitzgerald, Susanna, 117, 121
Fitzgerald, Thomas, 117, 121
Fleckinger, Jacob, 133
Fleckinger, Peter, 133
Fleckinger, Ulrich, 133
Flick, Juliana, 89
Flick, Margaretha, 11
Flick, Margreth, 100
Flick, Maria Margreth, 89, 94

152

Flick, Martin, 11
Flick, Paul, 89, 94, 100
Flick, Sara, 100
Flickinger, Adam, 61
Flickinger, Anna, 79
Flickinger, Anna Eva, 24, 25, 26, 29
Flickinger, Barbara, 11, 12, 13, 15, 21
Flickinger, Catharina, 13, 34, 37, 44, 55, 57, 59, 61, 65, 69, 72, 73, 74,, 76, 78, 92
Flickinger, Catharina Barbara, 6, 133
Flickinger, Catharina Elisabeth, 13
Flickinger, Catrina, 12
Flickinger, Christian, 15, 132
Flickinger, Daniel, 32, 63, 72, 73, 74, 76, 87
Flickinger, Elisabeth, 65
Flickinger, Eva, 15, 17, 21, 31, 37, 38, 40, 48, 50, 55, 58, 59
Flickinger, Eva Susanna, 17
Flickinger, Georg, 15, 17, 20, 21, 26, 31, 32, 37, 38, 40, 48, 50, 55, 58, 59, 66, 68, 70, 74, 78, 83, 87, 92
Flickinger, George, 5, 21, 29
Flickinger, Hans Georg, 7
Flickinger, J. Georg, 25
Flickinger, Jacob, 12, 13, 14, 15, 17, 18, 21, 24, 26, 42, 44, 49, 50, 51, 55, 57, 59, 65, 66, 69, 78
Flickinger, Joh. Georg, 24, 29
Flickinger, Joh. Jacob, 24
Flickinger, Joh. Michael, 12
Flickinger, Johan Peter, 15
Flickinger, Johann Georg, 13, 21
Flickinger, Johann Jacob, 12
Flickinger, Johannes, 17, 26
Flickinger, John, 72, 76
Flickinger, Lucae, 9
Flickinger, Luce, 6
Flickinger, Lucey, 7
Flickinger, Lucia, 5, 132
Flickinger, Lucin, 10
Flickinger, Lydia, 72, 74,
Flickinger, Magdalena, 47, 66, 68, 74, 78, 83, 87, 92, 70
Flickinger, Margareta, 23
Flickinger, Margreth, 15, 72
Flickinger, Maria Barbara, 12, 14, 15, 16, 17, 20, 23
Flickinger, Maria Elisabeth, 13, 17, 21, 24, 26, 42, 44, 49, 50, 55, 65, 66, 92
Flickinger, Maria Elisabetha, 15, 18
Flickinger, Maria Eva, 20, 21
Flickinger, Maria Magdalena, 14, 21, 26
Flickinger, Michael, 44
Flickinger, Peter, 11, 12, 13, 14, 15, 16, 17, 20, 21, 23, 26
Flickinger, Ruben, 83
Flickinger, Salme, 78
Flickinger, Susanna, 41, 44
Flickinger, Ulrich, 5, 6, 9, 12, 9, 132, 136
Fogel, Catharine, 144
Fohr, Jacob, 132
Fox, John Nicholas, 140
Fox, Margaret, 140
Frack, Anna, 122, 123, 124
Frack, Barbara, 48, 51
Frack, Catharina, 48
Frack, Daniel, 113, 114, 116, 124
Frack, Delila, 127, 128
Frack, Eleonora, 114
Frack, Elisabeth, 123

Frack, Hanna, 85, 86, 99, 101, 102, 120
Frack, Hannah, 78
Frack, Henry, 127, 128
Frack, Jacob, 48, 52, 123
Frack, Magdalena, 113
Frack, Maria, 114, 116
Frack, Maria Magdalena, 124
Frack, Michael, 78, 85, 86, 99, 101, 102, 120, 122, 124
Frack, Samuel, 124
Frack, Susanna, 104
Frack, Tobias, 52
Fraehn, Christina, 81
Fraehn, John, 81
Fraehn, Magdalena, 81
Frantz, Abraham, 123, 129
Frantz, Catharina, 129
Frantz, Christina Barbara, 11
Frantz, Elisabeth, 131
Frantz, Eva Elisabeth, 11
Frantz, Henrich, 121, 129
Frantz, Henrich Benjamin, 123
Frantz, Henry, 131
Frantz, Jacob, 23, 28, 45, 123, 130
Frantz, Jeanne, 13
Frantz, Joh. Georg., 23
Frantz, Joseph, 123
Frantz, Margreth, 23, 28, 45
Frantz, Margretha, 121, 129
Frantz, Peter, 11
Frantz, Polly, 123, 129
Frantz, Sally Anna, 121
Frantz, Salome, 121, 123
Frantz, Sarah, 130
Frantz, Susanna, 131
Frantz, Susanna Margreth, 28
Frantz, Thomas, 123
Frantz, William, 121
Franz, Abraham, 70
Franz, Carl, 95
Franz, Catharina, 59, 60,100, 110, 113
Franz, Christina, 73
Franz, Daniel, 75
Franz, Eli, 114
Franz, Elisabeth, 95, 103, 105
Franz, Eliza, 95
Franz, Esther, 107
Franz, Georg, 110
Franz, George, 60, 100
Franz, Henrich, 61, 63, 64, 70, 73, 75, 80, 82, 86, 89, 96, 105, 113, 114, 115, 117,
Franz, Jacob, 60, 61, 72, 73, 96, 101, 103, 107, 111, 112, 114, 118
Franz, Johan Georg, 59
Franz, John, 79
Franz, Joseph, 61, 108, 114, 117, 118, 120,
Franz, Lydia, 84, 112
Franz, Margreth, 60, 63, 64, 61, 70, 72, 73, 75, 80, 82, 84, 86, 89, 96, 105, 115,
Franz, Margretha, 114, 117
Franz, Maria Anna, 96
Franz, Mentor, 117
Franz, Peter, 60, 79
Franz, Ruben, 118
Franz, Salme, 79
Franz, Salome, 73, 96, 97, 101, 103, 107, 111, 112, 114. 117, 118, 120
Franz, Sarah, 101
Franz, William, 114, 118, 120
Frederick, Catharine, 144
Frey, Anna Maria, 41, 122
Frey, Barbara, 45
Frey, Catharina, 29, 30

Frey, Daniel, 122
Frey, Dennis, 122
Frey, George, 115
Frey, Jacob, 41
Frey, Leonhard, 29, 30
Frey, Magdalena, 115
Frey, Maria Elisabeth, 23, 45
Frey, Martin, 41, 45
Frey, Michael, 45, 122
Frey, Peter, 29
Frey, Sibilla, 41
Frey, Susanna, 41, 122
Frey, Sybilla, 45
Freyman, Barbara, 57
Freyman, Catharina, 61
Freyman, Christopher, 129
Freyman, Debora, 125
Freyman, Gideon, 129
Freyman, Johannes, 61
Freyman, Joseph, 125, 108, 129.
Freyman, Magdalena, 61
Freyman, Maria Eva, 129
Freyman, Salome, 125, 129
Freyman, William Tilghman, 113
Freymann, Abraham, 57, 59
Freymann, Barbara, 59
Freymann, Christoph, 79
Freymann, Daniel, 57
Freymann, Elisabeth, 76
Freymann, Eva, 79
Freymann, Franz Joseph, 117
Freymann, Johnn Georg, 59
Freymann, Joseph, 113, 117
Freymann, Michael, 76
Freymann, Salome, 76, 113, 117
Freyvoger, Anna, 8
Freyvoger, Johannes, 8
Fuchs, Andreas, 34
Fuchs, Eva, 34
Fuchs, Henrich, 34
Fuchs, Joh. Nicolas, 17
Fuchs, Johann Nickel, 15, 133
Fuchs, Margaretha, 15
Fuchs, Peter, 15
Fuhr, Anna Maria, 29
Fuhr, Catharina Elisabeth, 23
Fuhr, Johannes, 23, 29, 46
Fuhr, Joseph, 46
Fuhr, Juliana, 46
Fuhr, Maria Margreth, 23, 29, 32
Fur, Leonhard, 9
Fur, Maria Catharina, 9
Fur, Susanna Elisabetha, 9
Gangenwehr, Carl, 36
Gangenwehr, Georg, 36
Gangenwehr, Christina, 36
Gangenwer, Sibilla, 36
Gangewere, George, 143
Gangwehr, Abraham, 78, 114
Gangwehr, Anna, 73
Gangwehr, Carl, 97, 121
Gangwehr, Catharina, 87, 104
Gangwehr, Charles, 78, 81, 86, 109, 115
Gangwehr, David, 69
Gangwehr, Elisabeth, 68, 69, 73, 83, 86, 87, 102, 114
Gangwehr, Magdalena, 81, 83, 86, 97, 109, 115
Gangwehr, Maria, 102
Gangwehr, Moses, 109
Gangwehr, Ruben, 87
Gangwehr, Susanna, 101, 115
Gangwehr, Thomas, 69, 101
Gangwehr, Wilhelm, 68, 73, 83
Gangwehr, William, 102, 114
Gangwher, Jacobus, 69
Gangwher, Magdalena, 121

Gangwher, Maria Magdalena, 78
Gangwher, Susanna, 69, 83
Gangwher, Thomas, 83
Gangwher, Wilhelm, 69, 87
Garanflo, Charles, 128
Garanflo, Hanna, 128
Geck, Heinrich, 5
Geiger, Catharina, 84, 142
Geiger, Eva Catharina, 32, 33
Geiger, Jacob, 32, 33, 142
Geiger, Maria, 142
Geiger, Sarah, 142
Geiger, Susanna, 33
Georg, Abby, 128
Georg, Abraham, 113
Georg, Anna Elisabeth, 37
Georg, Anna Maria, 61
Georg, Catharina, 113
Georg, David, 125
Georg, Diana, 118
Georg, Eva, 113
Georg, Helena, 113
Georg, Henrich, 7, 87, 90, 91, 94, 98, 107, 108, 111
Georg, Isabella, 111
Georg, Johannes, 37, 98
Georg, John, 102, 107, 113, 114, 115, 118, 123, 125, 126
Georg, Joseph, 63
Georg, Kitty Ann, 128
Georg, Lea, 107, 114, 118, 123, 126
Georg, Lydia, 94
Georg, Magdalena, 70, 87, 90, 91, 94, 98, 108, 111
Georg, Margreth, 63
Georg, Maria Anna, 114
Georg, Owen, 107
Georg, Philip, 61, 63
Georg, Salome, 87
Georg, Sarah, 107, 115
Georg, Solomon, 70, 114, 116, 121, 128
Georg, Susanna, 98
Georg, Thomas, 115
Georg, Thomas Franklin, 126
Georg, Wilhelm, 98
Geringer, Johannes, 20
Geringer, Maria Elisabeth, 20
Gersler, Barbara Alimand, 8
Gersler, Heinrich, 8
Gersler, Philip Jacob, 8
Gerster, Barbara, 17
Gerster, Conrad, 27
Gerster, Maria Margreth, 25
Geyer, Eva Catharina, 66
Gilbert, Adam, 74, 80, 84, 88, 93, 96, 102, 114
Gilbert, Anna Lavina, 93
Gilbert, Caroline, 114
Gilbert, Catharina, 74, 96, 102, 114
Gilbert, David, 88
Gilbert, Esther, 80
Gilbert, Jacob, 78, 114, 119
Gilbert, Juliana, 102
Gilbert, Maria, 78, 96, 114, 119
Gilbert, Melvina, 119
Gilbert, Ruben, 78
Gilbert, Sophiana, 78
Gilbert, Susanna, 74, 84, 88, 93
Ginnert, Anna Mathilda, 128
Ginnert, Elisabeth, 128
Ginnert, John, 128
Gloeckner, Barbara, 44, 47
Gloeckner, Catharina, 91
Gloeckner, Elizabeth, 91
Gloeckner, Johannes, 47
Gloeckner, Nicklaus, 47
Gloeckner, Nicolaus, 44
Gloeckner, Solomon, 91

Gloeckner, Susanna, 44
Gobrecht, Elisabeth, 86, 102, 109
Gobrecht, Esther, 70
Gobrecht, Hanna, 70, 73, 74, 75, 76, 80, 83, 86, 88, 90
Gobrecht, J., 57, 75, 80, 83, 88, 90, 102
Gobrecht, John, 70, 73, 74, 76, 80, 86, 109, 128
Gobrecht, Juliana, 76, 131
Gobrecht, Maria Adeline Rosa, 109
Gobrecht, Rachel, 73
Gobrecht, Sara, 70
Gobrecht, Sophia, 80
Goebel, Johannes, 59
Goebel, Susanna, 59
Goldner, Georg, 24
Goldner, Gertrude, 24
Goranflo, Charles, 126
Goranflo, Hannah, 126
Goranflo, Henry William Alfred, 128
Gottfried, Elisabeth, 88
Gottfried, Peter, 88
Graeber, Elisabeth, 77
Graeber, Mattheus, 77
Graf, Anna, 62, 140
Graf, Anna Barbara, 17, 20, 22, 26
Graf, Barbara, 16, 18, 20, 24, 26, 32, 33, 39, 140
Graf, Elisabeth, 62, 65
Graf, Eva Catharina, 27
Graf, Georg, 16, 17, 18, 20, 26, 32, 62, 65
Graf, Johann Georg, 22
Graf, Louise, 65
Graf, Magdalena, 16, 24, 48
Graf, Maria Barbara, 18, 26, 27, 31
Graf, Martin, 20, 22, 24, 26, 27, 32, 33, 39
Graf, Peter, 27
Graf, Solomon, 20, 62
Graf, Stephanus, 39
Graff, Augustus, 69
Graff, Carl, 59
Graff, Carolina, 98
Graff, Catharina 57, 140, 144,
Graff, Elisabeth, 59, 69, 70, 74, 75, 85, 87, 90,98, 100, 104, 143
Graff, Elisabetha, 57
Graff, Georg, 57, 59,
Graff, George, 74, 85, 140, 141, 143
Graff, Hanna, 143
Graff, Hannah, 140
Graff, Jacob, 148, 140
Graff, Joseph, 140
Graff, Magdalena, 140
Graff, Maria, 85
Graff, Martin, 141, 143, 145
Graff, Mary Ann, 127
Graff, Peter, 69, 75, 85, 87, 90, 98
Graff, Polly, 127
Graff, Sara, 74, 149
Graff, Solomon, 69, 194, 145
Graff, Stephanus, 75
Graff, Stephen, 125, 127
Greenawald, Catharina, 124
Greenawald, Daniel, 124
Greenawald, Thomas, 124
Greiling, Elisabeth, 110
Greiling, George, 110
Greiter, Conrad, 30
Greiter, Regina, 30
Greuling, Elisabeth, 99, 101
Greuling, George, 97, 99, 101
Greuling, Hanna, 97
Greuling, Maria, 101
Griesemer, Anna Maria, 144
Griesemer, Catharina, 142

Grimm, Dina, 107
Grimm, Peter, 107
Grob, Adelaide, 143, 144
Grob, Anna Maria, 24, 25, 36, 39, 43, 64
Grob, Barbara, 107, 81, 111
Grob, Carl Georg, 100
Grob, Catharina, 97, 100, 104, 142
Grob, Daniel, 53, 72, 97, 100, 104, 138
Grob, Edmund, 97
Grob, Edwin, 107
Grob, Elisabeth, 68, 72, 74, 90, 94
Grob, Eliza, 111
Grob, Ephriam, 104
Grob, Henrich, 25, 33, 42, 39, 45, 47, 51, 55, 60, 68, 72, 74, 81, 90, 94, 107, 111
Grob, Henry, 142, 143, 144
Grob, Johannes, 20, 21, 24, 25, 33, 36, 39, 43, 47, 64, 72
Grob, John, 52, 53, 142
Grob, Jonas, 36, 42
Grob, Joseph, 25, 55
Grob, Lydia, 60
Grob, Margaret, 143
Grob, Margreth, 39, 42, 45, 47, 51, 55, 60
Grob, Maria, 33, 47, 52, 53, 72
Grob, Salome, 55
Grob, Sarah, 47, 143
Grob, Stephan, 81
Grob, Susanna, 51
Grob, Tobias, 43, 100, 140
Gros, J. Daniel, 146
Gros, Rev. 139, 146
Gross, Abraham, 101
Gross, Barbara, 101
Grubb, Daniel, 145
Grubb, George W., 143
Grubb, Jonas, 143
Grubb, Jonathan, 143
Grubb, Joseph, 145
Grubb, Perry D. 143
Grubb, Stephen, 145
Grubb, Tobias, 143
Gruber, Carolina, 123
Gruber, David, 120
Gruber, Elisabeth, 86, 101, 105, 106, 111, 112, 116, 120, 123, 131
Gruber, Eliza Ann, 106
Gruber, Jacob, 101, 105, 106, 111, 112, 116, 120, 123, 131
Gruber, Nicolaus, 99, 105
Gruber, Rosina Emilia, 131
Gruber, Ruben, 111
Gruber, Solomon, 78, 99
Gruber, Sophiana, 116
Gruber, Susanna, 99, 105
Gruber, Susanna Emilia, 105
Gruber, William, 101
Grueling, Catharina, 106
Grueling, Elisabeth, 97, 106
Grueling, George, 106
Grumbach, Eva Catharina, 133
Grumback, Conrad, 133
Gucker, Bardel
Gucker, Eva Elisabeth, 9
Gut, Abigail, 96
Gut, Catharina, 53, 63, 66, 93
Gut, Eva Catharina, 17
Gut, Fridrich, 49
Gut, Friedrich, 89, 94, 96, 102
Gut, Horace, 102
Gut, Jacob, 27, 53, 66
Gut, Lorentz, 6, 13
Gut, Magdalena, 49
Gut, Peter, 17

Gut, Salome, 5, 6, 7, 79
Gut, Sophia, 19
Gut, Susanna, 89, 94, 96, 102
Guth, Adam, 136
Guth, Eva Barbara, 136
Guth, Friedrich, 106, 130
Guth, Johannes, 130
Guth, Juliana Margaretha, 133
Guth, Juliana Margaret, 135
Guth, Lorent, 138
Guth, Lorentz, 6, 8, 133, 135,
Guth, Lydia, 130
Guth, Margaret, 136
Guth, Peter, 136, 141
Guth, Sophia, 106
Guth, Susanna, 106
Haag, Catharina, 31
Haag, Conrad, 31
Haag, Elisabeth, 31
Haag, Jacob, 31
Haag, Margretha, 30
Haas, Barbara, 50
Haas, Daniel, 74
Haas, Elisabeth, 89
Haas, Henrich, 49, 50, 71, 74, 76, 78, 79, 89, 97
Haas, John, 79
Haas, Joseph, 71
Haas, Juliana, 50, 71, 74, 76, 78, 89, 79, 97
Haas, Maria, 64
Haes, Eva, 92
Haes, Henrich, 92
Haese, Samuel, 80
Haeuse, Anna, 93
Haeuse, Elisabeth, 93
Haeuse, Samuel, 93
Hagenbuch, Elisabeth Susanna, 127
Hagenbuch, Polly, 127
Hagenbuch, Stephen, 127
Hahn, Anna Milia, 13
Hahn, Johannes, 11
Hahn, Maria Catharina, 11
Hall, Mary I., 119
Handwerk, Catharina, 95
Handwerk, Friedrich, 95
Hann, Maria Susanna, 141
Happel, Elisabeth, 88
Hardly, David, 125
Hardly, Eliza, 125
Hardly, John Carl, 125
Hardly, Thomas Peter, 125
Hartman, ____, 21
Hartman, Abraham, 27, 35, 40, 45, 51, 53, 57
Hartman, Andreas, 26
Hartman, Anna Maria, 60
Hartman, Anna Margreth, 17
Hartman, Barbara, 45, 51, 53, 57, 144
Hartman, Benjamin, 36
Hartman, Carl Peter, 17, 42
Hartman, Catharina, 23, 27, 49, 53
Hartman, Christian, 32, 33, 37, 39, 40, 44, 60
Hartman, Daniel, 22, 45
Hartman, Elias, 63
Hartman, Elisabeth, 27, 28, 30, 32, 34, 35, 36, 37, 39, 42, 43, 46, 50, 51
Hartman, Esther, 34, 42
Hartman, Eva, 29, 30, 35, 39, 42, 45, 46, 49, 50, 53
Hartman, Eva Catharina, 32, 63, 64,
Hartman, Georg, 32, 34, 36, 43, 50
Hartman, Isaac, 18
Hartman, J. Dider, 32, 37
Hartman, J. Dietrich, 35

Hartman, Jacob, 17, 18, 22, 26, 29, 28, 30, 31, 32, 33, 35, 36, 39, 42, 45, 46, 49, 50, 53, 64
Hartman, Joh. Dider, 30
Hartman, Joh. Dietrich, 27
Hartman, Johann Diedrich, 28
Hartman, Johannes, 36, 39, 46
Hartman, John, 42
Hartman, Jonas, 50
Hartman, Joseph, 28, 44,
Hartman, Lydia, 53
Hartman, Magdalena, 29, 37, 39, 40, 44
Hartman, Margreth, 22, 26, 28, 32, 36, 39
Hartman, Maria, 33
Hartman, Maria Dorothea, 32
Hartman, Maria Magdalena, 35
Hartman, Maria Margreth, 18
Hartman, Peter, 42
Hartman, Salome, 37
Hartman, Sara, 35, 39, 37
Hartman, Solomon, 30
Hartmann, Abraham, 114
Hartmann, Carl, 81
Hartmann, Catharina, 77, 79, 81, 83, 84, 87, 95, 114
Hartmann, Jacob, 74, 77, 79, 81, 83, 84
Hartmann, Luciana, 79
Hartmann, Margretha, 46
Harxel, Anna Maria, 95
Harxel, George, 95
Harzel, Samuel, 95
Hass, Elisabeth, 50
Hass, Henrich, 54, 58
Hass, Juliana, 54, 58
Hass, Margareth, 54
Hass, Peter, 54
Hauck, Catharina Margreth, 35
Hauer, Andreas, 34, 51
Hauer, Catharina, 34, 51
Hauer, Eva Catharina, 34
Hauer, Jacob, 34
Hauesli, Barbara, 17
Hauesli, Elisabeth, 18, 23
Hauesli, Henrich, 17
Hauesli, Jacob, 17
Hauesli, Joachim, 21
Hauesli, Johann Heinrich, 17
Hauesli, Margreth, 21
Hauser, Barbara, 19, 52
Hauser, Elisabeth, 44, 47, 51, 54
Hauser, Georg, 44,, 52, 54
Hauser, George, 51
Hauser, Heinrich, 7
Hauser, J. Georg, 47
Hauser, Magdalean, 51
Hauser, Nicolaus, 44
Hauser, Salome, 19
Hauser, Ulrich, 19
Hausknecht, Daniel, 96
Hausknecht, Gertraut, 96
Hausknecht, John 89
Hausknecht, Maria, 89
Hausknecht, Sally Anna, 96
Hausknecht, Sarah, 96
Hausser, Catharina, 57
Hausser, Elisabetha, 57
Hausser, George, 57
Heck, Peter, 41
Heck, Barbara, 19
Heck, Christian, 37
Heck, Elisabeth, 37, 39, 41, 43
Heck, Henrich, 37, 39, 41, 43
Heck, Johannes, 19, 39
Hecker, Adam, 35, 42, 88
Hecker, Adelina, 125
Hecker, Anna Maria, 35

Hecker, Carl, 60
Hecker, Catharina, 35, 99, 101, 106, 125
Hecker, Charles, 125
Hecker, Daniel, 46, 97, 102
Hecker, Elisabeth, 46, 72, 73, 97, 102
Hecker, Jeremias, 57
Hecker, John, 123, 130
Hecker, John Egidus, 143
Hecker, Jonas, 46, 44, 45, 48, 51, 54, 57, 60, 63, 67, 73, 84, 102
Hecker, Joseph, 51
Hecker, Jost, 57
Hecker, Jost Wilhelm, 41, 44, 46, 143
Hecker, Jost William, 143
Hecker, Julia, 131
Hecker, Juliana, 67
Hecker, Magdalena, 46, 48, 51, 54, 57, 60, 63, 67, 73, 102
Hecker, Maria, 123, 130
Hecker, Maria Magdalena, 84
Hecker, Peter, 73
Hecker, Rebecca, 125
Hecker, Regina, 42, 46, 44, 57, 143
Hecker, Robert, 99
Hecker, Sibilla Veronica, 31
Hecker, Stephen, 97
Hecker, Susanna, 88
Hecker, Wilhelm, 48
Hecker, William, 99, 101
Heckman, Maria, 61
Heckman, Maria Margaretha, 126
Heckmann, Adam, 61
Heckmann, Christina, 115
Heckmann, Daniel, 63
Heckmann, Elisabeth, 101
Heckmann, Georg, 59
Heckmann, George, 101, 106, 115, 120, 126
Heckmann, Johan Georg, 63
Heckmann, John, 59
Heckmann, Magdalena, 59, 63, 106, 115
Heckmann, Maria, 120
Heckmann, Melinda, 120
Heckmann, Polly, 101
Heckmann, Sally Ann, 106
Hefelfinger, Henrich, 59, 65
Hefelfinger, Maria, 43
Hefelfinger, Peter, 48
Heffelfinger, Henrich, 76, 79
Heffelfinger, Susanna, 59, 65, 76, 79
Heilman, Anna Margaretha, 134
Heilman, Joseph, 131
Helfrich, Anna, 109
Helfrich, Anna Maria, 104
Helfrich, Anne, 99
Helfrich, Catharina, 34, 35
Helfrich, Eliza, 128
Helfrich, Henrich, 47
Helfrich, Johannes, 35
Helfrich, Magdalena, 35
Helfrich, Samuel, 99, 104, 109
Heller, Anna Elisabth, 77
Heller, David, 66, 77, 88
Heller, Elisabeth, 66, 88
Heller, Margreth, 32
Hellman, Christian, 29, 31
Hellman, Georg Jacob, 31
Hellman, Rosina, 29, 31,
Hellmann, Christian, 33
Hellmann, Elisabeth, 29
Hellmann, Rosina, 33
Hemsing, Daniel 69, 70, 72, 74
Hemsing, Henrich, 72
Hemsing, Margreth, 69, 70, 74, 72
Hemsing, Sarah, 60
Heninger, Catharina, 79
Heninger, George, 79

Henrich, Georg, 48
Hensinger, Elisabeth, 90
Hensinger, Nicolaus, 90
Hering, Andreas, 34
Hering, Catharina, 40
Hering, Hanna, 37
Hering, Jacob, 40
Herman, Jacob, 142
Hermany, Abraham, 109, 113, 114
Hermany, Catharina, 79
Hermany, Isaac, 79
Hermany, Magdalena, 113, 114
Hermany, Maria, 109
Hermany, Maria Magdalena, 103
Hermany, Owen, 103
Hermany, Samuel, 109
Hertzog, Adam, 47
Hertzog, Anna Lisa, 10
Hertzog, Catharina, 24, 25, 29, 30, 34, 35, 42, 47
Hertzog, Daniel, 24
Hertzog, Johannes, 35
Hertzog, Magdalena, 24
Hertzog, Maria Catharina, 10, 25, 31
Hertzog, Maria Magdalena, 42
Hertzog, Nicolaus, 10, 25, 29, 25, 31, 35
Hertzog, Peter, 30
Hertzog, Theobald, 21, 24, 25, 30, 34, 35, 42, 47
Herzog, Anna Elisabeth, 20
Herzog, Anna Maria, 23
Herzog, Catharina, 51
Herzog, Isaac, 45
Herzog, Johann Theobald, 18
Herzog, Magdalena, 22
Herzog, Margreth, 45
Heussly, Anna Magdalena, 7
Heussly, Elisabeth, 7
Heussly, Joachim, 7
Hirsch, Catharina, 80
Hirsch, Jacob, 80
Hisky, Caroline, 121
Hisky, Edwin, 126
Hisky, Henry, 121, 126
Hisky. Eva, 121, 126
Hitz, Adelaide, 142
Hoerdli, Catharine, 33
Hoerdli, Elisabeth, 33, 38
Hoerdli, Robert, 33, 38
Hoffman, Anna, 11
Hoffman, Anna Elisabetha, 11
Hoffman, Barbara, 92
Hoffman, Catharina, 63
Hoffman, Catharina Elisabetha, 133, 135
Hoffman, Catrina Lisbeth, 5
Hoffman, Dina, 60
Hoffman, Eli, 126
Hoffman, Eliza Ann, 128
Hoffman, Eva, 10
Hoffman, Eva Catharine, 8
Hoffman, Eva Catrina, 5
Hoffman, James Washington, 118
Hoffman, Joel, 57, 128
Hoffman, Joh. Michael, 8
Hoffman, Johannes, 11
Hoffman, John, 57, 60, 63, 92, 96, 135
Hoffman, Juliana, 135
Hoffman, Julianna Catharina, 12
Hoffman, Lydia, 128
Hoffman, Magdalena, 70, 129
Hoffman, Margaretha, 8
Hoffman, Margreth, 67
Hoffman, Maria Barbara, 57, 60, 135
Hoffman, Maria Catharina, 11
Hoffman, Maria Magdalena, 67, 135

Hoffman, Michael, 5, 8, 11, 59, 67, 135
Hoffman, Peter, 67, 87, 88, 102, 116, 118, 125, 126, 129
Hoffman, Ruben, 102
Hoffman, Sara Anna Elisabetha, 126
Hoffman, Susanna, 87, 102, 113, 118, 125, 126
Hoffmann, Apollonia, 18
Hoffmann, Barbara, 52, 65. 68, 69, 75, 81, 93, 96, 98
Hoffmann, Carl Ludwig, 121
Hoffmann, Catharina, 67
Hoffmann, Daniel, 96
Hoffmann, David, 123
Hoffmann, Debora, 77
Hoffmann, Emilia, 107
Hofmann, Englebert, 13, 17
Hoffmann, Heinrich, 68
Hoffmann, J., 102
Hoffmann, Joel, 107, 111, 116, 121, 120, 123, 126
Hoffmann, Johannes, 35, 65, 67
Hoffmann, John, 18, 27, 43, 52, 55, 69, 75, 81, 93, 98
Hoffmann, Josia, 111
Hoffmann, Lea, 69, 89, 102,
Hoffmann, Lydia, 89, 107, 111, 116, 120, 121, 123, 126
Hoffmann, Michael, 81, 82
Hoffmann, Magdalena, 61, 65, 73, 77, 81, 82, 87, 90, 92
Hoffmann, Manasse, 81
Hoffmann, Maria Anna, 67, 116
Hoffmann, Marianne, 114
Hoffmann, Maria Barbara, 102, 110
Hoffmann, Maria Catharina, 18
Hoffmann, Maria Magdalena, 65, 73
Hoffmann, Michael, 18, 70, 73, 77, 82, 87
Hoffmann, Peter, 49, 61, 90, 96, 101, 104, 107, 110, 113, 121
Hoffmann, Rosina, 13
Hoffmann, Ruben, 120
Hoffmann, Salome, 70
Hoffmann, Sarah Ann, 126
Hoffmann, Solomon, 113
Hoffmann, Stephanus, 81
Hoffmann, Susanna, 51, 88, 90, 96, 101, 104, 107, 110, 116, 121
Hofman, Catharina, 36
Hofman, Engelbert, 21
Hofman, Georg Jacob, 21
Hofman, Magdalena, 13, 25
Hofmann, Barbara, 25, 49, 51, 52, 54, 55
Hofmann, Catharina, 22, 46, 52
Hofmann, Daniel, 17, 51
Hofmann, Engelbert, 25
Hofmann, Eva Catharina, 15
Hofmann, J. Georg, 52
Hofmann, Johann Peter, 13
Hofmann, Johannes, 14, 15, 16, 43
Hofmann, John, 22, 46, 49, 54, 55, 63
Hofmann, Lydia, 55
Hofmann, Magdalena, 17, 51
Hofmann, Maria Barbara, 13, 14, 15, 16
Hofmann, Maria Catharina, 27
Hofmann, Maria Magdalena, 16
Hofmann, Michael, 15, 65
Hofmann, Peter, 51
Holtzleiner, Ann Maria, 8
Holtzleiner, Anna Barbara, 8
Holtzleiner, Michael, 8
Homs, Anna Barbara, 22
Homs, Barbara, 14
Homs, Catharina, 26
Homs, J. Georg, 22

Homs, Johannes, 14
Horn, Elisabeth, 63, 66, 71, 82
Horn, Esther, 82
Horn, Jacob, 63, 66, 71, 82
Horn, John, 139
Horn, Louise, 66
Horn, Magdalena, 63
Horn, Maria Magdalena, 74
Horn, Susanna, 71
Hornung, Elisabeth, 45, 47, 50, 67, 85
Hornung, Joh. Georg, 50
Hornung, Johannes, 45, 47, 50, 67
Hornung, Joseph 67
Hornung, Salome, 45, 47
Huber, Heinrich, 10
Hubler, Abraham, 60
Hubler, Anna Margreth, 60
Hubler, Jacob, 60, 64, 65,
Hubler, Moses, 60
Hubler, Reuben, 65
Hubler, Salome, 65
Hubler, Susanna, 65
Huettel, Catharina Friederica, 83
Huettel, Georg, 81, 79, 83
Huettel, Maria, 83
Hunsecker, Christian, 14
Huston, Catharina, 61
Huston, William, 61
Hut, John, 112
Hut, Lydia, 112
Istmann Eva, 121, 98,
Istmann, Daniel, 98, , 102
Istmann, David, 102
Istmann, Sophia, 98, 102
Jacob, Abraham, 104
Jacob, Christian, 17
Jacob, Elisabeth, 104
Jacobi Jacob, 85, 87
Jacobi, Luciana, 85
Jacobi, Magdalena, 87
Jacobi, Maria, 85, 87
Jameson, Daniel, 79
Jameson, Jacobus, 71
Jameson, James, 71, 79
Jans, Christina, 71
Jans, Ruben, 71
Jans, Wilhelm, 71
Jehl, Andreas, 39, 77
Jehl, Anna Margareth, 42
Jehl, Catharina, 87
Jehl, Catharina Elisabetha, 47
Jehl, Elisabeth, 77
Jehl, Jacob, 42, 47
Jehl, Juliana, 39
Jehl, Margreth, 39, 47
Jehl, Maria Elisabeth, 42
Jehl, Peter, 87
Jehl, Susanna, 87
Johler, Daniel, 114
Johnson, Maria Barbara, 30
Johnson, Thomas, 30
Jones, Mary, 126
Jund, Abraham, 24
Jundt, Abraham, 59, 66
Jundt, Elisabeth, 59, 66
Jundt, Johannes, 11
Jundt, Joseph, 59
Kaemmerer, Anna, 120, 98
Kaemmerer, Daniel, 118
Kaemmerer, David, 98
Kaemmerer, Dorothea, 118
Kaemmerer, Friedrich, 98
Kaemmerer, Georg Adam, 71, 94, 95, 97, 195
Kaemmerer, George, 110, 120
Kaemmerer, Jacob, 118
Kaemmerer, Jonas, 91
Kaemmerer, Magdalena, 71, 114

Kaemmerer, Rosina, 70
Kaemmerer, Solomon, 114
Kaemmerer, Susanna, 71, 94, 95, 97, 105
Keck, George, 101
Keck, Johannes, 41
Keck, Sarah Anne, 101
Kehl, Benjamin, 130
Kehl, Sarah Ann, 130
Kehl, Susanna, 130
Kehler, Georg, 12, 16
Kehler, Maria Elisabeth, 13, 16
Keifer, Anna Susanna, 128
Keiper, Catharina, 24, 37
Keiper, Johannes, 26
Keiper, Ludwig, 37
Kelchner, Anna Emilia, 113
Kelchner, Anne, 113
Kelchner, Barbara, 38, 41, 44, 47, 94
Kelchner, Catharina, 52
Kelchner, Christoph, 38, 44, 47, 50, 52, 56, 58, 61, 65, 67, 69, 78, 83, 84, 98, 108
Kelchner, Elisabeth, 16, 17, 18, 20, 41
Kelchner, Elisabetha, 14
Kelchner, Georg, 50
Kelchner, Hanna, 58
Kelchner, Isabella, 88
Kelchner, Johann Christoffel, 14
Kelchner, Johannes, 47
Kelchner, John, 65, 88, 100
Kelchner, Joseph, 69
Kelchner, Juliana, 83
Kelchner, Levina, 94
Kelchner, Magdalena, 34, 65, 83, 88, 94, 106
Kelchner, Maria, 100
Kelchner, Maria Barbara, 50, 52, 56, 58, 61, 65, 67, 69, 79, 83, 84, 98, 108
Kelchner, Michael, 14, 17, 20., 61, 113
Kelchner, Michel, 18, 41
Kelchner, Paul, 78
Kelchner, Peter, 16, 38, 44, 83, 94
Kelchner, Stoffel, 41
Kelchner, Susanna, 44
Kelly, Elisabeth, 75, 85
Kelly, James, 75
Kelly, John, 75
Kemmerer, Anna, 1130
Kemmerer, Dorothea, 124
Kemmerer, Eliza Anna, 130
Kemmerer, George, 130
Kemmerer, George Adam, 129
Kemmerer, Jacob, 124
Kemmerer, Joshua, 124
Kemmerer, Magdalena, 126
Kemmerer, Maria Susanna, 189
Kemmerer, Sarah, 126
Kemmerer, Sarah Catharina, 126
Kemmerer, Solomon, 126
Kendel, Dewald, 16
Kendel, Jacob, 41
Kendel, Maria Magdalean, 16
Kennel, Joseph, 9, 10
Kennel, Maria, 9
Kennel, Maria Barbara, 10
Kennel, Sara, 9
Kepp, Johannes, 76
Kepp, Susanna, 76
Kerfass, Adam, 29
Kerfass, Maria Elisabeth, 29
Kern, Adelina, 123
Kern, Anna, 48
Kern, Barbara, 41

Kern, Catharina, 15, 16, 19, 21, 22, 23, 24, 25, 26, 27, 29, 30, 31, 32, 33, 34, 35, 36, 38, 42, 43, 44, 46, 48, 51, 54, 55, 57, 58, 62, 66, 73, 81, 84, 86,, 95, 112, 122
Kern, Catharina Elisabeth, 5, 6, 11, 18, 133,
Kern, Catharina Elizabetha, 6, 12, 139
Kern, Catrina Lisabeth, 5
Kern, Christina, 107
Kern, Christoph, 12, 18, 21, 23, 24, 26, 27, 29, 32, 33, 35, 36, 38, 43,
Kern, Christophel, 16
Kern, Cornela, 8
Kern, Daniel, 11, 18, 23, 32, 38, 42, 43, 53, 54, 101
Kern, David
Kern, Eli, 99
Kern, Elisabeth, 21, 127
Kern, Eva Catharina, 24, 25, 27, 142
Kern, Floriana, 86
Kern, Georg, 6, 7, 8, 28, 41, 133
Kern, Georg Jacob, 6, 7, 8, 11, 12, 13, 14, 15,
Kern, George, 5, 5, 82, 89, 94, 95, 106, 108, 109, 113, 127
Kern, George Jacob, 139
Kern, Gertrude, 28
Kern, Hanna, 86, 89, 90, 91, 95, 99, 107
Kern, Hannah, 92
Kern, Heinrich, 16
Kern, Henriette, 16, 115
Kern, Henry Joseph, 127
Kern, J. Nicolaus, 54, 66, 81, 84
Kern, Jacob, 8, 16, 18, 19, 26, 28, 29, 32, 34, 43, 53, 59
Kern, James, 123, 130
Kern, Jesse, 32
Kern, Joh. Michael, 19
Kern, Joh. Peter, 24, 27
Kern, Johan Nicolaus, 62
Kern, Johannes, 12, 16, 23, 29, 32
Kern, Johannetha, 11
Kern, John, 38
Kern, John Nicolaus, 55
Kern, Jonas, 26
Kern, Jonathan, 28
Kern, Joseph, 19, 38, 43, 86, 89, 90, 91, 92, 95, 99, 107
Kern, Juliana, 22
Kern, Nicolaus, 6, 57
Kern, Peter, 42, 111
Kern, Susanna, 42
Kern, Leonhart, 11
Kern, Levi, 62
Kern, Lydia, 55
Kern, Magdalena, 26, 32, 38, 42, 92
Kern, Manasse, 73
Kern, Margaretha, 5, 11, 13, 10, 13, 101, 106, 112, 130
Kern, Margreth, 11, 15, 18, 29, 38, 43, 89, 90, 95, 110, 111, 115, 127
Kern, Maria, 58, 95, 119, 130
Kern, Maria Barbara, 53, 55, 57
Kern, Maria Elisabeth, 13
Kern, Maria Gretha, 12
Kern, Maria Magdalena, 14, 53
Kern, Maria Margreth, 34, 59
Kern, Maria Margretha, 16
Kern, Mawdalina, 123
Kern, Michael, 53, 55, 57, 127
Kern, Michael, 127
Kern, Nicklaus, 46, 51
Kern, Nicolas, 6

Kern, Nicolaus, 5, 8, 43, 44, 43, 48, 58, 73, 84, 86, 95, 134
Kern, Owen, 90
Kern, Peter, 13, 16, 19, 21, 22, 24, 25, 26, 27, 31, 34, 38, 46, 90, 95, 101, 106, 110, 112, 115, 127, 130, 144
Kern, Salome, 31, 82, 89, 94, 95, 106, 108, 109, 113. 116, 127
Kern, Salome Anna, 89
Kern, Sara, 35
Kern, Sarah, 106
Kern, Stoffel, 13
Kern, Susanna, 15, 16, 18, 33, 34, 37, 130, 145
Kern, Thomas, 42, 116
Kern, Wilhelm, 51
Kern, William, 95
Kester, John, 55
Kester, Lorenz, 54
Kester, Peter, 86
Kester, Philip, 55
Kester, Polly, 55
Kester, Regina, 71
Kester, Salome, 71
Kester, Susanna, 105
Kester, Wilhelm, 71
Kestin, Elisabeth, 28
Kestin, Samuel, 28
Keurschner, Jeremais, 56
Keurschner, Magdalena, 56
Keurschner, Margreth, 56
Kichel, Catharina, 104
Kichel, John, 95
Kichel, John, 104
Kichel, Levina, 95
Kiefer, John, 92
Kiefer, Daniel, 92, 92
Kiefer, John, 92, 93, 94, 98, 128
Kiefer, Susanna, 92, 93, 94, 98, 128
Kieffer, John, 90
Kieffer, Susanna, 90
Kieffer, William, 90
Kirschner, Daniel, 130
Kirschner, Lea, 130
Kirschner, Susanna, 130
Kleder, Elisabeth, 3o
Kleder, Margreth, 32
Kleder, Maria Barbara, 54
Klein, Catharina, 34
Klein, Christina, 43
Klein, Samuel, 106
Klenberg, Carl, 95
Klenberg, Eliza, 95
Klenberg, Joseph, 95
Kleppinger, Anna Maria, 109
Kleppinger, George, 109
Klien, Elisabeth, 31
Knapenburger, Abraham, 126t
Knapenberger, Adam, 35
Knapenberger, Elisabeth, 66
Knapenberger, Jonathan, 35, 71
Knapenberger, Margreth, 32, 35
Knapenberger, Philip, 32, 35
Knapenberger, Robert, 66
Knapenberger, Solomon, 32
Knappenberger, Salome, 126
Knappenberger, Sarah, 125
Knappenberger, Thomas, 125, 126
Knaus, Anna Maria, 51
Knaus, Catharina, 29, 36
Knaus, Elisabeth, 99
Knaus, Eva, 6
Knaus, Gottfried, 51, 63, 133
Knaus, Jonathan, 99
Knaus, Ludwig, 6
Knaus, Maria, 63, 89
Knaus, Paul, 29, 36

Knaus, Philip, 21
Knaus, Ruben, 119
Knaus, Solomon, 89
Knauss, Anna Eva, 10, 137, 144
Knauss, Charlotte Barbara, 141
Knauss, Elisabeth, 34
Knauss, Eva Catharina, 145
Knauss, George, 141
Knauss, Godfrey, 137, 142
Knauss, Gottfried, 10, 144
Knauss, Paul, 142
Knauss, Philip, 141
Knauss, Salome, 144
Knedler, Andrew, 144
Knedler, Dorothea, 144
Knerr, Conrad, 106
Knerr, John, 129
Knerr, Maria, 106
Knoer, Andreas, 26
Knoer, Eva Catharina, 25
Knoer, Leonhard, 25
Knoer, Susanna, 25
Koch, Adam, 97
Koch, Anna Maria, 97
Koch, Catharina, 97, 104, 110, 114
Koch, David, 104
Koch, Eli, 110
Koch, Elisabewth, 36, 58
Koch, Ephriam, 93
Koch, Eva, 72
Koch, Georg, 58
Koch, George, 72, 97, 127
Koch, J. Georg, 36
Koch, Jacob, 97
Koch, Jacob, 104, 110, 114
Koch, John, 90
Koch, Jonas, 36
Koch, Joseph, 97
Koch, Lydia, 93
Koch, Magdalena, 90
Koch, Margreth,, 97
Koch, Maria, 54, 127
Koch, Sarah, 48
Koch, Tobias, 93
Kocher, Ann Barbara, 5
Kocher, Catharina, 36, 37, 42, 44, 47, 49, 52, 55, 108
Kocher, Daniel, 44
Kocher, Elisabeth, 47
Kocher, Eva, 55, 58
Kocher, Georg, 49
Kocher, Henrich, 52
Kocher, Johannes, 36, 37, 58
Kocher, John, 42, 44, 47, 49, 52, 55
Kocher, Martin, 5
Kocher, Peter, 42, 47
Kocher, Salome, 37
Kocher, Sara, 5
Kocher, Stephanus, 36
Koechlein, Catharina, 108
Koechlein, Peter, 108
Koehler, Elisabeth, 23
Koehler, Georg, 18, 23, 25, 30, 45
Koehler, George, 12, 143
Koehler, John Jacob, 138
Koehler, Maria Elisabetha, 14, 23, 25, 30, 45, 138, 143
Kohler, Aaron, 72
Kohler, Abraham, 35, 85
Kohler, Anna, 67
Kohler, Anna Levina, 84
Kohler, Anna Margaretha, 19
Kohler, Anna Maria, 15, 140
Kohler, Barbara, 15, 18, 25, 76, 140
Kohler, Benjamin, 33, 74, 76, 79, 82, 85, 88, 92, 95
Kohler, Carl, 114, 115

Kohler, Catharina, 12, 57, 58, 59, 61,
  62, 68, 70, 71, 72, 74, 76, 79,
  70, 80, 81, 82, 84, 85, 88, 92,
  93, 94, 95, 98, 98, 99, 100,
  102, 104, 107, 109, 115, 120,
  121, 122, 127, 130, 140
Kohler, Daniel, 39, 76, 84, 88, 90,
  97, 99, 104, 108, 118, 122
Kohler, Debora, 84
Kohler, Dorothea, 95
Kohler, Edmund, 118
Kohler, Edward, 124, 131
Kohler, Elisabeth, 99
Kohler, Eliza, 74
Kohler, Emilie, 131
Kohler, Ephriam, 90, 122
Kohler, Esther, 59
Kohler, Euphemia, 77
Kohler, Eva Catharina, 12
Kohler, Eva Maria, 28
Kohler, Floriana, 92
Kohler, Henriette, 88
Kohler, Horace, 107
Kohler, Isaac, 49, 99, 102, 107, 115,
  120, 122, 130,
Kohler, Jacob, 14, 17, 18, 19, 17, 18,
  25, 26, 27, 28, 30, 33, 35, 39,
  45, 47, 49, 53, 55, 62, 67, 67,
  70, 72, 77, 79, 82, 84, 85,
  134, 138, 139, 140, 145
Kohler, James, 120
Kohler, James Alfred Peter, 127
Kohler, Joh. Jacob, 25
Kohler, Joh. Peter, 12, 28
Kohler, Johan Jacob, 13
Kohler, Johannes, 14, 45
Kohler, Joseph, 53, 62, 99, 125, 130,
  131
Kohler, Josua, 81, 104
Kohler, Judith, 59
Kohler, Juliana, 13, 15, 17, 19, 28,
  32, 33, 39
Kohler, Juliana Margaret, 145
Kohler, Julianna Margaretha, 12
Kohler, Leanna, 130
Kohler, Lucas, 82
Kohler, Luciana, 85
Kohler, Magdalena, 13, 14, 84, 88, 90,
  97, 99, 104, 108, 114, 118,
  122, 125
Kohler, Manasse, 79
Kohler, Margreth, 82
Kohler, Maria, 16, 62, 67, 72, 77, 82,
  85, 94, 99, 122, 123, 125, 131
Kohler, Maria Barbara, 14, 16, 17, 19,
  26, 145
Kohler, Maria Catharina, 30
Kohler, Maria Elisabeth, 26, 27, 28,
  30, 33, 35, 39, 45, 47, 49, 53,
  55, 62, 70, 79, 84
Kohler, Maria Elisabetha, 15
Kohler, Mary, 127
Kohler, Peter, 12, 13, 15, 16, 17, 18,
  19, 24, 28, 32, 33, 39, 47, 53,
  56, 57, 58, 59, 61, 62, 68, 71,
  72, 74, 76, 80, 81, 82, 83, 84,
  85, 93, 94, 99, 100, 102, 104,
  109, 113, 121, 124, 127, 136,
  138, 139, 140, 145, 149
Kohler, Philip, 140
Kohler, Polly, 121, 130
Kohler, Ruben, 99
Kohler, Sarah Ann, 125
Kohler, Sophiana, 76
Kohler, Susanna, 17, 59, 81, 113
Kohler, Tilghman, 97
Kohler, William, 62, 102, 119, 122,
  127

Kohler, William Henry Michael, 127
Kohler, Wm., 123, 125
Kolb, Catharina, 34
Kolb, Elisabeth, 35
Kolb, Johann Adam, 89
Kolb, Susanna, 89
Kopp, Anna Maria, 11
Kopp, Joerg, 11
Kostard, Susanna, 40
Krailing, Elisabeth, 121
Krailing, George, 121
Krailing, Sarah, 121
Kratzer, Andreas, 62, 66, 69, 71, 74,
  80, 86, 97
Kratzer, Anna Maria, 52
Kratzer, Daniel, 52
Kratzer, David, 80
Kratzer, Eliza, 97
Kratzer, Joseph, 74
Kratzer, Magdalena, 52, 62, 66, 69,
  71, 74, 80, 86, 97
Kratzer, Peter, 66
Kratzer, Sara, 71
Kratzer, Wilhelm, 86
Kregli, Andreas, 108
Kregli, Daniel, 105
Kregli, John, 105
Kregli, Margreth, 105
Kregli, Mathilda, 108
Kregli, Susanna, 108
Kreidler, Daniel, 8
Kreidler, Johann George, 8
Kreidler, Sybilla, 8
Kreiling, Elisabeth, 117
Kreiling, George, 117
Kreiling, Ruben, 117
Kretschmann, Margareth, 72
Krum, Maria, 47
Kuerschner, Jeremias, 56
Kuerschner, Magdalena, 56
Kuerschner, Margreth, 56
Kuever, Catharina, 132
Kuever, Henrich, 132
Kuns, Catharina, 106
Kuns, George, 106
Kuns, Jacob, 65, 68
Kuns, Johannes, 68
Kuns, Salome, 116
Kuns, Solomon, 116
Kuntz, Adam, 20
Kuntz, Christina, 23
Kuntz, Daniel, 23
Kuntz, Georg, 26
Kuntz, Georg Jacob, 23
Kuntz, Margreth, 24
Kuntz, Wilhelm, 23
Labach, Adam, 71, 84, 103
Labach, Catharina, 88, 122
Labach, Christian, 98, 103, 113, 115,
  118,
Labach, Edward Christian, 122
Labach, Elisabeth, 98, 103, 113, 115,
  118, 122
Labach, Jesse, 118
Labach, Josua, 98
Labach, Margreth, 71
Labach, Maria Margreth, 84
Labach, Stephanus, 113
Lamp, Johannes, 9
Lamp, Susanna, 9
Lane, Mary Margareth, 119
Lane, Mathias, 125
Lane, Matthias, 119
Lane, Sally Ann, 125
Lane, Susan, 125
Lane, Susanna, 119
Lang, Edmund, 116

Lang, Joseph, 97, 101, 107, 110, 111, 116, 121, 126
Lang, Lydia, 97, 101, 107, 110, 111, 116, 121, 126
Lang, Sarah Anne, 121
Lang, Stephan, 101
Lang, Wilhelmine, 110
Larasch, Elizabeth, 77
Larasch, Hanna, 91
Larasch, Jacob, 77, 82, 86, 91, 105
Larasch, Jacob Ettwine, 105
Larasch, Leonard, 105
Larasch, Leonhardt, 100
Larasch, Luciana, 86
Larasch, Salome, 82
Larasch, Sara, 77, 82, 86
Larasch, Sarah, 91, 105
Larosch, Henrich, 123
Larosch, Jacob, 123
Larosch, Sarah, 123
Laub, Catharina, 30
Laub, Jacob, 30
Laubach, Conrad, 46
Laure, Elisabeth, 29, 32
Laure, Gottfried, 26, 29, 52
Laure, Margreth, 27, 42
Laure, Susanna, 26, 29, 52
Laure, Wilhelm, 32, 41
Lauri, Catharina, 48
Lauri, Elisabeth, 58
Lauri, Gottfried, 27, 44, 45, 48
Lauri, Joh. Daniel, 29
Lauri, Margreth, 53
Lauri, Maria Margreth, 29
Lauri, Susanna, 44, 45, 48
Lauri, Wilhelm, 29, 53, 56
Laury, Adam, 81
Laury, Barbara, 91
Laury, Catharina, 82
Laury, Daniel, 82
Laury, David, 63, 123, 126, 145
Laury, Elisabeth, 63
Laury, Gottfried, 63, 78
Laury, Jacob, 106
Laury, John, 63
Laury, Lydia, 129
Laury, Magdalena, 63
Laury, Maria, 126
Laury, Polly, 123
Laury, Susanna, 63, 78, 106
Laury, Susanna Ann, 106
Laury, Wilhelm, 57
Lautenschlaeger, Anton, 73, 77, 80, 83, 97, 99, 107
Lautenschlaeger, Caroline, 101
Lautenschlaeger, Elisabeth, 77, 78, 80, 83, 97, 99, 107
Lautenschlaeger, Eva, 55, 61, 65, 67, 70, 78
Lautenschlaeger, G. Jacob, 51, 54
Lautenschlaeger, Georg, 67
Lautenschlaeger, Georg Jacob, 65, 70
Lautenschlaeger, Jacob, 61, 78
Lautenschlaeger, John, 78
Lautenschlaeger, Jonathan, 67
Lautenschlaeger, Josua, 70
Lautenschlaeger, Margreth, 61, 78
Lautenschlaeger, Maria, 107
Lautenschlaeger, Peter, 89, 101, 103, 116, 129
Lautenschlaeger, Ruben, 77
Lautenschlaeger, Sara, 83
Lautenschlaeger, Stephan, 65
Lautenschlaeger, Susanna, 55, 101, 103, 116, 129
Leaser, Charles, 126, 128
Leaser, Margaretha, 126, 128
Leh, Carl, 100

Leh, Catharina, 93, 94, 100, 105, 111, 116, 119, 122
Leh, Daniel, 83
Leh, Eli, 116
Leh, Esther, 105
Leh, Henrich, 83, 84, 88, 90, 93, 94, 96, 100, 105, 111, 116, 122
Leh, Henry, 119
Leh, Henry William, 122
Leh, Horace, 110
Leh, James, 119
Leh, Magdalena, 93, 96, 101, 105, 116, 119, 124
Leh, Maria, 105
Leh, Maria Anna, 96
Leh, Ruben, 90
Leh, Samuel, 93, 96, 101, 105, 116, 119, 121
Leh, Sarah, 101, 122
Leh, Stephan, 94
Leh, Susanna, 83, 90, 94, 96, 100
Leh, Wilhelm, 93
Lehant, Carl, 55
Lehant, Magdalena, 55, 56
Lehant, Solomon, 55, 56
Lehr, Catharina, 55
Lehr, Eva, 55
Lehr, Eva Catharina, 141
Lehr, William, 55
Leibeguth, Anna, 78
Leibenguth, Christina Margaretha, 11
Leibenguth, Catharina, 13, 15, 96,
Leibenguth, Christian, 14
Leibenguth, Christina Margaretha, 133
Leibenguth, Georg, 13, 14, 15, 96,
Leibenguth, Hanna, 96
Leibenguth, Johann Peter, 13
Leibenguth, Magdalena, 14
Leibenguth, Maria Magdalena, 14, 15, 18
Leibenguth, Philip, 133
Leibenguth, Susanna, 15
Leibinguth, Christian, 18, 20, 23
Leibinguth, Johannes, 20
Leibinguth, Magdalena, 20
Leibingut, Maria Susanna, 18
Leibengut, Christian, 16
Leibengut, Maria Magdalena, 16
Leibengut, Michael, 16
Leibrod, Anna Barbara, 9
Leibrod, Christian, 9
Leienberger, Carl, 121
Leienberger, Peter, 121
Leinberger, Debora, 125
Leinberger, Diana, 127
Leinberger, Elisabeth, 121, 125, 127
Leinberger, Peter, 121, 125, 127
Leinberger, Susanna, 121, 125
Leisenring, Andrew, 142
Leisenring, Anna, 99
Leisenring, Anna Maria, 142
Leisenring, Barbara, 142
Leisenring, Catharina, 33, 41, 42, 45, 54, 69, 75, 81, 87
Leisenring, Conrad, 24, 27, 33, 34, 41, 42, 45, 69, 75, 81, 87, 118, 142, 143, 144
Leisenring, Daniel, 99, 117, 140, 142,
Leisenring, Elizabeth, 142
Leisenring, Eva, 142
Leisenring, Eva Catharina, 34
Leisenring, Eva Catharine, 142, 146
Leisenring, Johannes, 45
Leisenring, John, 143
Leisenring, John Sebastian, 142
Leisenring, Lydia, 52, 118
Leisenring, Margareth, 114, 115
Leisenring, Maria, 143

Leisenring, Peter, 36, 40, 41, 50, 52, 53, 54, 115, 142, 143, 144
Leisenring, Salome,
Leisenring, Sibilla, 142, 144
Leisenring, Sibylla, 24
Leisenring, Susanna, 50, 52 , 53,
Leisenring, Sybilla, 27
Leisinring, Anna Maria, 20
Lenz, Catharina, 99
Lenz, Esther, 99
Lenz, Magdalena, 99
Lenz, Salme, 78
Lenz, Stephan, 99
Lenz, Wilhelm, 99
Lerch, Abraham, 81
Lesar, John, 131
Leser, Catharina, 54
Leser, John, 54, 111
Leser, Magdalena, 54
Levan, Abraham, 62, 67, 126
Levan, Catharina, 67
Levan, John, 58
Levan, Lewis Fredinand, 67
Levan, Magdalena, 58, 62, 67
Levan, Maria, 47
Levan, Peter, 126
Levan, Solomon, 58, 62, 67
Levan, Susan, 143
Levan, Thomas, 62
Levi, Maria, 74, 79, 88,
Levi, Maria Anna, 79
Levi, Moses, 74, 79, 88
Levi, Nathan, 88
Levi, Sara, 74
Leyenberger, Jacob, 119
Leyenberger, Margreth, 119
Liebeguth, Alexander, 78
Liebeguth, Georg, 78
Liesenring, Anna Maria, 142
Liesenring, Anne, 117
Liesenring, Catharina, 34
Liesenring, Elisabeth, 25
Lindeman, Catherina Elisabeth, 45
Lindeman, Eva, 45
Lindeman, Jacob, 45
Lins, Elisabeth, 49
Lins, Johannes, 49
Lins, Martin, 49
Lobach, Abraham, 81
Lobach, Magdalena, 81
Lobach, Peter, 81
Loehr, Eva, 49, 53
Loehr, Jacob, 53
Loehr, Maria Magdalena, 53
Loehr, Philip, 49, 53
Loeser, Carl, 65
Loeser, Catharina, 58, 61, 65, 82,
Loeser, Elisabeth, 58
Loeser, Johannes, 58
Loeser, John, 61, 65, 82, 104
Lorash, Jacob, 127
Lorash, James William, 127
Lorash, Leonhard, 123, 127
Lorash, Sarah, 127
Lorash, Sarah Ann, 123
Lorash, Sophia Ann, 123
Lorash, Sophianna, 127
Lutter, Louise, 21
Maerz, Catharina, 111
Maerz, Dewalt, 111
Maerz, Jonas, 106
Maerz, Sabina, 106
Maerz, Salome, 106
Maier, Sarah, 121
Marck, Conrad, 28
Marck, Catharina, 30
Marck, Conrad, 16, 26, 30, 36,41, 140
Marck, Daniel, 25
Marck, Eva, 19
Marck, Margaretha, 26, 41
Marck, Margreth, 28, 30, 36
Marck, Maria Barbara, 28
Marck, Maria Magdalena, 26
Marck, Nicolaus, 25
Mark, Eva, 14
Mark, Catharina, 14
Mark, Conrad, 14
Mark, Joh. Nickel, 14
Mark, Nickel, 15, 14
Martin, Abraham, 17
Martin, Joh. Adam, 27
Martin, Joh. Jacob, 27
Martin, Margreth, 27
Marx, Conrad, 22, 24
Marx, Esther, 129
Marx, Eva, 16, 21
Marx, Gideon, 124, 129
Marx, Hetty, 124
Marx, Joh. Nichlaus, 21
Marx, Johan Peter, 21
Marx, Johannes, 22
Marx, Margreth, 22
Marx, Margaretha, 24
Marx, Maria, 129
Marx, Nicholas, 140
Marx, Nicolaus, 16, 22
Marx, Uriah Lewis, 124
Mattheus, Anna Caroline, 100
Mattheus, Esther, 100, 104
Mattheus, Mahlon, 104
Mattheus, Samuel, 100, 104
Maurer, Adam, 14
Maurer, Barbara, 21
Mayer, Abigail, 116
Mayer, Anna, 63
Mayer, Catharina, 66, 116
Mayer, Christina, 60, 62, 65, 66
Mayer, Daniel, 77
Mayer, Edward, 69
Mayer, Jacob, 60, 63, 62, 65, 66,
Mayer, Joseph, 69
Mayer, Magdalena, 66
Mayer, Margreth, 63, 66, 74
Mayer, Martin, 66, 74
Mayer, Peter, 60, 66, 116
Mayer, Salome, 66
Mayer, Stephanus, 66
Mayer, Susannah, 69
Mayer, Thomas, 62
McLachlen, Anthony W., 122
McLachlen, Christianna, 122
McLachlen, Lea, 122
McLachly, Anton, 130
McLachly, Lea, 130
McLachly, Maria Margaretha, 130
McLaughlin, Henrich, 119
McLaughlin, Lea, 119
Meckle, Jacob, 9
Meckli, Jacob, 133
Mehrkamm, Catharina, 11
Mehrkamm, Conrad, 11
Mehrkamm, Margaretha, 11
Meier, Abby, 129
Meier, Abraham, 121, 128
Meier, Catharina, 123, 125
Meier, Conrad, 126, 129
Meier, Daniel, 123, 124, 132
Meier, David, 126, 141
Meier, Elemina, 125
Meier, Elisabeth, 122, 126, 129
Meier, Eliza, 121
Meier, George, 126,128
Meier, Henry, 122
Meier, Hetty, 128
Meier, John, 141
Meier, John Nicholas, 141

Meier, Jonas, 129, 130,
Meier, Kitty Ann, 128
Meier, Magdalena, 121, 124, 128, 132
Meier, Margaret, 141
Meier, Margaretha, 126, 128
Meier, Peter, 125
Meier, Rebecca, 125, 129
Meier, Ruben, 122, 123
Meier, Susan, 128
Meier, Susanna, 123, 129, 130,
Meier, Thomas, 128
Mensch, Adam, 45
Mensch, Margreth, 45
Mertz, Elisabeth, 39
Mertz, Esther, 39, 128
Mertz, George Henry, 136
Mertz, Henrich, 39
Mertz, Joseph,. 128
Mertz, Magdalena, 124
Mertz, Theobald, 127
Metzgar, John, 121
Metzgar, Polly, 121
Metzger, Johannes, 79
Metzger, John, 92, 111, 115, 124
Metzger, Magdalena, 115
Metzger, Maria, 79, 92, 111,
Metzger, Polly, 124
Meuckley, Eva Catharina, 68
Mueckley, Jacob, 68
Meuckli, Catharina, 24, 27, 31, 36, 42, 46
Meuckli, Christian, 43, 47, 70
Meuckli, Elisabeth, 43, 47, 58
Meuckli, Eva, 29
Meuckli, Eva Catharina, 41, 38, 48, 68
Meuckli, Henrich,, 29
Meuckli, J. Jacob, 37, 38
Meuckli, Jacob, 29, 31, 35, 41, 46, 48, 53
Meuckli, Joh. Jacob, 27
Meuckli, Joh. Martin. 24, 31, 42
Meuckli, Johannes, 42
Meuckli, John, 49
Meuckli, John Jacob, 43
Meuckli, John Martin, 27
Meuckli, Joseph, 31, 53
Meuckli, Maria Barbara, 31
Meuckli, Maria Salome, 53
Meuckli, Peter, 22, 24, 29, 47, 49, 53, 56
Meuckli, Salome, 47, 49, 53, 56
Meuckli, Susanna, 18, 29, 31, 37, 38, 43, 55
Meuckly, Edward, 72
Meuckly, Elisabeth, 58, 70, 78
Meuckly, Henrich, 72, 81
Meuckly, Jacob, 60
Meuckly, Magdalena, 72
Meuckly, Peter, 69, 70, 83
Meuckly, Salome, 69, 70, 78
Meuhlhausen, Ann Kunigunda, 93, 99, 102
Meyer, Abraham, 100, 103, 105, 112, 113, 116,
Meyer, Abigail, 87
Meyer, Adeline, 109
Meyer, Andreas, 37
Meyer, Angeline, 98
Meyer, Anna Maria, 49, 53, 78
Meyer, Barbara, 22, 43, 85
Meyer, Carl, 75, 81, 87, 91, 100
Meyer, Casper, 85
Meyer, Catharina, 22, 24, 28, 25, 26, 29, 30, 31, 32, 34, 36, 39, 40, 41, 46, 49, 53, 55, 59, 66, 68, 71, 74, 77, 79, 81, 82, 85, 87, 89, 94, 95, 98, 104, 106, 109, 113, 118, 132

Meyer, Christina, 70, 71, 74, 79, 80, 81, 82, 86, 92, 104
Meyer, Conrad, 41, 84, 87, 89, 95, 96, 102, 105, 109, 113 117, 113
Meyer, Daniel, 35 , 36, 69, 78, 80, 81, 82, 89, 91, 98, 102, 112, 118
Meyer, David, 74, 84
Meyer, Debora, 77
Meyer, Dorothea, 46, 77
Meyer, Eli, 117
Meyer, Elias, 88
Meyer, Elisabeth, 24, 31, 33, 35, 39, 41, 45, 48. 50, 54, 56, 59, 62, 81, 84, 87, 88, 89, 92, 94, 95, 97, 102, 105, 109, 113, 117
Meyer, Eliza, 85, 89
Meyer, Emilia, 110, 117
Meyer, Eva, 31, 32, 35, 82, 84, 89, 92
Meyer, Georg, 33, 44, 78, 113,
Meyer, George, 53, 70, 88, 89, 92, 98, 106
Meyer, Gideon, 113
Meyer, Gottfried, 45
Meyer, Hanna, 49, 72, 113
Meyer, Henrich, 89, 94
Meyer, Jacob, 28, 33, 31, 35, 39, 45, 48, 50, 56, 59, 70, 71, 74, 79, 80, 81, 82, 86, 89, 92
Meyer, Jacob Ettwine, 109
Meyer, James, 80
Meyer, Jesse, 105
Meyer, Joel, 95
Meyer, Joh. Georg, 41
Meyer, Joh. Jacob, 21
Meyer, Joh. Nicolaus, 21, 49
Meyer, Johannes, 25, 29, 31, 32, 33
Meyer, John, 35, 71, 74, 77, 82, 84,89, 92, 102, 110, 113
Meyer, Jonas, 50, 78, 89, 90, 98, 104, 111, 113, 117
Meyer, Joseph, 39, 59, 72, 75, 77, 80, 82, 86, 87, 90, 92, 94,
Meyer, Jost, 44
Meyer, Juliana, 17, 36
Meyer, Lea, 53
Meyer, Levina, 97
Meyer, Luciana, 92
Meyer, Lucinda, 98
Meyer, Lydia, 84, 105
Meyer, Magdalena, 11, 39, 47, 71, 74, 80, 81, 82, 89, 94, 98, 100, 102, 103, 105, 110, 112, 116, 118
Meyer, Manasse, 74
Meyer, Margaretha, 13
Meyer, Margreth, 32, 33, 35, 36, 38, 51, 52, 67, 80, 82, 84, 87, 88, 95, 92, 97, 98, 102, 104 , 106, 113
Meyer, Maria, 44, 84, 102, 106
Meyer, Maria Magdalena, 32, 37, 44
Meyer, Maria Margreth, 72
Meyer, Martha, 37
Meyer, Martin, 11, 20, 24, 28, 32, 33, 36, 38, 46, 52, 67, 74, 132, 142
Meyer, Mary, 112
Meyer, Paul, 82
Meyer, Peter, 22, 25, 28, 29, 30, 31, 32, 34, 36, 39, 40, 49, 51, 53, 55, 59, 66, 68, 71, 77, 74, 80, 81, 82, 84, 85, 87, 89, 94, 95, 97, 98, 102, 104, 106, 109, 113, 118
Meyer, Rebecca, 89
Meyer, Rosina, 31
Meyer, Ruben, 77, 102

Meyer, Salme, 80
Meyer, Salome, 33, 71, 86
Meyer, Sara, 60, 69
Meyer, Sarah, 34, 98
Meyer, Simom, 94
Meyer, Solomon, 85
Meyer, Sophiana, 113
Meyer, Stephan, 36
Meyer, Stephanus, 21
Meyer, Susanna, 36, 75, 77, 78, 80, 81, 82, 86, 87, 90, 91, 94, 98, 104, 111, 113, 117
Meyer, Thomas, 104
Meyer, Wilhelm, 68, 78, 80, 82,
Meyer, William, 37, 113
Michael, Catharina, 23
Michael, Hoffman, 133
Michael, Johannes. 23
Michel, Adam, 71
Michel, Elisabeth, 64
Michel, Henrich, 23
Michel, Maria, 53, 64, 71
Michel, Peter, 53
Michel, Ulrich, 53, 64, 71,
Mickle, Jacob, 15, 139
Mickle, Johann Jacob, 13
Mickle, Magdalena, 13
Mickle, Martin, 14
Mickle, Susanna,
Mickle, Susanna Margaretha, 13
Mickley, Esther, 78
Mickley, Jacob, 140
Mickley, John Jacob, 136
Mickley, Magdalena, 140
Mickley, Sarah, 145
Mickley, Susanna, 143
Mickli, Daniel, 23
Mickli, Elisabeth, 11
Mickli, Jacob, 23
Mickli, Peter, 23
Mickli, Susanna, 23
Mickly, Jacob, 102, 119
Mickly, Abraham Tilgham, 111
Mickly, Anna, 90
Mickly, Anna, 90, 93, 95, 96, 101, 102, 104, 106, 107, 110, 113, 111, 114, 117, 119, 122, 123, 131,
Mickly, Anna Levina, 90
Mickly, Anne Caroline, 119
Mickly, Carl, 101, 125
Mickly, Carl Mathias, 125
Mickly, Catharina, 75, 96, 98, 99, 100, 101, 105, 110, 115
Mickly, Catharina Anna, 122
Mickly, Charles, 119
Mickly, David, 110
Mickly, Debora, 76
Mickly, Edward, 119, 121
Mickly, Edwin, 119
Mickly, Elisabeth, 78
Mickly, Eliza, 131
Mickly, Eliza Amanda, 115
Mickly, Elizabeth Barbara, 139
Mickly, Ephriam, 110
Mickly, Eva Catharina, 90, 114
Mickly, Francisca, 106
Mickly, Franklin Peter, 123
Mickly, Henrich, 76, 90, 94, 96, 98, 105, 110, 111
Mickly, Jacob, 90, 95, 101, 106, 107, 114, 117, 122, 131
Mickly, James, 110
Mickly, James William, 114
Mickly, Jedda, 119
Mickly, Jetta, 125
Mickly, John Jacob, 139

Mickly, Joseph, 78, 96, 98, 99, 100, 101, 105, 110, 115
Mickly, Lydia, 126
Mickly, Magdalena, 76, 90, 94, 96, 98, 105, 110, 111,
Mickly, Maria, 95, 98
Mickly, Peter, 80, 88, 90, 93, 101, 104, 105, 111, 113, 115, 119, 123, 125, 131
Mickly, Rebecca, 102
Mickly, Salome, 80, 88, 90, 105, 115, 119,
Mickly, Stephanus, 90
Mickly, Susan, 125
Mickly, Susanna, 105, 116
Mickly, Thomas, 93, 94
Mickly, William, 105
Miller, Abraham, 64, 81, 93, 96, 108, 110
Miller, Anna Elisabeth, 20, 25
Miller, Anna Maria, 47, 49, 50, 52, 57, 60, 61, 63, 64, 69, 74, 76, 79, 87
Miller, Barbara, 18, 31, 35, 45, 60, 62, 65
Miller, Anna Maria, 42, 45, 50, 53, 54, 65
Miller, Andreas, 25
Miller, Caroline, 109
Miller, Catharina, 17, 18, 20, 22, 25, 27, 29, 30, 31, 32, 34, 37, 40, 54, 57, 89, 109, 112, 115, 119, 122.
Miller, Catharina Elisabeth, 20
Miller, Charles, 109
Miller, Christian, 18
Miller, Christina, 48, 50, 52, 54, 56, 61, 64, 68, 74, 80, 100
Miller, Conrad, 38, 39
Miller, Daniel, 108, 122
Miller, David, 106
Miller, Edward, 108
Miller, Elisabeth, 19, 30, 35, 49, 50, 54, 75, 104, 108
Miller, Eliza, 122
Miller, Esther, 120
Miller, Eva, 14, 28, 30, 44, 51, 56, 57, 58
Miller, Eva Catharina, 18, 41, 139
Miller, Eva Maria, 33
Miller, Ferdinand, 140
Miller, Georg, 33, 41, 61, 77, 80
Miller, Georg Jacob, 20, 24, 31, 35, 62
Miller, George, 84, 88, 100, 104, 109, 115, 117, 126, 127, 130
Miller, Harrison Walter, 119
Miller, Henrich, 83
Miller, J. Georg, 50
Miller, Jacob, 14, 19, 27, 35, 40, 42, 47, 49, 50, 53, 54, 57, 60, 64, 70, 75, 80, 81, 83, 108
Miller, James, 114
Miller, Joh. Adam, 27
Miller, John Georg, 51
Miller, Joh. Jacob, 22
Miller, Johannes, 14, 19, 31, 33, 38, 48, 50, 65
Miller, John, 28, 48, 49, 50, 52, 54, 57, 60, 61, 63, 69, 74, 76, 79, 87, 124, 131, 139
Miller, Jonas, 33, 47
Miller, Jonathan, 34
Miller, Joseph, 61, 64, 65, 104, 108, 109, 115, 123
Miller, Judith, 120, 122, 127, 128
Miller, Juliana, 26
Miller, Leonhard, 60

165

Miller, Levina, 93
Miller, Lorenz, 82
Miller, Louisa, 127
Miller, Lydia, 69, 106, 114, 127, 130
Miller, Magdalena, 18, 60, 100, 104, 109, 115, 117, 126, 130
Miller, Margreth, 38, 56, 57, 82
Miller, Maria, 40, 57, 70, 72, 75, 81, 83, 93, 109, 120
Miller, Maria Barbara,, 54, 72, 77
Miller, Maria Eva, 32, 133
Miller, Maria Elisabeth, 35
Miller, Maria Magdelana, 44, 70
Miller, Maria Margaretha, 53, 58
Miller, Maria Margreth, 54
Miller, Maria Salome, 56
Miller, Margreth, 39
Miller, Mary Anna, 130
Miller, Mattheus, 77
Miller, Michael, 30, 32,44, 51, 56, 57, 74
Miller, Michel, 33
Miller, Peter, 14, 27, 37, 40, 48, 52, 54, 56, 61, 64, 65, 68, 72, 74, 80, 100, 112, 114, 119, 120, 122, 127, 128, 133
Miller, Philip, 18
Miller, Polly, 123
Miller, Polly Iona, 131
Miller, Rebecca Elisabeth, 50
Miller, Reuben, 126, 131
Miller, Rosina, 33
Miller, Salome, 35, 37, 41, 54, 64
Miller, Samuel, 108, 131
Miller, Sarah, 109, 124, 131
Miller, Sarah Ann, 124
Miller, Sebastian, 17, 18, 20, 22, 25, 27, 29, 30, 31, 32, 34, 37, 40, 54, 56, 57, 58, 60, 65, 72, 77
Miller, Simon, 64
Miller, Stephan, 109
Miller, Susanna, 25, 42, 48, 64, 74, 84, 88, 93, 96, 108, 110, 115
Miller, Susanna Margaret, 139
Miller, Thomas, 100
Miller, Wilhelm, 93
Miller, William, 84, 112
Minnich, Adelina, 112
Minnich, Edwin, 115
Minnich, John, 111
Minnich, Maria, 112, 115, 125
Minnich, Michael, 112, 115, 125
Minnich, Rueben, 125
Minnich, Sarah, 125
Minnich, Susanna, 111
Moharter, Jacob, 66, 77, 82
Moharter, Magdalena, 77
Moharter, Margreth, 66, 77, 82
Moharter, Salome, 82
Moll, Peter, 67
Moll, Salme, 67
Moran, Esther, 120
Moran, Mathilda Sophia Catharina, 120
Moran, P., 120
Moritz, Johannes, 13, 15, 20, 22, 25, 32, 33, 37, 42, 45
Moritz, Magdalena, 20, 25, 33, 42, 45
Moritz, Maria Magdalena, 37
Moser, Catharina, 64
Mosgenung, Christina, 21
Mosgenung, David, 17
Mosser, Anna Barbara, 9
Mosser, Tobias, 9
Muckli, John Jacob, 137
Mueckli, Anna, 51
Mueckli, Anna Catharina, 17
Mueckli, Catharina, 16, 19, 21, 22, 25, 26, 27, 33, 35, 51, 56

Mueckli, Christian, 38, 51, 52, 56
Mueckli, Daniel, 22, 27
Mueckli, Elisabeth, 51, 52, 56
Mueckli, Eva Catharina, 17, 41, 53
Mueckli, Hanna, 56
Mueckli, Hans Jacob, 19
Mueckli, Hans Martin, 19
Mueckli, Henrich, 21, 36, 55
Mueckli, J. Jacob, 25
Mueckli, Jacob, 18, 29, 37, 51
Mueckli, Joh. Jacob, 21, 27
Mueckli, Joh. Martin, 21, 22, 25, 27
Mueckli, Johann Peter, 18
Mueckli, Johann Martin, 35, 36
Mueckli, Jon. Martin, 33
Mueckli, Juliana, 25
Mueckli, Magdalena, 25, 38, 40
Mueckli, Maria Magdalena, 16
Mueckli, Martin, 16, 17
Mueckli, Peter, 51
Mueckli, Salome, 53
Mueckli, Sara, 19, 21, 25, 27, 31, 35, 36, 37, 41
Mueckly, Anna, 66
Mueckly, Carl, 60
Mueckly, Christian, 58, 60, 78
Mueckly, Christina, 69
Mueckly, Daniel, 66
Mueckly, Debora, 70
Mueckly, Elisabeth, 60, 64
Mueckly, Eva Catharina, 60, 62, 71
Mueckly, Henrich, 61, 66
Mueckly, Jacob, 57, 60, 62, 66, 68, 71
Mueckly, Joseph, 58
Mueckly, Magdalena, 60, 61, 66, 81
Mueckly, Peter, 58, 60, 64, 73, 78
Mueckly, Salome, 58, 60, 64, 73, 83
Mueckly, Susanna, 57, 66, 70, 78
Mueckly, Susanna Catharina, 66
Mueckly, Thamar, 66
Mueckly, Wilhelm, 81
Muehlhausen, Anna Kunigunda, 96, 105
Muehlhausen David, 104
Muehlhausen, Elisabeth, 96
Muehlhausen, Henrich, 93, 96, 99, 102, 105
Muehlhausen, Susanna, 93
Muenich, Magdalena, 54
Muenich, Peter, 54
Muennich, Magdalena, 82
Muennich, Peter, 82
Mufli, Johannes, 39
Mufli, Barbara, 39
Mufli, Peter, 39
Muschlitz, Catharina, 118
Muschlitz, Peter, 118
Muschlitz, Sophiana, 118
Muselmann, Magdalena, 70
Muselmann, Peter, 70
Musgenung, Anna Maria, 33
Musgenung, David, 33
Musgenung, Jacob, 33
Music, Catharina, 48
Music, David, 48, 144
Music, Dorothea, 144
Music, Elisabeth, 48
Music, Samuel, 144
Mussellmann, Elisabeth, 103
Mussellmann, Jonas, 103
Mussellmann, Michael, 103
Mussellmann, Salome, 103
Mussellmann, Thomas, 103
Musselmann, Aaron, 109
Musselmann, Eli, 117
Musselmann, Elisabeth, 115
Musselmann, Jonas, 115
Musselmann, Michael, 109, 117
Musselmann, Salome, 109, 117

Myer, Peter, 16
Nagel, Catharina, 81
Nagel, Gutilia, 128
Nagel, Joseph, 128
Nagel, Salome, 128
Nass, Christian, 72
Nass, Christina, 72
Nass, Michael, 72
Naumann, Anna Maria, 47
Naumann, Michael, 47
Nehlich, Nicolaus, 10
Nelson, Robert, 66
Neudardt, Sara, 62
Neuhard, Anna Catharina, 9
Neuhard, Apollonia, 20, 22, 25, 27, 28, 30, 34, 42,
Neuhard, Appollonia, 23, 24, 33, 36, 49, 51
Neuhard, Barbara, 22, 23, 25, 27, 28, 31, 32, 38, 43, 45, 51, 52, 55
Neuhard, Catharina, 26, 34, 37
Neuhard, Cath. Elisabet, 7
Neuhard, Catharina, 26, 34, 40, 44, 47, 51, 53, 54, 55, 84
Neuhard, Catharina Elisabeth, 20, 40
Neuhard, Catharina Elisabetha, 15
Neuhard, Conrad, 30
Neuhard, Daniel, 30, 32, 36, 38, 39, 42
Neuhard, Elisabeth, 8, 24, 43, 46, 47, 48, 50, 51, 53
Neuhard, Elisabetha Margaretha, 133
Neuhard, Eva, 41
Neuhard, Eva Catharina, 30, 32, 36, 39, 42
Neuhard, Fridrich, 15, 20, 22, 23, 24, 25, 27, 28, 30, 33, 34, 36, 42, 47, 51, 55,
Neuhard, Friedrich, 46, 48, 49
Neuhard, Georg, 9
Neuhard, Jacob, 16
Neuhard, Joh. Fridrich, 24
Neuhard, Joh. Jacob, 30
Neuhard, Joh. Peter, 22
Neuhard, Johann Peter, 13
Neuhard, Johannes, 9, 20
Neuhard, John, 46, 46, 50, 51, 52, 55
Neuhard, Jonas, 52
Neuhard, Juliana, 23, 46, 47, 49
Neuhard, Magdalena, 15, 22, 23, 24, 30, 36, 43
Neuhard, Maria Barbara, 13, 15, 17, 19, 20, 23, 24, 26, 27, 54
Neuhard, Maria Catharina, 36
Neuhard, Maria Magdalena, 15, 20, 33
Neuhard, Maria Marg., 7
Neuhard, Maria Margreth, 26, 42
Neuhard, Maria Salome, 28, 39
Neuhard, Michael, 8, 13, 15, 19, 22, 24, 25, 26, 27, 34, 43, 45, 46, 49, 50, 51, 52, 53, 55, 133
Neuhard, Michel, 20, 23, 25, 31, 32, 38
Neuhard, Peter, 13, 14, 15, 20, 22, 23, 24, 26, 32, 34, 37, 40, 43, 44, 46, 47, 51, 53, 54, 55
Neuhard, Salome, 40, 46, 50, 51
Neuhard, Sara, 52, 67
Neuhard, Sarah, 51
Neuhard, Susanna, 49
Neuhardt, Aaron, 106
Neuhardt, Abraham, 78
Neuhardt, Apollonia, 18, 69, 71
Neuhardt, Barbara, 93
Neuhardt, Catharina, 61, 63, 64, 65, 67, 68, 71, 72, 74, 76, 78, 80, 82, 84, 85, 89, 92, 95, 100, 102, 106, 112, 114, 116

Neuhardt, Daniel, 72, 84, 93
Neuhardt, Elisabeth, 57, 58, 92
Neuhardt, Eliza, 85
Neuhardt, Eva, 83
Neuhardt, Friederick, 6, 7
Neuhardt, Friderich, 18, 69, 71
Neuhardt, Jacobus, 100
Neuhardt, Johannes, 58, 59
Neuhardt, John, 62, 67, 72, 78, 80, 83, 84, 89, 95, 109, 116
Neuhardt, Jonas, 83, 85, 89, 92, 95, 100, 105
Neuhardt, Joseph, 64, 67, 116
Neuhardt, Julianna, 12
Neuhardt, Levina, 89, 116
Neuhardt, Lydia, 76, 83
Neuhardt, Magdalena, 61, 92, 105, 116,
Neuhardt, Margaretha, 6, 35,
Neuhardt, Margreth, 72
Neuhardt, Maria, 62, 72, 74
Neuhardt, Maria Barbara, 7, 17, 18, 58
Neuhardt, Maria Magdalena, 17
Neuhardt, Maria Margaret, 7
Neuhardt, Marianna, 105
Neuhardt, Michael, 6, 18, 57, 58, 62, 67, 74, 105, 106, 112, 116
Neuhardt, Michel, 7
Neuhardt, Owen, 7, 17, 57, 61, 63, 64, 65, 67, 68, 72, 74, 76, 78, 82, 84, 89, 92, 100, 106, 109, 110, 112, 114, 116
Neuhardt, Regina, 82
Neuhardt, Ruben, 103, 116
Neuhardt, Sally Anne, 112
Neuhardt, Salome, 68, 104, 106
Neuhardt, Sara, 55, 58, 59, 72, 78, 80, 83, 84, 89, 95, 109, 112, 116
Neuhardt, Susanna, 106, 109, 110
Neuhardt, Wilhelm, 95
Neuhardt, William, 106
Neuhart, Anna Barbara, 8
Neuhart, Barbara, 16
Neuhart, Frederich, 6
Neuhart, John Michael Lorentz, 6
Neuhart, Lorentz, 11
Neuhart, Maria Barbara, 6, 10, 16
Neuhart, Maria Magdalena, 10
Neuhart, Maria Margaretha, 5, 8
Neuhart, Michael, 10, 16
Neuhart, Michel, 6
Neuhardt, Sara, 80
Newhard, Barbara, 136
Newhard, Carlotta Lucetta, 131
Newhard, Catharina, 124, 127
Newhard, Edwin, 122
Newhard, Ezra, 127
Newhard, Frederick, 135, 136, 141
Newhard, Georg Adam, 128
Newhard, George, 135
Newhard, George Jacob, 140
Newhard, Henry, 131
Newhard, John, 124
Newhard, John Hiram, 131
Newhard, Jonas, 127
Newhard, Joseph, 122
Newhard, Lorentz, 135
Newhard, Magdalena, 15, 122, 131, 140
Newhard, Margaretha, 126, 128
Newhard, Maria, 122
Newhard, Mary Ann, 122
Newhard, Michael, 122, 131, 135, 136, 140
Newhard, Peter, 122, 124, 126, 140
Newhard, Rachel, 131
Newhard, Sarah, 122, 131
Newhard, Susanna, 122, 126

Newhard, Tilghman, 126
Neyhard, Fridrich, 51
Neyhard, Juliana, 47
Neyhart, Barbara, 16
Neyhart, Michael, 12, 28, 139
Neyhart, Michel, 12, 13
Nitschman, Johannes, 20, 22
Nitschman, Margreth, 22
Nitschman, Maria Margreth, 20
Oblinger, Catharina, 91
Oblinger, Nicolaus, 91
Oblinger, Salome, 91
Odenwaelder, Catharina, 45
Odenwaelder, Philip, 45
Ohl, Andreas, 9
Ohl, Anna Catharina, 9
Ohl, Elisabeth Barbara, 9
Ohl, Eva Catharinaa, 9
Ohl, Henrich, 9
Ohl, Michael, 9, 137
Orsenbach, Catharina, 50
Orsenbach, Henrich, 50
Osmun, Magdalena, 93, 98
Osmun, Paul, 93
Osmun, Ruben, 98
Osmun, Samuel, 93, 98
Ott, Benjamin, 24
Ott, Dorothea, 21
Ott, Magdalena, 24
Ott, Maria Magdalena, 24
Otterson, John, 126
Otterson, Lydia, 126
Otterson, Mary Ann, 126
Owen, Rebecca, 130
Paillet, Paulus, 6
Paljet, Maria Magdalean, 9
Paljet, Paulus, 9
Palliet, Eva, 12
Palliet, Magdalena, 12
Palliet, Paulus, 12
Palyet, Joh. Jacob, 9
Palyet, Maria Magdalean, 9
Palyet, Paulus, 9
Paul, Anna, 100
Paul, Eli, 105
Paul, Elisabeth, 93
Paul, Esther, 78, 79, 83, 86, 93, 100, 105, 111
Paul, Hannah, 86
Paul, John, 78, 79, 83, 86, 93, 100, 105, 111
Paul, Margreth, 93
Paul, Maria, 111
Paul, Ruben, 79
Paul, Thomas, 86
Pelz, Juliana, 39
Peter, Anna Elisabeth, 24
Peter, Anna Magdalean, 10
Peter, Casper, 25, 26, 29, 77
Peter, Catharina, 77, 82, 93
Peter, Daniel, 93, 118
Peter, Elisabeth, 25, 26, 29, 77, 82, 92, 93, 94, 96, 97, 105, 107, 109, 108, 111, 118
Peter, Elisabetha, 10
Peter, Gottfried, 11, 26, 77, 82, 92, 93, 94, 96, 105, 107, 108, 109, 118
Peter, Jacob, 10
Peter, Joh. Daniel, 25
Peter, Johannes, 30
Peter, John, 82, 99, 101
Peter, Margreth, 30
Peter, Maria Magdalena, 10,
Peter, Maria Elisabeth, 26
Peter, Mathilda, 99
Peter, Rebecca, 118
Peter, Rudolph, 10

Peter, Susanna, 99, 101
Peter, Violetta, 101
Peter, Wilhelm, 93
Pfeiffer, Barbara, 21
Pfeiffer, Catharina, 34
Pfeiffer, Elisabeth Barbara, 17
Pfeiffer, Henrich, 17, 21
Pfeiffer, Johann Nicolaus, 21
Pfeiffer, Sybilla, 36
Plessli, Samuel, 18
Preis, Charles, 117
Preis, John, 117
Preis, Regina, 117
Prengel, Anna Barbara, 7
Prengel, Christian, 7
Prengel, Lorentz, 7
Preston, Catharina, 59
Preston, James, 59
Preston, Magdalena, 59
Queer, Angelina, 130
Queer, Daniel, 84
Queer, Eva, 84
Queer, Eva Elisabeth, 84
Queer, Jonas, 130
Queer, Mary, 130
Ramstet, Nicolas, 133
Rauch, Anna Margreth, 20, 23
Rauch, Catharina, 23
Rauch, Johannes, 18
Rauch, Margreth, 18
Rauch, Peter, 18, 20, 23
Rauch, Susanna, 7, 20
Reg (?), Johan Deis, 133
Reg, Elizabetha, 133
Reichel, Christina, 102
Reichel, Henrich, 102
Reichel, William, 102
Reigy, Peter, 98
Reinert, Catharina, 15
Reinert, Christian, 15
Reinhard, Anna Margretha, 8
Reinhard, Elisabet Maria, 8
Reinhard, Johann Henrich, 8
Reinhardt, Joh. Hen., 9
Reis, Daniel, 129
Reis, Peter Michael, 129
Reis, Sophia, 129
Reiswig, Catharina Margreth, 19
Reiswig, Conrad, 19
Reiswig, Johannes, 19
Reiswig, Maria Susannna, 19
Reit, Aaron, 88
Reit, Benjamin, 114
Reit, Daniel, 114
Reit, Esther, 100
Reit, George, 88, 91, 97, 95, 94, 100, 105, 114, 118, 130
Reit, Leanda, 130
Reit, Magdalena, 88, 95, 97, 91, 94, 100, 105, 114, 118
Reit, Moses, 118
Reit, Polly, 130
Reit, Sophiette, 105
Reit, Stephanus, 91
Reit, Susanna, 114
Reit, William, 94
Remeli, Anna Maria, 46
Remeli, Catharina, 46
Remeli, Elisabeth, 30, 32, 50, 53
Remeli, Georg, 30, 50, 53
Remeli, J. Peter, 53
Remeli, Johannes, 46
Remeli, Jonas, 46
Remelli, Maria, 47
Remelli, Barbara, 45
Remelly, Ambrosius, 34
Remelly, Christina, 37
Remely, George, 91

Remely, Ambros, 75
Remely, Ambrosius, 52
Remely, Elisabeth Barbara, 52
Remely, George, 73, 78, 83, 101, 113
Remely, Hannah, 124
Remely, Lydia, 73, 119
Remely, Magdalena, 57, 103
Remely, Peter, 92, 105, 124
Remely, Regina, 73, 78, 91, 101, 113
Remely, Wilhelm, 103
Remely, William, 121
Remley, Elisabeth Barbara, 75
Remley, Regina, 83
Rendscheimer, Jacob, 110
Rendscheimer, Margreth, 110
Rendscheimer, Rebecca, 110
Rendsheimer, Jacob, 118
Rendsheimer, Joseph, 118
Rendsheimer, Margreth, 118
Rentzheimer, Franklin, 124
Rentzheimer, Jacob, 124
Rentzheimer, Margaretha, 124
Reub, Andreas, 44
Reub, Eva, 44
Rex, Bernhard Jacob, 137
Rex, George, 137
Rex, Hannah, 130
Rex, Jacob, 10
Rhoads, Daniel, 117
Rhoads, Erastus Daniel, 117
Rhoads, John, 137, 140
Rhoads, Peter, 134, 137, 139, 140
Rici, Barbara, 107
Rici, Henrich,
Ricker, George, 125
Ricker, Judith, 125
Riebelet, Barthol, 11
Riebelet, Johannes, 11
Riebelet, Maria Catharina, 11
Ries, Johannes, 13
Rincker, Eva, 47
Ringeiser, Whilelmina, 130
Ringer, Carolina, 123
Ringer, Catharina, 112, 130
Ringer, Chr., 10
Ringer, Daniel, 107, 108, 112, 117
Ringer, George, 101, 105
Ringer, Johannes, 30
Ringer, John, 101
Ringer, Julia, 123
Ringer, Juliana, 103, 116
Ringer, Margreth, 15
Ringer, Maria, 101, 105
Ringer, Michael, 10, 14, 15, 23
Ringer, Michel, 30
Ringer, Salome, 107, 108, 112, 117
Ringer, Sarah, 108
Ringer, Sarah Anna, 103
Ringer, Stephen, 107
Ringer, Susanna, 116
Ringer, William, 103, 116, 123
Rinker, Abigail, 99
Rinker, Catharina. 35
Rinker, Daniel, 89, 91, 94, 95, 99, 103, 106
Rinker, Elisabeth, 40, 89, 102
Rinker, Esther, 96
Rinker, Eva, 35, 81
Rinker, Georg, 35, 40, 85
Rinker, George, 88, 91, 95, 99
Rinker, James, 91
Rinker, Jeremias, 88
Rinker, John, 102
Rinker, Jonas, 85
Rinker, Joseph, 106
Rinker, Juliana, 77, 87, 88, 96
Rinker, Margreth, 21
Rinker, Maria, 85, 88, 91, 95, 99

Rinker, Maria Anna, 95
Rinker, Maria Eva, 21
Rinker, Michel, 21, 35
Rinker, Paulus, 103
Rinker, Ruben, 91
Rinker, Salome, 89, 91, 94, 95, 99, 103, 106
Rinker, Wilhelm, 77, 87, 88
Rinker, William, 81, 96
Rischel, Anna Maria, 17
Rischel, Georg, 17
Rischel, Maria Catharina, 17
Rith, Charles, 115
Rith, Peter, 133
Rittenhaus, Jacob, 38
Rittenhaus, Maria Salome, 38
Ritter, Andreas, 48, 50
Ritter, Anna, 50, 127
Ritter, Anna Maria, 48
Ritter, Barbara, 61
Ritter, Carl, 102
Ritter, Casper, 32, 40
Ritter, Catharina, 48, 94
Ritter, Charles, 107
Ritter, Christina Messina, 119
Ritter, Daniel, 48, 83, 88, 89, 92, 98, 102, 106, 110, 117, 132
Ritter, Elisabeth, 35, 36, 50, 80, 83, 89, 92, 98, 102, 106, 107, 109, 110, 111, 117, 132
Ritter, Esther, 98
Ritter, Hanna, 80, 130
Ritter, Hannah, 119, 122
Ritter, Henrich, 80, 83, 98, 107, 109, 117
Ritter, Henry, 127
Ritter, Jacob, 107
Ritter, Jeremiah, 130
Ritter, Jeremias 68, 115, 119, 122
Ritter, Johann, 98
Ritter, Johannes, 44, 57, 63, 68, 75, 83, 94, 100, 101, 103
Ritter, John, 48, 59, 106, 110, 111
Ritter, Jonas, 63
Ritter, Joseph, 100
Ritter, Louise Carolina, 130
Ritter, Magdalena, 42, 107, 143,
Ritter, Margreth, 32, 104
Ritter, Maria, 57, 59, 63, 68, 75, 83
Ritter, Marianne, 111, 117
Ritter, Martin, 32
Ritter, Michael, 104
Ritter, Ottilia, 32, 40
Ritter, Rebecca, 132
Ritter, Salome, 86, 110
Ritter, Sarah, 94, 98, 100, 101, 103, 106
Ritter, Sarah Anne, 122
Ritter, Susanna, 48, 50, 120, 115
Ritter, Tilghman, 120
Ritter, Wilhelm, 92, 94
Ritter, William George, 127
Rockel, Anna Maria, 67
Rockel, Catharina, 27
Rockel, J. Peter, 32
Rockel, Johann Georg, 67
Rockel, Johannes, 27
Rockel, Magdalena, 69
Rockel, Maria, 63
Rockel, Maria Catharina, 63
Rockel, Melchoir, 63, 67
Roeder, Anna Margaretha, 8
Roeder, Catharina, 19
Roeder, Elisabeth, 132
Roeder, Henrich, 8, 9, 132
Roeder, Maria Susanna, 19
Roeder, Martin, 19
Roether, Adam, 12

Roether, Margaretha Maria Susanna, 12
Romig, Hanna, 63, 117
Romig, Peter, 63, 117
Ross, Catharina, 89
Ross, Eliza, 89
Ross, Hanna, 78
Ross, John, 78, 89
Ross, Regina, 77
Roth, Abraham, 94, 96
Roth, Anna, 58, 108, 122
Roth, Anna Elisabeth, 77
Roth, Anna Maria Elisabeth, 122
Roth, Anna Margaretha, 5
Roth, Anna Maria, 122
Roth, Anna Magdlaena, 136
Roth, Anne, 113, 114, 119, 120
Roth, Barbara, 94, 96
Roth, Catharina, 20, 27, 53, 57, 90, 91, 95, 100, 103, 108, 119, 145
Roth, Catharina Margaret, 144, 145
Roth, Cathrina, 16
Roth, Christian, 73
Roth, Daniel, 5, 75, 93, 100, 133, 134, 144, 145
Roth, David, 68
Roth, Dorothea, 10
Roth, Elisabeth, 62, 68, 73, 77, 82, 86, 93, 110, 111, 114, 116, 119; 120,
Roth, Eliza, 110
Roth, Eliza Melvina, 114
Roth, Eva, 5
Roth, Eva Catharina, 10, 137
Roth, Georg, 67
Roth, George, 110, 111, 114, 119, 120,
Roth, George Jacob, 137, 145
Roth, Godfrey, 137
Roth, Hannah, 116
Roth, Henrich, 121
Roth, Jacob, 10, 53, 62, 73, 77, 82, 86, 93, 108, 113, 114, 119, 120, 122, 133
Roth, James, 78, 119, 122
Roth, Joel, 63
Roth, Joh. Jacob, 27
Roth, Joh. Philip, 20, 27
Roth, Johannes, 10
Roth, John, 90, 91, 95, 100, 103, 108, 122, 137, 145
Roth, Joseph, 62, 116
Roth, Josia, 108
Roth, Magdalena, 61, 100, 137
Roth, Margreth, 82
Roth, Maria, 57, 61, 63, 67, 71, 75, 78, 103, 121
Roth, Paul, 95
Roth, Peter, 5, 12, 15, 16, 47, 57, 61, 63, 67, 71, 75, 78, 134
Roth, Philip, 16, 58, 61, 66, 140
Roth, Rebecca, 61
Roth, Salome, 71, 105, 108, 116
Roth, Sarah, 108
Roth, Solomon, 86
Roth, Sophia Dorothea, 145
Roth, Susanna, 19, 58, 61, 66
Roth, William, 66, 114
Rother, Jacob, 68
Rothrock, John, 101, 108
Rothrock, Maria Magdalena, 108
Rothrock, Polly, 101
Ruch, Catharina, 21
Ruch, Charlotte, 19, 21, 23, 24, 28, 30, 32, 34, 41, 42, 63, 68
Ruch, Conrad, 30
Ruch, David, 68, 126
Ruch, Elisabeth, 34, 37, 39, 42, 62
Ruch, Georg Henrich, 33

Ruch, George, 6, 132, 136, 141
Ruch, Hanna, 30, 53
Ruch, Henrich, 30, 33, 37, 39, 42
Ruch, Joh. Henrich, 42
Ruch, John, 132
Ruch, Joseph, 41
Ruch, Lorentz, 21, 23, 24, 28, 30, 32, 34, 41, 42, 63, 68, 113, 141
Ruch, Lorenz, 19, 145
Ruch, Lucianna, 128
Ruch, Lucy Ann, 127
Ruch, Lydia, 128
Ruch, Maria, 33, 35, 125, 126, 128
Ruch, Maria Susanna, 24
Ruch, Peter, 54, 58, 62, 65, 68, 71, 78, 96, 107, 114, 123, 124, 127, 128, 145
Ruch, Salome, 39
Ruch, Susan, 123, 128
Ruch, Susanna, 6, 62, 65, 68, 71, 78, 96, 107, 114, 124
Ruch, Wilhelm, 39
Ruch, William, 39, 65
Ruch, William Henry, 123
Rueb, Catharina, 39
Rueb, Isaac, 39
Saeger, Abigail, 73, 86
Saeger, Anna Barbara, 21, 135, 143
Saeger, Anna Catharina, 145
Saeger, Anna Elisabeth, 135
Saeger, Anna Eva, 23
Saeger, Anna Maria, 20, 58
Saeger, Anna Mary, 135
Saeger, Barbara, 55, 64, 84, 87, 89, 102, 115, 141
Saeger, Catharina, 35, 56, 62, 64, 81, 84, 87, 95, 141, 142
Saeger, Christian, 21, 23, 30, 39, 41, 64, 73, 135, 141
Saeger, Christina, 29, 141
Saeger, Christina Barbara, 135
Saeger, Daniel, 44, 59, 62, 66, 84, 88, 93, 102, 108, 110, 111, 115, 120, 123, 125, 141
Saeger, Edward, 66
Saeger, Eli Joseph, 91
Saeger, Elisabeth, 44, 64
Saeger, Eva, 20, 28, 30, 33, 42, 43
Saeger, Eva Catharina, 18, 19, 20
Saeger, Isaac, 62
Saeger, J. Jacob, 38
Saeger, Jacob, 48, 50, 68, 70, 73, 76, 80, 81, 97, 141
Saeger, Joh. Jacob, 21
Saeger, Johann Jacob, 87
Saeger, Johannes, 33, 44, 56, 73, 93
Saeger, John, 55, 87, 135, 143, 145
Saeger, John Jacob, 135
Saeger, John Nicholas, 141. 143
Saeger, John Nicolaus, 135
Saeger, John Peter, 55
Saeger, Jonathan, 143
Saeger, Joseph, 82, 86, 91, 92, 103, 107, 120, 123, 126,
Saeger, Magdalena, 44, 48, 55, 64, 65, 73, 82, 83, 86, 87, 91, 92, 103, 106, 107, 120, 123, 141
Saeger, Margaret, 141
Saeger, Margaretha, 10, 24, 59, 62
Saeger, Margreth, 48, 50, 66, 68, 70, 73, 76, 80, 81
Saeger, Maria, 67, 73, 80, 81, 83, 84, 89, 107, 131
Saeger, Maria Charlotte, 23
Saeger, Maria Magdalena, 43
Saeger, Maria Susanna, 23, 28
Saeger, Mary Margaret, 135
Saeger, Mathilda, 125

Saeger, Nathan, 64, 112
Saeger, Nicholas, 64, 67, 83, 143
Saeger, Nicolaus, 22, 24, 28, 33, 39, 42, 43, 48, 55, 56, 58, 62, 64, 65. 73, 81, 82, 84, 86, 87, 95, 135
Saeger, Peter, 56
Saeger, Ruben, 84
Saeger, Salanda, 82
Saeger, Salome, 39, 50, 56, 64
Saeger, Samuel, 20, 23, 64, 78, 84, 89, 102, 115, 135, 141
Saeger, Stephanus, 73
Saeger, Susanna, 21, 30, 38, 39, 41, 88, 93, 102, 108, 110, 111, 115, 120, 123, 125
Saeger, Tilghman, 84
Sahm, Johannes, 82, 85, 88
Sahm, Johannes Jacob, 84
Sahm, Maria, 82
Sahm, Susanna, 82, 85, 88
Sauerwein, Charles, 120
Sauerwein, Elisabeth, 120
Sauerwein, Maria Anna, 125
Sauerwein, Sarah, 125
Sauerwein, William, 120, 125
Sauerwine, Charles, 131
Sauerwine, Elisabeth, 131
Sauerwine, Henry William, 131
Sauerwine, Ludwig, 131
Sauerwine, Nathan, 131
Sauerwine, Sarah, 131
Sauerwine, William, 131
Schaad, Abraham, 113
Schaad, Carolina, 126
Schaad, Henrich, 113
Schaad, John, 126, 132
Schaad, Josiah, 129
Schaad, Lorentz, 129
Schaad, Magdalena, 113, 129
Schaad, Maria, 126, 132
Schaad, Sophiana, 113
Schaad, Susanna, 113
Schaad, Tilghman, 132
Schaal, Elisabeth, 91
Schaal, Maria, 91
Schaal, Michael, 91
Schad, Abraham, 104, 107, 118, 120, 125, 128, 130
Schad, Benjamin Henry, 110
Schad, Caroline, 104
Schad, Catharina, 71
Schad, David, 107
Schad, Debora, 88
Schad, Delila, 75
Schad, Edwin, 108
Schad, Elisabeth, 61, 79
Schad, Esther, 92, 119
Schad, Franklin, 117
Schad, Georg, 61, 62, 75,
Schad, George, 58, 68
Schad, Hanna, 102
Schad, Henrich, 88, 99, 103, 107, 110, 119, 123
Schad, Henry, 122, 129
Schad, Johannes, 61, 79
Schad, John, 69, 92, 97, 102, 104, 107, 112, 117
Schad, Lea, 62
Schad, Lenora, 118
Schad, Lorentz, 124
Schad, Lorenz, 84, 87, 88, 93, 97, 102, 103, 107, 108, 113, 118
Schad, Luciana, 107
Schad, Magdalena, 69, 74, 75, 84, 87, 88, 93, 97, 99, 102, 103, 107, 108, 110, 112, 113, 118, 119, 124

Schad, Margretha, 97
Schad, Maria, 92, 97, 102, 104, 107, 112, 117, 122, 123, 128, 129
Schad, Maria Anna, 93
Schad, Monroe
Schad, Moses, 113
Schad, Owen, 104
Schad, Peter, 75
Schad, Ruben, 84
Schad, Salome, 58, 61, 62, 69, 75
Schad, Sarah Anna, 103
Schad, Susanna, 74, 104, 107, 108, 110, 116, 118, 120, 124, 125, 128, 130, 144
Schad, Thomas, 120
Schad, William. 99
Schadt, Johannes, 139
Schadt, John, 111
Schadt, Maria, 111
Schaefer, Anna Maria, 88
Schaefer, Daniel, 88
Schaefer, Elisabeth, 73
Schaefer, Jacob, 73
Schaefer, James, 73
Schaefer, Louise Friderica, 88
Schaefer, Lydia, 73
Schaefer, Peter, 73
Schaeffer, Adam, 131
Schaeffer, Jacob, 131
Schaeffer, Juliana, 131
Schanz, Peter, 114
Scheerer, Clarissa, 114
Scheerer, Hanna, 111
Scheerer, Hannah, 114
Scheerer, John, 111, 114
Scheerer, Marianda, 111
Scheldon, Andrew, 131
Scheldon, Anna, 104, 131
Scheurer, Anne
Scheurer, Alfred, 128
Scheurer, Amandus, 105
Scheurer, Caroline, 109
Scheurer, Catharina, 74, 77, 79, 81, 82, 84, 86, 89, 92, 93, 97, 98, 99, 102, 107, 109, 114, 118, 129
Scheurer, Charles, 105
Scheurer, David, 93, 99, 109, 115, 119, 128,
Scheurer, Dorothea, 89, 93, 96, 98, 102, 106, 110
Scheurer, Eli, 93
Scheurer, Elisabeth, 75, 80, 85, 87, 93, 96, 99, 100, 105, 106, 109, 115, 117, 118, 119, 120, 128
Scheurer, Eliza, 93
Scheurer, Erwine, 95
Scheurer, Eva, 64, 103
Scheurer, Georg, 68
Scheurer, Georg Adam, 129
Scheurer, George, 80, 85, 87, 96, 100, 106
Scheurer, George LaFayette, 106
Scheurer, Hanna, 85
Scheurer, J. Jacob, 81, 97, 99, 102, 109, 107
Scheurer, Jacob, 79, 82, 97
Scheurer, Jacobus, 74
Scheurer, Johann Jacob, 74
Scheurer, John, 64, 103, 114, 118, 129,
Scheurer, Jonas, 89, 93, 96, 98, 102, 106, 110
Scheurer, Lydia, 63, 117
Scheurer, Maria, 115, 117
Scheurer, Mariane, 99
Scheurer, Marianne, 118
Scheurer, Moses, 110

Scheurer, Nicolaus, 75, 80, 85, 95, 120
Scheurer, Owen, 114
Scheurer, Paulus, 90
Scheurer, Peter, 77, 79, 82, 89
Scheurer, Reuben, 126
Scheurer, Salme, 79
Scheurer, Solomon, 74, 80, 84, 85, 86, 90, 92, 93, 99
Scheurer, Susanna, 80, 85, 90, 95, 120
Scheurer, Thomas, 102
Scheurer, Tilghman, 89
Scheurer, William, 117
Schifferstein, Nathan, 131
Schlosser, Anna Margaretha, 133
Schlosser, Barbara, 8
Schlosser, Conrad, 133
Schlosser, Leonhard, 133
Schlosser, Stephanus, 117
Schmid, Catharina, 133
Schmid, Christian, 8, 133
Schmid, Joh. Henr., 8
Schmidt, Carl, 79, 112
Schmidt, Catharina, 75, 78, 79, 92, 97, 112
Schmidt, Daniel, 79, 92, 97
Schmidt, Hanna, 111
Schmidt, Hannah. 101
Schmidt, Jacob, 112
Schmidt, John, 101, 111
Schmidt, Lewis, 115
Schmidt, Ludwig, 144
Schmidt, Rolamd, 6
Schmidt, Sally Ann, 97
Schmidt, Salme, 78
Schmidt, Salome, 115
Schmidt, Samuel, 92
Schmidt, Stephanus, 101
Schmidt, Wilhelm, 75, 78
Schmoll, Catharina, 75, 107
Schmoll, Charles, 111
Schmoll, George, 64
Schmoll, Levi, 111
Schmoll, Peter, 88, 103, 107
Schmoll, Salome, 88, 107, 111
Schmoll, Sara, 64
Schmoll, Sarah, 103
Schmoll, Simon, 103
Schmoll, Susanna, 64
Schneck, Adam, 83
Schneck, David, 131
Schneck, Elisabeth, 131
Schneck, Eliza, 93
Schneck, John, 81, 93, 131
Schneck, Magdalena, 78, 81, 93
Schneck, Peter, 78
Schneck, Ruben, 81
Schneck, Susanna, 83
Schneid, Johannes, 7
Schneider, ___, 21
Schneider, Ann Elisabeth, 18
Schneider, Ann Elisabetha, 14
Schneider, Anna Margaretha, 9
Schneider, Anna Maria, 6, 7
Schneider, Catharina, 10, 60, 64, 66
Schneider, Christophel, 14, 18
Schneider, Conrad, 27
Schneider, Daniel, 10, 60, 64, 66, 111
Schneider, Elisabeth, 22, 111
Schneider, Eliza, 110
Schneider, Eva, 6, 7, 12
Schneider, Friederich, 6
Schneider, Georg Jacob, 6
Schneider, Hanna, 93
Schneider, Hannes, 13
Schneider, Henrich, 110
Schneider, Henry, 124
Schneider, Joh. Friederich, 7

Schneider, Joh. Nicolaus, 7
Schneider, Johann Nicolaus, 6, 12
Schneider, Johann Samuel, 7
Schneider, Johannes, 7, 8, 9, 12
Schneider, John, 140
Schneider, Julianna Catharina, 7
Schneider, Margaretha, 13, 124
Schneider, Margreth, 110
Schneider, Maria, 99
Schneider, Maria Barbara, 6
Schneider, Maria Barbel, 10
Schneider, Peter, 7, 93, 99
Schneider, Salome, 95, 106, 114
Schneider, Samuel, 95, 106, 114
Schneider, Sara, 9
Schneider, Stephan, 11
Schneider, Susanna, 13
Schneider, Wilhelm, 23
Schnerr, Anna, 113
Schnerr, Georg, 64
Schnerr, George, 77, 113
Schnerr, Jacob, 64
Schnerr, Levi, 64, 129
Schnerr, Lydia, 129
Schnerr, Magdalena, 64, 77, 113
Schnerr, Peter, 113
Schnerr, Thomas, 129
Schnerr, William, 113
Schneyder, Christian, 133
Schneyder, Maria Christina, 133
Schoenebruch, Eva, 101, 116
Schoenebruch, Johannes, 101, 116
Scholl, Henrich, 99
Scholl, Jacob, 99
Scholl, Regina, 99
Schlosser, Leonhard, 8
Schreiber, Aaron, 75
Schreiber, Adam, 104
Schreiber, Barbara, 71, 75, 91, 93, 99, 102, 104, 110, 116
Schreiber, Catharina Elisabetha, 14, 16
Schreiber, Christina, 104
Schreiber, Daniel, 71, 75, 91, 93, 99, 102, 104, 110, 116
Schreiber, David, 116
Schreiber, Edward, 68, 121
Schreiber, Elisabeth, 24, 104
Schreiber, Elisabeth Amanda Melvina, 102
Schreiber, Eliza Juliana, 100
Schreiber, Eva, 64, 68, 87, 92, 100, 112, 117
Schreiber, George, 100, 140
Schreiber, Horace, 104
Schreiber, Jacob, 8, 13, 16, 21, 24, 64, 68, 87, 92, 100, 112, 117, 133, 136, 140, 142, 146
Schreiber, Johann Jacob, 13
Schreiber, Johannes, 17
Schreiber, John Jacob, 139
Schreiber, Juliana, 13, 100
Schreiber, Maria, 68, 87, 93
Schreiber, Maria Magdalena, 14, 133
Schreiber, Peter, 66, 68, 73, 84, 88, 102, 104, 110, 127
Schreiber, Philip Jacob, 8, 11, 14, 139, 145
Schreiber, Philippus Jacobus, 13
Schreiber, Ruben, 71
Schreiber, Salome, 64, 146
Schreiber, Susanna, 21, 24, 66, 68, 73, 84, 88, 102, 127, 145
Schreiber, Theresia, 99
Schriber, Catharina, 12
Schriber, Jacob, 12
Schrieber, Abigail, 121
Schrieber, Apollona, 79

Schrieber, Barbara, 79
Schrieber, Catharina Elisabetha, 15
Schrieber, Daniel, 79
Schrieber, Elisabeth, 17
Schrieber, Jacob, 17, 133
Schrieber, John, 80
Schrieber, Johann Georg, 133
Schrieber, Peter, 79
Schrieber, Philipp Jacob, 15
Schrieber, Salme, 80
Schrieber, Susanna, 79
Schriebler, Anna Margareth, 17
Schriebler, Johann Carl, 17
Schuerer, Anna, 68
Schuerer, Catharine Elizabeth, 68, 70
Schuerer, Johann Jacob, 68
Schuerer, Magdalena, 64
Schuerer, Maria Catharina, 68
Schuerer, Susanna, 63, 75
Schumacher, Adam, 119
Schumacher, Barbara, 58, 60
Schumacher, Catharina, 12, 21, 24
Schumacher, Daniel, 117, 119, 122,. 124
Schumacher, Esther, 117, 119
Schumacher, Friedrich, 58, 60
Schumacher, Henrich, 58
Schumacher, Jacob, 60
Schumacher, Luciana, 117
Schumacher, Lucinda, 124
Schurer, Nicolaus, 63
Schutter, Maria Christina, 11
Schwab, Anna Barbara, 14
Schwab, Daniel, 131
Schwab, Jacob, 131
Schwab, Johann Martin, 14
Schwab, Maria, 131
Schwager, Elizabeth, 144
Schwager, Peter, 144
Schwartz, Elisabeth, 76, 110
Schwartz, John, 110
Schwarz, Christian, 76
Scotlan, Andreas, 95
Scotlan, John, 95
Scotlan, Maria, 95
Seager, Maria, 53
Seager, Nicolaus, 53
Seeger, Christian, 11
Seeger, Margretha, 11
Seeger, Nicolaus, 132
Seeger, Samuel, 8. 132
Segar, Christian, 13
Segar, Susanna, 13
Seger, Anna Barbara, 6
Seger, Anna Maria, 13
Seger, Barbara, 7
Seger, Christian, 12, 17, 31, 34
Seger, Elisabetha, 11
Seger, Eva, 32, 37
Seger, Joh. Nicolaus, 7
Seger, Johannes, 39
Seger, John, 13
Seger, Maria Susanna, 12, 17, 31, 34
Seger, Niclaus, 5
Seger, Nicolas, 6, 62, 37,
Seger, Samuel, 7
Seger, Susanna, 34
Seibel, Jacob, 63
Seibel, Jonas, 63
Seibel, Sarah, 63
Seiberling, Juliana, 23
Seider, Catharina, 97
Seider, John, 97
Seiger, Elisabeth, 107
Seigfried, Andreas, 41
Seigfried, Anna Elisabeth, 41
Seigfried, Catharina, 130
Seigfried, Elisabeth, 126

Seip, Georg Jacob, 24
Seip, Susanna, 24
Seip, Wilhelm, 24
Sem, Georg, 50
Sem, Margreth, 50
Semel, Johannes, 70
Semel, Maria, 70
Semm, Georg, 20
Semm, Margreth, 20
Semm, Maria Magdalena, 20
Semmel, Catharina, 82, 83, 100, 117
Semmel, Martin, 82, 83, 100, 117
Sensinger, Cathrina, 6
Sensinger, Joh. Peter, 6
Sensinger, Ulrich, 6
Seyp, Susanna, 22
Seyp, Wilhelm, 22
Shad, Abraham, 54
Shad, Anna Maria, 49
Shad, Catharina, 45
Shad, Catharina Elisabeth, 21
Shad, Elisabeth, 34, 37, 38, 41, 45, 48, 54, 56
Shad, Georg, 35, 40, 51, 53, 57,
Shad, George, 52
Shad, Henrich, 49
Shad, Johannes, 25, 34, 37, 38, 41, 45, 48, 49, 54, 56
Shad, John, 38
Shad, Jonas, 34
Shad, Jonathan, 57
Shad, Lorenz, 41
Shad, Magdalena, 43
Shad, Peter, 37
Shad, Salome, 35, 37, 40, 41, 43, 45, 49, 51, 52, 53, 57
Shad, Susanna, 45
Shaed, George, 65
Shaed, Margreth, 65
Shaefer, Anna Maria, 17
Shaefer, Antoni, 22
Shaefer, Catharina, 22
Shaefer, Dewald, 20
Shaefer, Magdalena, 20
Shaefer, Marie Catharina, 20
Shantz, Daniel, 49
Shantz, Elisabeth, 42
Shantz, Hanna, 39
Shantz, Johannes, 30
Shantz, John, 39, 42, 49
Shantz, Magdalena, 39, 42, 49
Shantz, Philip, 34
Shed, Hans Georg, 17
Sheirer, Hannah, 122
Shenck, Jacob, 40
Shenck, Magdalena, 40
Shettel, Henry, 142
Sheuer, Adam, 41
Sheuer, Catharina Elisabeth, 41
Sheuer, Joh. Georg, 41
Sheurer, Anna Elisabeth, 21
Sheurer, Adam, 21, 30, 35, 41, 43, 44, 47, 51, 56
Sheurer, Catharina, 42, 43, 44, 56, 126,
Sheurer, Cath. Elisabeth, 35
Sheurer, Catharina Elisabeth, 23, 30, 41
Sheurer, David, 105
Sheurer, J. Adam, 23
Sheurer, Joseph, 44
Sheurer, Maria Magdalena, 35
Sheurer, Peter, 23, 48, 56
Sheurer, Thomas, 126
Shick, Georg Emmerich, 19
Shick, Johannes, 19
Shick, Maria Margreth, 19
Shmoll, Carl, 55

Shmoll, Catharina, 45
Shmoll, Georg, 34, 36, 45, 47, 55, 56
Shmoll, Peter, 47
Shmoll, Susanna, 45, 47, 55, 56,
Shneck, Joh. Peter, 35
Shneck, Magdalena, 35
Shneck, Peter, 27
Shneider, Conrad, 28, 31, 39
Shneider, Daniel, 25. 40
Shneider, Eva, 39
Shneider, Hanna, 33
Shneider, Maria Eva, 31
Shneider, Michel
Shoch, Reuben, 128
Shreiber, Anna Maria, 19
Shreiber, Catharina Elisabeth, 19, 43
Shreiber, Elisabeth, 21, 26, 28, 29, 46, 47
Shreiber, Daniel, 33
Shreiber, Eva, 29
Shreiber, Eva Catharina, 26, 34
Shreiber, Georg, 22
Shreiber, Jacob, 13, 19, 26, 28, 29, 43, 46, 47,
Shreiber, Juliana, 22
Shreiber, Maria Margareth, 19
Shreiber, Peter, 30, 31, 33
Shribeler, Anna Margreth, 19, 22
Shribeler, Johann Carl, 19
Shribeler, Jon. Carl, 22
Shrieber, Barbara, 51
Shrieber, Elisabeth, 33, 44
Shrieber, Georg, 17
Shrieber, Jacob, 33, 44
Shrieber, Juliana, 17
Shrieber, Peter, 31
Shumacher, Barbara, 56
Shumacher, Christina Margreth, 55
Shumacher, Fridrich, 54, 56
Shumacher, J. Henrich, 55
Shumacher, Jacob, 22
Shumacher, Magdalena, 56
Shumacher, Salome, 55
Shumacher, Susanna, 54
Shumacher, Wilhelm, 56
Shumacker, Barbara, 54
Shwager, Elisabeth, 47
Shwager, Peter, 47
Shwander, Barbara, 25, 28
Shwander, Catharina, 28
Shwander, Friderich, 28
Shwander, Heinrich, 25
Shwander, Jacob, 25, 28
Shwartz, Anna Elizabeth, 31
Shwartz, Christian, 37, 39, 43, 51, 54
Shwartz, Christina, 31
Shwartz, Daniel, 28, 31
Shwartz, Elisabeth, 31, 37, 39, 51
Shwartz, Margaretha, 31
Shwartz, Maria Eva, 31
Sieder, Catharina, 97
Sieder, John, 97
Sieder, Levina, 97
Sieger, George, 107
Siegfried, Aaron, 60,
Siegfried, Andreas, 25, 26, 29, 30, 32, 34, 38, 44, 48, 54, 60, 61, 67, 77, 81, 87, 90, 91, 94, 100
Siegfried, Anna Elisabeth, 25, 26, 29, 44, 48, 54, 67, 77, 100
Siegfried, Anna Margaretha, 22
Siegfried, Carl, 68
Siegfried, Carolina, 126
Siegfried, Caroline, 99
Siegfried, Catharina, 34, 68, 71, 76, 79, 87, 99, 128
Siegfried, Daniel, 30, 63, 65, 68, 70, 72, 87, 92, 128, 129, 130

Siegfried, Elisabeth, 30, 32, 34, 38, 59, 60, 61, 81, 91, 99, 120, 129
Siegfried, Eliza, 111
Siegfried, Henriette, 71
Siegfried, Isaac, 75, 77, 99
Siegfried, Jacob, 94
Siegfried, Jacobus, 71
Siegfried, Joh. Andreas, 44
Siegfried, Johannes, 38
Siegfried, John, 63, 64, 100
Siegfried, Jonathan, 54
Siegfried, Joseph, 48, 61, 63, 64, 67, 72, 85, 91, 99, 111, 120, 126
Siegfried, Juliana, 74
Siegfried, Madgalena, 85, 87, 90, 91, 94, 111
Siegfried, Margareth, 32
Siegfried, Maria, 64, 100
Siegfried, Maria Barbara, 26
Siegfried, Maria Elisabeth, 44
Siegfried, Maria Magdalena, 82
Siegfried, Peter, 27, 59, 60, 64, 67, 71, 76, 79, 81, 85
Siegfried, Ruben, 94
Siegfried, Salome, 41, 85
Siegfried, Sara, 63, 72
Siegfried, Sarah, 92
Siegfried, Solomon, 71, 72, 74, 77, 82, 85,
Siegfried, Susanna, 59, 60, 61, 63, 64, 67, 68, 71, 72, 74, 76, 77, 79, 81, 82, 85
Siegfried, Thomas, 87
Siegfried, Wilhelm, 90
Siegfried, William, 94
Sies, Johann Georg, 21
Sies, Maria Magdalena, 21
Sigfrid, Andreas, 51
Sigfrid, Anna, 51
Sigfrid, Anna Elisabeth, 51
Sigfried, Andreas, 27, 35
Sigfried, Elisabeth, 27, 35
Sigfried, Eva Elisabeth, 18
Sigfried, Peter, 18, 27
Sigfried, Solomon, 35
Sigli, Elisabeth, 46
Small, George, 143
Sneider, Peter, 38
Snyder, Elizabeth, 145
Snyder, John, 138
Sohn, Albertina, 30, 34, 38, 40, 45, 47, 56, 82, 105, 108
Sohn, Apollonia, 105
Sohn, Catharina, 34
Sohn, Daniel, 40. 82, 83, 118
Sohn, Elisabeth, 45, 83, 105, 118, 122
Sohn, Friedrich, 83
Sohn, Jacob, 34, 38, 40, 45, 47, 56, 81, 105, 122,
Sohn, Jesse, 122
Sohn, Joh. Jacob, 30
Sohn, Magdalena, 118
Sohn, Margaretha, 38
Sohn, Maria, 82, 83
Sohn, Maria Barbara, 47
Sohn, Peter, 56
Sold, Daniel, 8
Sold, Henrich, 8
Solt, ____, 10
Solt, Daniel, 10
Solt, Johannes, 12
Solt, Maria Catherina, 12
Solt, Melchoir, 11
Spaed, George, 74
Spaed, Margreth, 74
Spaengler, Caroline, 112
Spaengler, Catharina, 112

Spaengler, George, 112
Spaet, George, 70, 73
Spaet, Margreth, 70, 73
Sped, Anna Maria, 19, 40
Sped, Hans Georg, 17
Sped, Johannes, 19
Stapp, Anne, 107
Stapp, Christina, 118
Stapp, Jacob, 107, 118
Stapp, Mary, 107
Steckel, Abraham, 72, 113
Steckel, Aegidius, 106
Steckel, Alexander, 103
Steckel, Amos, 126
Steckel, Anna Maria, 69, 75, 76, 79, 93, 100, 110, 112, 116, 121, 123, 124, 131
Steckel, Carl, 99
Steckel, Caroline, 115
Steckel, Catharina, 86, 145
Steckel, Clarissa, 108
Steckel, Colette, 112
Steckel, Daniel, 15, 74, 84, 86, 89, 93, 95, 99, 103, 106, 110, 111, 115, 118, 123, 126, 131
Steckel, David, 119
Steckel, Debora, 83
Steckel, Dorothea, 142
Steckel, Edward, 124
Steckel, Eli, 93, 99
Steckel, Elisabeth, 64, 66, 69, 75, 77, 79, 80, 83, 85, 86, 87, 89, 93, 94, 95, 99, 102, 103, 108, 111, 113, 115, 118, 119, 123, 126, 127, 131
Steckel, Elisabetha, 15
Steckel, Emelia, 115
Steckel, Ephriam, 111
Steckel, Esther, 75, 118
Steckel, Eva Catharina, 59, 62
Steckel, Henrich, 58, 66, 69, 79, 83
Steckel, Henriette, 113
Steckel, Jacob, 62, 79, 81, 142
Steckel, James, 89
Steckel, Johann Peter, 69
Steckel, Johannes, 58
Steckel, John, 69, 74, 76, 85, 86, 89
Steckel, Joseph, 58, 103, 111, 115, 118, 119, 124
Steckel, Levina, 93
Steckel, Magdaleana, 58, 69, 74, 76, 85, 86, 89
Steckel, Margaret, 142
Steckel, Maria, 58, 66, 69, 80, 81, 83, 95, 100, 103, 104, 108, 111, 115, 118, 119
Steckel, Maria Salome, 87
Steckel, Maria Susanna, 145
Steckel, Mary, 124
Steckel, Peter, 9, 15, 64, 66, 69, 75, 77, 79, 80, 83, 85, 86, 87, 89, 93, 94, 95, 99, 102, 103, 108, 111, 113, 118, 119, 127, 136, 142
Steckel, Rebecca, 113
Steckel, Regina, 50
Steckel, Ruben, 123
Steckel, Sally Ann, 127
Steckel, Sally Anne, 111
Steckel, Salome, 65, 66, 86, 89, 93, 95, 99, 103, 106, 110, 111
Steckel, Solomon, 69, 75, 76, 79, 80, 93, 100, 104, 108, 110, 112, 113, 116, 121, 123. 124, 128, 131, 142
Steckel, Thomas, 94
Steckel, Wilhelm, 80
Stein, Himan L., 130

Stein, Julia, 130
Stein, Peter, 35
Stein, Sarah Ann, 130
Steinberger, Elisabeth, 76
Stemmler, Henrich, 34
Stettler, Catharina, 70
Stettler, Jacob, 70
Stichler, Eva, 120
Stichler, Jacob, 120
Stichler, Maria Catharina, 120
Stoeckel, Abraham, 32
Stoeckel, Anna Elisabetha, 18
Stoeckel, Catharina, 56
Stoeckel, Elisabeth, 22, 50, 49, 54
Stoeckel, Eva Catharina, 27, 28, 29, 32, 34, 35, 38, 40, 46, 48
Stoeckel, Daniel, 40
Stoeckel, Henrich, 3, 25, 27, 28, 29, 33, 38
Stoeckel, Jacob, 21, 27, 28, 29, 31, 32, 33, 34, 35, 40, 46, 48
Stoeckel, Johannes, 31, 34, 36
Stoeckel, John, 40, 43, 50
Stoeckel, John Jacob, 38
Stoeckel, Magdalena, 36, 40, 43, 50
Stoeckel, Margaretha, 24
Stoeckel, Maria, 33, 38
Stoeckel, Maria Susanna, 27
Stoeckel, Peter, 7, 16, 18, 22, 33, 43, 49, 50, 54
Stoeckel, Salome, 36
Stoeckel, Solomon, 38
Stoeckel, Susanna, 51, 53
Stoeckli, Elisabeth, 20
Stoeckli, Peter, 20
Stoeri, Gertrude, 21
Stofflet, Eva, 44, 46, 53
Stofflet, John, 44, 46, 53
Stofflet, Jonas, 53
Stofflet, Ludwig, 41, 56
Stofflet, Magdalena, 41
Stofflet, Maria, 44, 45, 50
Stofflet, Susanna, 41, 56
Stofflet, William, 56
Stoflet, Caroline, 111
Stoflet, Catharina, 95
Stoflet, Deborah, 116
Stoflet, Elisabeth, 73
Stoflet, Eva, 37, 60, 73, 85, 101
Stoflet, Hanna, 60
Stoflet, Johannes, 101
Stoflet, John, 37, 60, 75, 85, 101, 139
Stoflet, Jonas, 95, 101, 106, 111, 116, 120, 129
Stoflet, Ludwig, 37
Stoflet, Margaretha, 129
Stoflet, Margreth, 95, 101, 106, 111, 116, 120
Stoflet, Maria Magdalena, 101
Stoflet, Nathan, 129
Stoflet, Susanna, 106
Storb, Albert, 143
Storb, Sarah, 107
Storb, Theodore, 107, 143
Stras, Simon, 75
Straus, Carl, 60
Straus, Catharina Andrea, 92
Straus, Clara Catharina 115
Straus, Clarissa, 115
Straus, David, 84
Straus, Elisabeth, 60, 70, 75, 90, 91
Straus, Eva, 125
Straus, Henrich, 92
Straus, John, 125
Straus, Peter, 115
Straus, Philip, 72, 84, 115
Straus, Regina, 72

Straus, Salome, 72, 84
Straus, Simon, 60, 70, 90, 91
Straus, Thomas, 91
Strauss, Catharina, 64, 65, 66, 71, 75, 82
Strauss, Elisabeth, 64, 65, 66, 75, 78, 83, 86
Strauss, Johann Peter, 71, 75
Strauss, John, 76, 118
Strauss, Jost, 65, 66
Strauss, Lydia, 118
Strauss, Magdalena, 80, 115, 119
Strauss, Maria, 86
Strauss, Marianne, 119
Strauss, Peter, 65, 71, 82, 120
Strauss, Philip, 76, 78, 80, 89, 93, 119
Strauss, Ruben, 78
Strauss, Salome, 76, 77, 80, 89, 93
Strauss, Sara, 66
Strauss, Simon, 64, 66, 75, 78, 83, 86, 93
Strein, Jacob, 39, 43, 47
Strein, Maria Barbara, 39, 47
Stricker, Friedrich, 83
Strieby, Catharina, 72
Strien, Jacob, 49
Strien, Maria Barbara, 43, 49
Swartz, Christina, 45
Swartz, Elisabeth, 43, 45, 54
Swartz, Jacob, 31
Symonds, Assah, 49, 50
Symonds, Assah, 49
Symonds, Magdalena, 49
Symonds, Margreth, 49, 50
Tanner, Christina, 7
Taylor, Sarah, 92
Taylor, Sem, 92
Taylor, William, 92
Teichman, George, 70
Teichman, John, 57, 129
Teichman, Susanna, 57
Teichmann, Abraham, 59
Teichmann, Catharina, 62
Teichmann, George, 84, 97
Teichmann, John, 59, 60, 72, 73, 85, 87, 90, 92, 96, 104, 108, 113
Teichmann, Susanna, 59, 60, 72, 73, 84, 85, 87, 90, 92, 96, 97, 104, 108, 113
Teschler, Adam, 7, 16
Teschler, Maria Catharina, 16
Teschler, Maria Barbara, 16
Teschler, Peter, 7
Texchler, Apel, 7
Texchler, Hann Apel, 7
Theichmann, John, 57
Theichmann, Susanna, 57
Theil, Margaretha, 23
Thimm, David, 92
Thomas, Conrad, 44
Thomas, Elisabeth, 44
Thomas, Peter, 44
Thormeyer, Andreas, 17, 19
Thormeyer, Anna Maria, 17
Thormeyer, Catharina, 19
Thormeyer, Maria Magdalena, 19
Thurburn, Jenny, 67
Toeschler, Apolonia, 8
Torchius, Peter Henrich, 6
Torner, Catharina, 75
Torner, Jacob, 75
Torner, Stephanus, 75
Trachsel, Maria, 52
Trachsel, Adam, 24, 27, 28, 31
Trachsel, Anna Maria, 27, 28, 31
Trachsel, Catharina, 13, 14, 15, 23
Trachsel, Christian, 31

Trachsel, Elisabetha, 14
Trachsel, Eva, 15
Trachsel, Joh. Adam, 19
Trachsel, Joh. Peter, 19, 21
Trachsel, Joh. Niclaus, 27
Trachsel, Johann Peter, 8
Trachsel, Maria Barbara, 13, 28
Trachsel, Michel, 12
Trachsel, Nicolaus, 27
Trachsel, Nikel, 13, 15
Trachsel, Peter, 8, 28
Trachsel, Sibilla, 50
Trachsel, Stephan, 52
Traxel, Abraham, 125
Traxel, Adam, 34, 36, 42, 45, 46, 61, 63, 65, 67, 69, 70, 77, 123, 129, 139, 142
Traxel, Amandus, 97
Traxel, Anna Mary, 6
Traxel, Anna Maria, 7, 34, 36, 42, 45, 46, 124, 136, 131, 119
Traxel, Anna Mary, 6
Traxel, Anna Susanna, 88
Traxel, Catharina, 34
Traxel, Barbara, 69, 70, 67, 73, 78, 80, 91
Traxel, Carl, 72, 77
Traxel, Catharina, 35, 37, 48, 61, 67, 80, 106
Traxel, Catharina Elisabeth, 12
Traxel, Charles, 114, 132
Traxel, Chrietian, 114
Traxel, Christian, 5, 67, 69, 70, 73, 74, 78, 80, 101, 103, 105, 112, 133
Traxel, Christina, 72, 73, 77, 80, 88, 91, 92, 97, 107, 119, 128
Traxel, Daniel, 11, 134, 138
Traxel, David, 5
Traxel, Drucilla, 92
Traxel, Edmund, 116
Traxel, Edward, 80, 90
Traxel, Eleonora, 118
Traxel, Elias, 61
Traxel, Elisabeth, 66, 90, 91, 93, 94, 103, 116, 123, 125, 124, 126, 127
Traxel, Elisabetha, 14
Traxel, Eliza, 97
Traxel, Emilia, 109
Traxel, Emmelina, 124
Traxel, Eva, 139
Traxel, Eva Catharina, 100
Traxel, George Friederich, 6
Traxel, Hanna, 34, 60, 67
Traxel, Hans Nickel, 12
Traxel, Isabella, 84, 128
Traxel, J. Nicolaus, 62, 66, 76, 84, 95, 99, 100, 105
Traxel, Joh. Michael, 12
Traxel, Johann Nickel, 37
Traxel, Johann Nicolaus, 63, 70, 71, 139
Traxel, Johannes, 5, 6, 37
Traxel, John, 61, 90, 94, 96, 98, 100, 106, 109, 114, 118, 119, 124, 126, 131, 135
Traxel, John Nickel, 35
Traxel, Jonas, 45, 74, 83, 84, 86, 90, 93, 94, 95, 105, 117, 118, 119, 121, 122, 123, 124, 142
Traxel, Jonathan, 90, 91, 93, 94, 97, 103, 116, 125
Traxel, Joseph, 95, 113
Traxel, Juliana Catharina, 5, 6, 7, 8
Traxel, Juliana Margaretha, 5, 133
Traxel, Julianna, 6, 67
Traxel, Leanda, 118

Traxel, Levina, 90
Traxel, Lydia, 84, 123, 129
Traxel, Magdalena, 101, 103, 105, 112, 114, 119, 129, 139
Traxel, Margaretha, 8, 10, 12
Traxel, Margreth, 78
Traxel, Maria, 42, 61, 62, 63, 65, 67, 66, 67, 69, 70, 71, 73, 76, 77, 80, 84, 85, 88, 95, 97, 99, 100, 105, 106, 115, 119
Traxel, Michael, 10
Traxel, Michel, 10
Traxel, Milton, 98
Traxel, Nicholas, 34, 69, 73, 76, 77, 80, 84, 85, 88, 97, 100, 106, 115
Traxel, Owen, 100
Traxel, Paul, 105
Traxel, Peter, 5, 6, 7, 8, 37, 38, 44, 58, 61, 67, 72, 73, 76, 77, 80, 88, 92, 97, 106, 107, 119, 123, 129, 131, 133, 134, 136, 138,
Traxel, Polly, 131
Traxel, Robert, 75
Traxel, Rufus, 124
Traxel, Sally, 131
Traxel, Sally Ann, 123, 131
Traxel, Salome, 90, 94, 96, 98, 100, 104, 106, 109, 118, 124
Traxel, Samuel, 70
Traxel, Samuel Peter, 129
Traxel, Sara, 73, 84, 86, 90
Traxel, Sarah, 93, 94, 95, 105, 113, 117, 118, 119, 121, 122, 123, 124
Traxel, Sibilla, 48
Traxel, Sibilla Veronica, 37, 38, 44, 58, 61
Traxel, Sofia, 13
Traxel, Solomon, 104
Traxel, Sophia, 103
Traxel, Stephan, 84
Traxel, Susanna, 114, 132
Traxel, Thomas, 96
Traxel, Wilhelm, 74
Traxel, William, 106
Traxel, William Henry, 119
Traxsel, Joel, 59
Traxsel, Peter, 59
Traxsel, Sybilla Veronica, 59
Triesbach, Adam, 19
Triesbach, Elisabeth, 19
Triesbach, Johannes, 19
Triesbach, Susanna, 19
Troxell, Solomon, 143
Trumer, Engel, 6
Trumer, Simon, 6
Turn, Johannes, 11
Umbehauer, Catharina, 74
Vaudring, Abraham, 14
Vaudring, Johan Nickel, 14
Vaudring, Maria Margaretha, 14
Vaudring, Nickel, 14
Vehl, Jacob, 130
Vehl, Magdalena, 130
Veit, Sibilla, 142
Verbilger, Catharina, 50
Verbilger, Henrich, 50
Voiturin, Abraham, 19, 23, 135
Voiturin, Daniel, 23
Voiturin, Johannes, 19
Voiturin, Margreth, 19, 23, 28
Voiturin, Nicolas, 19, 28
Waeber, Daniel, 15
Waeber, Margaretha, 15
Waeber, Maria Elisabeth, 15
Waeckerly, Abraham, 7
Waeckerly, Johannes, 7

Wagenmacher, Elisabetha, 133
Wagenmacher, Georg, 133
Wagenmann, Susanna, 56
Walb, John, 40, 42
Walb, Jost, 40
Walb, Margareth, 40, 42
Walb, Maria Catharina, 40
Walb, Wilhelm, 42
Walter, Elisabeth, 99
Walter, John, 84, 99
Walter, Solomon, 99
Wannemacher, Peter, 11
Wasser, Eliza Ann, 121
Wasser, Catharina, 97
Wasser, Edward, 116
Wasser, Eli, 104
Wasser, Magdalena, 88, 92, 97, 104, 116, 118, 121
Wasser, Thomas, 88, 92, 97, 104, 116, 118, 121
Watring, Maria Barbara, 116
Weber, Anna Maria, 6, 101
Weber, Christina, 99
Weber, Elisabeth, 91, 99, 104, 114
Weber, Johann Michael, 6
Weber, Johannes, 6
Weber, Michael, 6
Weber, Philip, 91, 104
Weida, Elisabeth, 114
Weida, George, 114
Weiss, Anna Maria, 132
Weiss, Georg, 132
Welsh, Charles, 127
Welsh, Feyanna, 127
Welsh, Margaretha, 127
Wenner, John, 124
Wenner, Polly, 124
Werz, John, 77
Werz, Caroline, 104
Werz, Eliza, 77
Werz, Magdalena, 77
Werz, Maria, 104
Werz, Peter, 104
West, Friderich, 21
West, Georg, 21
West, Maria Elisabeth, 21
Wetherbold, Henry William, 121
Wetherbold, Sophia, 121
Wetherbold, William, 121
Wetherhold, Alfred Peter, 124
Wetherhold, Sophia, 120, 124
Wetherhold, Sophia Ann, 127
Wetherhold, William, 120, 124, 127
White, George, 129
White, Hetty, 129
White, Mary, 129
Widdes, Isaac, 87
Widdes, Maria Anna, 87
Widdes, Rebecca, 87
Widerstein, Anna Maria, 133
Widerstein, Johann Henrich, 133
Wike, Scott, 143
Willauer, Joseph, 46
Willauer, Margreth, 46
Willauer, Maria, 46
Williams, John, 75
Williams, Maria, 75
Williams, Peter, 75
Williamson, Elisabeth, 46
Williamson, Jacob, 46
Williamson, Samuel, 46
Wint, Daniel, 130
Wirth, Anna Barbara, 133
Wirth, Jacob, 133
Wiser, Sarah, 143
Wisser, Jonathan, 106
Wissler, Johannes Jacobus, 8
Wissler, John Jacob, 146

Wolf, Georg, 61
Wolf, N., 17
Wolff, Christina, 11
Wolff, Jacob, 11
Wolff, Maria Margaretha, 11
Woodring, Cain, 126
Woodring, Lewis David, 126
Woodring, Margaret, 126
Wotering, Jacob, 36
Wotring, Abraham, 135, 137
Wotring, Anna Barbara, 135
Wotring, Anna Margaretha, 135
Wotring, Barbara, 11
Wotring, Cain, 112, 116
Wotring, Elisabeth, 38, 85, 90, 94, 135
Wotring, Eva, 94, 135
Wotring, Henrich, 116
Wotring, Jacob, 38
Wotring, Joh. Peter, 11
Wotring, John, 90
Wotring, Jonathan Franklin, 116
Wotring, Magadalena, 38, 135
Wotring, Margaretha, 11, 43
Wotring, Margreth, 48
Wotring, Maria Anna, 112
Wotring, Mary Anne, 116
Wotring, Maria Barbara, 47
Wotring, Maria Magdalena, 136
Wotring, Nicholas, 140
Wotring, Nicolas, 43, 48, 54
Wotring, Peter, 11, 85, 90, 94, 135
Wotring, Ruben, 112
Wotring, Samuel, 11, 45, 47, 94
Wotring, Stephan, 103
Wotring, William, 11, 38, 135
Woutring, Abraham, 133
Woutring, Anna Barbara, 133
Wright, George, 86
Wright, Luciana, 86
Wright, Magdalena, 86
Wudling, Abraham, 57
Wudring, Anna Barbara, 5
Wudring, Anna Margreth, 5
Wuertz, Joh. Conrad, 7
Wuess, Anna Maria, 17, 18, 20
Wuess, Elisabeth, 20
Wuess, Georg, 17, 18, 20
Wuess, Johan Jacob, 18
Wutring, Abraham, 132, 133
Wutring, Elisabeth, 61, 66, 74
Wutring, Jacob, 64
Wutring, Johann Wilhelm, 133
Wutring, Magdalena, 64
Wutring, Margreth, 68, 73
Wutring, Maria Margreth, 58
Wutring, Nicolaus, 58, 68, 73
Wutring, Peter, 61, 66, 74
Xander, Daniel, 109
Xander, Susanna, 109
Yehl, Anna, 65
Yehl, Henrich, 65
Yehl, Jacob, 124
Yehl, John, 91
Yehl, Jonas, 92
Yehl, Magdalena, 65, 124
Yehl, Maria, 91
Yehl, Salome, 92
Yehl, Samuel, 91
Yehl, Tilghman, 124
Yohe, Catharina, 86, 96, 100
Yohe, John, 86, 96. 100
Yohe, Jonas, 86
Yohe, Maria, 100
Yohe, Sarah, 96
Yundt, Abraham, 60, 62, 65, 83, 86 117
Yundt, Anna, 98
Yundt, Anna Elisabetha, 11

Yundt, Carl, 87
Yundt, Catharinaa, 62
Yundt, Elisabeth, 60, 62, 65, 83, 86, 117
Yundt, Esther, 65, 91
Yundt, Georg, 62
Yundt, George, 145
Yundt, Hanna, 87
Yundt, Henrich, 83
Yundt, Jacob, 145
Yundt, John, 87, 98
Yundt, Jonas, 91, 94, 144
Yundt, Lydia, 91, 94
Yundt, Magdalena, 98
Yundt, Maria Ann, 94
Yundt, Mathilda, 86
Yundt, Ruffina, 62
Yung, Elisabeth, 64
Yung, John, 64
Yung, Maria, 64
Zellner, Judith, 131
Zellner, Peter, 131
Zerfass, Abraham, 47, 58, 63, 75
Zerfass, Adam, 22, 45
Zerfass, Christina, 124
Zerfass, Clorai, 125
Zerfass, Daniel, 124
Zerfass, Elisabeth, 41
Zerfass, Georg, 56, 63
Zerfass, George, 59, 63
Zerfass, Hanna, 58, 63, 75
Zerfass, Henrich, 86
Zerfass, J. Adam, 25
Zerfass, John, 59, 125, 130
Zerfass, Jos. Georg., 25
Zerfass, Margreth, 33
Zerfass, Maria Elisabeth, 25, 45
Zerfass, Marie Elisabeth, 22
Zerfass, Peter, 63
Zerfass, Sarah, 125, 130
Zerfass, Susanna, 59, 63, 86, 130
Zink, Catharina, 57
Zoellner, Anna Carolina, 115
Zoellner, Catharina, 87, 92, 103, 109, 115, 122
Zoellner, Elias, 92
Zoellner, Michael, 44, 87, 92, 103, 109, 115, 122
Zoellner, Michel, 33
Zoellner, Tilghman, 122
Zoellner, Tillera, 103
Zoellner, William, 109

www.ingramcontent.com/pod-product-compliance
Lightning Source LLC
Chambersburg PA
CBHW051100160426
43193CB00010B/1261